THE WORKING MEN'S COLLEGE

AUSPICIUM MELIORIS

ÆVI· MDCCCLIV·

PURCHASED

R.E.Tyler Del. 1913. C.H.Perry Sc.

THE VULGAR HEART

By Doris Langley Moore

Novels

A WINTER'S PASSION
THE UNKNOWN EROS
THEY KNEW HER WHEN . . .

Non-Fiction

ANACREON, TWENTY-NINE ODES
THE TECHNIQUE OF THE LOVE AFFAIR
PANDORA'S LETTER BOX
E. NESBIT : A BIOGRAPHY

By June and Doris Langley Moore

THE PLEASURE OF YOUR COMPANY
OUR LOVING DUTY

THE VULGAR HEART

An Enquiry into the Sentimental Tendencies of Public Opinion

by

DORIS LANGLEY MOORE

A habitation giddy and unsure
Hath he that buildeth on the vulgar heart.
2 Henry IV : WM. SHAKESPEARE.

CASSELL AND COMPANY LTD.

London, Toronto, Melbourne and Sydney

To my dear friend
MARGARET LANE

First published 1945

THIS BOOK IS PRODUCED IN
COMPLETE CONFORMITY WITH THE
AUTHORIZED ECONOMY STANDARDS

Printed in Great Britain
by T. and A. Constable Ltd., Hopetoun Street,
Printers to the University of Edinburgh
F. 445

CONTENTS

AUTHOR'S NOTE

I FORMED the intention of writing this book in 1935 and began in a rather desultory way to collect material. Three years later, in 1938, I wrote the first chapter, and took the best part of three years more to reach the last. The typescript was then sent to the publishers, and disappeared with their offices in one of the great fire raids on the City of London. By the time a new copy was prepared—a substantial task—the paper shortage had made it necessary to postpone publication.

During this long passage of time there have been many changes, chiefly of a degenerative character, in the social order, creating among their million graver problems some difficulty in connection with the examples scattered throughout my text. A number of these I have banished in favour of newer specimens in finally revising the script, but I have been obliged to risk the possible obsolescence of others. In the appendices—which I wanly hope will not be altogether ignored—I have placed among various kinds of matter which could not be incorporated some of the illustrations most likely to need bringing up to date if this book is to be more than ephemeral. But it was never intended to be a topical survey, and the general validity, if any, of the thesis will not be overthrown by time's invalidation of particular instances.

It is desirable to emphasize, since so many of my conclusions are an explicit or implicit appeal for rationalism—using the word in its ordinarily understood meaning of a habit of preferring the guidance of reason to the guidance of emotion—that I am aware our reason, in its probably still embryonic stage of development, is so entwisted with our sentiments as to be at times a very unreliable guide. But I know of none better; and I believe in the ultimate possibility, and the urgent necessity, of bringing deceptive emotion under control.

Finally, the current zest for political labels makes it probable that, on the strength of expressing views which are supposed to belong to this 'ideology' or that, I shall be credited with having politics of some certain definite colour. I therefore think it well to describe my political tendencies with candour and clarity. I mix a good deal with Conservatives and I am inclined to share a number of their conclusions; I have always been sympathetic to Labour, though I deplore the subservience and toadyism of the party since it joined hands with its antagonists; I dislike Communism in its subjugation of the individual to the State, but I have no doubt at all of the value of many of the measures it proposes; I have always had an aversion from Fascism, yet I am prepared to admit that it produces a certain costly efficiency; I feel a good deal of sincere admiration for the Independent Labour Party, which nevertheless seems to me to idealize 'the workers' and over-simplify difficulties; the doctrines of Anarchism have much to recommend them in my eyes, but I am not sure about its means of achieving its ends. In short, there is no political creed which I have ever been able to accept whole and entire, and I have therefore never belonged to a political party. If there were a Rationalist Party and it were seriously attempting to be rational, I should belong to that.

D. L. M.

The laws of Society are stronger than the will of mankind.
Adolphe: BENJAMIN CONSTANT.

THERE is, I believe, a stage in the growth of every intelligent being's perceptions when he realizes with a mixture of gratitude and dismay that individuals are more rational and certainly far kinder than the institutions which are supposed to represent their collective conscience—that is to say, than the law, the government, the press, the organized churches; when he discovers, in short, that private opinion is immeasurably more liberal than public opinion, which in its turn usually outstrips the slow machinery of Church and State.

Having reached this understanding, he will become increasingly aware that the rulings of corporate bodies, civic, professional, religious, and even artistic, are often based upon anomalies, archaisms, and empty conventions, and are in certain instances so repugnant to reason as to be upheld almost apologetically by the persons who administer them. The judge frequently directs the jury not to consider whether an act has been justifiable upon humane grounds or otherwise, but to decide only if it is a violation of law; the medical man cannot always follow the dictates of his conscience if he follows the dictates of his Council; the priest, trying to reconcile the antiquated theology favoured by the mass with the altogether more ethical tenets of the individual, entangles himself in a maze of sophisticated arguments. On every side tragi-comic divergences between public principles and private thought and conduct offer themselves for inspection.

But after the novelty of astonishing or exasperating himself with such disparities has worn off, it is probable that our 'intelligent being' ceases to inspect and learns to acquiesce instead, sinking little by little into a position of tolerance from which only the grossest evidences of unreason can move him. It is not comfortable, he finds, to live at loggerheads with public principles; not restful to spend one's days being shocked and worried by them. In youth he had energy enough to rebel, and optimism enough to make rebellion seem worth while, but as time goes on he grows languid, sceptical, nervous of change, careful for what he conceives to be his interests; by an imperceptible process he joins the ranks of those who prefer not to question established systems. His private behaviour remains benevolent and sensible—it may even increase signally in virtue—but he thinks it well to endorse the public policies of his class and kind, and at last may be only dimly aware when such policies are at variance with his own code. That code itself becomes confused through the confusion in which it must operate. The rational mind succumbs, the rational creature stealthily gives place to the sentimentalist.

This brief inglorious history does not pretend to be universally applicable. We are not all discerning enquirers in our youth and muddle-headed escapists in maturity. Sometimes the process is reversed, and having first been willing to adopt our standards ready-made, we achieve the strength of mind to investigate and reject only after much painful experience and laborious effort. Sometimes the capacity for dispassionate observation persists through life and develops rather than decays. But in general it will be conceded that an inclination to criticize the accepted order manifests itself in youth and is likely to subside in middle age.

There are some in every class who are never troubled by this inclination at any period of their existence, but intellects of so inveterately low a quality are not, I fancy, as numerous as the backward state of social ethics might lead one to suppose. It is part of my thesis that men are made of better material than often appears, so ugly are the designs to which they allow themselves to be cut. They are shaped by public opinion even as they help to shape it. The circle is a singularly vicious one.

A definition now becomes necessary, and I will risk the scorn of those who like such business to be transacted in impressively obscure language by choosing the simplest and most obvious. Public opinion is the synthesis of those views which, presumably, are held by the majority of any given populace. The adverb has not been dropped in at random. It is one of the most disconcerting aspects of public opinion that it must nearly always be a matter of speculation. There is seldom any absolute proof that a majority of the populace is of one mind or another: one can only, as a rule, deduce the current trend from sporadic symptoms, and the conclusion is by no means infallibly reliable. Those whose arduous task it is to keep their fingers on the public pulse grow inured to uncertainty. The crowd is fickle and easily persuaded; moreover, detached sections of it which are not really representative have a way of making so much clamour that they drown the voices of the true Demos.

More bewildering still, even when a majority verdict is so indicated as to be unmistakable, there is no guarantee that it is the true projection of a natural and artless impulse, since bad training, want of courage, and self-interest combine to lead many people into modes of thinking actually foreign to them and to seduce them into believing they hold the views it seems convenient to hold. However, when all the difficulties in the way of forming an estimate have been allowed for, there remains a wide range of topics on which it is fairly safe to predict what the findings of the majority will be, and fairly safe again to assume that they will be less generous than the findings of the same body of people if each were individually given an opportunity of exercising his discretion.

And here is the point at which I can begin, rather tortuously I fear, to explain the theme and intention of this book.

Public opinion is a composite and largely artificial product which, even at best, could illustrate only the Lowest Common Denominator of taste and judgment. In effect its relationship to taste and judgment is extremely obscure, because many private opinions are moulded by the real or imagined pressure of public conviction and help to swell its tide though they do not genuinely express the sentiments of the individuals concerned—or rather they do not express what those sentiments would have been if the desire to conform had been absent. This desire to conform, is, however, an immensely powerful motive in all but highly exceptional entities, and is fostered by every device of conventional education throughout the whole community; so that the effort of independent thinking is most exhausting and is seldom sustained beyond a more or less deciduous phase.

Besides an anxiety to keep within the fold, springing from so many recognizable sources that there is no need to trace its origin, there is in most people's method of dealing with non-personal issues, a habit of laziness which favours drastic simplifications. Through this weakness, problems of peculiar intricacy are reduced to a few bare outlines; codes are set up for the easy classification of every species of human activity; systems are devised under which cases requiring to be considered on their separate merits are disposed of by rule of thumb; religion assumes a most ignoble pettiness; superstition, which almost invariably reflects some tendency to over-simplify, produces a multitude of harmful follies. If to the infirmity of laziness we add another infirmity still more widespread—namely, that reluctance to face unpalatable facts which is one of the major premises of modern psychology—it will hardly come as a surprise that reason is given little inducement to flourish. (It may be argued that these defects are inherent in the mental constitution of mankind and are not more evident in a public opinion than in a private one, but I hope to show that a failing which has general sanction is very much more serious than the same failing shared by the same number of people without one another's approbation.)

The intellect being discouraged from free functioning, both by social custom and the weaknesses touched upon, man will form his judgments chiefly upon his feelings—feelings, it must be remembered, which have been subjected from earliest childhood to strong external influences and are therefore hopelessly adulterated. In consequence, his outlook is the antithesis of rational; it is extremely sentimental, deliberately sentimental. The more he wishes to avoid coming into conflict with public opinion, the more assiduously will he be obliged to cultivate sentimentality.

Another definition is called for here, and it is one which I must ask the reader to examine somewhat carefully, since upon it hinges the whole validity of the theory I am about to put forward.

The dictionaries are agreed that sentimentality means the quality or state of being sentimental, and that to be sentimental in the less agreeable sense of that sometimes ambiguous word is to give way to mawkish or superficial emotions, to address oneself to easily swayed feelings and predilections, or to indulge in extravagant or affected sentiment. I would particularly draw attention to the qualifying adjectives, for otherwise occasions of misconstruction will arise. Sentiment is not opposed to reason *in itself*, but only when an undue emphasis is laid upon its claims.

There are, of course, many different views as to what constitutes undue emphasis. Some extremists despise every manifestation of strong feeling, even denying merit to a work of art if it is not primarily intellectual in conception. Others actually take a pride in emotional judgments and look upon the intellectual approach as something dangerous and reprehensible. These types, though both sufficiently common, are outnumbered, however, by that more moderate order of humanity which includes myself and probably my reader.

Assuming it is well understood that here 'sentimental' is always related to sentimentality and not to sentiment in its purer form, and that no one is likely to quarrel with the dictionary interpretation, I will avow at once that my ultimate design is by a sort of anatomical survey to reveal how many of our emotions are mawkish or superficial, how many of our feelings and predilections are easily swayed, and how seldom even those which spring from the most genuine sources are untainted with extravagance or affectedness by the time their little weight is thrown into the scale of public opinion. But for the present I must attempt to trace more minutely the process of mind by which the sentimental attitude first comes to be adopted.

As I have already implied, it is the result of the desire for simplification working in conjunction with the ingenious mechanism by which the brain strives to protect itself from the full glare of disquieting truths. To reduce the complex operation to its barest elements, it is as if the owner of the mechanism were being told, first: 'It would be more agreeable to you if such-and-such unpleasant possibilities did not exist.' Then, 'They *ought* not to exist.' And finally, 'If they do exist, it can only be by a deplorable aberration in the scheme of things.'

At first this will seem a far-fetched illustration, but a little reflection may make it apparent that it does, in a crude fashion, point the course of an enormous variety of moral and aesthetic judgments. To apply it to a particular instance, let us imagine the mental condition of one who sanctions religious persecution [1]—an evil which, being remote from most contemporary lives, may be examined with a measure of detachment.

[1] Religious persecution should not be confused with racial persecution, which has a different genesis.

The desire for simplification makes this man pledge his faith to some system claiming to expound a divine plan of justice under which every puzzling circumstance in the universe can be accounted for—if not here, hereafter. Having once chosen his creed—we will suppose a Christian creed—or accepted it at the bidding of others, he is spared a thousand perplexities which must beset the mind which still gropes and questions. He can leave his problems in the hands of God, lay his burdens on the shoulders of Christ, let the Blood of the Lamb atone for his sins, and resign himself in all misfortunes to the Lord's will; or at least he is able to aspire after this holy tranquillity with some hope that it might be attained. Those sufferings of others which he is indisposed or powerless to redress he can dismiss with the assurance that sooner or later God, in His infinite wisdom and mercy, will set matters right, and meanwhile the wind will be tempered to the shorn lamb.

Now, in order that this believer may feel secure in his enjoyment of what have so aptly been called 'the consolations of religion,' he must be spared from the disturbing influence of those who find flaws in His divine plan or who cast contempt on it mutely by preferring another. The fanatic who seeks martyrdom thrives upon opposition, but the fanatic who persecutes is made of frailer material and must defend his more vulnerable faith against potential onslaughts. His protective mechanism works on the lines sketched out, demonstrating, first, that alien doctrines are a threat to his peace; next, that they ought not to exist; and ultimately, that they do not exist except among those whose wickedness justifies the sternest means of suppression.

On the topic of religion at least—and it is hardly likely that he will stop short there—he judges not with his intellect but with his biased emotions, and in so far as he does so he is sentimental instead of rational. His reasoning powers are used perversely to supply a warrant for an activity quite incompatible with the teaching he professes to follow; unless he receives some deflecting shock, they will continue to function corruptly, bribed by his wishes, cowed by his fears.

The habit of thinking in terms of wish fulfilment or fear evasion seems to be resorted to by all human beings from the age of infancy, and no doubt it serves many useful purposes, though the best intelligences struggle to grow out of it, or only to yield to it with conscious intention. But a form of self-deception which is harmless, more or less, to the individual may be most dangerous when a crowd is induced to share it. Religious dogmas, criminal and civil laws, codes of sexual morality, policies of government at home and abroad, based on wish-fulfilment fantasies instead of what we know, or might discover, of objective reality, must necessarily prove causes of great hardship. Yet these fantasies invariably travel even further from fact when they are approved and promoted by the mass. The simplifications are more ruthless, and on such subjects as crime, patriotism, and sexual 'decency,' the desire

13

—indeed the necessity—to conform renders us still more incapable of arriving at an impartial estimate.

Now, at the risk of seeming to labour the point, I must repeat what I will describe in future as the Sentimentality Formula, for it is well that it should be fixed in the reader's memory, so that whether he agrees with my arguments or not, we shall remain in accord as to my meaning.

This time we use our example as a method of approach. Let us briefly analyse why it is that such an institution as Mother's Day, on which numbers of Americans regale their mothers with flowers, gifts, and loving messages, proves so distasteful, in a ludicrous way, to anyone who attempts to be a rationalist. Not, certainly, because he despises filial affection, as the supporters of Mother's Day would probably allege (for sentimentalists have a way of inferring that if one is not in their camp, one must be in some camp diametrically opposite). What he must despise is the grotesque simplification which seeks to draw all women who happen to have borne children into a single class to receive simultaneous honours, and the wish-fulfilling assumption that such honours will be deserved. The sponsors have assented, even more eagerly than the rest of mankind, to the proposition that, because it would be a pleasanter world if all mothers were devoted women beloved by their children, therefore all mothers *are* devoted and beloved by their children—with a few shocking exceptions whose abnormality is taken to be a matter of wilfully evil disposition.

The underlying principle of belief may be compressed thus : 'It would be pleasanter. . . . It ought to be. . . It is.' That is our formula.

The successful establishment of Mother's Day furnishes a specimen of sentimentalism so blatant that, through it, I am able to show the twin processes of simplifying and idealizing with more clarity than complex examples might allow. There will be subtler variations upon the same theme in the pages to come. The present fashion for emotional reserve among Englishmen makes it unlikely that a general festival of filial observances would appeal to their sense of decorum. It would have had a better chance of popularity—supposing it to have been conceivable at all—in the eighteenth century, when the visible expression of emotion was thought admirable; only then it would have been celebrated as Father's Day.

The objection may be raised that there is no great harm in a faith, unfounded though it may be, which occasions many parents and children who would otherwise be on the worst of terms to make a show of caring for one another. But I am persuaded, and shall try to persuade the reader, that any good which may result from such a pretence (not usually, of course, a conscious pretence) is heavily outweighed by several ill effects.

Having thus indicated, in what is admittedly a rudimentary fashion, the nature of the sentimental attitude—its basis in a need for plain, easily understood standards coupled with a preference for those aspects of things which reflect flatteringly upon the human race or any chosen fragment of it—I may pass on to the detailed discussion of its results: but first I had better pause to clear the ground of one or two possible sources of misapprehension.

As I have said in a parenthesis, sentimentalists usually presume that if one does not hold the same opinion as themselves one must hold a positively opposite opinion. This is the familiar habit of minds addicted to narrowing down all issues and to closing themselves tight against the danger of conversion by putting into the mouths of their opponents whatever arguments sound most objectionable. Thus a Tory of low-grade intellect will suspect that if one does not favour the *status quo* one must be an out-and-out 'Red,' while Communists are ready to convince themselves that all who dislike their political outlook are sycophants of capitalism. Even in the sphere of taste there is a very general tendency to fancy that a liking for one sort of work must produce a complementary aversion from another. There are critics who talk as if it were impossible to admire Bach if one is pleased with Tchaikowsky, or as if no one could appreciate Emily Brontë who feels any affection for Charlotte.

Now I think it extremely unlikely that there will be a high proportion of sentimentalists among the readers of this book, because it is a regrettable but not at all remarkable fact that one is usually obliged to preach to the converted: people being prone to give their careful attention solely to those ideas which are congenial. But in case I have been so fortunate as to entrap a few waverers who are not unreasoning on principle, may I urge them to abstain, even if with an arduous struggle, from any kind of surmise founded upon a prepossession?

My intelligent reader will not conclude that since I find so many of our present institutions deplorable, I see the institutions of the past through a rosy glow, nor that, if I criticize England, I must be enamoured of the world outside. He will not imagine that I throw every notion of morality overboard because I would like to destroy existing codes of morals. On the contrary, he will realize that my primary anxiety is to avoid all wholesale judgments, since I have made it my business to prove that they are extremely pernicious, and my book is essentially a plea for the consideration of every case upon its merits.

To sum up briefly, my thesis is that public opinion is a synthetic and perishable concoction only remotely connected with private opinion. It is almost always irrational, being based upon a form of sentimentality, and is demonstrably not entitled to respect, and the deference at present accorded to it by a pandering press [1] and innumerable institutions and individuals holding themselves dependent on its favour is calamitously

---

[1] The press panders to public opinion, I am well aware, only to exercise the more control over it.

misplaced. It is deference to a mere shifting and elusive shadow. There is no firm substance in any opinion which is not the result of the nearest approach separate men, women, and children can make to careful and detached thinking.

If it were a more general habit to form opinions carefully and with detachment, many crude emotional situations which recurringly give rise to strife and slaughter in their most abominable forms would have no existence. A thousand lesser, but still very great, evils could be eradicated. Much private, indeed secret suffering, caused through the difficulty of adjusting one's sentiments to fit into the expected convention, would find permanent relief.

Unfortunately, honesty of thought is given scant welcome in a society which, with whatever ultimately unhealthy effects, prefers soothing fictions to astringent truths. The suppression of honesty begins in the nursery and is continued without relaxation until adulthood, by which time there is usually not much of it left to suppress.

It is very painful when one reflects upon the wonderful ingenuity of man, his thirst for beauty, and his good and generous impulses, to see him at every turn stultifying and defeating himself because, in his love of ease, he makes himself a party to the pitiful conspiracy of self-deception. The ensuing chapters compose a tiny fragment of the counterplot initiated when the human mind was first submitted to dispassionate study, a tardy event in scientific history.

Incapable of apprehending things in all their complexity, they [the masses] tend always to assign to them a single cause, easily presented and, so to speak, tangible and visible.

La Psychologie des Masses: DR. ANDRÉ JOUSSAIN.

IN my first chapter I paved the way for an investigation of the many evils which arise from a non-rational mode of thinking, and fixed upon two forms of ease as the reason why such a mode proves generally congenial: first, the ease of simplicity, to be found in accepting definite and readily ascertainable, if inaccurate, explanations, standards of value, and principles; then, the comfort of glossing over with illusions what is unpleasing. With the reader's forbearance, I shall consider separately these widely adopted though, in the long run, strikingly unsuccessful precautions against mental disturbance. When they are taken together the equation is sentimentality, but, that we may thoroughly know the elements of the danger, it is well to go to the trouble of looking at them apart.

The question is reiterantly asked—whether mankind has made progress or is deteriorating. It must, of course, be futile to answer unless we are agreed as to what the word progress shall mean in this context. If it stands for scientific knowledge and invention, then the verdict cannot be for an instant in doubt except among those childish minds which cling to the belief that everything was much better done and much more wisely understood in the remote past. If it means an increase of happiness, we shall need data now hardly procurable, since happiness appears to be, like heat and sweetness, a relative affair. When your hands are very cold, tepid water will seem hot; when you have been eating chocolate creams, your coffee, sweetened to its usual degree, will taste bitter: happiness is likewise affected by contrasts and dwindles or grows great according to the balance of your other emotions, so that to show an improvement in the external conditions of life is not quite conclusive as to the feelings of the people affected.

If you suppose, as some still do, that it is retrogression to question the veracity of the Bible, then in your eyes we are retrogressing. If, on the other hand, the tendency to enquire and criticize commends itself to you as a desirable one, you will consider that we make visible progress from generation to generation.

I am myself strongly of this persuasion, since I hold that every movement away from rough-and-ready appraisals, every attempt to recognize the complexity and diversity of the phenomena we are capable of observing, is a movement towards justice and benevolence—which I do not, however, conceive to be absolutes.

The history of human development is, I think, demonstrably a history of such recognitions, each leading actually or potentially to useful knowledge, fairer judgments, and the abandonment of malpractices based on over-simple assumptions. These recognitions are first achieved by persons of exceptional intelligence or intuitive power who usually have much difficulty in prevailing upon their fellow-creatures to retract from time-honoured and perhaps more immediately satisfying beliefs. But, little by little, other open-minded experimenters uphold the new findings, and as the circle widens and the number of convinced authorities grows more impressive, larger and larger sections of people make the effort involved in acknowledging, or at least pretending to acknowledge, the truth of the discovery.

Every branch of science will provide us with illustrations showing how appearances of the simplest kind, when skilfully probed, reveal intricacies of design and varieties of material which the layman at first cannot credit. The earth seems more or less flat, and certainly stationary, covered by a pleasing, changeful dome above which may be easily imagined the abode of supernatural beings: it is tiresome—or was at the beginning, for we are inured to it now—when expert observers present evidences of a vast, unhomely, complicated universe in which nothing is exactly what our senses apprehend. Tiny points of fire in the sky are stupendous whirling suns inconceivably larger than our native planet. There are rays of light we cannot see, sounds we cannot hear, mysterious forces and activities which we have harnessed to our use but whose very existence was unsuspected for thousands of years. Earth, air, fire, water, the four substances out of which everything was said to be made, are not, it turns out, the only elements—indeed they are not elements at all! And so it goes on, one act of recognition succeeding another with constantly increasing rapidity as the spirit of research is liberated more and more effectively from the restrictions formerly imposed.

My business is with social science, which, compared with such impersonal studies as chemistry or physics, is in an early stage of its infancy. Mathematics had reached a very fair degree of advancement at a time when it was still thought that public executions with every attendant painful circumstance were a highly salutary spectacle. Remarkable feats of engineering had been accomplished long before most educators noticed that to exact servile obedience under the discipline of the birch was not a first-rate way of forming a child's character. Men who could prophesy the movements of a comet with great precision were accustomed to the idea that a woman's honour resided in her vagina, from whence it could be, with or without her own consent, removed. And even today, when the ever-multiplying ' wonders of science ' (that is to say, the practical uses to which we put extending recognitions) are becoming commonplaces, knowledge of human reactions is still so primitive that we behave as if disputes between large groups of people could be settled by mutual carnage.

Nevertheless, depressing as the gaps in our understanding may be, many that existed almost universally in the past are being filled or partially filled. Though our delusive emotions have prevented us from making headway as fast as the astronomers, we do not see human relations and dispositions in quite the same flat primary colours as our forefathers. Life is no longer treated altogether as if it were a comedy or tragedy of Humours even by the insensitive machinery of the law courts.

In the old days—let us, for definition and ease of reference, say two centuries ago—there were conceptions of right and wrong, merit and demerit, so perfectly straightforward, so untrammelled by refinements, that those whose task or pleasure it was to sit in judgment over others were seldom in doubt as to the steps that should be taken. Certain people chose to be bad and must be punished. For instance, a man who stole was bad, irrespective of circumstances conducing to the offence. A man, or a boy in his early teens, who stole goods worth more than a few pence was bad enough to be hanged. There existed upwards of two hundred crimes for which both adults and children could be, and frequently were, considered so wicked that they deserved to die. The simple state of badness demanded the simple remedy of death : if not death, transportation or imprisonment upon terms that would make life as irksome as possible. Such penalties would not only satisfy society's just demand for vengeance against malefactors, but would obviously deter others from pursuing similar courses. Few ventured to suppose that perhaps these arrangements might be rather too plain-sailing, and that the obvious inference was (as it often falls out) a fallacious one.

A woman was bad if she lay with any other man than her lawful wedded husband. Although the death penalty was not imposed (we are confining ourselves to England), this was looked upon, or at any rate constantly referred to, as by far the most shocking crime in the power of females to commit, and one inducing a depravity to which death was preferable. Known unchastity in low life was punishable by bridewell imprisonment, in middle and high life by total exclusion from respectable society. Adultery, practised by a wife, was even worse than other forms of immorality. No temptation was allowed to excuse it ; yet it was an age when temptations must have been heavy, since fashion encouraged men to be rakes, and custom authorized parents to marry their daughters 'advantageously' to suitors physically incompatible or even repulsive. The woman guilty of dishonouring her marriage bed was universally accounted unfit to associate with her own children, and at least one moralist [1] looked wistfully back to the ancient Saxon custom of marking her off from the rest of humankind by mutilating her face. Theoretically at least, the whole business was simplicity itself.

[1] The anonymous author of *A Treatise Concerning Adultery and Divorce*, 1700.

The social order was another simple matter. It had been organized by God. Not to believe in the designs of God as interpreted by orthodox religion was wickedness. It was His clear and evident intention that some people should be rich and great, and others poor and industrious. A man should not repine against his destiny or attempt to move himself, except through a few restricted channels, out of his allotted station. The good poor 'knew their place'; malcontents were bad and did not deserve the charity which it was the virtue of the rich to administer. It was true that the immense inequalities of the social scale led to many apparent unfairnesses, but these were only superficial, because, God having ordained everything, fundamentally the system must be right. God admittedly moved in a mysterious way. So much the more reason for maintaining simple faith.

God, for all His mysterious movements and triune constitution, was Himself a Being of simple tastes. Like a childish man, He demanded to be loved and feared. His power must be constantly acknowledged, otherwise He was liable to grow angry and to start manifesting His might —in cruder words, showing off. In the character of the Son, He was mild and kindly; but as the Father, He was expected to be vindictive, petty, tyrannical, a stickler for formalities, and addicted to favouritism— no doubt very like the earthly despots on whom His legendary personality had long ago been modelled. Ecclesiastically, domestically, and legally, God the Father carried much more weight than God the Son, though nominally they were equal. The two characters did not hang together at all well, and the presence of an incomprehensible Holy Ghost shed little light: but then, the Trinity was a mystery, and from mysteries of religion the intellect was freely permitted to retreat.

Religious observances might be exacting and details of dogma controversial, but religion itself was, for most of its exponents, an affair of clear outlines and simple issues. So were patriotism, courage, honour, purity, and the rest of the abstract qualities. A man who would not readily risk physical injury was a coward. Honour could be sullied by a word and appeased by a wound. Purity was sexual innocence, without which female charms were at a serious discount. Patriotism demanded a belief in the superiority of one's own country and a respect for certain symbols by which that country was represented, royal personages, flags and banners, mythical figures like Britannia.

It is possible to argue that there is only a slight improvement in our outlook on most of the topics mentioned, and that as to one or two we have been travelling in a backward direction. The law has somewhat abated its ferocity, but it still takes the view that criminality is a way of life deliberately chosen, rather than an outgrowth of social conditions and psychological equipment largely beyond the control of the subject; and it receives with the utmost scepticism every evidence of the inadequacy of punishment as a deterrent. Chastity remains legally the most prized virtue of women, and the suspicion of its absence so grave a stigma that a counsel,[1] without being laughed out of court, was, in quite recent times, able to say on behalf of a client: 'There was alleged against her the most terrible thing that could be alleged against any woman—that she was unchaste.' Our divorce laws to this day put the castigation of adultery before the necessity of restoring lives damaged by matrimonial error, and it is common for judges to decide that a woman is an unsuitable person to have the care of her own children not because she is ill-tempered, ignorant, or neglectful, but because she has had a lover.

The social order is relaxed but not radically changed: what has been gained in one direction has sometimes been lost in another, and God is publicly invoked as the responsible agent oftener than most of us notice, so unquestioningly do we take these archaic references for granted. The Churches grow old but do not grow up. Their exposition of the mind of God continues to be, on the whole, bewilderingly silly and full of contradictions. The teaching of new or newly adapted religions, of which Spiritualism, Theosophy, and Christian Science are specimens, is as infantile as anything inherited from the past. The old stock categories for human actions and emotions have been only slightly enlarged. Patriotism indeed is interpreted on narrower lines than the eighteenth century dreamed of, and is capable of promoting cruelties far and away beyond the scope of that cruel age.

These objections to the theory of progress have much plausibility, yet they are answerable. The persistence of some evils, the extension of others, will be found to be an effect *incidental* to the development of mechanical invention, which has not only vastly increased our facilities for welding people into great masses but has furnished us with weapons more violent and undiscriminating than any known in earlier times. Such weapons have rather evolved through folly and greed than been devised by conscious malignity, and who that has studied the eighteenth century, or any other, will suppose the instruments of policy we now adopt (protesting and deploring) would have been rejected then had they then been available?

It is not fiendish spite against the human race which impels a man to devote his ingenuity to the perfecting of bombs and poison gases and the research for death rays; his motives are more generally small prosaic ones—commercial ambition, the desire for promotion, and so on, justified by reasoning on the lines of: 'The more frightful the armaments at our disposal, the less likelihood of our having to use them.' In each age, offensive and defensive nations have amassed the deadliest materials they had means to obtain. Our ancestors knew less about the arts of wholesale destruction than we do; that cannot be said to prove they were morally better.

[1] W. Gorman, K.C., in 1937.

That patriotism has degenerated into blaring nationalism is not because we are less liberal and more bigoted than of old, but through the employment on an immense scale of machinery which enables the stupidest and least educated sections of the community to speak with the loudest voice.[1] The ignorant brutalized lower classes of a hundred or two hundred years ago had no popular press to consult their tastes and give expression to their views. Had it been otherwise, we might be able to see very plainly what we can now only gather through indirect channels, that they were even more addicted to national self-aggrandizement and raucous contempt for foreigners than the worst of their successors.

But though we have come a long way, we have an immeasurably longer way to go. Public affairs of every species, and hence to an extent difficult to estimate private affairs also, are still moulded to fit egregiously over-simplified patterns. If I devote a great part of this chapter to displaying the yet simpler framework of beliefs we have abandoned, it is not with the intention of sneering at the past and inviting complacency over the present, but for two much better reasons. First, we can look at the past more or less dispassionately, which is good practice for a study of the present. And then, the past holds up a lamp which may illuminate the future.

Had it not been for the growth of power and solidarity among the masses traceable, as I say, to the unforeseen consequences of mechanical proficiency, we might now be moving away from our old puerile observances and assessments with a rapidity unequalled since the end of the Middle Ages, for we are on the further side of a Rubicon our forefathers lacked the courage to cross.

As it is, progress in recognitions continues to be much swifter than progress in the application of them. That is to say, recognitions of immense potential value have been made, but are not yet put to much practical use, because of the obstacles opposed by huge groups of common minds.

The point I would stress is that, until the last few decades, neither common minds nor fine ones—with certain extremely rare and remarkable exceptions—had as yet achieved the detachment and expansion necessary for the discoveries of which I speak. Even men of first-rate talents failed completely to perceive how many ideals accepted as noble, how many traditions held to be rooted in timeless standards of honour, were nothing better than an ingenious means of giving countenance to quite discreditable passions, how many lawful and established customs were barbarous and barbaric, how often piety was a mere feeble clutching on to the skirts of protective power.

Thus—to gather in a handful of the least subtle examples—though it may well happen that reactionary fashions will gain votaries and have

---

[1] The outbreak of Jingoism at the end of the nineteenth century coincided exactly with the growth of a press designed to cater for ' the masses.'

their day, it seems to me to be recognized once and for all by persons of respectable mental capacity that a woman can feel sexual desire and gratify it without having 'shame, guilt, and sorrow as her continual attendants'; [1] that sexual perversion is not invariably vice and, even in its most distasteful manifestations, is more likely to be a diseased condition than a wilful iniquity; that fear produces ultimate effects the very opposite to what is usually intended by those who employ it as a method of admonishing either children or adults; that there is nothing inherently 'sacred' about matrimony, parenthood, family life, monarchy, or the constitution of any country; and that animals were not expressly created (as a Catholic nun once blandly informed me) 'for the use and pleasure of man,' thus exempting our consciences from the need to reckon with their sufferings.

These aspects of enlightenment, probably so taken for granted by my intelligent reader that he will think it superfluous to mention them, were nevertheless beyond the grasp of highly brilliant intellects a few generations ago. We may imagine Dr Johnson, one of the most realistic thinkers of his age, confronted with any of those, to us, almost self-evident propositions. The suggestion that feminine chastity could be less than an absolute standard of virtue would have shocked and annoyed him profoundly. Homosexuality, to name but one form of sexual aberration, would certainly have provoked condemnation in his severest vein. He believed and stated that children could 'only be governed by fear,' [2] and that 'to impress fear' was one of the first duties of those who had the care of them; and as he thought the threat of eternal punishment compatible with Divine Goodness, it may be assumed that terrorism seemed to him an equally proper corrective for adults. The sanctity of institutions blessed by the Church and upheld by the State was something he never appears to have called into question, and it is improbable, to say the least of it, that he would have approved of those modern usages which encroach upon 'sacred rights.' He was regardful of the welfare of animals, being in this matter an exceedingly humane man, in advance of most of his contemporaries,[3] but we know from his amused scorn for the theories of the interesting Lord Monboddo that the notion of sharing with beasts a common primeval ancestry would have been repulsive to him: he considered such speculations useless and foolish.

Dr Johnson was admittedly a stubborn conservative and a moralist, but his views on the particular subjects I have mentioned were universally

---

[1] The doom pronounced for female sinners by Edward Cobden in a sermon on chastity preached before the King in 1748.

[2] See his 'Argument on Behalf of Hastie the Schoolmaster, Prosecuted for Undue Severity.'

[3] Instances of his active kindness to animals are well known, but his remarks concerning vivisection appear to have escaped the general notice. In his edition of Shakespeare's *Cymbeline*, he takes occasion to speak of being shocked at experiments published 'by a race of men that have practised tortures without pity, and related them without shame, and are yet suffered to erect their heads among human beings.'

held in his time, and I have only selected him as my specimen because his opinions are so readily accessible. The whole of eighteenth-century England will hardly, I think, yield a dozen minds equal to *all* the acts of recognition involved in accepting the very modest hypotheses I have enumerated.

As each one of these hypotheses gives rise, when permitted to influence conduct, to a widening of the field of sympathy and a lessening of the field of autocratic power, I regard them as evidences of progress. Each, it may be seen, necessitates the rejection of the simple and obvious inference, the narrow and unalterable line of demarcation. Each acknowledges the existence of problems where our precursors found none. This is to advance in courage and candour, even as our precursors in their turn advanced, amending a little the still more rudimentary judgments of earlier times; and our descendants, it is to be hoped, will travel much further forward than ourselves.

The eighteenth century is called the Age of Reason. It would be more accurately described as the Age of Rationalization. Until that time such emotions as vindictiveness, cupidity, and lust had been acted upon fairly frankly, or, if reasoning was used to extenuate them, it was of a very primitive or else a mystical kind. (Mystical and primitive modes of thought usually, of course, have much in common.) The metaphysicians of the seventeenth century, with their taste for allegory and symbolism, evolved into the ratiocinators of the eighteenth, masterly at the tortuous and sophisticated art of 'proving' that Divine sanction corresponded exactly with the human tendencies of those holding authority.[1] In the eighteenth century we may say people employed reason to support what they wanted to believe. Not until late in the nineteenth was it customary for reason to be adduced in support of what people did *not* want to believe. That is the Rubicon of which I spoke a little while ago.

Tortuous and sophisticated though the logic of the moralizing philosophers may have been, the assumptions upon which it was based were nevertheless very much too simple. Fear, pain, and humiliation, for instance, produce an immediate and visible effect in the training of children. What more obvious than that these must be turned to account 'for the child's own good'? It requires patient skill to discern that a postponed and *in*visible effect makes such expedients sources of grave danger. A still acuter penetration is needed to track down the secret relish that some adults feel in inflicting fear, pain, and humiliation, and the dark spring from which that pleasure flows.

The glorification of virginity affords another example of the ornamental flourish of reasoning which often disguises a mental line of least resistance. The chastity of women was naturally guarded with care when

---

[1] Undeniably there were two or three secular philosophers whose scientific detachment remains above criticism, but I am outlining the general trend. For every Hume there were twenty Paleys.

24

sexual freedom was liable to promote indiscriminate breeding; that was logical and sound. The over-simplification consisted in identifying virginity with virtue—a confusion which had always been widespread, but which was carried to such fanatical lengths by the rationalization experts of the eighteenth century, and the overt sentimentalists of the nineteenth, that it will take generations to shake off the remnants of entangling nonsense.

If the study of the past inclines us, as I suggested, to approach the present dispassionately, a survey of fiction may very well prepare us for a survey of facts. The course taken by the English novel since it became established as a popular literary form (that is, after Richardson, Smollett, and Fielding, who had the freedom conceded to pioneers) [1] seems to me to illustrate with peculiar clarity our slow but sure extension of recognitions, our growing willingness to accept reality in all its complex and fortuitous shapes, instead of ascribing to it a false shape that is easier to understand.

The principal characters in early novels, with certain exceptions outstanding because of their rarity, were painted in the most extreme colours the writer had at his command. Goodness and wickedness were depicted entirely without half measures. The 'villain' fell, as a rule, into one of two categories, the fashionable libertine or the lawless recreant. If the latter, he was villainous without mitigation. His motives were evil, his deeds were evil, his outward aspect was evil. He thoroughly deserved the unpleasant death that awaited him. The debauchee, on the other hand, was not without soft moments of relenting. Sometimes he laid traps for the seduction of the heroine with a tear stealing down his cheek. Yet passion compelled him to pursue his course of infamy as earnestly as if life afforded no other occupation. Indeed, it was very probable that it did not, for this was the era when villains, heroes, and heroines were generally drawn from the leisured classes, persons in high life being supposed, by another simplification, to taste experience upon a larger scale than common mortals. (For the same reason, the chief actors in tragedy on the stage were kings and queens.)

The heroine was flawlessly beautiful, exquisitely graceful and accomplished, and of a spotless purity that she would at any time die to defend. No fault was ever allowed to appear in her worse than a slight excess of sensibility and an indiscreetness which was solely due to her artless ignorance of the world.

The hero was handsome, brave, magnanimous, and well-bred. If *he* had a fault, it was in his generous impetuosity, or the touchiness of his high honour. True, he was not always as chaste as the heroine; he might, at some time in his headstrong youth, have committed acts occasioning remorse; but chastity in males was a virtue praised only by tepid lip

---

[1] Defoe's work was done before the Age of Rationalization and he had yet more freedom than the later experimentalists whom I have named as my starting-point. Rationalization, being a mode of self-deception, stultifies frankness of vision.

service. A hero, as Tom Jones had proved, was none the less attractive for a superabundance of virility.

The plot invariably hinged upon difficulties caused by circumstances. No problem ever arose from the mind or spirit. Though one or other of the lovers might be tricked (if female) or tempted (if male) into behaviour which bred misunderstanding, their *sentiments* were in rigorous accord with every conventional demand. Even writers of genius exempted themselves but seldom from this law.

But from the last quarter of the century onward the pattern became more subtle. Minor figures had always been sketched with a free hand, but now there were innovators too numerous to mention whose experiments brought the deportment of heroes and heroines themselves a little nearer to real life. Young ladies in Regency novels are beautiful and good, very good indeed, but they have not the spectacular perfection of the Clarissas, Emilias, Cecilias, and Isabellas who had gone before. Heroes develop weaknesses less engaging than a turn for gallantry. As the tendencies of individual character are more and more convincingly expressed, plots are no longer mechanical in structure. It is not the machinations of his enemy so much as Darcy's own snobbish arrogance which at first alienates him from Elizabeth Bennet. Marianne Dashwood is human enough to fall deeply in love with a man who has only been flirting with her, and to behave very rashly over it. Wickham, like Willoughby, is no satanic scoundrel, but only a rather unscrupulous light-minded young egocentric who probably deceives himself nearly as much as he deceives others. Henry Crawford can be genuinely kind and chivalrous as well as selfish and irresponsible.

It is perhaps unfair to cite instances from so unique a realist as Jane Austen. No such faithful observation was to be brought into play again for many years, but lesser talents and talents of a different order were steadily augmenting and elaborating the novelist's material. Dickens carried the process several stages further with his heroes in humble ranks of life, his colloquial dialogue, and the extraordinary variety of his canvas. Charlotte Brontë repudiated the facile attraction of beauty, never till that time denied, as far as I am aware, to any heroine, and made Jane Eyre a fascinating and memorable creature despite her plainness, her caustic tongue, and the rebellious independence then considered most undesirable in women.

The habit of trying to represent things as they were, instead of as it was deemed polite to pretend they were, grew and grew upon the more serious kind of writers, despite the many lingering prohibitions of taste and custom. The career of Dickens holds up a clear glass to the expansive temper of the age. How flat and static are the figures of Harry Maylie and Nicholas Nickleby compared with Pip in *Great Expectations*, who is portrayed so 'roundly' that he can excite the reader's pity, contempt, and affection at the same moment! How much more plausible is the faulty heroine, Bella Wilfer, good-natured and lively but common and petulant, than Mary Graham, the immaculate granddaughter of old Martin Chuzzlewit! The characters in the later novels experience shades of feeling the earlier ones give no hint of. They have foolish, aimless passions, like the passions of people in real life . . . Pip's Estella obsession, which Dickens never meant to justify by marriage, Eugene Wrayburn's half-mischievous, half-genuine desire to be loved by Lizzie Hexam. They are susceptible of change, not in the unlikely manner of Mr Pickwick, who begins as an amiable buffoon and ends as an heroic crusader, but with the fidelity to nature of Mrs Gummidge, whose self-centred grumblings quietly subside in the face of real calamity—an accurate glimpse of psychology.

It was not merely that Dickens's great powers gathered scope with maturity—though that is also true—but that the novel itself had gathered scope. Literature was taking a less and less *simple* view of life. Soon there was a small legion of novelists who carried research into verities of one kind and another further than Dickens—writers who, like Hardy, Butler, and George Moore, questioned the beneficence of Providence or claimed sympathy for transgressors against a moral code that had seemed fixed and incontrovertible; writers like Henry James and Meredith, who in their different ways analysed more exquisite nuances of emotion than any of their predecessors; writers like Anstey, Gissing, Stevenson, and later H. G. Wells, who specialized in the air of verisimilitude.

The resemblance of fiction to reality continually gained ground as practices destructive to the illusion were one by one abandoned—rhetorical flights of dialogue, humorously descriptive names for characters, apostrophes and irrelevant asides from the author, and the doling out of rewards and punishments.

After the novel of analysis comes the novel of suggestion, initiated by Henry James and brought to its full delicate fruition by E. M. Forster. Here undertones and overtones are used to convey impressions so fine, so tenuous, that they might elude direct transcription. Next there begins with Dorothy Richardson a more minute representation of the workings of the mind and of sensory perceptions than anyone has yet attempted, while the story grows amorphous and inconclusive as life itself. Her methods are now imitated by many disciples, and, seeking to penetrate deeper still, James Joyce and others attempt to display the subconscious regions of thought in all their probable incoherence, grotesqueness, and libidinousness.

Meanwhile, one taboo after another has been broken down, timidly, tremblingly at first, then with bolder and bolder impetus. Physical functions and misfunctions usually ignored or referred to in euphemisms now sometimes receive a disproportionate emphasis. (I do not think, to give one instance, that nausea is felt quite so often and so actively in real life as modern authors would lead one to suppose.) The so-called coarseness of the novel before gentility took possession of it belonged to a bawdy, jesting vein which is still tapped liberally by raconteurs said to be connected with the stock exchange : its humour depends very largely on the premise that sexual pleasure is an amusing sin and a sinful amusement—an idea which must irresistibly arise where a practice condoned in one sex is looked upon as degrading to the other. Though some have striven, rather smirkingly, to revive the ribaldry of the early eighteenth century, sexual experience has, on the whole, been treated by the writers of our time in an earnest and sometimes solemn spirit of enquiry.

To say that there has been a striking advance in naturalism even among the ephemeral rank and file of fiction writers will not be construed, I hope, as implying that any new novel is better than any old one. Naturalism is not the sole merit of a work of art. There are times when it is not a merit at all, and when a clearer perception of essential elements may be obtained by sifting them, as it were, into unnatural separateness, like light broken by a prismatic glass. The wit and fancy of Swift, the infectious gusto, the manly vigour of Fielding, Sterne's drollery, Fanny Burney's adroitness at keeping the reader on the *qui vive* with a series of harrowing dilemmas—such qualities as these are not easily thrown in the shade by the highest degree of literal exactness.

I have made this light survey of the trend of fiction, not as art, but as a record—clearer and more compact than history provides—of a change in outlook which has modified the conditions of life very visibly within a quite brief space of time. It is a record which might inspire us to look towards the future with optimism if we were not living in an age when public opinion can be moulded more surely than ever before by organized propaganda, and when the most efficient instruments of that propaganda are (as they inevitably would be) in the hands of the reactionaries.

While national and international affairs are transacted with a contempt for individual feeling which must be viewed with great alarm, the laws, legal and social, governing private relations continue to yield, an inch here, the fraction of an inch there, to the exertions of those who perceive that our old simple standards are the standards of lazy or greedy or cruel ignorance.

Already the arguments used—and often successfully used—against reforms now completely accepted begin to astonish us with their childish absurdity. When we read that Lord Brougham opposed legislation to improve the appalling conditions under which children slaved in factories, on the grounds that such an interference would be 'contrary to the order of nature and the direction of Providence' [1] which had willed that only a child's parents had the right to protect it, we marvel at his naïveté. A statement in the *Saturday Review*,[2] typical of many which appeared

---

[1] Speech in the House of Lords, 1844. Quoted in *Lord Shaftesbury*, by J. L. and Barbara Hammond.
[2] In 1857. Quoted in *The Cause*, by Ray Strachey.

whenever the question was raised whether a married woman should be entitled to own property, brings to our lips a faint, incredulous smile. The proposal, it said, 'set at defiance the common sense of mankind, and would revolutionize society. There is besides a smack of selfish independence about it which rather jars with poetical notions of wedlock.' We cannot but smile again, somewhat wryly, when the same paper dismisses thus the economic difficulties of unmarried women desirous of earning their living: 'Married life is woman's profession; and to this life her training—that of dependence—is modelled. Of course, by not getting a husband, or losing him, she may find she is without resources. All that can be said of her is, she has failed in business and no social reform can prevent such failures.' [1]

It is absurd in a still more dreadful way to find the agitation to repeal the Contagious Diseases Act stigmatized [2] as a 'disgrace to the country' because 'it flooded gentlemen's breakfast tables with abominable literature, not addressed to themselves only, but also to their wives and daughters'; and we are shocked without any vestige of amusement at all when we learn that Samuel Solly, twice a vice-President of the Royal College of Surgeons, described syphilis, then virtually incurable, as a blessing, since, without it, there would be more fornication!

We have reached a stage of advancement where, *on these particular subjects*, the fatuity of such reasoning is no longer in dispute, and not only the Shaftesburys, the John Stuart Mills, and the Josephine Butlers, but also average citizens of middle-grade intellect uncomfortably suspect, if they cannot see at a glance, that some unsound short cut has been taken for the sake of ease.

In the case of the factory children, the ease required was a salve for conscience. The industrialists believed that their prosperity, and in consequence the prosperity of England, depended on cheap labour; starvation wages forced parents to send their children out to work as soon as their services became marketable; dire need rendered it impossible for them to bargain or lay down conditions. What more artlessly artful than to exalt the parents' 'sacred right' to be sole arbiters of the child's welfare, while slyly ignoring their powerlessness to exercise that right?

The muddle-headedness of the anti-feminists, which provides some of the most laughable examples of false prophecy in existence, was due, partly no doubt to certain sexual prepossessions, but partly also to their shivering fear of change. Convinced that the social order would collapse if women were granted the means of being independent, they were seized with panic and took refuge in any hole and corner of argument. Thus in nervous desperation the same writer who esteemed marriage as too poetical to be jarred by sordid notions when a wife wanted money, became capable of describing it as woman's 'profession,' her 'business'

[1] In 1857. Quoted in *The Cause*, by Ray Strachey.
[2] By Osborne Morgan, M.P., in a House of Commons Debate, 1872.

and the only business she should have, when spinsters claimed the right to earn.

As for Mr Osborne Morgan, M.P., he wished to be free, and to keep his fellows free, from the compulsion to bring intelligence to bear upon a very hateful squalid problem hedged about with every kind of taboo. It seemed less difficult to connive—tacitly—at prostitution and to treat prostitutes as a sub-human species than to reconsider the whole moral code and have ideas put into the heads of his wife and daughters. Lecky's famous burst of eloquence [1] on the prostitute as a mainstay of society represented the genuine and sincere belief of many moralists and most men of the world. 'That unhappy being,' he said, 'whose very name is a shame to speak, who is scorned and insulted as the vilest of her sex, and doomed for the most part to disease and abject wretchedness and an early death . . . is ultimately the most efficient guardian of virtue. But for her the unchallenged purity of countless happy homes would be polluted. . . . On that degraded and ignoble form are concentrated the passions that might have filled the world with shame.'

Given the simple postulate that any price, absolutely any price, was worth paying to preserve the chastity of women who belonged to the wives-and-daughters class, there is nothing wrong with the conclusions of Mr Lecky or even of Mr Solly.

Mr Solly shared with numbers of his contemporaries, and not a few of ours, a most peculiar sense of proportion. He thought an odious disease, the ravages of which were then most terrible, preferable to the evil of illicit sexual intercourse, and he was glad that the disease should exist if it made illicit sexual intercourse less tempting. He even deduced that it must have been invented by his benevolent Maker for that end. What he refused to recognize was that God's kindly plan was *not working*. The blessing of syphilis and the curse of fornication did not cancel each other out, but on the contrary each actually tended to promote the other.[2] For syphilis was (when it was decently allowed to be) an obstacle to holy wedlock, and yet had singularly little effect as a preventive of sexual desire and fulfilment. Once again the obvious inference turned out a fallacy.[3]

The fact that an inference is simple, however, does not mean that it will be explained or defended in simple terms. I have spoken of 'the ornamental flourish of reasoning which often disguises a mental line of

[1] In his *History of European Morals*, vol. ii., 1869.

[2] I learn from the National Society for the Prevention of Venereal Disease that there is still an appreciable number of persons who object to its work for hygiene on grounds that would have been approved by Mr Solly, but I hardly think those can be classified as 'average citizens of middle-grade intellect' or better. Though some of them are highly placed, they belong to a palpably retrogressive minority.

[3] That fear was not efficacious as a deterrent was one of the useful discoveries of the Trevethin Committee, appointed by the Government in 1922 to report upon venereal diseases. Twenty years after this investigation, however, the State campaign against the alarming increase of contagion has still been largely a bogy-bogy affair.

least resistance.' Incapable of admitting that he clings to a hard-and-fast belief because it would be a prolonged and perhaps a disillusioning effort to make fresh appraisals, the rationalizer will become more ingenious in designing a structure to support his error than he would need to be to pursue elusive truth.

Edmund Gosse's father, the zoologist, supplies an admirable paradigm of this confusion. A man of very brilliant and eminent attainments, he had acquired learning at a time when it was still possible for scientists to believe that the world had been created, whole and entire with all its animal and vegetable life, in precisely six days. Simple faith being necessary to his happiness, he maintained the literal accuracy of every statement in the Bible. Unfortunately his career coincided with those of Darwin, Wallace, Huxley, and their followers, whose enquiry into the origin of the species cast doubt, quite incidentally, on the Book of Genesis. There came a stage when Philip Gosse was compelled to wrestle with himself: he must either accept the evidence of modern geology and revise his view of the Bible as history—which was tantamount to questioning its divine inspiration—or else he must find means to refute that evidence. He chose the latter course and produced a most elaborate theory which could only bear one interpretation—though not the one he had intended: namely, 'that God had placed the fossils in the rocks in order to tempt geologists into infidelity.' Thus, in the words of his son, 'he took one step in the service of truth, and then he drew back in an agony, and accepted the servitude of error.'

Had he lived in a less analytical age, he might have been spared from the contrivance of distressing subterfuges. Anthony Nesbit, confronted with the remains of prehistoric animals a generation sooner, had dismissed the matter without a qualm. Noah, it seemed, must have omitted to take specimens of these into the Ark.

But we had better beware how we make fun of our ancestors, for it is probable that in another hundred years or so their nonsense will not seem so much worse than ours. How often, glancing through some old magazine or album, do we gibe at the fashions of a few years ago, ourselves wearing clothes which will be the laughing-stock of a few years hence!

I had thought to end this chapter with a selection of modern examples of the vice of over-simplifying, and indeed my cutting-books yield riches embarrassing in more senses than one. There is the Dean who would make adultery a criminal offence and send any person convicted of it to hard labour for a year (simple moral code and simple plan for enforcing it); the seaside vicar who describes 'the present world-wide dementia, the orgy of lust and passion for killing,' as being caused by the cult of the body and especially its exposure at holiday resorts (simplicity of explanation); the country vicar who tells us that if Nature had intended milk to be pasteurised, 'she' would have pasteurised it (simple-

minded personification of Nature and conviction of 'her' infallibility);
the Attorney-General who says in court: 'The book deals with what
everybody will recognize as an unsavoury subject—gratification of the
sexual appetite' (simple assumption that something which is unsavoury
to the Attorney-General must be unsavoury to everybody); the judge
who propounds the view that judges do not need sociological knowledge
and the less such knowledge is brought to bear on legal questions the
better (tenacious adhesion to simple rule-of-thumb methods); and the
statesman who, though he was Prime Minister during the last war,
remarks that if hostilities had broken out in September 1938 'we should
have suffered here at the beginning, but the totalitarian states would have
been crushed like an eggshell in the end' (simplification of every conceivable issue for the sake of rhetorical effect—i.e. appeal to emotion
instead of reason).

The shoddy treasure-trove of puerilities is inexhaustible, but to linger
there would be mere dalliance, since we have as yet examined only half
the ingredients of sentimentality. The other half, which happens to be
the more recognizable, I must keep for the next chapter.

What's the use of pretending? None? All the same, I shall continue
to pretend. To pretend that in the end the world will be as it was in the
beginning, a garden.
> BEVERLEY NICHOLS, in the *Sunday Chronicle*, June 2nd, 1939.

THE tendency to idealize is, I submitted, more recognizable than the
tendency to simplify; because, paradoxically enough, over-simplification often gives rise to complexity. Idealization also disguises itself,
but not in forms so nearly impenetrable. It has been, to some extent,
acknowledged as a natural bias of the outlook from ancient times, as
numerous proverbs and colloquial phrases testify, but on the whole it
was regarded either as a comical vanity ('seeing one's own geese as
swans') or a meritorious rosiness of vision ('looking on the bright side'),
and it was left to modern psychology to discover—or begin to discover—
the full reach and depth of its significance. The mind, according to the
demands of its weakness, evolves a technique of self-protection, sometimes
raising a barrier or series of barriers between itself and the objects presumed to be distasteful, and sometimes using, as it were, distorting
glasses which give reality an appearance more closely in keeping with
the idealist's wishes.

Self-protection by barrier can hardly find a clearer illustration than
Queen Victoria's alleged reply to one who had raised a question concerning prostitutes: 'In my realms there are no such women.' Defences
as palpable as this are rare and can be sustained only by persons who
are conceded a special right to rebuff intrusion. Beings not so privileged
usually camouflage their entrenchments. Self-protection by distorted
vision may be studied at its most obvious in the crude loyalties of those
who imagine that wherever their own lot has been cast is the most
desirable of all environments.

These methods of evasion need not be employed separately. One will
tend to promote the other, and indeed it is probable that there is always
some reciprocity between them. The Yorkshireman who sturdily
maintains that Yorkshire produces the salt of the earth is not only seeing
his own country through a lens which blurs all its defects; he is also
cutting himself off by barriers from a just appreciation of the outside
world. The queen who denies the existence of prostitution in her own
realm is setting up a fanciful picture of that realm as well as shutting
away an unpleasant topic.

In the same way, idealization converges upon simplification, and the
two ease-giving anodynes—to change a little the metaphor—become so
mingled that it is almost impossible to resolve them back into their

C   33

elements. If you glance again at Lord Brougham's pretext for opposing factory legislation, you will observe that besides being based on an acceptance of the simplest faith—namely, that Providence has 'implanted in the bosom of the mother and the father' all the care that can be necessary for a child's welfare—it implies a highly idealized view of the virtues and capacities of parents.

Reading further, you will find the proposal for regulating the sweated labour of women attacked in these terms: 'Cannot a woman make a bargain? Cannot a woman look after her own interests? Is not a woman a being capable of understanding those interests, and saying whether or not she have stamina and strength for work?' And after rebuking the humanitarians for cruelty and injustice because they forget how healthful it is 'to be able to appease the cravings of hunger by the sweat of the brow,' he proceeds, quite carried away with chivalrous indignation, to address the working classes: 'Make such contracts as you please with your master, carry your labour to the best market where you can get the greatest share of that abundance which Providence has prepared for you, and employ all the hours of the day in working with perseverance and spirit and honesty, while you retain the power and the will.'

Here we have a specimen of pure and unmistakable sentimentality. As the biographers of Brougham's adversary, Shaftesbury, remark, the message has 'a good, manly, sensible ring'; but in the simplicity and ideality of its reasoning it entirely missed the vital fact that the factory drudge had no power to make such contracts as he (or she) pleased, and that 'the abundance which Providence had prepared' for men, women, and children in the labour market was a fourteen-to-sixteen-hour day's work under the foulest conditions the body could endure for the lowest wage that would sustain it alive.

Presently we shall come to modern examples of this use of well-blended anodynes. We must first, however, look further into the anti-reality principle.

Idealization has an unfortunate corollary in the shape of a habit of irrational condemnation. If certain objects enjoy more than their fair share of praise, others, deemed to be opposite in character, are likely to receive more than their fair share of blame, and the propensity to over-simplify will make the selection of these objects somewhat haphazard. Through the same infirmity, the whole will often be condemned for the part, for it is much easier to reject things, people, or opinions in one comprehensive operation than to submit them to an analysis which may yield perplexing results. There is a natural eagerness for assured beliefs; indecision is burdensome. Those who are not trained in some form of scientific discipline like to feel they have 'made up their minds' even if it brings them down on the side of resentment and opprobrium.

And such emotions are not, of course, altogether disagreeable. That there is a satisfaction to be obtained from dislike may be seen in the fact that conversations in which someone is being criticized adversely nearly always last much longer and are far more animated than those in which there is nothing but kindness to be uttered. The destructive impulse, which is a very general, perhaps a universal one, requires infinitely less skill to gratify than the constructive.

But there is a point beyond which the pleasures of disapprobation wear thin. When personal security seems threatened, irate complacency gives place to fear. In short, the distortion of vision which produces deceptive beauties may be at least equally apt to produce deceptive horrors. If, to change the metaphor again, you believe in fairies, there is a pretty good chance that you will believe in bogies too.

I offer some glimpses both of enjoyable delusions and their customary obverse.

OPTATIVE IDEALIZATION (the fairy-tale):

'So successful has the Public School system of education been in producing men who are anxious to give the world unselfish service that it might be assumed that the segregation common to our Public School system is all that St James meant when he used the words "unspotted from the world."'

(The Headmaster of Felstead School in a University sermon reported in the *Cambridge Review*.)

'Lord Sandhurst in replying to a toast of the Houses of Parliament said the House of Lords was "the finest body of men on any subject." It could always produce the necessary expert. He found, though, a disinclination among the Lords to vote in their own propertied interests. He himself, he said, tried to persuade them that in voting in their own interests they would be voting in the interests of the country.'

(Report of a public dinner in the *Manchester Guardian*.)

'Twice in your leading article in last Wednesday's paper there occur the words British cowardice. One wonders what is the nationality of the man who wrote it, as the combination of these two words, together, is unknown in the English language, or in the tongue of any country in the world. In the present delicate situation in Europe would not the words "British Diplomacy" be more appropriate?'

(A letter in the *News Chronicle*, signed 'A Britisher, and Proud of it.')

'Hunting is really a kindness to the fox. . . . Instead of being the scum of the earth—as low in the opinion of man as a rat—he has become almost a king, respected by nearly everyone.'

(Major V. D. Williams, chairman of the Institute of the Horse and Pony Club, in a lecture on fox-hunting, reported in the *Daily Herald*.)

OBVERSE IDEALIZATION (the ghost-story) :

'The thoughtful man realizes in a moment that "Genesis" is imagination run riot, but there will be hundreds of thousands who see this monstrosity who will never allow their wives to become mothers.'
(Comment on a work of Epstein in the *Manchester Evening News*.)

'Rabbit trappers were looked upon as a most barbarous class of people, whereas they were most humane. All this "paper talk" going on against spring traps was nothing but nonsense, and it was his opinion it was Bolshevik money running it.'
(From a farmer's speech reported in the *Exeter Express and Echo*.)

'I have recently been very much struck by the low opinion which the Italians seem to hold of the British nation in general. Is it not possible that this contempt was first aroused by the example set by the poets Byron and Shelley when they lived at Lerici, near Leghorn, with Claire and Mary Godwin? Such proceedings can hardly have aroused feelings of admiration or respect for the nation which had produced them.'
(From a letter in the *Oxford Mail*.)

'Sir,—I heartily agree with "Retired Colonel." Every day in Kensington Gardens I notice the steady deterioration in manners of the rising generation, and their utter lack of consideration for either the beauties of Nature surrounding them or their fellow creatures— Yours, etc. "Better Days," Kensington W.8.'
(Letter in the *Daily Telegraph*.) [1]

Of the four positive examples, the first two give us, if I may use the paradox, stark *couleur de rose*; in the third there is a certain evasiveness —a resort to protective word-magic very typical of the fairy-tale world; the fourth offers as plain a specimen of magical personification as it would be possible to find outside the nursery. To justify enjoyment of the chase, the hunting enthusiast attributes to the hunted animal the feelings and knowledge of a man (a man, moreover, afflicted with an acute form of masochism). We find a similar ingenuous—or is it ingenious?— outlook on the part of those who assume that what is sport to human beings will be sport to their animal victims. Thus, one hears devotees speak of the 'unfairness' of shooting an animal instead of giving it a sporting chance—that is, using all the skill of huntsmen and trained hounds in a lethal chase of several hours.

Our negatives show us how sources of irritation are turned into bogies, and may even have powers imputed to them that verge on the miraculous. That we may recognize the emotional approach under less obvious aspects, let us, by way of preliminary exercise, briefly conjecture what

[1] All from *This England* edited by Gerald Barry, 1933, and *This England* edited by V. S. Pritchett, 1937 and 1940.

is going on in the minds of these four hyperbolists, each confronted with something that casts a shadow, great or little, on the way of life he prefers.

The critic of 'Genesis' is offended, I surmise, on two counts. First, the work in which so many profess to see wonderful excellences is to him quite incomprehensible; second, it symbolizes pregnancy in a fashion which violates his idealistic picture of that condition. Thus doubly dismayed, he represents the statue as a sort of mysterious and frightful totem which can produce celibate marriage beds, or an epidemic of abortions, or possibly merely a more determined use of contraceptives. (The means by which disgusted husbands are to prevent their wives from becoming mothers have not, we gather, been worked out on a practical basis. This vagueness is characteristic of evils prophesied under the stress of emotion.) But realizing, even in his wrath, that some will say he is going to extremes, he ascribes these dread effects only to the common herd, and classes himself as one of that small 'thoughtful' group among whom the processes of genitation will go on unimpaired.

That is one interpretation. Another is that the outburst is purely vituperative, the speaker being quite aware that he is talking nonsense. The direction taken by rhetoric, however, is by no means insignificant.

In our next case, we see, as often happens, positive and negative idealizations in conjunction. On the positive side, there is a roseate view of the sensations of trapped rabbits, consonant with the farmer's belief that the gin-trap is the cheapest and easiest means of dealing with a pest; on the negative, the worst view possible of anyone who threatens him with the prospect of having to change his methods. The worst view possible!—that leads him inevitably to the bogy of all bogies, Bolshevism, a fearful Russian cult whose fanatics are pledged to undermine the whole known order of everything. Like many of his countrymen, before the first great *volte face* of 1939,[1] he finds in Bolshevism a universal scapegoat, and, since he is in good practice, it is not at all a difficult feat for him to imagine the deep-scheming Russians, bent upon the ruin of British agriculture, financing a humane trapping campaign. Compared with some of the suspected activities of 'Russian gold' during the boom period of anti-Communism—say about 1930—his is a fairly sober hypothesis.

The example which follows is so very inane that at first it seems completely unaccountable. The suggestion that a race with such a tradition of gallantry as exists in Italy must feel towards a Shelley or a Byron

---

[1] This came about when we were seeking an alliance with Russia and for a few months Russian stock stood pretty high. The second great *volte face* was due, of course, to the loss of our potential ally to the enemy, when we reverted to our original position, later consolidated by events in Poland and Finland. Further remarkable somersaults have since been turned.

exactly the same reaction as English puritans is singularly naïve, and more so yet the presumption of a legacy of undying contempt left by their illicit loves. My theory of this curious recrimination will not, I fancy, be disputed by any reader acquainted with the effect Byron and, in a lesser degree, Shelley still have upon those who take exception to their morals. Here is a person with the notions of morality that are at home in a fourpenny novelette contemplating in fascinated horror a group of beings whose loves, after much more than a century, retain a strange power of disturbing. Risk, excitement, glamour, passion, the sense of memorable adventure—Byron stood, and still stands, for these. A figure of dark romance, he quickens a secret trauma in the idealist whose own sexual life has been anything but rich, and the throb becomes a throb of indignation. In the particular instance cited, the trauma is evidently unusually profound, for the Byron-Shelley circle is elevated to a very special degree of bogydom and the assailant has rushed to the attack quite wildly, not troubling to be accurate on a single point.[1]

The gentleman who signs himself 'Better Days' rather tamely brings up the rear. His complaint is a very old and very ordinary one and can be diagnosed at a glance. Regretting his own lost youth, he idealizes it and gets what bitter consolation he can out of vilifying the youth of the present. In such a frame of mind as this, there can be little doubt that he magnifies every evidence he can find of inconsiderateness, indifference to beauty, and so forth, and shuts his eyes firmly against all contrary manifestations.

I once, in the course of preparing another work, accumulated so many diatribes against the younger generation, dating consecutively from the most ancient times, that I formed the purpose of making an anthology of them, in hopes that it might induce a few readers to avoid the same error—for if it is not an error, then the human race has never ceased to grow steadily worse since it departed from some golden age of which there is no contemporary record. But with increasing realization that the task would be both melancholy and thankless, I abandoned it.

People, I suppose, will always fall into two main character groups, the strong and agile who will try to adapt themselves to the real conditions of life, hard as they may be, and the timid indolent who will look for life to adapt itself to them, and when that does not happen, will cherish such illusions as may comfort them. Thus the realist, as youth recedes from him, will prepare, it may be not without sorrow, to fit himself as best he can for his changed estate; the idealist will either refuse to acknowledge the advancing years or else will flatter himself with having been young at a time when virtue, courage, taste, gallantry—

[1] Mary Godwin and Shelley had been married for some years before they came to Lerici, and Byron never lived with Claire Clairmont either there or anywhere else in Italy. Byron and Shelley, so far from arousing contempt, were and have remained among the few Englishmen whom the Italians thoroughly like and admire.

whatever, in short, he holds in esteem—shone with a lustre unknown to these decadent days; and though you should prove to him conclusively that his opinion is one which has been common to most of the elderly in every place and age, he will persist in his faith that, no matter who was wrong, he, at any rate, is right.

So much for our first selection of object lessons, all the materials of which bear some easily traceable relation to the needs or wishes of the subject. But idealization is not always so perceptible in its motive power. Many of the illusions cherished most lovingly would appear, superficially, more likely to sadden than to bring comfort. The blessings of home life are nowhere so highly idealized as by the homeless, while those upon whom domestic ties press heavily think with deluded envy of the untrammelled liberty enjoyed by the free. Notwithstanding that there has never so far been any mortal creature who, when examined intimately, failed to reveal reasonable or unreasonable discontentments, each believes some other to be favoured with an almost carefree lot. Of another genre, but still less calculated, one might assume, to promote happiness, there are idealizations of conditions positively unattainable— of the past (that is, the past before one's own time), or the savage, an innovation of the eighteenth century, or of the nature and habits of animals, a speciality of the twentieth.

Yet if we ask ourselves what purpose these superstitions serve—for it is very certain that an inclination so widespread cannot be merely wanton—we shall find that they are not, after all, without their consoling function. The persuasion, in an unhappy world, that life has been, even at some distant time, or is, even in some distant place or among some alien species, healthy, wise, and good, becomes a sort of reassurance, a sustenance for pride of spirit. Or, on a more personal plane, the belief, when our own destiny seems painful or boring beyond endurance, that in propitious circumstances serenity would have been attainable (if we were rich! if we were bound by loving ties! if we were free!) does in some degree mitigate the despair with which, otherwise, we might be tempted to survey the whole human scene.

Vicarious illusions and illusions concerned with remote objects afford a channel of escape from known evils different from the distorted vision which misrepresents the life we actually have to live, but both kinds of idealization are equally a product of wishful thinking, taking their shape from the defects of reality.

It was the growing artificiality of the eighteenth-century world which brought about a vogue for hermits and a veneration for 'the noble savage,' ingenuous, untutored, uncorrupted, and full of natural goodness. (Our modern adaptation of this picture emphasizes physical fitness rather than virtue, and there are many who seriously imagine, regardless of all the evidence available, that natives from the wilds are invariably proof against disease, or in possession of tribal remedies immensely more effective than anything known to medical science.) [1] The still greater artificiality of our existence today leads certain harassed would-be fugitives to expatiate on the perfect health, the inward harmony, the immunity from all the morbid effects of civilization, which they tell us are characteristic of wild animals. Zoologists and naturalists, on the other hand, find disease and suffering among wild animals as among tame ones. I myself, in a South African museum, once strayed into a room devoted to parasites knowing no discrimination between wild creatures and tame, the only difference being that the tame are better protected from them; and I received an impression which has made me sceptical of the animal ideal ever since.

It is my experience that fantasies of this impersonal kind are often indulged in without a very radical attempt at self-deception. Faced with the opposition of facts, the enthusiast will say, in irritation rather than anger, 'Surely we can be allowed to have *some* illusions!' And inasmuch as he admits illusion at all, he is safe from its worst effects: a sufficiently urgent call for realistic judgment may cause him to emerge from his haze. Idealizations, positive or negative, which have a more immediate bearing upon the individual's own situation, and those which are fostered from childhood by social and ethical training, are naturally maintained with greater passion. Illusion cannot be admitted, and the danger becomes serious.

It is a twofold danger, reaching outward to society and inward to the detriment of the individual himself. Society is injured because institutions which it is customary to regard with undue optimism are thereby chartered to withstand criticism and correction, while adverse idealizations lend support to prejudices most damaging to the community in other directions. The individual for his part is usually given occasion—if he would but take it!—to discover that his protective mechanism was built upon a coiled spring. The world of facts is painfully insistent. Weave fantasies as we may, reality will keep breaking in.

The effect of this intrusion is to make some people bitter, stupidly sceptical of beauty and goodness, and addicted to belittling whatever is or has been or might be admired: others take refuge behind further and higher barriers until at last the opacity of their minds becomes impenetrable. Only a very few learn from disagreeable enlightenments to cultivate a more sober and searching outlook for the future.

Between our two great wars, the embittered class grew strikingly large and was catered for in sections of the press by a special kind of writer known in ugly slang as a 'debunker.' The word, which originally meant 'anti-idealist' in no uncomplimentary sense, now rather describes the would-be iconoclast who, if he has not the power to break an

---

[1] 'In spite of the much-insisted-upon wear and tear of modern life, the average city worker of northern latitudes lives nearly twice as long as the easy-going savage.'—E. G. Boulenger, in an essay on *Longevity*.

image, will defile it. It is part of the debunking method seldom to refer to any eminent or respected person, particularly among the dead who are unprotected by libel laws, without working in some touch of be-spattering ridicule, while what has hitherto been regarded as of little worth will be exalted to some surprisingly lofty level. (A similar technique, applied to art criticism, produced some years ago the *chi-chi* vogue.) This interesting reaction to disillusionment is the one most natural to the twentieth century, when progress in recognitions enables the critic and his audience to admit the weaknesses and absurdities of the great, the merits of the vulgar, without any corresponding increase of that honesty of vision which gives sound perspective.

For it is an unhappy fact that the slow but sure revolt against over-simplification has not been paralleled by a movement of equivalent impetus away from make-believe. To fulfil wishes and evade fears is still one of the most widely exercised functions of thought, and the majority of us persevere, to use the words of Lowes Dickinson, in 'our habitual refusal to look straight at realities in the light of the values we profess to hold.'

Now perhaps this is the point at which the reader may feel inclined to make a protest on these lines: 'But there are aspects of reality so distressing to some of us as to be hardly bearable. Surely a certain use of protective mechanism is essential? What good is there in "facing up" to truth when, as a result, the mind is so bruised as to be permanently damaged? A measure of illusion may be a necessity.'

The argument is one which has my particular sympathy since I am—if a personal confession will be tolerated—of a squeamish disposition, and the pain I have experienced in acquiring certain pieces of knowledge seems to me to have been out of all proportion to the good such know-ledge has enabled me to do. Indeed, there are states of mental disturb-ance so acute that a sort of paralysis ensues, when, with the best will in the world, the observer becomes helpless. I cannot conceive, therefore, that it is desirable, even if it were possible, for us to acquaint ourselves with every repellent fact about which information may be to hand. But what facts we do examine we should examine honestly. A measure of *ignorance* may be requisite, but I question the general necessity for illusion.

If it be asked why illusion is condemned when ignorance is to be permitted, I offer an important distinction. Illusion (in this context) is a glossing over of reality so as to conceal its evils or to lay them upon the shoulders of selected scapegoats, and it is therefore full of deceptions and dangers, whereas ignorance when it is deliberate implies an admission of evil, which is, in itself, potentially a step towards mitiga-tion. Many who subscribe to a society formed for the protection of children or animals would not be equal to making a detailed study of the cruelties they assist in suppressing. Their usefulness is certainly less great than it would be if their nervous constitution were more

41

robust, but they are not quite ineffectual. Their very horror has often served to stimulate valuable exertion.

The chief danger of not being able to stomach the whole truth is that one may espouse causes from humanitarian motives without sufficient knowledge of their merits, or may, on the other hand, refrain from espousing causes altogether because they might involve unnerving kinds of research. But here is no active obstructiveness such as we find in those who believe that animals enjoy being hunted, or that parents, however inferior in other respects, are endowed with a magical aptitude for behaving wisely and justly to their children.

Deliberate ignorance does not, in short, inevitably proceed from a violation of that reality principle which appears to most philosophers and scientists to be the best foundation for a life worth living—a principle which has been defined as one of 'basing our satisfactions upon a fundamental recognition of the real world, and not upon a distortion of it, or a denial of its less pleasant aspects.' The same authority,[1] with whom I am not often in such comfortable accord as now, has insisted that

> 'conscious investigation and assessment constitute the ultimate test as to whether or not a given tendency is in harmony with the reality principle. If it fails to pass this test, we cannot give it our approval, however greatly it is buttressed by tradition, or however strongly it appeals to the potent but dimmer forces of intuition and emotion.'

'*Conscious investigation and assessment,*' this is what denotes and has always denoted an honest and energetic mind; the scrupulous enquiry of reason instead of the blind surrender to sentiment, which, thus encouraged, unfailingly develops into sentimentality. The following chapters will, I hope, exhibit the pernicious effects of this surrender, and the degree to which approved custom exacts it.

Let us see what part the reality principle is allowed to play in the formation of those opinions which it is convenient to hold in public, and which are therefore very widely cultivated in private.

---

[1] Professor J. C. Flugel, in his *Psychology of Clothes*. I should mention that I use the term 'reality principle' in the obvious sense which accords with the definition above quoted, and not with the specialized connotation attached to it by Freud himself.

Wealthy people are, as a class, better than impoverished people, more moral, more intellectual, more well-behaved. There is only one class in the community that thinks more about money than the rich, and that is the poor. The poor can think of nothing else. That is the misery of being poor.

The Soul of Man Under Socialism: OSCAR WILDE.

I AM sensible as I write the word Demos at the top of this chapter that it is an abstraction, that there is no simple conglomerate 'people' any more than there are simple conglomerate popular opinions, but only collections of individuals capable of startling variations from the types to which we assign them. Everyone talks about the masses, but no one, it seems, belongs to them. So, when Malthusian doctrines were in favour, the surplus population was discussed as if it were a well-defined fringe of the social order, and no one supposed himself to be a member of it.

Whoever writes a book about the public without keeping it perpetually in mind that the 'many-headed monster' is a creature altogether fabulous can disseminate little but harmful error. Yet the research worker's situation is not entirely plain-sailing. Though the monster is fabulous, there is sometimes a very convincing projection of its appearance. People are individuals and there is no evidence that their identities can be merged, but it is not enough to study individual reactions if we are to take the temper of a crowd or a mass.[1] Something happens which gives the impression that separateness has been lost.

Here an analogy will prove useful. If you listen to a throng of chattering people—say at a party or in a well-patronized restaurant—the many intermingled voices will sound in your ears like one strident and strepitous noise. Beyond the circle of your nearest neighbours not a word is articulate, not a tone is distinguished for beauty or graciousness. The chirping and buzzing of a swarm of insects could not be more impersonal. Yet when you switch away your attention to join in the talk of your companions, what you hear is so wonderfully different in quality that you can hardly believe your voices too are contributing to the general din. They are still, to you, detached from the rest and perfectly recog-

---

[1] The structure, as well as the mentality, of masses and crowds has been admirably analysed by Dr Gustave Le Bon (*La Psychologie des Foules*) and Dr André Joussain (*La Psychologie des Masses*), and I do not propose to attempt a new anatomy. The difference is, briefly, that the crowd is a large assembly whose members are in direct contact with one another, but not necessarily united in intention, while the mass is a body of people which, though dispersed, is composed of individuals who have some strong community of purpose, of interests, or of ideas.

nizable—a little louder than usual perhaps, to be audible above the clamour, or a little softer, so as not to be caught by strangers, but certainly incapable, you would think, of becoming mere cacophony.

The crowded room reflects the world at large where, while your own separateness and that of those closely known to you are never lost, others seem to undergo some fusion. And in fact, although no real merging occurs, the overwhelming illusion of it is to be reckoned with. Nobody consenting to be part of a multitude can remain unaffected in his behaviour and opinions by what he supposes it to be. I say 'by what he *supposes* it to be' because the same assortment of persons, encountered or imagined one by one, would perhaps carry little weight: he submits to be influenced only because he is picturing it as a corporate entity, far greater and more powerful than himself. Each member of the mass— and by that I mean everyone who is thus willing to submit himself—is under a similar misapprehension about the collective character of the others.

It is towards that instinct of submission, commonly known as the herd instinct, that propagandists direct so many of their most telling suggestions. 'The vast majority of thoughtful men are agreed . . .'; 'None but a few cranks and faddists are likely to deny . . .'—by interlarding their statements with affirmations such as these, or by more subtly taking the weight of numbers for granted, they can usually bring all but the sturdiest independents into the selected fold. Sheep, we know, are inclined to follow other sheep: men will follow other men without so much sensory evidence as sheep require, being stirred by the mere report —and sometimes false report—of their movements.

And there is some justification for identifying these herd-like masses with the most plebeian sections of the community, for in them deliberate separateness demands far more effort and courage than among those born and bred to a little freedom. The rich and the well-born, the intelligentsia, even the class-disowning 'Bohemians,' are likewise inclined, much more than many of them realize, to run in droves, but their numbers are less unwieldy, there are better opportunities of breaking away, and they are not subjected to such a barrage of propaganda from classes outside their own to keep them doing and thinking the same things.

But no man inevitably belongs to 'the masses' by reason of being a plebeian, and no man is insulated from them by reason of having money, education, or good lineage. The masses are composed of persons who are content, whether through indolence, suggestibility, or lack of moral courage, to hold or pretend to hold opinions which come to them ready-manufactured. Whatever a statistical reckoning might make of him, no labourer, no artisan, no clerk, no shop assistant is to be counted with the masses whose conclusions are the product of his own reasoning powers, swayed only by such influences as expand those powers rather than contract them. There are many, certainly, who have a pleasing notion, very artfully fostered by their shepherds, that they 'think things out for themselves,' but who always arrive notwithstanding at the conclusions deemed expedient in their flock. There are also others who are so anxious to assert their separateness that they reject even a rational verdict when it is likely to be congenial to the majority. Lately these have been a sufficiently flourishing group to demand a good measure of the sociologist's attention.

Doubtless in every epoch some artists and critics exist whose attempt to be original takes the form of self-conscious perverseness, but in our time the number has been particularly striking and the resulting work strange without precedent. This is, I think, a not unnatural reaction against the mass-production of taste and feeling effected by the daily press, the cinema, and other popular modes of instruction and amusement. The degree of rebellion is proportionate to the degree of coercion, and it is beyond controversy that never before have the means of influencing the public outlook been so overwhelming. We cannot wonder that artists of gifts more than mediocre but less than first-rate should segregate themselves into little refractory cliques proclaiming, in effect, 'Whatever the public admires we despise.' There is nothing in common between this strained aloofness and the genuine detachment of originality, but unfortunately they are easily confused.

Defiant poets and painters, *chi-chi* critics and mocking philosophers are seldom found, however, below the middle grades of society. It is upon the lower grades, constituting, not by any means the only herds, but the largest and the most ready to be led or driven, that our enquiry must now be focussed. What they are and what they are assumed to be is of much greater importance to the rest of the social order than is usually understood, and probably no aspect of sentimental evasion has been so disastrous as that which we shall presently explore.

.   .   .   .

There is a generally prevalent idea that sentimentalists are benevolent while rationalists are hard and calculating. It is the custom of seekers after public favour to exalt the heart at the expense of the head, and one frequently hears people confess to emotional prejudices with complacency. Warm-hearted muddlers feel immensely superior in charity to those conscientious investigators who try to understand what they are doing and what the effects are likely to be. Frankly distrustful of efficiency—which they stigmatize as 'cold'—and taking credit to themselves for gullibility, they constitute a menace to the advancement of mankind, and preen themselves upon it. 'I'm not ashamed to be old-fashioned!' they proclaim as they oppose the cleaning of some time-honoured Augean stables, or, like that arch-emotionalist, Mr Beverley Nichols, when he admitted having been hoaxed and in turn hoaxing his readers with a peculiarly drivelling war-story of kindness rewarded: 'I was born credulous—and thank God for it.'[1] The assumption is that to be non-credulous—i.e. to apply the test of reason—is to be ill-natured.

In the words of Leonard Woolf, whose views diverge greatly from those of Mr Nichols, 'It seems almost to be assumed that a belief you have no reason for believing is more spiritual than and ethically superior to one for which you can give a reason.'

'Thank God I am credulous' is one of those sentiments which has the flavour we label Victorian, because the attitude it expresses reached the zenith of its cultivation during the nineteenth century; that epoch when, if novelists may be believed, elderly gentlemen of immense credulity were constantly wrought upon to wipe lachrymal mists from their eye-glasses, and were very much admired for it. The eighteenth century had its own forms of sentimentality, generally personal and patriarchal; by the nineteenth there had developed, under pressure and with marked reluctance, a social conscience, and to assuage it, a series of comforting idealizations kept pace. In the eighteenth century, prostitutes were sent to the treadmill; in the nineteenth, they were called unfortunates and unctuous tears were shed over them even by their patrons. Neither method was of much value in ridding society of a pest produced by its own unhealthy constitution. In the eighteenth century, the rich had made little attempt to disguise the fact that they regarded the poor as an unbounded nuisance and a bad lot; in the nineteenth, 'poor' was an adjective habitually associated with 'honest,' sweated labour was 'honest toil,' euphemisms were invented to designate what had formerly been bluntly called the lower orders, and there was a huge output of free tracts and red flannel petticoats.

In adopting these new manners, a number of people who profited by the hideous industrial conditions of the time were able to feel they were behaving handsomely towards the downtrodden. No doubt it was an indication of progress that they found it desirable to make concessions at all, but the great works of Victorian philanthropy were hindered rather than helped by such smug gestures. Although the reformers were usually obliged to talk the sentimental language their audiences approved, and were sometimes carried away by it, their approach to the particular evils which they had elected to fight was necessarily realistic. Social physicians, they did not delude themselves that they could cure disease by masking the symptoms.

The writers of the *Life of Lord Shaftesbury* [2] tell us that, when appeals were made to housewives not to allow young children to do the cruel and dangerous work of cleaning chimneys (a machine being on the market which should have rendered the climbing method obsolete), the chief effect was actually to encourage the employment of the 'dear little boys,' since the uneasy feeling awakened prompted gifts of pennies and

<hr>

[1] *Sunday Chronicle*, October 15th, 1939.   [2] J. L. and Barbara Hammond.

food which made them more than ever profitable to their masters. Thus was conscience tranquillized at small cost without agitation for a reform deemed inconvenient.

The nineteenth century may be said to have specialized in this inexpensive mode of appeasement, the wretched results of which we see clearly enough in perspective. Poverty is a difficult condition to eliminate at the best of times, but when it is called 'honest poverty' and made to sound an almost enviable state, and when those who have been degraded by it are flattered into believing that they have some special nobility denied to the more comfortable, the difficulty is likely to become overwhelming. When the devastation of childhood in factories is defended on the grounds that the employer is fond of children and likes to have them about him,[1] when the miserable little dwarfs thus produced are gaily described as 'lively elves,'[2] when an overcrowded slum cottage is said to present 'a gratifying picture of social comfort,'[3] when a disease-ridden street-walker is looked upon as 'the most efficient guardian of virtue,'[4] the reformer may justly pride himself on having undertaken gigantic labours. Cold-blooded cruelty is easier to vanquish than hypocrisy, and the hypocrisy by which one deceives oneself is the most incorrigible of all.

Unhappily, substantial relics of the Victorian talent for self-hood-winking still impede the movements of the public intellect. And in nothing does it work with more insidious effect than in the glorification of the lower classes.

I am not unaware—indeed I am only too well aware—that it is considered snobbish and unmannerly to refer to the lower classes under that name. Indeed, there is almost a taboo upon the mention of the words. An exactly similar taboo was once adopted in the Southern States of America, 'where gentlemen who vaguely felt, or knew that they ought to feel, that it was wrong to keep human beings in servitude but had no intention of ceasing to do so, would never refer to their slaves otherwise than as "hands," "negroes," "my people," or "the force." They found that these paraphrases proved admirable conscience-salves.'[5] The slaves themselves doubtless endured their slavery a little more resignedly because this courtesy was accorded them.

[1] In Richard Beamish's Memoir of the Life of the Elder Brunel we find a reference to the engineer's 'high gratification' (as well as to the 'important economic advantages to the public') in his being able to employ children in mechanical sawmills. 'The love of the young,' remarks his biographer, 'was a distinguished and abiding feature of Brunel's character.'

[2] Dr Andrew Ure, in The Philosophy of Manufactures, 1835, quoted in The Englishman's Food by J. C. Drummond and Ann Wilbraham. Dr Ure thought the ills of labourers were due to 'high wages which enabled them . . . to pamper themselves into nervous ailments by a diet too rich and exciting for their indoor employment.'

[3] Dr William Morrison, reporting on the housing conditions of colliers to the Children's Employment Commission, 1841.

[4] W. E. H. Lecky, in his History of European Morals, supra.

[5] From It Isn't Done : Taboo Among the British Islanders, by Archibald Lyall.

47

Now, at the risk of giving displeasure to several different sorts of readers, I assert bluntly that, in every country where inequalities of wealth and opportunity are strongly marked, there are lower classes, and that, in England at any rate, they are very low indeed. The presence among the poor of a few shining exceptions to the generally dismal standard of health, beauty, and intelligence is naturally exploited on both the upper and under levels of society—by the rich because they like to believe that bad food, bad houses, and a general state of disadvantage are not so destructive as sociologists assume; by the poor because the exaltation of one of their number sheds a little light and dignity upon themselves. But this rare survival of good attributes against heavy odds proves nothing except a certain sportiveness in nature.

The terms 'rich' and 'poor' in such a connection as this are, of course, ill-defined and crude, but I think they will be understood to indicate the disparity between those who may to some extent choose their way of life and those who belong to that world in which the compulsion of necessity is always evident. Oscar Wilde sketches the situation vividly, if with some rhetorical exaggeration, in his neglected essay, *The Soul of Man Under Socialism*:

'At present, in consequence of the existence of private property, a great many people are enabled to develop a certain very limited amount of Individualism. They are either under no necessity to work for their living, or are enabled to choose the sphere of activity that is really congenial to them, and gives them pleasure. These are the poets, the philosophers, the men of science, the men of culture—in a word, the real men, the men who have realized themselves, and in whom all Humanity gains a partial realization. Upon the other hand, there are a great many people who, having no private property of their own, and being always on the brink of sheer starvation, are compelled to do the work of beasts of burden, to do work that is quite uncongenial to them, and to which they are forced by the peremptory, unreasonable degrading Tyranny of want. These are the poor; and amongst them there is no grace of manner, or charm of speech, or civilization or culture, or refinement in pleasures, or joy of life. From their collective force Humanity gains much in material prosperity. But it is only the material result that it gains, and the man who is poor is in himself absolutely of no importance. He is merely the infinitesimal atom of a force that, so far from regarding him, crushes him: indeed, prefers him crushed, as in that case he is far more obedient.'

Although it would be ludicrous to pretend that the so-called rich habitually develop into poets, philosophers, and men of science, it is true that this class of people—that is the upper and middle class, those who have some slight experience of freedom—has always contained a far greater number of artistic and intellectual workers, individuals of distinctive value to the race, than the propertyless masses. It is also true (and it seems absurd to have to make the statement) that well-nourished, well-housed people are more elegant, pleasanter in form and feature, cleaner, more honourable, and better able to control themselves. Ostensibly it is kind and polite, actually it is expedient, to ignore these well-known facts, and to pretend that the man who has had none of the advantages conferred by money is, if anything, superior to one of higher caste—sturdier, more straightforward, more gifted with human understanding. The popular press, the popular novel, the popular theatre, the cinema, and innumerable periodicals all support this view, so congenial to the majority, so acceptable even to the minority whose sympathies take comfort from the fairy-tale.

Yet an impartial enquirer cannot fail to be struck with the degree to which sustained poverty and near-poverty undermine the character, corrupt the manners, and destroy the physical well-being of those who must contend with it. The rarity of plebeian good looks, to name an aspect of the matter which I think only the superficial will dismiss as unimportant, is in itself a depressing proof of the extensiveness of the damage. I have not noticed that in infancy the children of the poor are less pretty than those more fortunately born, though their attractions tend to be obscured by dirt and matted hair, and the want of pocket-handkerchiefs. But whatever qualities the child may have are usually laid waste almost before the end of adolescence. Defective teeth, stunted growth,[1] deformities which are the aftermath of neglected adenoids or rickets, pasty faces mature beyond their years, figures destined quickly to run to seed—these have become melancholy class distinctions.

Even when good features remain unimpaired till adulthood, their effect is likely to be marred by ugly little expressions, twistings of the mouth, grins and sneers, sudden slackenings of the facial muscles, which reveal origin to the observant eye as surely as an accent will reveal it to the observant ear. To overcome these lifelong mannerisms is a wonderful feat, performed only by the specially gifted and ambitious, and involving a strain upon the personality which may vitiate it. To make believe on the other hand that class distinctions are of no account and not worth bothering about is a foolish form of inverted snobbery which does no service to those who suffer because of them.

Through the fundamental fact of economic differences, other differences exist, physically, mentally, visibly and covertly, which are a reproach to civilization. It is an altogether false humanitarianism which seeks to persuade us that the makeshift life imposed by poverty does not debase its victims. The present system must remain exactly so long as there is this mutual conspiracy between high and low to deny its disgusting evils.

For a long while past it has been customary to denigrate the rich,

[1] See Appendix 1.

many of whom have lent themselves with willingness and perhaps even with relish to the business of sitting for a highly coloured picture of follies and vices : it is a simple and amusing way of satisfying the mingled feelings of the poor—their pardonable spite, their envy, and their sensationalism. In consequence it has come to be widely accepted that moneyed people are either brainless or wicked—a fiction which is soothing to the poor in much the same way as it is soothing to a plain woman to suppose that pretty ones are empty-headed and heartless. In truth, the rich, though most of them display the inveterate selfishness which our system engenders, have virtues the poor cannot be expected to emulate.

Their education, far from good though it is, yet has merits not found in the education of the humble ; their homes afford some privacy, their lives some leisure, for the development of taste and the acquisition of knowledge. That few of them make the best use of these privileges is very obvious, but even with less than the best use, some benefit can hardly fail to be realized. The rich, having been spared so many embittered struggles, so many mean little shifts and stultifying discomforts, are, as they well might be, comparatively tolerant and enlightened. Their training makes it unusual for them to practise sordid forms of cruelty, dishonesty, and interference with liberty. At close quarters they are more considerate as employers. (I say 'at close quarters' because they are accustomed, with enterprises that can be controlled from a distance, to turning promoted members of the lower classes into overseers and shutting their eyes to the method by which profit is obtained.) They are not so much given to ill-using their children,[1] to prying into and meddling with each other's lives,[2] to sniggering at what is new and strange, to releasing bad temper in bouts of physical violence, and to becoming the prey of such petty vindictiveness and irrational antagonisms as people of happier breed know only from the feuds of their servants.

In the statement of these dreary facts there is no reflection upon the poor, in whom the existence of any merits at all is remarkable : the reflection is upon the privileged classes who prefer flattering the creators of their wealth and keeping them low, to acknowledging their wretched condition and raising them up. If there is any blame to be laid on the shoulders of the dispossessed, it is because they bear the desperate injustice so tamely—these people who, in the words of Mirabeau, 'produce everything, and to be formidable have only to stand motionless.' Wilde's essay contains the exonerating answer : 'Misery and poverty are so absolutely degrading, and exercise such a paralysing effect over the nature of men, that no class is ever really conscious of its own suffering. They have to be told of it by other people, and they often entirely disbelieve them.'

The monstrosities of our economic system—which is perhaps the most

[1] See Appendix 2.   [2] See Appendix 3.

*un*economic system that purblind greed could have contrived—have been so often analysed and arraigned that I will crystallize all my own indictment into the oblique observations recorded here. It is a system which ensures that large sections of the populace shall be uneducated, ugly, and displeasing in their habits. If to this number we add another mass almost as great in size and, although slightly better in physical quality, rather more backward mentally, namely the lower middle class, which, in its anxiety to dissociate itself from the class just beneath its own, supports with enthusiastic loyalty the worst nonsense of the obsolescent order,[1] we shall see that the stupid and ignorant are a vastly preponderating majority.

.   .   .   .

It is part of the technique of keeping potentially dissatisfied groups quiet by playing upon their vanity—and of allaying conscience at the same time—to give them a little nominal power and a few rights not likely often to be asserted. Thus, in England and some other countries where the division of wealth is palpably unequal, great stress is laid on the democratic constitution—government by the people, a catchword which has been infinitely useful to the forces of reaction. Whether government by the people would be desirable if it could be achieved is very doubtful in view of their striking want of the requisite abilities: that it *has* been achieved is a delusion astonishing even to a specialist in delusions.

Now a catchword is one which, generally as the result of some interested party's propaganda, has developed emotional connotations likely to cloud over its literal meaning; and unless there is agreement as to that meaning, there cannot be any reasonable discussion of the issues involved. Let us therefore very briefly examine what democracy signifies. To the opponents of the Reform Bills in the eighteen-thirties the term was one of opprobrium and contempt; it meant mob law, dissent from the Church, rebellion against the Landed Gentry who had been England's God-sent rulers from time immemorial, and the 'intimidation and audacity which always accompany revolutionary proceedings.'[2] A persecutor of early Christians could hardly be more amazed, confronted with the Vatican, than the Duke of Wellington would be to learn that democracy had become the battle-cry of the English. (The parallel can be carried further; for the nineteenth-century democrats themselves would, I suspect, take much the same view of modern democracy that the early Christians would take of modern Christianity.) To represent

---

[1] It is from this stratum that most of the teachers in elementary and secondary schools are drawn.

[2] Words used by Wellington to describe the democratic movement in a letter to J. W. Croker, 1833. Croker considered 'that a democracy, once set a-going, must sooner or later work itself out till it ends in anarchy and that some kind of despotism must then come to restore society.' Quoted by G. J. Renier in *The English: Are They Human?*

democracy as an ancient tradition of these realms, as our publicists so blatantly attempt to do, is the purest fantasy.

Wellington no doubt ascribed to the word nothing more than the meaning it derives from Greek, and his opinion of Demos was much poorer than that which it is thought humane to hold today : but now the idea of government by the people has gathered, for those who favour it, certain very important associations. Among the values which have been added to it are freedom, equality, social and legal justice, the dignity of the individual. Thus Clarence Streit feels able to give this definition : [1]

'Democracy to me is the way to individual freedom formed by men organizing themselves on the principle of the equality of man. That is, they organize government of themselves in the sense that their laws operate on them individually as equals. They organize government by themselves, each having an equal vote in making law. They organize government for themselves, to secure equally the freedom, in the broadest possible sense of the term, of each of them. By democracy I mean government of the totality by the majority for the sake equally of each minority of one, particularly as regards securing him such rights as freedom of speech, press and association.'

Mr Streit, an American, flatters us prodigiously when he assumes that our Parliament of big business men, hereditary peers, Church of England bishops, trade union champions, and obscure party yes-men—with how thin a sprinkling of disinterested public servants !—has really had as its prime object any such noble notions. Equality is a mere verbal flourish when inherited rank confers privilege, when the dignitaries of a favoured Church are allowed to be legislators, when poverty subjugates millions to a thankless slavery, and when distinctions of caste—through distinctions of income—are so pronounced as usually to be recognizable at a single glance. And if these violations of Mr Streit's democratic principles are patent in England, they are a hundred times more so in the countries which England rules, or partially rules, from a distance. The tens of millions of citizens of the British Empire who are completely without franchise probably take a somewhat jaundiced view of the glorious ideal of political freedom as interpreted in Westminster. Our system of government has been described by its foreign critics as plutodemocracy : it might with even more reason be called leucodemocracy—government (theoretically) by the people ; but only if they are white.[2]

Another sentimental evaluation has been given by Mr Winston Churchill, who, in January 1939, shortly before peacetime conscription was brought into effect, remarked that : 'The essential aspects of demo-

[1] In *Union Now*, a Proposal for Federal Union of the Leading Democracies.
[2] See Appendix 4.

cracy are the freedom of the individual, within the framework of laws passed by Parliament, to order his life as he pleases, and the uniform enforcement of tribunals independent of the executive.' Mr Churchill, with his long experience as a politician, knows the power of suggestion and is aware no doubt that it stirs a little heart-warming pride in a semi-illiterate voter who went to work at fourteen to believe that he is ordering his life as he pleases. 'Freedom within the framework of laws passed by Parliament'—he has been told so often how grateful he ought to be for having that, that when Parliament passes laws threatening the removal of his freedom altogether, putting him at the disposal of the State for uses that may be totally against his wishes, his interests, and the interests of his class and kind, he still proclaims himself the inhabitant of a free country. 'The uniform enforcement of tribunals independent of the executive' —that is one of those phrases of cloudy import which seem the natural mode of utterance for statesmen. Whatever its precise meaning may be, if the enforced tribunals maintain the same standard of independence from the executive as—for example—the tribunals for conscientious objectors, I think the executive need not much fear to be overruled.

Sir Nevile Henderson goes so far as to think democracy compatible with actual tyranny, for in his White Paper, immediately after referring to Herr Hitler's 'detestable tyrannical methods,' he remarks that many of his social reforms, '*in spite of their complete disregard of personal liberty of thought, word or deed*, were on highly advanced democratic lines.' (I need hardly say that I am responsible for the italics.)

Democracy frequently seems to be regarded, even by those who think themselves its most ardent supporters, as no more than a readiness to level down class distinctions on some specific government occasion, as when food is to be rationed or men are to be conscripted for the army. In the press campaign for compulsory military service—which began in the form of an appeal for 'physical training' to benefit the youth of the nation —there were reiterant allusions to the democratic character of the measures proposed, since all would be treated alike. (In point of fact, public school boys with an O.T.C. record do not seem to remain indefinitely in the ranks; nor is their promotion unreasonable, since, as Bertrand Russell affirms in his analysis of *Power*: 'There is no doubt that the habit of command makes it easier to bear responsibilities and to take quick decisions.' The indignation aroused over any candid acceptance of this obvious fact, such as Colonel Bingham's celebrated letter to *The Times*, is misguided on the part of the ruled and spurious on the part of the rulers.)

It is hard to see on what grounds conscription has been held to be democratic in England and America and anti-democratic in Germany and Italy. I concede that it has spared us from frantic recruiting appeals and public insults to men not wearing uniforms, but to speak of democratic conscription remains a contradiction in terms, whether we take the literal meaning of the adjective or the significance habitually given to it as descriptive of government based on the individual's right to freedom of action and conscience. If the people's will is overwhelmingly in favour of military service, is it necessary to compel them to serve? If a majority is in favour of it, while a large minority is adverse, can it be democratic to submit that large minority to coercion? A small minority, leaving the ethical aspect in abeyance, would hardly be worth coercing.

As a matter of deplorable truth, multitudes of people do not know what they want—or rather, they are prepared to want anything that propaganda urges upon them, being ignorant, emotional and untrained in the art of dispassionate reasoning. We have at hand an appropriate example of their extreme suggestibility. On May 8th, 1939, the *News Chronicle*, reporting, 'Ten days have sufficed to cause a complete reversal in public opinion on conscription,' gave the results of an investigation by Dr Gallup's Institute, whose findings on this topic have been substantiated by events, in so far as substantiation can be possible. Between the 21st and 26th of April, 53 per cent. of the selected cross-section 'representative of the whole population' claimed to prefer voluntary recruitment; 39 per cent. were in favour of compulsion; the remainder would express no opinion. On April 27th the House of Commons approved Mr Chamberlain's conscription plan. Between the 2nd and 5th of May, the British Institute of Public Opinion took another survey and found this time that 58 per cent. applauded the new measure, while 38 per cent. were against it, and 4 per cent. were indifferent or uncertain. Nothing had occurred in the meantime to change the outlook except a Parliamentary debate and a vigorous newspaper ' crusade.'

These figures may serve a double purpose. They show, not only that public opinion shifts and veers about at the instigation of politicians and journalists, but also that the coercion of the minority by the majority is particularly unfair, considering how that majority may be arrived at. If the cross-section is really representative, the number of persons in a hundred who may be presumed to have altered their view within a few days is about fifteen; while four who had no view suddenly acquired one. These fifteen turn the scale to make a working majority; yet who that remembers the activities of publicists at that time can doubt whence the conversion came, or that equally intensive propaganda to the opposite effect could have produced the opposite verdict? Had the change been brought about over a period of years or months, it might have been accepted as the legitimate outcome of a sincere enquiry (not that the sincere enquiries of people who obtain their information from daily papers, popular magazines, and radio or news-reel commentaries are likely to be very enlightening to the mind); but a *volte face* achieved in ten days suggests either a childish malleability on the part of the converted or a miracle.

In short, on the conscription question as in most other matters of first-rate importance to the nation, the extent to which the people have any genuine powers of decision, or indeed any will to decide, is exceedingly limited. Government by the masses is a sentimental myth.

But, I may be asked by some reader who is trustful rather than reflective, what of our electoral system, the votes for everybody, the criticisms so freely permitted, the various checks upon government domination? Let us give a moment's attention to these matters. It is perfectly true that the Members of Parliament are elected by the people : that is to say, in each constituency it has usually (not by any means invariably) [1] been agreed by a majority that a certain man or woman is better fit to govern than the one or two others who offered their services, but the choice may have been a choice of evils and quite lacking in the elements of spontaneous preference. The electors can only vote for the candidates who have presented themselves, and those candidates are likely to belong to a few very restricted categories, adhering to party programmes of a stereotyped character. Those who cannot give one of these programmes an unqualified support are often left with no alternative but to refrain from voting.

Though there is now complete adult suffrage, only a fraction of the individuals constituting the electorate is represented, in anything approaching a *real* sense of the term, in the House of Commons. First among the unrepresented are the voters, an enormous percentage, whose candidate was beaten at the polls.[2] Then there is that other immense mass, those who did not vote at all, either because they were indifferent, or because both or all the protagonists seemed equally unsatisfactory. Represented in name only are the groups which have helped to send to Parliament a man who, once there, does nothing or does what they never bargained for—the latter no trifling number since members of supposedly advanced factions have taken, on such a wholesale basis, to endorsing policies they were pledged to resist. Again—though this is only indirectly the fault of the system—there are the millions of enfranchised citizens who vote without knowledge, enquiry, or interest, because family or friends persuade them, because they can think of no reason for refusing someone who has canvassed them, or because an intensive election campaign gives them a momentary feeling of obligation. Add to

[1] Sometimes a candidate stands unopposed (there were 40 in the last General Election and have since been others) and the people have no choice but to return him : while in a three-cornered contest the two who are rejected may together have acquired a far greater number of votes than the one who is returned.

[2] In the General Election, 1935, the supporters of the National Government polled 11,792,332 votes, and returned 431 members, while the supporters of opposition parties polled 10,209,505 votes and only returned 184 members. The total electorate was about 30,000,000, so that some 8,000,000 did not register their opinion.

all this that such representation as there may be is not proportional, constituencies being unequal in population, that there is an Upper House which is not subject to election at all, and that the Cabinet itself, the very head and front of government, is not chosen for office by the House of Commons nor are its members even necessarily persons who have reached the legislature by public suffrage,[1] and it must surely be a believer at once very tenacious and very docile who still maintains that the people rule.

A bird's-eye view of our political institutions given by Dr G. J. Renier in his penetrating and sympathetic study, *The English: Are They Human?*, contains some relevant comments:

'. . . Outside the Greek city-states it is doubtful if democracy ever existed. Government of the people, by the people, for the people, would have been impossible even in the Greek city but for its exiguous size and the institution of slavery. The renowned medieval democracies were rank oligarchies. In the modern world democracy is bound to be a sham, because the citizens are unknown to each other and unable to check in detail the activities of their unwieldy administrative machine. . . .

The main reason that renders the verdict of the electorate highly unreal is that only a few simple issues are put before it. All those that arise after the verdict has been given are settled in a way which accords with the general trend of thought of the supporters of the executive. England, therefore, cannot be said to be a country governed by its own people. The people's only political privilege is that of expressing, at intervals, their determination not to be governed for some time to come by people holding the general views of the executive that is in power at the time the electorate is consulted.

The English system of Government may therefore be called a dictatorship modified by the free expression of public opinion and by the intermittent veto which is the only actual power possessed by the bulk of the nation.'

Dr Renier was writing in 1931, and perhaps later developments have modified his opinion of the freedom permitted to Englishmen in respect of their opinions. I fear a certain element of illusionism now invests— perhaps always invested—this right to untrammelled expression of opinion, a right which reflects so honourable a lustre that it is not surprising nations should mendaciously claim to bask in it. Free press, speech, and association, even when there is no 'emergency,' flourish in radiant theory rather than in reliable practice, as anyone who has espoused a thoroughly unpopular cause can probably bear witness. Ever since some sagacious newspaper manager first discovered that more profit was

[1] In *Tory M.P.* by Simon Haxey there are some rather startling figures showing the extent to which the Cabinet has always been recruited from the peerage.

to be made from the advertisement columns than from the actual sale of copies, and that it was extremely well worth while to keep in with the men who have goods to sell, the press has been largely controlled by certain persons and groups of persons with an axe to grind. Described with hypnotic reiteration as free, it exists in perpetual enslavement [1]— enslavement to advertisers, to press lords and their policies, to conjectural public opinion, and to the various government departments which, for a long while before the war, were in the habit of issuing requests that 'discretion' might be observed about this subject or that [2] —not to speak of the Official Secrets Act and the highly repressive laws which, by partitioning the guilt of a libel among the author, printer, publisher, editor, and distributor, ensure that a great deal of material likely to make one or another a little uneasy never gets as far as the printing presses.

Those who have had the experience of writing for money know what an immense range of important subjects must be accounted taboo or treated in a manner fundamentally dishonest. Vested interests of one kind and another have long ensured that the great bulk of the people's reading matter shall be very adequately censored,[3] and dependence upon public favour imposes a further censorship by making editors with an eye upon circulation chary of admitting views which may run counter to those held by absurdly ill-informed patrons.

'That would offend far too many of our readers!' 'I'm afraid *that* wouldn't go down very well with our advertisers!'—the writer who has hoped to avail himself of the vaunted freedom of the press soon learns from such rebuffs as these how hard it is to find a platform for unconventional opinions. Only contributors whose names carry an enormous prestige are given opportunity, from time to time, to break the childish discipline. Yet while the people are so carefully protected from the shock of knowing the real verdicts of many philosophers, the real findings of many scientists, in international affairs their feelings are manipulated with a callousness to their welfare which is horrifying.

Whenever any voice is raised to protest against these notorious abuses, we are sure to be reminded how much worse they are elsewhere, as if black and grey made white. The state of things elsewhere seems to me to provide a cogent series of reasons for our adopting the most different methods possible.

Freedom of speech and association varies greatly in degree from one

---

[1] There are exceptions in the shape of a very few weekly and monthly 'reviews,' some special periodicals not often found on the bookstalls, and one rebel daily paper, also seldom found on the bookstalls : but the circulation of all these together is not as great as that of one 'national' newspaper.

[2] 'Not the least praiseworthy thing about the British Press is the degree of voluntary censorship it imposes on itself in the national interest, and observes in peace as well as in war.'—*Propaganda in the Next War*, by Sidney Rogerson, 1938.

[3] See Appendix 5.

region to another,[1] being largely in the power of the Chief Constables and other local authorities. London, for instance, allows, or did allow, much greater latitude than many provincial centres. One law will occasionally serve to cancel out another. Thus meetings which could not be banned frankly as subversive have been prevented from taking place on the grounds that they were liable to cause a breach of the peace or might obstruct the traffic—grounds sometimes distinctly unconvincing. It is true that the legality of such prohibitions has been successfully disputed in a number of cases, but on the whole the local organizers of movements which are in disfavour naturally prefer to avoid challenging the police. Many are not conversant with their legal rights; and many shrink from putting a tax upon the moral courage of their followers.

Often, in cases of another kind, the meeting contemplated would be genuinely likely to create a breach of the peace—that is, to be violently broken up by ruffians who dislike the policy to be advocated—and this possibility again must be opposed to the fond illusion of freedom. In an educated community, a community which was, in the literal sense of the term, well-bred, it would be unusual, to say the least of it, to express disagreement in so irrelevant a fashion. One perceives the dilemma of the authorities, but the existence of unfortunate persons too inarticulate to know any argument but force is not a satisfactory motive for suppressing the liberties of others. The perfectly impartial respect of the law could do much, and in many districts has done much, to raise the level of public good manners.

The press offers a trickier problem, since many daily and Sunday papers have abused what freedom they have had with striking irresponsibility, and have lent themselves to such detestable uses as fomenting national hatreds, deliberately encouraging morbid sensationalism, and glorifying the most dangerous forms of sentimentality. I would restrain the press in exactly those directions in which it now enjoys almost unbridled licence, namely, the *manner* in which news is presented and commented upon, and the various methods of influencing, or seeking to influence, public opinion: I would, on the other hand, permit all available news to be printed. There should be no censorship, only a liability to prosecution in the event of news being over-coloured, distorted, or written about in the terms rather of propaganda than of criticism. Strict rules defining the styles to be avoided would, of course, be impossible to formulate, but it should not be much more difficult in a court of law to deal with a charge of tendentious journalism than to decide what con-

---

[1] It will be understood that I am referring to peacetime conditions. The Emergency Powers Act has made all freedom a matter of doubtful sufferance. On the day of my sketching out this (November 20th, 1939) I read that a young man belonging to an unpopular political movement was sent to prison for three months for making what I should have judged to be a very innocuous speech against Mr Winston Churchill. Since then there have been numerous cases—particularly concerned with ' Alarm and Despondency '—which may be startling to look back on in the years to come.

stitutes insulting words and behaviour, slander, obscenity, incitement to disaffection, and many other offences which from time to time come up for trial.

Reporting would lose a good deal of its dramatic quality and editorial language would no longer be noted for its magniloquence, but the gain in accuracy of statement would be immense. Picturesque writing on non-fictional topics would become suspect; the use of stirring phrases without exact referents would be frowned upon by the authorities. Little by little, papers would begin to vie with each other in the making of cool, detached, and lucid reports and commentaries. It might even be esteemed necessary for journalists to take a degree in semantics before being allowed to practise publicly; and students of social history, in a century or so, would be as shocked to think of newspaper men allowed to treat the gravest concerns of the nation in loose emotional terminology as we are ourselves today to learn how persons without training or erudition were once able to set up as schoolmasters and inflict their miserable teachings and canings on unprotected youth.

. . . .

In this chapter I have attempted to show that the idealization of the lower classes can do them nothing but disservice, since only by candid recognition of their unhappy state will the system under which they suffer eventually be overthrown; from there I went on to consider, very briefly, the implications of democracy, a natural transition, since the lower classes are in the majority and therefore form the mass of the people who are supposed, so very erroneously, to rule. To make the obvious assertion that they are not fit to rule, however, is by no means to imply that there is some other ready-made class which *is* fit. Various castes have had the opportunity of demonstrating what they can do with the tremendous tasks of government—royal families, priests and nobles, country squires, industrial magnates, and others. The one qualification which has never in England been given an adequate trial is the possession of a good intellect.

It would be interesting to see what would be the upshot of a few years of government by first-rate intelligences. There is, and doubtless always has been, a sprinkling of clever individuals at the head of affairs, but intelligence has never, in any shape or form, been made an essential to membership of the legislative body; at least, not more intelligence than it takes to get elected, a triumph which may depend on several extraneous advantages. I shrink from imagining the confusion, prejudice, mis-information, and stone-blind loyalty to irrational standards, that cloud the minds of many M.P.s whose utterances I have heard and a few whom I have personally known. Yet it would not be a feat of unthinkable magnitude to arrange examinations which would indicate, even with some exactness, the talents and attainments of those who aspire to govern us, and would certainly weed out the grossly intemperate, the senile, and the complacently stupid who have long helped to bring politics into contempt.

If every member of the (literally) ruling class were one who had survived the ordeal of a stiff competitive examination as well as election, we might ultimately have a government as efficient as the Civil Service at its best and containing elements far more brilliant than are often found in the legislature of today. The condition exacting a large money deposit which can be fulfilled so easily by some potential candidates and is so prohibitively difficult for others—especially the independents whose presence in the Commons is exceedingly desirable—would be altogether superseded, since the necessity for passing difficult tests would make frivolous nominations very much more unlikely than they are now. To become a Member of Parliament would no longer be, as it so often is at present, a matter of personal popularity, or family influence ensuring the support of a party, or wealth, or a good platform manner, but would invariably indicate the possession of specialized knowledge and reasoning powers above the average.

Just as now we expect a solicitor or barrister to be versed in law, a doctor to be well trained in medicine, a stockbroker to have an expert grasp of market operations, so then we should demand from those whose errors can make millions wretched, a thorough grounding in sociology, group psychology, and whatever aspects of history shed particular light upon the trend of modern events. Naturally some would acquire more skill in the application of this learning than others, but even the worst of the elect would satisfy certain basic requirements as yet wholly ignored. Thus encouraged, the social sciences would probably move forward at a pace comparable with that attained by mechanical invention in the nineteenth century, and the various economic and psychological maladies which break out periodically in symptoms of hideous disruption would be traced to their sources and effective remedies found.

But though the highest standard must obviously be looked for in those who have the widest powers, the electorate itself should not be allowed to be stupid. The one essential qualification for a voter, as for a ruler, should be intelligence. A few very elementary tests repeated at intervals of years could determine in an approximate fashion the fitness or unfitness to vote of all who might choose to apply for the privilege. Simple questions set for unambiguous answers and brought up to date at each election could establish beyond any reasonable doubt whether a candidate for admission to the voter's register could at least understand the anatomy of government and the principal issues liable to be influenced by his vote.

Tests of intelligence are not, of course, infallible, but they have proved an excellent guide for many industrial and educational purposes, and have been successfully used on a wide scale in the Forces. A good deal, in fact, is already known about the technique of investigating mental capacity; and it is to be very confidently expected that, with only a few of such opportunities and inducements as have hitherto been reserved chiefly for armaments experts, much more would be learned.

The first results would probably be a series of painful disclosures reminiscent of those produced by the medical examination of recruits during the Boer War, when the public conscience is said to have been chasteningly shocked at the degree of physical defectiveness revealed. The voters' register as it improved in quality would suffer a proportionate diminution of volume: for elections in Great Britain probably differ little, except in method, from the American variety, described by one observer [1] as being 'fought out on the basis of issues about which the voters have no intelligent conception whatsoever, nor could a majority of them acquire such a conception even if there were time and machinery for their education.'

With the general acceptance of the new standards (I am assuming that the arts of persuasion could be employed as skilfully in getting them accepted as in exalting financial success or military glory or any of the other standards to which the public has paid homage, often against its own interests), twenty or thirty years would suffice to show the beginnings of a change. Only two full generations have had time to develop since the Boer War, yet already, physical fitness having then become a national aim—even though on the most moderate and limited scale— the gain in health has been appreciable. The nation's health is by no means a subject for complacency, but it is certainly better than in 1900, and this is due, not merely to progress in medicine but also to progress in the people's attitude, without which medicine, like psychology, may press forward in vain. If to be well informed and politically rational were an acknowledged necessity for complete citizenship, as much energy would be expended in the propagation of intelligence as on the cult of the body—notably in the last twenty years—for the purpose of taking part in games or wars, or of increasing sexual attraction. To be an elector, to rear children equal to passing the electoral test, would be a matter for pride. Juvenile education, we might hope, would gradually jettison its old bad habit of inculcating a blind respect for nationalistic tradition and pseudo-religious authority and would direct itself to the eradication of prejudice and the creation of liberal and speculative modes of thought. The *trend* would be towards evoking the people's good sense as, now, it is towards flattering their stupidity.

In the course of weeding out mentally crippled electors it would inevitably be necessary to inflict certain humiliations—though, as I conceive it, there would be no compulsion upon anybody to submit to the tests, and many would take refuge in professions of disapproval or indifference, enough of them sincere to keep the others in countenance. But in any case, it is unfair and absurd to set the footsteps of the whole

[1] See Appendix 6.

61

community in the wake of its lamest members. That all men are equal in political judgment is as nonsensical a pretence as that they are all equal in beauty or in stature. Until the human race is produced in robot fashion, Nature will continue to equip some of the species very much more generously than others, and those who have been badly furnished with brains must bear with the obviousness of their deficiency as they would bear with being unlovely in appearance.

The writer who has undertaken to analyse what is objectionable in some popular practice or system or series of beliefs must fall recurringly upon a dilemma. If he simply displays the evil, he is said to be adopting the easy rôle of a destructive critic; if he proposes remedies, he may be accused of taking upon himself functions beyond those of pure criticism, like a surveyor who condemns a row of houses in order to become the architect of the next lot. 'Your affair,' the reader may admonish me, 'is to explain the sentimentality of the public mind. You needn't trouble to remould the social order for us.' There is, however, an implicit method of criticism; the rough outline of a new structure will indicate the weaknesses of the old. Believing with Seneca that 'our chief bane is that we live not according to the light of reason,' I seek to show what change would be made in our institutions if reason were given scope, and if comfortable illusions and their corollary *un*comfortable illusions about the human race were treated as childishnesses to be outgrown instead of being dignified with such names as loyalty, patriotism, and idealism.

Thus it does not seem to me that I am overstepping the proper limits of my subject when I suggest, not only that dull and uninformed persons should be disqualified from governing or choosing governors, but also that the entire system of representation should be changed. I have already quoted a remark by Dr Renier on the unwieldy size and character of the electorate and the consequent over-simplification of the few issues which are put before it. Another learned critic, Richard Gregg, sums up the verdicts of a number of historical authorities in these words:

'. . . It is possible that great size in any executive organization in-evitably results in bureaucracy, ignorance, moral irresponsibility, pretence, psychological strain, injustice, and eventually in coercion and violence of thought and action. This might mean that small-scale, decentralized, largely autonomous units with different and perhaps new modes of integration into larger units would give us sounder forms of human association and group life.' [1]

Our destiny while we remain faithful to the traditional political patterns is, and must inevitably be, in the hands of those who know how to manipulate the emotions of crowds, a craft which, though some great men have mastered it without self-destruction, is most congenial

[1] From *The Power of Non-Violence.*

to the vulgar and the superficial. If there is one point upon which psychologists are perfectly agreed (and I fear it must be the only one), it is that the temper of the crowd or the mass is essentially irrational: and the men who get and keep power, whether in a dictatorship State or a make-believe democracy, are such as can appear, or better still, can *be* as unreasoning as their audiences.

'The small chance of success [says Dr André Joussain [1]] which moderate intellects have in hostile crowds is due precisely to their having a sense of the difficulties and knowing the complexity of problems. Counsellors of violence and narrow-minded beings whose solutions are radical and whose utterances are trenchant easily carry all before them. What is true of assemblies is also true of masses: resentful of subtle distinctions, they judge by appearances and adhere to simple solutions.'

And in another passage:

'It is inevitable that all superiorities of mind and heart must cancel one another out in the masses, where individuals can only agree among themselves and act in concert through their inferior faculties. . . . The most complicated operations of the intelligence cannot be carried out by all at the same time and in the same manner; the simplest can. You may be able to make a large number of men execute the same movement at the same time, such as raising their arm at the word of command; but if you require a series of very complicated and extremely exact movements you must renounce the attempt at unity and let each one take his time, choose his means and get on as best he can. One could hardly expect a hundred men to be capable of disentangling the Gordian knot if they were all obliged to keep time with one another. Now, to form an opinion on questions as complex as political, economic, financial, and social problems, is decidedly to undo a Gordian knot, and one can only manage it by a series of very personal reflexions. It follows that, in masses as in crowds, the most sketchy ideas and the most primitive instincts predominate: whatever is mechanical or instinctive in our mental or affective functioning will overwhelm thought and considered voluntary activity: association of ideas will be more powerful than reason, spontaneous imagination than rational and constructive imagination, blind faith than critical intelligence, and emotion and passion will prove a barrier to self-possession.'

Government which treats the population as one mass, and which is adapted to suit the mass, or to delude it into believing it is suited, is not likely to display much subtlety in analysis or depth of penetration when dealing with the abstruse ills of that immensely varied organism, the body

[1] In *La Psychologie des Masses*.

politic. Some experiment in self-government by groups, as opposed to self-surrender by crowds, is, one would think, worth the trial.[1]

I have, rather wistfully, relegated to an appendix [2] my own notion of how these small-scale units, so frequently envisaged by reformers, might operate and what mode of integration could be used, yet I cherish little hope that even the series of disasters which prevailing systems of government have brought upon us will inspire sufficient resolution to produce the necessary changes. The majority will prefer to cling to the symbols by which they are so treacherously reassured. 'The Mother of Parliaments' will doubtless continue to be cluttered up with the rubbish of its bad antiquity, fictitious rights and liberties will be treasured at the expense of those which might have become real, the old gibberish about the help of God, the will of God, and the grace of God will be reverently declaimed by persons whose policies are a defiance of the teachings they profess to believe, children will learn to suspend their reasoning faculties when certain gestures are made and certain slogans uttered, and the wealth of sterile traditions will accumulate while men decay.

The ensuing chapter contains a cursory examination of the almost universal form of sentimentality which occasions my despondent prophecy.

---

[1] 'A crowd is a lot of people; a group is a few. A crowd has a mental life inferior in intellectual quality and emotionally less under voluntary control than the mental life of each of its members in isolation. The mental life of a group is not inferior, either intellectually or emotionally, to the mental life of the individuals comprising it, and may, in favourable circumstances, actually be superior.'—Aldous Huxley: *Ends and Means*.

[2] Appendix 7.

Words are wise men's counters; they do but reckon by them. But they are the money of fools.

Leviathan: THOMAS HOBBES.

Cinna	Truly, my name is Cinna.
First Citizen	Tear him to pieces; he's a conspirator.
Cinna	I am Cinna the poet, I am Cinna the poet.
Fourth Citizen	Tear him for his bad verses, tear him for his bad verses.
Cinna	I am not Cinna the conspirator.
Fourth Citizen	It is no matter, his name's Cinna. Pluck but his name out of his heart. . . .

Julius Caesar: WM. SHAKESPEARE.

IN his amusing and, fortunately, successful book, *The Tyranny of Words*, Stuart Chase follows up the work of various pioneers in a new, or newish, form of research, the science of semantics, prospected by Ogden and Richards as *The Meaning of Meaning*. Chase, whose exposition is conspicuously easier to read than those of his precursors, attributes many, if not most, of the social ills of mankind to what he calls 'bad language,' the careless, inaccurate use of words, the use of words without referents, the passion for abstract words and figures of speech posing as factual statements. He shows with admirable examples how certain expressions which have the profoundest effects upon the passions of multitudes contain so little exact meaning that scarcely any two people will give the same interpretation of them. 'Fascist,' a name derived from a symbol intended to signify Roman unity, came to mean more or less anyone whom radicals disliked. 'Bolshevik,' 'communist,' 'democrat,' 'socialist,' 'totalitarian,' 'republican,' all are words which have been used as mere general terms of abuse by hundreds of millions who would be highly embarrassed if compelled to explain, with precision, what they stood for and why that referent was obnoxious.

Similarly loose and vague language is the medium of exchange for ideas on almost every subject which does not *obviously* and *immediately* require an accurate terminology. (I stress those adverbs, because they indicate the reason why small commerical transactions, for instance, can generally be dealt with in terms which mean the same to all parties concerned, while large-scale economics are discussed in a cloud of debatable abstractions. The need for clarity is, if anything, greater among economists offering solutions to world problems than among shopkeepers pricing their goods, but the consequences of failure to achieve understanding are unhappily not so obvious, nor so immediate, therefore it is not achieved.) [1]

[1] See Appendix 8.

The difficulty has been accounted for by the fact that all modern languages have, imbedded in their structure, 'vestiges derived in the course of long ages from primitive beliefs and pre-scientific views of life and the world,'[1] and that being thus 'infected by metaphysics and myth,' by personifications of abstractions and confusions of the levels of abstraction, they are ill adapted for scientific communication. This seems to me only a partial explanation, nor is it, I dare say, intended for a complete one. We must ask ourselves not only *how* but *why* these vestigial remains are allowed to clutter up our speech until it becomes unfit for its proper functions. The answer, I think, is to be found in two interesting psychological features of 'bad language'; first, it is almost invariably a short cut, a labour-saving device, a substitute, sometimes for thinking, sometimes for articulately arranging one's thoughts; second, it is seldom without an element of idealization, positive or adverse.

Bad language, therefore, is usually *sentimental* language, the tongue of the stupid who use ready-made phrases and tropes hallowed by time 'as a respectable screen for dogmatism, prejudice, and vacuity,' the tongue of the lazy who want 'distilled truth put up in capsules, wisdom concentrated and simplified for easy consumption,'[2] and, most of all, the tongue of the self-deceiving who clothe their primitive fears, angers, lusts, and vanities in flattering nomenclature and are able to regard them as virtues. (This positive idealization is, of course, accompanied by its obverse; an unflattering nomenclature enables one to dispose summarily of claims and pretensions that run counter to one's own.)

The art of propaganda is very largely the art of exploiting the misuse and misdevelopment of language and encouraging those unreasoning impulsive responses which it should have been the business of education to discredit. The tendency to regard words as things, with an independent reality of their own and meanings fixed, as it were, by immutable law, the habit, derived no doubt from savage ancestors, of 'objectifying' abstractions, the readiness to believe anything that is stated in terms sanctified by association,—it is upon such weaknesses of the mind as these that propagandists rely for their effects. Nor must it be imagined that the reporters, leader-writers, politicians, advocates, preachers, pedagogues, and demagogues, who make the claptrap vocabulary especially their own, enjoy a cynical awareness of the methods by which they succeed: they have been trained to be deliberately irrational like the rest of mankind, and are seldom capable of analysing their own cant.

One must conquer a natural reluctance to question authority—the authority of long custom as well as present power—before one can perceive how great a proportion of the characteristic idiom used for debating public affairs has an almost wholly emotional significance and

---

[1] The quoted words are from Cassius J. Keyser's *Scripta Mathematica*.
[2] The inverted commas denote a small debt to E. S. Fosdick, author of *The Old Savage in the New Civilization*.

means nothing verifiable. It is a discovery at once tragic and comic. The psychological reactions of simple, greedy, credulous savages masquerade so happily in high-flown metaphors and soothing euphemisms that almost no one has the heart to strip them of their finery. One hears, says Stuart Chase, 'grown men and women, presumably sane, trying to describe and settle social and political problems in words which have no more application to the grave situations at issue than the bedtime stories of children. The dream world which the eager imagination of the child builds may or may not assist the child's development. When one hears adults solemnly employing similar fantasies in trying to cope with wars, strikes, depressions, one stands appalled at the thought of where this infantile process will lead.'

Foremost among the several kinds of linguistic dangers which must occupy the student of public opinion are the quicksands of word-magic, especially the verbal taboo. The cult of word-magic is based upon the widespread and apparently primeval delusion that to change the name of a thing is to change its nature, while what is not mentioned at all practically ceases to exist. An extension of this belief is the idea that what is mentioned in sufficiently impressive terms by a sufficiently powerful entity will forthwith come into being. The creation of the world in six days from 'the Word' is our most notable example of this superstition; the utterance of curses and blessings is a slighter form of it. In civilized communities it develops into the self-hypnotizing assurances of journalists, divines, and politicians of the ultra-complacent school, those who reiterate in time of scarcity that there is no real hardship, in time of war that there is no profiteering, no grumbling, no want of confidence, in time of doubt and strife that 'the country is firmly united' in support of authority.

Verbal taboo, the attempt to remove objects of distaste by never naming them, was very much more widely practised in the nineteenth century than it has been, so far, in the twentieth. By comparison with the Victorians, who banned an immense range of topics and cast out from the tribe all breakers of the taboo, it may seem that we are almost grown up. Nineteenth-century propriety screened away appalling slum areas in the social order, and I fancy that our progress in clearing them has corresponded very thoroughly with the degree to which free discussion has been permitted. The squalors of prostitution, for instance, though by no means expunged, are certainly not so dreadful as in the day when W. T. Stead suffered imprisonment for ventilating the evil in a newspaper and supporting his assertions with evidence.[1]

There has been a campaign against venereal disease in which, though the psychological approach has been, in my view, most unfortunate, the infections have at least been publicly given their names, and this in respectable periodicals as well as underground lavatories.

[1] See Appendix 9.

A substantial number of years ago a distinguished hygienist [1] wrote:

'I know of no disease which is at the mercy of the human race so completely as venereal diseases: they are waiting to be wiped out and they could be exterminated without much difficulty or much expenditure.'

In order, however, to set about this extermination, it was necessary to break our lifelong habit of not discussing the subject, or discussing it only as a ribald joke or an unthinkably remote nastiness. There were many who felt passionately concerned to uphold the taboo, not so much out of a desire for the continuance of the disease, as out of a confused hope that if one kept it dark it would somehow disappear. I quote from *The Tyranny of Words* an example which happens to be American; but the primitive logophobia which inspires it is quite as potent in Great Britain.

'State Senator John McNaboe of New York bitterly opposed the Bill for the control of syphilis in May 1937, because "the innocence of children might be corrupted by a widespread use of the term. . . . This particular word creates a shudder in every decent woman and decent man."' [2]

We need not know the merits or demerits of the Bill in question to perceive that the Senator either regards the name of the thing as worse than the thing itself, or else expects to cast out the disease by casting out its name—both regrettable delusions in a legislator.

But let us not imagine that superstitious concealment on this topic has been altogether brought to an end by the sharp exigencies of war. Though we may now speak of cure, we must not allude to prevention. No reference to medical means of prevention has been made in the press and poster campaign, chemists are still forbidden to give information on prophylactics to their customers, the National Society for the Prevention of Venereal Disease was not permitted to exhibit its name to the public by means of a fascia signboard, and it is only in the armed Forces that obscurantism is not given full possession of the field. Yet a new generation has grown up since experts trained in the hard school of the last war proved the efficiency of methods which could make this contagion as rare as smallpox.

'The evidence in favour of practical prevention [wrote Dr Lyster] is overwhelming, absolutely and completely overwhelming, and must convince everyone who approaches the subject without prejudice. . . . Taking the laboratory evidence together with the administrative

[1] Dr Robert A. Lyster, a Medical Officer of high scientific eminence whose range of experience includes a period as Sanitary Specialist and Venereal Diseases Officer for a wide area of the Southern Command.
[2] See Appendix 10.

evidence, we can say that the proof is more complete than with any other disease in the world. I am satisfied as a public health officer that that is an absolute fact. . . .'

Yet, decades after this discovery, the only precaution which the Ministry of Health has seen fit to recommend to the public is that which, in time of war above all, is quite certain not to be taken—sexual abstinence.

It is true that this taboo is not primarily verbal, since there is a large number of people who, for various reasons, disapprove of prophylaxis, and resent the diffusion of knowledge: but what is very interesting is that some of those who know the value of preventive measures and have found them essential to the health of men in their care prefer to call them anything but what they are.

Dr James H. Sequeira, one of the foremost authorities on syphilology, has written [1] of the pernicious ban on the word 'prevention' in the last war, directly traceable to the influence of the Churches, which did not wish it to be known that prevention was possible, their official attitude at the time being that disease was a punishment for sin. By 1916 the infection was spreading at so terrible a rate that it became imperative, Churches notwithstanding, to give the Forces prophylactic instruction, and even to establish venereal ablution rooms. But they were called 'early treatment centres,' thus salving the conscience, Dr Sequeira tells us, of the opponents of prevention.

'It was a miserable subterfuge, for one does not "treat" non-existent disease, and no one would dream of calling a prophylactic dose of diphtheria anti-toxin "early treatment."'

The misnomer was a serious obstacle to acceptance of the hygienic facilities provided.

Verbal taboos grow strict or die away in accordance with the waxing and waning of the fears and distastes they are intended to negate. There is seldom, except vestigially, a taboo upon the mention of anything which has lost its immediate terrors or its association of moral obloquy. It will be remembered that between 1914 and 1919, plays and novels which dealt with war invariably treated either its humours or its glories, and, like the battle-paintings at Versailles, contained only a general effect of martial enterprise with little or nothing in detail that could upset the most squeamish, whereas when the last of the alarms had died down, authors, playwrights, and film producers vied with each other in portraying warfare with hideous, stomach-turning realism. We are in the first

---

[1] In a paper on *Venereal Disease in the Great War* (i.e. 1914-1918). Since there is still a widespread reluctance to believe that prevention is possible, I append here his opinion: ' As to the efficiency of prophylaxis, we are absolutely agreed that it is wonderful in its efficacy, if used properly. There is no question about it.'

phase of this typical cycle as I write: the second will doubtless have its day later.

As an example of moral mutation, consider the lifting of the silence which formerly shrouded every recognizable aspect of sexual abnormality. The trial of Oscar Wilde was spoken of by his contemporaries—when they ventured to speak of it at all—in shivering whispers and thickly disguised language. By the time of the last war, homosexuality had so far lost its dark and diabolical implications as to become the object of many smirking jokes. Jesting intolerance was followed by jesting tolerance, until at last, with the growing disinclination—outside police stations, assize courts, and other such old-world environments—to brand every homosexual as a wicked monstrosity, the joke has worn thin and, except in very precious forms, is confined to unsophisticated circles.

From non-mention to veiled mention, and thence to facetious mention (facetiousness being a kind of euphemism), and from jocosity at first savage then gradually developing good-humour to an ultimate taking-for-granted—this is the usual destiny of a moral veto.

The banning of words as a method of getting rid of the things they stand for is, of course, very closely interlinked with the practice of changing or misapplying words in order to change (or modify) the things they stand for; to make things we wish to hate more hateful, things it suits us to revere more venerable, things we are afraid of less alarming, things we might be ashamed of more acceptable. Thus Germans are effectively, if not accurately, named Huns by the chief word-magicians; Frenchmen under the name of 'Vichy men' have been killed without compunction; armaments in every country are described as weapons of defence; and to dispose by murder of one's political opponents is, in some circles, to liquidate them, which sounds quite a cool and agreeable process. It is much easier to say, 'Liquidate that man!' than 'Have that man killed!' and morally much less disturbing to use weapons of defence than weapons of attack, even when they are physically indistinguishable from one another.[1]

When policies of violence come to be worked out, 'dainty terms for fratricide'[2] are very good emollients for the conscience. Humorous terms are also lenitive, both to fear and to disgust. Now, for instance, we 'mop up' enemy soldiers, just as in an earlier war or two we 'wiped

[1] I am aware that a case may be made, and is made in every heavily armed country, for regarding one's own bombers, marine mines, etc., as purely defensive, but it hangs upon sophistries and verbal tricks: 'The best defence is attack,' and so forth. An anti-aircraft gun is rightly called a weapon of defence, but a bomber can only be, at best, a weapon of counter-attack.

[2] '... All our dainty terms for fratricide,
　　Terms which we trundle smoothly o'er our tongues
　　Like mere abstractions, empty sounds to which
　　We join no feeling and attach no form!
　　As if the soldier died without a wound;
　　As if the fibres of this godlike frame
　　Were gored without a pang; as if the wretch

70

them out' (but that phrase, through long practical experience, has lost its original comic overtone). Our airmen sportively 'bag' enemy machines. Bombs are known to those who drop them as 'eggs' and 'cookies.' Raids in which homes and lives are blown to fragments take a touch of airy comedy from being known as a 'blitz.' The gay and whimsical style in which some of our journals depict the more inhuman types of military operation helps many to discard the scruples that might otherwise afflict them.[1] War itself can be shorn, theoretically, of all its barbarities and squalors, by referring to it as if it were a straightforward game: 'We must hit the other fellow and hit him hard,' and 'If a certain gentleman over the other side of the water wants to fight, this country is ready to meet him,'[2] language which removes all the complexities of the situation and calls up gratifying images of direct reprisals against one highly tangible offender. A general described the impending invasion of Europe in the terms of a tug-of-war, and promised the public that it would be 'a magnificent party.'[3]

The old proverb which said, or implied, that to give a dog a bad name was a step towards destroying him contains wisdom of which propagandists have always liberally availed themselves. At a time when there was great hostility towards the Pope it was a good move for keen Protestants to label Roman Catholics 'papists,' but better still to apply the epithet indiscriminately to all persons, adherents of the Papacy or otherwise, whose religious views were not compatible with their own. The author of *Mein Kampf* early recognized the value of this technique and wrote of it with exasperating frankness: 'It is of the genius of a great leader to represent even widely differing enemies as belonging to only one category, because to realize several enemies at a time may, in feeble and uncertain minds, easily engender doubts.' Thus, in 1938, all Catholics became, according to the German press, Communists—a bewildering state of affairs because all Communists had for some years been Jews.

A similar proposition in favour here until Russia became our ally was that pacifists were either in the pay of the Nazis or else were financed by that ubiquitous metal 'Russian gold'; and as Nazis and Communists were notoriously 'anti-God,' the inference was that all pacifists, including

---

Who fell in battle, doing bloody deeds,
Passed off to Heaven, translated and not killed;

... And what if all-avenging Providence,
Strong and retributive, should make us know
The meaning of our words, force us to feel
The desolation and the agony
Of our fierce doings?'
                    (From *Fears in Solitude*, by S. T. Coleridge, 1798.)

[1] See Appendix 11.
[2] Sir Walter Kirke and Lord Nuffield respectively at a Territorial Army dinner in the House of Commons, July 1939.
[3] General Alexander at the Mansion House, March 1944.

the Christian sects, were atheists, just as, in Germany, all Catholics were Jews.

I must not confine my rudimentary outline of verbal self-deceptions,[1] however, solely to those which are concocted under the strong temptation occasioned by war and preparations for war. Peace too has her euphemisms, and, if I may coin an ugly word, her cacophemisms.

Probably the largest class of these is that collection of oral fig-leaves which drape a number of the physiological functions. In the sculpture galleries of the Vatican every naked male figure, even to the tiniest cupid, has been furnished at considerable trouble and expense with a coy ornament. I have heard of a very young lady of prudish upbringing and small experience who went away with a vague impression that procreation was achieved by means of a leaf-shaped organ, and was rather surprised when she came to Florence to find that there it was quite a different matter. In one way and another life is full of these surprises, some of which are needlessly disturbing. But sexual and functional evasions have lately been investigated with painstaking care by a varied assortment of research workers, and I for one am a little exhausted with the subject. Moreover, there has been a striking improvement of outlook which begins to affect even the lower middle classes.

Word-magic is resorted to with greater or less eagerness not only from one epoch to another but also from one class to another, evasion being naturally in higher favour where reality is more distasteful. Thus in those circles where it is customary for money to be, on the whole, plentiful, and where debt does not take sordid shapes, people talk freely of their incomes, their overdrafts—an indication, after all, of good credit —and what they can afford and not afford. But in that class which is not very far above the poverty level or in which abundance is a novelty, money may be an uncomfortable subject seldom mentioned by name. A variety of devices is in use for making it sound unreal and its absence less serious. Instead of 'He is poor,' the comment will be 'He hasn't many pennies' (a phrase subtly different from the blithe exaggeration, 'He hasn't a penny,' which might be applied to the same case by someone more at ease). Instead of 'I can't spare the money,' one will hear 'I'm a little bit short just at the moment': while slang words, such as 'dibs,' 'spondulics,' 'the wherewithal,' and 'L.S.D.' lend the requisite air of fantasy. In a state of actual poverty, these flippancies are seldom encoun-

---

[1] I speak of *self*-deception even in connection with consciously propagandist activities, for it seems to me that those who devote themselves to promoting certain ideas will ultimately become their own victims, however cynical the spirit in which they set out. It is hard to be convincing without being convinced. I may quote Mr Harry Pollitt's statement in the *Daily Worker*, November 23rd, 1939, explaining why, after supporting the war, he had ceased to do so:

'My hatred of Fascism had developed by five years' intensive anti-Fascist propaganda which led to a position where I did not see in time the true rôle of British Imperialism, as the main enemy of the working-class movement.'

As one commentator puts it, 'The Chief Medicine-Man was poisoned by his own Ju-Ju.'

tered, for the evil is not a lurking shadow but a visible fact and evasion is impossible. It is in this respect and several others like it that the speech of the lower classes approximates to the speech of the upper; for the one, evasion is impossible, for the other, unnecessary.

Lower and upper class people will use words signifying awareness of a definite social status, as 'lady' and 'servant,' but in the middle grades there are uncertainties which make such clean-cut designations rare except in special contexts—e.g. 'a public servant,' 'a lady cook.' Many members of the upper classes are still waited upon by employees who go to a Servants' Ball and sit in a servants' hall, whereas in the middle classes there are only 'staff sitting-rooms' occupied principally by 'maids.' The word-magic of calling a servant by some other name to render servitude more endurable [1] was probably started by wily masters and mistresses; it is carried on vehemently by the lesser ranks of servants themselves, and when Fowler of *King's English* fame enjoins us to cast aside this genteelism,[2] one gathers that he has lost touch with the urgencies of the domestic situation.

The passion of the humble for refined speech is comparable with their craving for refined flour and sugar, and is as deleterious to their mental as the other is said to be to their physical development—perhaps much more so. A mild vitamin deficiency can hardly impair the body as thoroughly as a perpetual refusal to deal with the world as it is impairs the mind. What frail qualifications for forming realistic judgments may we expect to find in the author of this letter in the *Daily Express*?

'With the approaching butter rationing, why not give margarine a more atractive name? I suggest "butterine" or "art butter." This would help the proud housewife out of her difficulty.' [3]

It is not clear who is to be deceived, or rather, distracted from the truth, by this camouflage, the shopman or the purchaser. In either case, the price to be paid for reassurance is, as it so often must be, an eager suspension of the intelligence.

The fear of words is nowhere more touchingly demonstrated than by the avoidance of direct terminology for death and its painful accompaniments. Affectionate children will say 'If anything should happen to mother,' when they mean 'If mother should die.' A grave is called a

---

[1] It is not of very modern origin. There were 'retainers' and 'abigails' long ago, and 'the male domestic of Mrs Boffin' will not be forgotten.

[2] See Appendix 12.

[3] From *This England*, 1940, edited by V. S. Pritchett. The writer is, incidentally, on a psychologically wrong track. People do not like names which remind them that the goods they are purchasing are a substitute for something more expensive. The rayon industry laboured for years to prevent its fabrics from being called artificial or 'art' silk. The less costly furs sell much more easily when they have altogether fancy names invented for them instead of being called 'imitation sable,' 'foxaline,' 'coney seal,' etc.

The naming of commercial products, and their subsequent success or failure, would in itself be a profitable study. Also meriting consideration is the re-naming of colours every few years in order to give them a new fashion value.

'resting place,' and undertakers will be merely hinted at as 'they.' 'The funeral is tomorrow' becomes 'They are going to put him away to-morrow.' The Americans know a coffin as a casket. A friend of mine sent three telegrams from a village post office: 'Mother died this morning.' On arrival they all read: 'Mother passed away this morning,' changed (certainly not with the sanction of the G.P.O.) by a kindly assistant who must have hoped, in softening the word, to soften the fact.

A variable taboo also bans the blunt naming of those illnesses which have peculiar terrors for the imagination in any given period. Reading novels of the nineteenth century—a time when the ravages of disease were calamitous in every rank of life—we cannot but be struck by the enormous number of characters who die, and die lingeringly, without any specified malady. When a young female goes into a decline, fades away like a flower, and descends gently to the grave, we are doubtless intended to assume an exceedingly rarefied kind of tuberculosis. Coarser disorders only found their way into the more robust sort of literature. The number of ailments which are euphemistically treated in conversation and writing today is much less than it used to be—an evidence of the progress of medicine and the lowered death-rate; but it is still not thought quite delicate to refer openly to cancer unless the allusion is general and impersonal. When we no longer feel impelled to seek roundabout ways of denoting this enemy, it will be because we are near to mastering it.

I ventured to use the word cacophemism—I shall not do so very often —to describe that kind of verbal conjuring which makes an object of dislike look gratifyingly worse instead of better. There are some evils it suits us to mask in mellowing language, and others to which we give names which nourish our hatred or contempt. Stuart Chase instances the word 'dole' as a specimen of misapplication for this purpose. It was selected—in England to begin with—as a weapon to attack a new kind of social service which was objectionable, and remained objectionable, to certain classes of taxpayers; and having a strong satirical undertone— as well as being easier to say than Unemployment Benefit—it was soon taken up by the class which might have been expected to resent it. Apparently, at a later time, indignant Americans followed the example of indignant Englishmen. The 'baleful word . . . was thrown like a bomb against measures for State and federal relief. The immensity of human need prevented the barrage from being successful.'

When we search out true referents for this insulting epithet, we find, as Mr Chase explains, that a dole from the Government is merely a community benefit comparable with a hundred others which are now acceptably furnished out of public funds. Free police protection might as well be called a dole to property-owners, roads provided by taxation a dole to motorists, pavements and street lighting a dole to pedestrians, council schools a dole for children, buoys and lighthouses a dole for navigators. If the State subsidy for the unemployed had been known by its literal name, I think it probable that between 1920 and 1930 there would have been a large-scale and concerted effort to solve the problem of unemployment, since we should have had the irritating topic constantly on our lips undisguised either by grim comedy or—dare I say ?—uncalled-for dolefulness.

A less durable and less effective cacophemism was the expression 'Flapper Vote,' scornfully indicating the proposal to extend the franchise to women between the ages of twenty-one and thirty. Whoever was responsible for this catchword when the issue was before Parliament made a blunder, for the absurdity of suggesting that any woman under thirty must be in an early stage of adolescence was palpable to all but the most reckless anti-feminists, and the shaft of ridicule was easily turned upon its authors. Word-magic must be handled with a modicum of skill. Praise and abuse should have their air of conviction. Only in contexts which evoke emotions deemed to be supra-rational—e.g. concerned with religion or patriotism—is it unnecessary for words to have any ascertainable relation to facts at all.

Another kind of bad language—though, to be sure, all kinds are nearly related and one lapse makes many—is produced by that desire for definiteness which, having ascribed to words narrow and exclusive meanings charged with the user's prejudices, proceeds to employ them as labels for the rapid classification of persons and objects. Plain, if somewhat out-of-date, examples are 'a good woman' in the sense of 'a sexually inexperienced woman'; 'a religious man'—a man of censorious outlook; 'a failure in life'—one who has not acquired money Perhaps this habit which the French call 'simpliste' is at its most incorrigible in the law courts, where policemen intone records of 'good characters' and 'bad associates' and judges speak of 'unpardonable crimes' and 'utterly worthless lives' with as much assurance as a cashier adding up columns of unmistakable figures.

Very nearly as facile are the estimates the public forms of its artists. Dead or alive, these are always gratefully welcomed if they can be made to slip smoothly into categories. Versatility is a serious impediment unless the artist has, so to speak, specialized in it from the outset. 'Even the lettered public,' writes Dr Joussain,[1] 'loves one to be *absolutely* what one is. It wants an author defined by an epithet like a label stuck on a bottle to make it recognizable at a glance and easier to use. It does not readily allow a man mastery in opposing directions.' The derogatory effects of an ill-contrived or misapplied label need hardly be elaborated. The bottle, which contains, it may be, a vintage of the rarest or the most variable quality, is inscribed with an inadequate and often an inaccurate phrase, and is accepted or rejected at that valuation by all who cannot

[1] In *La Psychologie des Masses.* For a full-length study of the 'labelling' tendency in literary criticism, I know no better work than Stephen Potter's *The Muse in Chains.*

trust their own palate. And certainly none but a connoisseur can rely upon his private judgment sufficiently to distinguish noble burgundy under the title of—say—'Medicated Tonic Wine,' or *vice versa*.

The little tags affixed to works of art and hung about the necks of the personalities which create them are searching and subtle, however, compared with those which are used to characterize whole huge classes and kinds of people. The entire French nation was once supposed to be 'frivolous,' while the Germans were 'scientific' and 'intellectual'— adjectives which could have been mutually exchanged without the smallest loss of aptness. The Chinese, formerly almost invariably 'sinister,' are now allowed to be highly 'honourable'; while, through phases of villainy and virtue alike, they have retained their 'Oriental impassiveness' (an attribute decidedly out of keeping with the boisterous mirth and noisy vehemence of the Chinese I have had an opportunity of knowing). The Japanese are, in a reprehensible way, 'clever.' The Portuguese are 'cowardly,' the Spaniards 'cruel'; half-castes are addicted to crime; coolies of all descriptions can live on a handful of rice—a very unfortunate label, like many others which affect the wages and working conditions of native labourers.

Domestic servants have long borne a name for gratuitous troublesomeness. Soldiers are all bravery and heroism, except when they are fighting for a cause we disapprove, in which case their daring, if acknowledged at all, is usually put down either to desperation or to ferocity. Actresses used to be known as 'fast': it was matter for surprised comment if they turned out to be not so. Hospital nurses are 'devoted and selfless women': I have heard a lady express keen disappointment because she had read a biography portraying Florence Nightingale as a strong determined rebel against existing conventions instead of a sweet and gentle female saint.

I do not say that such generalizations as I have selected are altogether without foundation. It is probably true that the well-bred Chinese aspire to be impassive; there is undoubtedly a great deal of cruelty to animals in Spain; half-castes, through the miserable ambiguousness of their social status rather than through any inherent anti-social leaning, may tend to become members of an underworld; Indian and other Oriental workers are possibly able, owing to their greater portion of sunshine, to subsist on a lower diet than is good for Europeans. *But a more or less vague basis of truth is not truth*, and when this is forgotten generalization becomes pernicious. The cruel Spaniard is said by those who have lived in his country to be much kinder to children than the Teutonic people who are, on the whole, humane to animals. Domestic servants are an uncommonly motley assortment of good, bad, and indifferent, and a reiterated statement, though only made in private, that they are usually bad induces a most fallacious approach to the whole problem of service. The selfless devotion we look for in nurses has supplied a pretext for low wages, long hours, and waste of energy in childish discipline, to the ultimate detriment of the profession.

There is a difference between generalizations which are a mere expression of personal opinion, wrong-headed and ill-grounded as it may be, and those which pass themselves off as known and established verities. Personal opinions would not, I conceive, so often be wrong-headed and ill-grounded but for the crude formulae which help to keep the mind travelling in attractively familiar grooves. 'Verbal habits,' we read in *The Meaning of Meaning*, 'overpower the sense of actuality even in the best philosophers.' If this happens to the best, we may imagine the effect upon the debilitated minds of the many.

No single aspect of human affairs displays so startlingly the capacity of men to bemuse and deceive themselves with words as the naming of causes for which wars are undertaken. In the last war, our fight was chiefly 'to save democracy'; we were assisted by anti-democratic countries such as Russia and Japan. Engaged now, as we have been told a hundred times by the persons who are, as it were, public labellers, in a crusade to preserve Christian civilization, we seek the aid of large populations of Hindus and Mohammedans, and have as allies the de-Christianized Russians. To defend Europe against further aggression by dictators, we guaranteed a military dictatorship with a history of aggression condemned by the League of Nations.[1] Raging on behalf of the persecuted Jews, we went to war (so the label said at the time) to support this nation whose record for persecution was unsurpassed; many of the Jews in Germany and Austria having originally gone there to escape from Polish cruelties.

'God' and 'anti-God' are tags frequently applied with quite ludicrous effect. During the Spanish war, Franco was upheld by Catholics and Church adherents generally as fighting on God's side against the forces of 'anti-God.' An appreciable share of the struggle on God's behalf was borne by German troops at the command of Hitler, who was 'anti-God,' however, in Germany!

Some labels there must be; we cannot do without them. It may be said that every word is a docket of one kind or another. What is to be desired is that these dockets should be handled with honesty and as much precision as we can attain with them, time being against us. Above all, it should be realized they have no power to change for better or for worse the objects to which they happen to be attached—no power indeed of any kind except what power we give them to express meaning and to create illusion.

We now come to the most serious part of this thin outline of a thesis, the enquiry into the confusion of abstractions with real entities, and metaphorical processes with real processes. (The reader will not, I trust, feel that before we can proceed, we are obliged to agree upon a definition

[1] See Appendix 13.

77

of reality. It will be enough for the purpose in hand if, as we go on, we remain in accord as to what is *not* reality.) A few simple specimens will avert much tedious explanation. I will take first a poster which, in the initial months of the war, must have been seen by most of the inhabitants of Great Britain. Decorated with a picture of the Nelson column, it contained these words:

'YOUR COUNTRY STILL EXPECTS YOU TO DO YOUR DUTY.'

People read it, and some of them, it would appear, hazily supposed it to be a statement of a literal fact. It was so authoritative; it was placed there by the Government; it was hallowed by the Nelson column, and anyone disputing its factual significance would have been unworthy the name of Englishman ('the *name* of Englishman' being, according to the rules of word-magic, something which in itself ennobles the possessor). Others, of a slightly higher level of intelligence, knew that the country was not literally in a state of expectation regarding individual passers-by, but they considered, nevertheless, that the pronouncement was invested with a kind of mystical veracity. For them the country has—vaguely of course—the attributes of a personality, and, like God, but with more pressing, more evident claims, it demands loving allegiance whether it has bestowed happiness and privilege or not. The call to patriotic duty, the reminiscence of a national hero, could be relied upon to stir sentiments they had been taught to take pride in, and that was enough.

Others, more detached, recognized with satisfaction, with indifference, or with irritation, that the statement was propaganda.

Let us try to connect this propaganda with what we know of facts, as distinct from theories, speculations, or emotions. I inhabit a portion of the earth, a geographical area, which for convenient reference is called Great Britain. The division to which I belong, England, consists of upwards of 50,000 square miles. If this amorphous and highly variegated mass of land has any intentions, expectations, or desires, they have never been communicated. It could not have been my country in the concrete sense to which the Government's poster referred. But there is an accepted metonymical usage by which, when we say 'country,' it is to be inferred that we are talking of the inhabitants. Did the sentence mean, then, that the inhabitants of England expected me to do my duty? Which inhabitants? Certainly not all of them. Many were young children without an idea of duty in their heads; some, though adults, were mentally incapable of coherent expectation or ideas of duty; some were completely engaged in coping with private misery, while great numbers always are unable to agree as to what a citizen's duty is and whether it is primarily to a concept called the State or a concept called God or another called Humanity. It is greatly to be doubted—it could not possibly be proved—that a majority, let alone a totality, had spontaneously decided upon the true nature of my duty and had lived in hopes of my performing it.

'Your country' did not literally stand for the people of my country. Perhaps then it was a way of saying 'the State.' The State, according to dictionaries, is a word which means either the population, the territory, and the Government, all considered together, an abstract amalgam which cannot, as I have shown, be supposed to have unanimous expectations; or 'the bodies which constitute the legislature of a country.' And now, of course, we are getting down to it: duty was being urged upon me by the legislative bodies. But even that is not exactly true, for the legislative bodies consist of individuals, and these were frequently in dispute amongst themselves. There were several at that time who were publicly at variance with the others on this very question of duty. Did not the message come then merely from a section of the legislative bodies, and possibly only a small section—a department concerned with 'ideas which must be propagated'?

And what about this duty? We can whittle 'your country' down to something fairly tangible, but where and what, in this world or any other, is 'your duty'? Is it not a moral obligation—which itself is a high order abstraction—and if so, how can it be determined but by the operations of our own conscience? Philosophers once believed in Absolutes. Love, Beauty, Virtue, Fidelity, had, like Heaven and Hell, a mysterious but scarcely disputed real existence as entities, and set the standard of perfection to aspire to; the only matter for argument being which artists, priests, and men of learning were most correct in interpreting glimpses of these elusive Goods. 'Duty' was whatever obligation the authorities laid upon one from their knowledge of divinely revealed law and religiously guided social custom, just as among unenquiring savages it was, and still is, whatever is prescribed by tribal ritual and totemic restriction. But now an absolute conception of duty, duty fixed and unchanging, duty by rule of thumb, seems as archaic as an absolute conception of beauty. There is a theory of relativity for ethics as well as physics, and it is widely believed that what would be good and appropriate conduct for one would be quite the wrong thing for another.

It may be, however, that duty according to the poster was an abstraction of a somewhat lower order, indicating only the performance of some task specifically undertaken. Thus it was that Nelson presumably meant it, addressing sailors who had accepted, or been pressed into, the duty of manning ships and guns. Yet, as I had not given any promise, implicit or explicit, to engage in a particular form of activity for the men who called themselves my country and who subsequently lost 'the country's' confidence, I consult the dictionary again and am reduced to the opinion that duty in this instance was probably no more than 'obedience and submission due to superiors,' and that raises a whole new set of questions.

The citizen who cares to understand what he is reading might translate the sentence into less high-flown English on these lines: 'The Government expects (or 'hopes', or 'urges') that the population will be obedient and submissive.'

By abstractifying this admonition and casting it in a mould which evokes memories of heroism, an entirely different complexion has been given to it.[1]

My next illustration shows the effect of confusing the levels of abstraction. In October 1939, Colonel Lindbergh broadcast a speech in which he deplored the possibility of the United States being dragged into the war through Canada. Such versions as I read were all too concentrated to be faithful, but, rightly or wrongly, he was reported to have proposed that Canada should cut adrift from the British Empire. Naturally the comment in the English press was unfavourable and newspaper after newspaper broke into angrily satirical headlines: 'HOSPITALITY REWARDED,' 'LINDBERGH REPAYS DEBT OF GRATITUDE,' and so forth. Mr Beverley Nichols was one of many who felt impelled to express his sense of grievance: [2]

> 'Lindbergh, who chose this country for his wife and his family as a refuge from the perils of America, chose to show his gratitude by endeavouring to split up the British Empire.'

The general verdict was that as Lindbergh had received British hospitality he was indebted to England and should have refrained from utterances which could not be approved here. Now this accusation hinges upon the unconscious shifting of 'hospitality' to a purely metaphorical level. Properly the word is an abstraction belonging to a comparatively 'solid' order, that is to say, an order representing experiences, attributes, sensations, etc., about which agreement may fairly easily be reached because the referents are in one way and another open to clear demonstration. Thus when someone says, 'The dentist's drill gives me pain,' there is far less likelihood of our going astray in comprehension than if the remark had been, 'Unseemly language gives me pain,' for the first kind of pain is—alas!—more responsive to evidential tests than the other.

The hospitality of a home where generous friends exert themselves to provide food, drink, comfort, and conversation affords pleasure of a high

---

[1] A good deal of government propaganda has been in the hands of the publicity experts who made such a sweeping success of advertising Guinness, Gold Flake, Johnnie Walker, and other famous commodities, so one would expect it to be managed with skill.

[2] In the *Sunday Chronicle*, October 29th. Under the headline 'THE HERO WHO WAS A BORE,' Mr Nichols very naïvely reveals his own suggestibility:

'Years ago, in common with every other author who met him, I wrote enthusiastically about Lindbergh. In those early days we were all swept away.

After all, he was on a pedestal with a great deal of limelight playing round him, and a large number of pretty women grouped in decorative attitudes at his feet . . . and in addition he *had* just performed a very brave and remarkable deed.'

order, but it is not a 'high order abstraction.' The hospitality of a country is a very high order abstraction indeed. A semantically disciplined reader would ask himself: In what way could the geographical area known as England be said to have given Colonel Lindbergh and his family hospitality? Were they prevented from paying money for the goods and amenities they enjoyed here? Did their presence demand sacrifices from an appreciable number of the inhabitants? Did they take up so much room as to be in the way? Did their entertainment call for so much unrewarded effort that they may justly be said to owe the nation a debt? If they were received in the houses of friends who showed kindness to them, are they thereby committed to emotions of gratitude towards the whole population, indeed the whole British Empire? Is everybody who visits a foreign country and receives courteous treatment from the individuals he meets there so deeply indebted to that country and its Government that he is not entitled to speak freely about it ever after? Or is the requisite degree of gratitude conditioned by one's motive in making the journey, so that if it was a temporary escape from a scene of distress and disturbance, the country has higher claims than if one had come to amuse oneself?

When all these questions are answered the enquirer will probably conclude that whether Colonel Lindbergh's views on Canada were sound or unsound, he was not guilty of any ingratitude in giving expression to them. The unwitting use of 'hospitality' on a figurative plane is, of course, facilitated by the equally unwitting personification of countries and nations—a simplifying and idealizing device which has long been recognized as dangerous.

Another, and this time a very subtle, example of deluding metaphor deserves attention. In the early days of the present war, the papers carried a number of news items typified in the following headline: MAHARAJAH OFFERS ONLY SURVIVING SON TO KING-EMPEROR.[1]

The paragraphs below explained how the Maharajah of B—— had approached the Viceroy and placed at his disposal the sword and personal services of Captain Maharaj-Kumar S—— B——. Charmed by picturesque allusions, stirred by impressive titles ('King-Emperor' is especially glittering), the reader for whom this kind of paragraph has been artfully composed has little chance of seeing what a meretricious piece of work it is. The offers of liberty-loving patriots to 'give' their near and dear ones in wartime can only be literally justified if those near and dear ones are chattel slaves. In the absence of a system of slavery, the most realistic claim to offering and giving must come from those who successfully bring pressure to bear upon unwilling dependants; but no one yet, to the best of my recollection, ever announced with pride that he had

[1] All references to the contents of newspapers are literal and genuine, though I have not encumbered the text with names and dates when they are used as mere general instances.

coerced a son to serve king and country. That is not what the maharajah's panegyrists would have us believe. If the son is free and has not been coerced, we are left to conclude that his father makes a gesture of giving him, though in point of fact the son himself is the real giver. The gesture, if the parent is waiving some valuable right *which it is in his power to exercise*, is perhaps a costly one: but in many cases when fathers boast of giving their sons and wives of giving their husbands, the gesture is empty for they have had no choice.

We see from the following openly sentimental passage to what a tiresome extent the giving illusion can be carried.[1] The mother of Louisa Alcott's *Little Women* in repeating a conversation with an old, poor, and tired man:

'"Have you sons in the army?" I asked. . . .

"Yes, ma'am; I had four, but two were killed; one is a prisoner, and I'm going to the other, who is very sick in Washington hospital," he answered quietly.

"You have done a great deal for your country, sir," I said, feeling respect now instead of pity.

"Not a mite more than I ought, ma'am. I'd go myself, if I was any use; as I ain't, I give my boys and give 'em free."

He spoke so cheerfully, looked so sincere, and seemed so glad to give his all, that I was ashamed of myself. I'd given one man and thought it too much, while he gave four, without grudging them.'

Abstract terms quite meaningless in the light of demonstrable facts are nowhere more persistently used than in the speeches and writings of statesmen, who cannot in all cases be acquitted of knowing the sort of material they are handling. In *The International Anarchy*,[2] the abuse of figurative language may distinctly be traced among the numberless tangled threads which went to make the Gordian knot of 1914, as we may judge here from one or two representative passages:

' . . . What are we to say about "national honour"? Honour is one of the words which excite so much passion that it is difficult to discover precisely what the passion is about. An American writer [Leo Perla] has collected over a hundred instances of the use of the word by politicians, historians, and the like, and some of his examples are surprising. Thus, according to Maximilian Harden, German "honour" demanded the annexation of Belgium. French "honour" demanded that the question of Morocco should *not* be submitted to an international conference. On the other hand, German "honour" required that it *should*. Japanese "honour" demanded that Japan should pre-

[1] Another form of it is evident in the statement, not seldom heard on the lips of wives and mistresses, that they have given the best years of their lives to a man. The assumption is that the years were a boon to the receiver, but a thankless sacrifice to the giver.

[2] G. Lowes Dickinson's still incomparable study of the origins of the first Great War.

dominate in eastern Asia. Other examples of what honour prescribes are: Breaking a treaty when it no longer expresses the actual relations between Powers (Treitschke). Breaking the American Peace Commission treaties, for these "it would be dishonourable to break, but far more dishonourable to keep" [Theodore Roosevelt]. Going to war against your ally. Italy did this in the Great War, and D'Annunzio said: "Blessed are the young men who hunger and thirst after honour, for their desire shall be fulfilled." When the Russians in 1914 mobilized against Austria they gave the reason that "Russia is offended in her honour as a Great Power...."

Such examples do not leave the observer with a very clear notion of what governments and nations understand by honour. It may, perhaps, help us in our quest if we note that the sentiment never seems to operate if it is divorced from interest; a fact which leads to the conjecture that it is only a mask thrown over interest to make it look attractive to generous or scrupulous spirits. ... It is, in fact, a word without content, employed to excite or to sustain emotions.'

And, as a tailpiece to honour, annihilation:

'"Isolation," said Baron Sonnino, "means annihilation." What "annihilation" means he did not discuss. In the language of statesmen it is apt to mean being weaker than another Power, though who is "annihilated" in that position is not clear. Not, one would suppose, the men and women who really *are* annihilated in war, but that curious abstraction "the State." ' [1]

From 1914 to the present day, the spokesmen of peoples have maintained an almost unremitting willingness to sacrifice peoples for symbols (for even those 'interests' which are disguised with noble-sounding names often turn out to be symbols in effect—symbols of the prestige and power which are actually enjoyed by only a small minority). Fantastic nonsense about the destiny of Aryan blood has been a pretext for shedding the very real blood of Germans; Englishmen are conscripted in order that they may defend the right to be free. As of old, men die in legions to win or save frontiers which never had any existence until they were drawn on maps. Mythical figures, like the French Marianne with her Phrygian cap, Gretchen with her flaxen braids, Britannia holding Neptune's trident, are accounted of infinitely higher value than sentient human beings.

Pictorial symbolism is a most potent method of inducing that habit of

[1] Compare this sort of language in the Parliamentary Blue Book on the Outbreak of Hostilities, 1939: 'Sir H. Kennard also reported his opinion that the Polish Government could not be induced to send a representative immediately to Berlin to discuss a settlement on the basis proposed by Herr Hitler. They would certainly sooner fight and perish than suffer such humiliation.' The Polish Government, which afterwords took root in London, neither fought nor perished; it was the people who did that.

personification which I have so far only glancingly touched upon. The picture may vanish from the conscious mind, but probably not before it has served its turn in strengthening the trend towards animism—a simplifying and emotionally gratifying legacy from aboriginal modes of thought. Cheap and easy printing, with constantly improving facilities for distribution, has increased the propensity just when it might have been expected that we would begin to grow out of it. The allegorical paintings which once so profusely adorned the walls and ceilings of the great have now developed into the political cartoons from which millions take their primary ideas of national and world affairs.

The Women's Movement was personified for many years in comic drawings of female policemen, soldiers, and doctors looking and behaving ridiculously : the Suffrage Campaign was discredited by the portrayal of a screaming virago contrasted, sometimes literally, sometimes by inference, with a gracious young mother rocking a cradle. When we feel friendly, 'the gallant little Jap' [1] is depicted as a sturdy warrior contending with some monster usually larger than himself; when unfriendly, we represent him as a species of yellow devil. Nations whose rulers are better known to us are subjected to a yet more convincing personification, the attention being all focussed on the character and aspect of certain leaders. This is particularly effective when relations are hostile, since popular ideas of aggressiveness, cunning, and ruffianism lend themselves to vivid imagery.

I well remember how, in my childhood, the cruel and arrogant figure of the Kaiser, the rat-like countenance of the Crown Prince (known then as Little Willie), the brutal bulk of Hindenburg, as interpreted by cartoonists who had never seen any of them, embodied Germany for me, playing much the same rôles as are now allotted to Hitler, Goebbels, and Goering—Hitler, of course, predominating just as the Kaiser predominated in his time. (Those old enough to recall the last war who protest that, after all, no one ever thought the Kaiser quite as bad as Hitler, seem to me to be infatuated in the same manner, though not the same direction, as lovers who retain no memory of earlier passions when they claim to be *really* in love at last.)

Nor is it surprising that these men—princes and dictators—should take the praise and blame for a whole nation, since that is what their supporters apparently desire and they consent to. The Archbishop of York told us, before the Coronation in 1937, that the King was 'incarnate of the community,' and Goering is reported to have said in a momentous speech, 'Hitler is Germany.' It is not surprising, but it is very regrettable, for it means, to name no other consequence, that anger and hate can be centred upon one target in a fashion which tragically eclipses the essential issues. Thus in wars pugnacity is always directed emotionally against

[1] These adjectives were constantly applied to the Japanese during their war with Russia in 1904, which we approved of, and the first Great War, when they were our allies.

the leaders, and it is felt that every blow is aimed at them,[1] whereas they are likely to be in fact the best-protected individuals in the whole populace.

The visible representation of a country as a person or a quasi-human animal prepares the way, as I have already suggested, for animism of a more subtle but equally mischievous type, affecting the outlook of even the intelligent. Nations are perpetually referred to as if they had, not national characteristics, which are a genuine phenomenon, if frequently an overstressed one,[2] but personality, and that of a most simple and compact order. England will not tolerate this. . . . Russia is out to gain that. . . . Japan is affronted. . . . America is in doubt. . . . Germany is proud. . . . Few who make currency of such phrases pause to reflect what they mean—which people in England are the ones refusing to tolerate, how many in Japan are aware of the conjectural affront, and so on. It is partly, of course, a matter of quick and convenient allusion; though sometimes it would only cost a word or two more to achieve approximate correctness—'the Cabinet Ministers of England,' 'several newspaper writers in America,' etc. But there is also, especially in reference to one's own race, a substantial remnant of totemism.

'Twentieth-century political thinking [writes Aldous Huxley] is incredibly primitive. The nation is personified as a living being with passions, desires, susceptibilities. The National Person is superhuman in size and energy but completely sub-human in morality. Ordinarily decent behaviour cannot be expected of the National Person, who is thought of as incapable of patience, forbearance, forgiveness and even of common sense and enlightened self-interest. Men, who in private life behave as reasonable and moral beings, become transformed as soon as they are acting as representatives of a National Person into the likeness of their stupid, hysterical and insanely touchy tribal divinity.'[3]

Statesmen and diplomats are as reckless as journalists in treating huge populations, unthinkably large and diversified groups of individuals, as if they were entities of one mind and one voice. To illustrate, I have chosen almost at random a passage from Harold Nicolson's Life of his father, *The First Lord Carnock*. It is out of Sir Arthur Nicolson's diary in 1909, when he was our entirely well-meaning ambassador to Russia, and it is concerned with those combinations and alliances which led to the first Great War, or, at any rate, made it considerably greater.

---

[1] Nothing could demonstrate this more obviously—or more touchingly—than the bombs and shells marked ' One for Adolf ' (as, in the last war, ' One for Kaiser Bill ') which could only by a miracle reach that destination, and may, on the other hand, reach destinations the senders could ill bear to think about.

[2] How greatly overstressed is suggested in Hamilton Fyfe's book, *The Illusion of National Character*.

[3] In *Ends and Means*.

'France has settled Morocco with Germany : Russia is thus isolated. Evident that Austria intends to have a military execution in Serbia, as the result of her feeling safe that France and England will not budge. I tried to convince him [Iswolsky] that there was no question of our deserting Russia. He would not have this : he repeated that Pourtalès was always rubbing in to him that Germany would march with Austria : he would have it that we had thrown over Russia and that France had done likewise. This meant complete collapse of his policy : he would have to admit that he had steered the wrong course, to abandon alliance and entente, to take another line. Berlin had always told him he was on the wrong tack and making combinations which at the critical moment would prove of no value. He doubted whether Germany would preach peace and moderation at Vienna, as both Germany and Austria thought Russia would do nothing and could be ignored. Serbia was perfectly quiet : it was a wanton act which Austria was preparing to commit. Russian opinion would be incensed and a general conflagration might follow.'

It would be an interesting exercise to find the real referents for all these glib references. Incidentally, we have here a dismal reminder, such as diplomatic memoirs will constantly afford, of the preposterous influence exercised by a few men in shaping the future of myriads. This mad confidence would probably not be reposed in statesmen if the nebulous faith in a tribal divinity did not cause the leaders to be looked upon as inspired high priests.

As well as nations, qualities, attitudes, and states of being are personified, again with signal help from the pictorial artist, and again to the great disadvantage of human relations and the prospects of happiness. Superficially the figure of Victory holding out a crown of laurels, or Justice with her blindfold and her scales, or Peace with her olive branch, or Charity sustaining a brood of infants, may not seem very dangerous symbols, but they tend to rigidify beliefs as to the nature of extremely remote abstractions, and the outcome has been disastrous to humanity.

Absolute Justice, 'positively living and moving in a remote and ethereal region,' [1] demands Absolute Laws. Laws made by men thus come to be administered as if they had been written on tables of stone ; indeed, even those which relate to wholly secular affairs seem, when they have the prestige of antiquity, to be solemnly regarded as of more than earthly origin. It is very reassuring to men to think so, for they naturally fear their own judgments and demand, in the words of Jerome Frank, 'a magical source of decisions. The early modes of trial—the ordeal, the judicial duel, the oath, the compurgation—were considered to be

---

[1] Samuel Butler's phrase in *Erewhon*, where he satirizes the habit of deifying modes of human thought and action.

uncontaminated by human elements. The judgment was the judgment of the supernatural.' [1]

Long after trial by ordeal had been, with difficulty, abolished, so great an authority as Blackstone was able to write : 'This, then, is the general signification of the Law : a rule of action dictated by some superior being.' And to this day one can scarcely read any batch of cases from a court of justice without finding among them one or two in which the verdicts have been based upon sheer legalisms and lag far behind our present views of right or wrong—behind even the views held by the lawyers themselves, though, through their constant enslavement to words and forms, they are notoriously liable to be in the rearguard of progress. The curious rituals of the court, and the quaint unchanging attire of the judge and advocates, support—as they are meant to do—the impression of a process not quite upon the ordinary human plane.

But it is not only the laws of the courts which are 'entangled with the ghosts of divine sanction.' Our sentimental reverence for abstractions has fathered an unremitting tyranny of systems, codes, and ideologies, many of which are upheld at the cost of incalculable suffering. Codes of morals, codes of honour, and codes of etiquette have been enforced with utter disregard of their arbitrary character. We are menaced by theoretical laws of nature and stultified by artificial laws of supply and demand. Fallacious Malthusian laws of population gave excuse for fatalistic resignation to growing slums and multiplying ills of poverty. Deluding economic laws, proven in the abstract to be irrefragable, made it 'impossible' to reduce working hours in the worst epoch of sweated labour, 'impossible' later to raise wages, 'impossible' later still to increase taxation, to go off the gold standard, or in short, to perform a hundred operations which have, when at last carried into practice, turned out perfectly feasible.

Besides religious, ethical, economic, and pseudo-scientific dogmas, there are the systems of principles for governments, which, once accepted, are elevated to a definitely sacred status. The Americans are hag-ridden by their Constitution, which again and again is referred to by men of great public position as if it had been, like Britannia's charter, received from guardian angels at Heaven's command.[2] Fortunately, the divine licence given to Britain was merely to rule the waves, and our Consitution being blessedly unwritten has always shown a very fair degree of the adaptability so desirable in human organizations. Our mystical consecration of the Crown, however, and the enormous variety of hallowed emblems and solemn forms connected with it, should remind

[1] Quoted in *The Tyranny of Words*.
[2] E.g. in his dissenting opinion on the Social Security Act, Mr Justice Reynolds said :
' We should keep in mind that we are living under a written Constitution. No volume of words and no citation of irrelevant statistics and no appeal to feelings of humanity can expand the powers granted to Congress. Neither can we . . . view the situation differently from that seen by the Fathers of the Constitution.'—Quoted in *The Tyranny of Words*.

us to think twice before calling other races superstitious, being, as we are, the inhabitants of a veritable Crystal Palace.

The custom of paying lip service to doctrines and enactments which have been preserved, through having been originally 'dictated by some superior being,' when they are secretly no longer esteemed useful or apt, gives rise to those purely verbal shifts and evasions which characterize so many of the rulings of authority. This unlovely form of dishonesty is occasionally used after Portia's fashion, to avert legally permissible harshness, but far more often affords a means of justifying some action or belief which stands gravely in need of justification.

A disingenuous recourse to the sanction of Biblical texts is the most familiar way of quibbling, and there are, I should think, enough ludicrous examples available to make an anthology. The pleasantest I can offer is the rejoinder of the late Dr Lyman Abbott, an eminent theologian in the United States, to those who doubted whether it was right, on Christian principles, for Americans to devote themselves so ardently to the amassing of money :

> 'Jesus did not say "Lay not up for yourselves treasures upon earth." He said "Lay not up for yourselves treasures upon earth *where moth and rust corrupt and where thieves break through and steal.*" And no sensible American does. Moth and rust do not get at Mr Rockefeller's oil wells, and thieves do not often break through and steal a railway. What Jesus condemned was hoarding wealth.' [1]

Mere verbalism, again, is often resorted to by political strategists where they are trying to explain tergiversations in policy or retreat from promises. Not everyone would have the honesty to say, like the late Mr Chamberlain, 'I have changed my mind.' The astonishing shufflings of the international cards since shortly before the outbreak of this war have promoted a series of conjuring tricks with abstract nouns and metaphorical verbs which are perhaps unparalleled since the days when lives, careers, and fortunes could depend upon the adroit handling of religious dicta. The editorial writers, even of comparatively enlightened sections of the press, have performed miracles of emergency logic.[2] One is inclined to think, until one remembers their record, that the bishops also have excelled themselves.[3] As for philosophers—I mean, of course, that large class of them which suffers from verbomania—they have not had

[1] The authors of *The Meaning of Meaning*, where I found the specimen, comment thus :
' When moth and rust have been eliminated by science the Christian investor will presumably have no problem, but in the meantime it would seem that Camphorated Oil fulfils most nearly the synoptic requirements. Burglars are not partial to it ; it is anathema to moth ; and the risk of rust is completely obviated.'

[2] See Appendix 14.

[3] In 1930, at the Lambeth Conference, they decided that war as a method of settling disputes was incompatible with the teaching and example of Christ. Today some of them seem to think rather more highly of it than the military experts, and particularly as a means of sustaining Christian values.

to shift their ground very much because, being altogether abstract, it is as peripatetic as the floating island of Laputa.

And now I hope it will not be inferred from anything I have written that I am so silly as to condemn, out of hand, all figurative language and words that do not indicate tangible objects. That would reduce our speech to an imbecile level, and indeed everyone may see, from the number of abstractions which appear in these pages, that I for one have not tried to do without them. The evils I have striven to exhibit are, chiefly and briefly, the identification of words with things, and the confusion of assumed properties with verifiable properties and of verbal forms with facts. 'Simile, metaphor, poetry,' says the invaluable Chase, 'are legitimate and useful methods of communication, provided speaker and hearer are conscious that they are being employed.' The same applies to any kind of abstraction or label derived from an abstraction.

It happens, unluckily, that the illusion of simplicity, and whatever other illusions the not very highly evolved mind finds comfort in, are served best by *not* being conscious of abstractification—by accepting the well-worn materials that are to hand without enquiry as to their nature. Conventional education has always encouraged this acceptance, upholding orthodoxy, frowning upon scepticism, bestowing its highest rewards on those who are most adept in academic formalities. Well-educated people, when they lose contact with reality, are more dangerous, more untrustworthy, than ignorant ones. 'The ablest logicians are precisely those who are led to evolve the most fantastic systems by the aid of their verbal technique.' [1]

So imperfect is our present means of communication, rather through prolonged misuse than any defect inherent in the symbols themselves, that it is sometimes almost a relief to deal only with those topics where the 'obvious and immediate' need of comprehension precludes all fanciful and artificial language. Nor can we be surprised that there are some who fling themselves with ardour into situations where the pressure of necessity must, as they think, break through the webs of speech. For it is true that, under the sharpest compulsions of anxiety and relief, suffering and happiness, human beings who had seemed quite wanting in high qualities will suddenly appear to shine with a natural goodness; and a few have thought it worth the loss of every urbane and civilized pleasure to feel and to inspire this nobility. But for most of us, ideas, emotions, sentiments, will remain 'strangely hidden in the covert of ambiguous words that . . . serves to beget nothing but matters of distrust and labyrinths of errors.'

[1] From *The Meaning of Meaning*.

You may not believe, as I believe, that Christ was God. Life would be simpler and sweeter if you did, but that is not my affair.
        BEVERLEY NICHOLS, in the *Sunday Chronicle*, April 28th, 1940.

REVERENCE for tradition is a fairly overt form of sentimentality and one which, most people feel, needs little defending. A mild and generalized ancestor worship, the repetition of time-honoured practices, the incantation of old formalities which gain charm in proportion as they lose in aptness—these will seem to many readers harmless emotional gratifications which it is captious to criticize, and to others even a valuable assurance of security. Nevertheless I believe that the retention of customs which are fully and widely recognized as archaic is always paralleled by the retention of customs which are not so recognized, with effects of varying evil, ranging from tiresomeness to tragedy, from the infliction of minor discomforts to barbarous cruelty. I shall begin to illustrate from a somewhat personal angle.

A few years ago I went to the most delightful of English watering-places to recuperate from a serious illness. I was suffering badly from insomnia—no very uncommon disorder, I imagine, where there are so many invalids—and my first prescription was to get more rest than had been possible in my previous surroundings. For a day or two all was well, but one evening, which I have good reason to know was a Saturday, neurasthenia again took the form of an incorrigible wakefulness, and I was alert the whole night long. (For the enlightenment of those who have a cheerful conviction that insomnia is largely imaginary, and that its professed victims usually get much more sleep than they realize, I will mention that I had taken refuge in a novel which I finished at about six in the morning.) Towards seven I fell asleep, gratefully assuring myself that I could rest, if I pleased, till eleven. I had not dozed for much more than an hour, I fancy, when I was aroused by the ringing of a church bell near at hand. It banged away on one note, as far as I can remember, for a long infuriating spell and then abruptly subsided. I stopped my ears as well as I could and succeeded at last in recapturing sleep, only to have it wrested from me again by a renewed clangor, which ceased and was resumed at intervals till somewhere near eleven o'clock, breaking out riotously into chimes that seemed to rake the room.

The exact sequence in which the bells were rung and the exact hours at which they were rung, both on that Sunday and the two following when I again had the exasperation of listening to them, I cannot pretend to recollect, but the thoughts that ran through my head are not likely to escape my memory, for they were the first clear foreshadowing of this book.

Church bells, I reflected, properly belong to that age when a very large majority of the population was in the habit of going to church, and a very small minority had accurate means of telling the time. Then they performed a function which was regarded as useful; now they are a pure anachronism, and one which, though lovable and delectable to many, is to at least as many more a recurring nuisance, and to a few under certain conditions a source of almost unbearable irritation—irritation far more intense in degree, to judge not from my own feelings alone, than any potential enjoyment. Why, I asked myself, should a world so belaboured with inescapable noises tolerate this perfectly gratuitous percussion? Why should it not be relegated to a convenient hour on occasions of special festivity?[1] Or why, if churches are permitted to advertise their ceremonies without consideration for the sensibilities of objectors, do we not find the same privilege granted to theatres, concert halls, and dance palaces? What steps would be taken if they should begin to announce their sessions with beating of drums, like ancient Oriental taverns, with blaring of amplified music, or even with a carillon? Clearly a thousand protests would be launched and the papers would be filled with letters signed 'Indignant Ratepayer,' and 'Pro Bono Publico.' Unless the police took action, private prosecutions would flood the courts, and rightly so.[2]

But churches, though only a small percentage of the population in towns and cities actually attends them, and fewer still give practical application to their doctrines, are treated with very nearly as much deference as if people believed in them. The Church of England is established as part of the State, it is subsidized,[3] its bishops take an official place in the legislature, it enforces laws made hundreds of years ago for the collection of taxes on certain lands, it owns vast possessions some of which are absolutely incompatible in their nature or their management with a straightforward interpretation of the Christian faith,[4] it is accorded the unprecedented facilities of the radio for pouring out its propaganda, it influences our laws and customs in a hundred diverse and often devious ways. Together with other highly organized communities, chiefly Catholic and Nonconformist, it exercises a power over public affairs immensely out of proportion with its power over private conduct: and for no better reason than that religious authority has a very long past and the education of most of us has been such as to compel at least the externals of respect for orthodoxy.

Orthodoxy, in fact, is highly valued even by many who quite con-

[1] Church bells, since I recorded this train of thought, were silenced for the purposes of the War Office, but the relief proved to be only temporary, so strong is the power of tradition.

[2] See Appendix 15.

[3] This is spoken of as 'endowment.'

[4] E.g. slum properties and blocks of shares which, to say the least of it, are difficult to reconcile with the Sermon on the Mount.

sciously do not share in any orthodox beliefs, because they look upon it, correctly enough, as a prop for the existing order of things in general: while others who have nothing to gain from the existing order support it willy-nilly through the emotional reactions induced by training and association. Thus people who freely admit that they 'never put their foot inside a church from one year's end to another' can be stirred to violent indignation against governments attempting to limit ecclesiastical influence, and will give the ready credence of resentment to palpably exaggerated accounts of religious persecution. Relying on this bias, in times of crisis propagandists usually claim to be defending some religious ideal, use symbolic figures, nuns and priests, as the principal victims in atrocity stories, and report the damage done to churches and sacred paraphernalia as if these were the most heinous crimes of war and revolution and far more serious than the destruction of secular property.[1]

(I do not suggest that every atrocity story involving nuns and priests must be fabricated. No doubt the same symbolism which hallows the church and the monastery for conservatives renders them outstandingly provocative to the more impassioned members of the opposition. But it is certain that many versions of sacerdotal outrages have a bad pedigree and should be cautiously received.)

Now, while to be shocked by persecution of any faith may indicate a very desirable progress in tolerance, if that sympathy is accompanied by a corollary eagerness to endorse every cause which claims to have a religious basis, it is only evidence of aimless, diffused, and sentimental convictions.

To pay some sort of verbal tribute to religion, even if one does not belong to any sect, is a habit so widely and deeply inculcated that, except from those who are naturally unconventional, it hardly elicits any form of self-enquiry. This willing veneration is often supposed to illustrate the inborn religious tendency of the human mind, but the conduct of man discloses very clearly that it is lip service. In describing the manners of the Erewhonians, Samuel Butler names it as 'one of their peculiarities that they very often do not believe or mean things which they profess to regard as indisputable.' And indeed, glancing over the history of human (as of Erewhonian) institutions, one is driven to conclude that the more emphatically societies have professed to regard a thing as indisputable, the more absolutely has their behaviour shown they do not

---

[1] The regular readers of the Rothermere Press during its Franco 'crusade' must have become connoisseurs of this kind of extravagance. Newspaper reports of German conquest in Poland have also abounded in tales of nuns forced to desecrate 'the Sacrament,' churches invaded by Nazi hordes, and praying peasants warned rudely, but perhaps not inappositely, to save their breath.

There is a striking reticence, however, about the terrorism indulged in by the champions of faith. Little has been heard of the 'armed Masses' which Franco's prisoners were forced to attend under the menace of fixed bayonets with machine-guns covering the exits. Yet these reports seem at least as well authenticated as the others.

really believe or mean it.   I will support this paradox with a few of the most obvious examples.

When the omnipotence, the omniscience, and the infallible justice of the Deity was held to be beyond question except by those doomed to eternal misery, crimes such as murder, blasphemy, and sacrilege were actually far more common than they are today, as may be seen in any study of a well-documented period such as the Renaissance ; and Rome, the very centre of Christendom, was worse, not better, than the outposts. When men were unanimous in asserting the existence of this personal God, who would take inexorable vengeance against sinners and who had created for this purpose a vast torture-chamber known as Hell, so far from leaving the business of elaborate punishment to the next world and confining their own efforts merely to ridding themselves of the evil-doer, they were at this very time most ingenious in devising penalties, and the executions of criminals and heretics were carried out by hideously painful methods.[1]   When matrimony was deemed so sacred as to be irrevocable, a holy union which it was mortal sin to dishonour, betrothals were frequently contracted between persons who had never seen each other for reasons of a purely mundane character, the aggrandizement of fortunes, the succession of titles, and so forth.   When the lusts of the flesh were classed among the deadliest of sins, men took an extravagant pride in sexual virility.   When there was most talk of the superiority and grandeur of the human species, each man being an immortal soul made in the image of his Maker, there was most contempt for the individual's dignity, most widespread enslavement and basest degradation.

Moreover, it is not to be imagined that the talking was done by one set of people, the contrasting deeds by another : those who were loudest in admiring the prevailing code often showed greatest indifference to it by their actions, as if, having made a gesture of respect to it, they felt they had done everything that was required of them.

In our time, this lip service has been at its most audible in the advocacy of peace, the organization for war meanwhile continuing on a scale without precedent even among nations proud to be warriors.

Emptiness of profession, hollow pretences of adherence to beliefs which in practice constantly go for nothing, these are a feature of social adaptation in every civilized community—and, it may be, of every savage community too if *to conform* is the unspoken golden rule.   Savages are perhaps as sceptical fundamentally of their ancient gods and tribal magic as most Christians are of the oft-recited statements in the Apostles' Creed. For people, even when schismless, do not believe in God and his awful

---

[1] That the spectacle of suffering was looked upon as a deterrent does not in itself provide an adequate motive.   Punishment was explicitly stated to be part of the intention.   Nor was it always assumed that by destroying the body the soul might be saved.   Condemned heretics were sometimes excommunicants—that is to say, absolutely assured of Hell.

Day of Judgment as they believe that fire burns or that water quenches thirst; they have no confidence in the practical wisdom of Christ; they have no inward assurance that the Gospels deal with facts in the sense that a bank-book or a Blue Book deals with facts. In Bridgman's *Logic of Modern Physics* we read: 'The true meaning of a term is to be found by observing what a man does with it, not what he says about it.' By that test the terms used by upholders of the Churches do not usually mean very much. This has been remarked so exceedingly often, both by the sincere believers and the agnostics (it is not their only common meeting-ground) that I could hardly say anything more hackneyed.

The innumerable reiterations have not been wholly without effect. It would be perverse not to acknowledge a great improvement in the last century, a great narrowing—in peacetime, at least—of the gap between preaching and practice. There is, for one thing, much less preaching. But muddle-headed self-deception and the indolence that loves grooves still play a very appreciable part in both private and public, and especially public, affairs. The gesture of respect to the prevailing code ensures that the code shall prevail long after all but the stupidest have seen that it is not appropriate to extant conditions. My church bells are the emblem of a multitude of surviving archaisms.

If we give evidence in a court of law, we are called upon to lay our hand on the Bible and swear by Almighty God. If we send our children to a public school, the chances are that they will be herded to church two or three times on Sundays and at least once on week-days: at elementary schools they are taught 'Scripture' as if every part of the Old Testament were historically true and ethically sound. Soldiers and sailors are marched to 'Divine worship' under orders. Patients in hospitals are asked as part of the routine whether they are R.C. or C. of E. The British Broadcasting Corporation regales, or endeavours to regale, its huge public with psalms, prayers, hymns, and sermons,[1] and permits no anti-religious utterance whatever.

Either the men responsible for the conduct of these institutions really maintain—I borrow Leonard Woolf's words—'that absolute truths about the nature of the universe were revealed divinely to savage tribes and primitive peoples thousands of years ago and must be accepted as such because they are recorded in books of which the origin and authors are unknown,' or else they wish quite cynically to keep others wedded to ideas they have broken away from themselves, for the reason that religious

---

[1] On January 1st, 1940, immediately after the chimes of Big Ben had dismissed a year in which our country had plunged into total warfare, we heard from Broadcasting House a sanctimonious apostrophe and the ironically chosen hymn, *The King of Love My Shepherd Is.*

In his book of reminiscences, *Ariel and All His Quality*, R. S. Lambert states that one of Sir John Reith's first questions in interviewing him for a perfectly secular post with the B.B.C. was: 'Do you accept the fundamental teaching of Jesus Christ?'

conservatism fathers social and political conservatism,[1] and the force of law and order is thus strengthened.

How curious, almost in the middle of the twentieth century after Christ, to find a war ushered in with a King, a Prime Minister, a Foreign Minister, and two Leaders of the Opposition, all invoking God to bless our arms![2] Can it be possible that these decorous persons, and the numberless others who publicly call for divine assistance, really and literally believe in the sort of god they address themselves to? A god whose intentions may be diverted by flattering appeals[3] and who is prepared to lend his aid to naval, military and aeronautical authorities to ensure the victory of his favourite nation? And if they do not believe, what is the point of praying? No one seems to place the smallest reliance on this Bronze Age god in private: surely it would be more honest and more dignified to refrain from making calls upon his name in public!

After Jehovah, but generally mentioned with less confidence and in a rather *sotto voce* manner, we have Jesus—but a Jesus who would assuredly provide many unpleasant surprises for the sensitive philosopher of Nazareth. The currently accepted Jesus has suffered the rigidifying change which so unfortunately affects persons who become symbols. He is, in his public or semi-public capacity, a machine which produces texts, texts sometimes interpreted so as to justify courses which are completely discredited by his whole mode of living and dying. A few isolated phrases and one isolated anecdote are used to negate everything else that has been told of him. True and beautiful as the metaphor must be to one who has experienced the terror of a spiritual struggle, I could wish—since so many fools have turned the words into a sanction for so many wars—that Jesus had never said he brought not peace but a sword. I could wish there were no record of his whipping the money-changers out of the temple, seeing that this one act has been taken as a licence for every species of punitive and revengeful violence.[4]

One of the most repulsive of the minor unpleasantnesses to be endured when Christian countries go to war is the very ancient and very nauseous practice of using false analogies to 'prove' that Jesus would not merely

[1] This was the observation of Mme Curie in a letter to her sister in 1887. She thought conservatism of both kinds 'incomprehensible.'

[2] See Appendix 16.

[3] That prayers, even when they contain a request for some boon, are not an attempt to divert the intentions of the Deity has long been contended by theologians, but their arguments are full of verbal mystifications and anything but convincing. The plain speaker is left wondering what is the motive for addressing petitions to an infinitely wise and righteous God if they are not genuine petitions at all but only an expression of pious resignation to what has already been ordained.

[4] 'Critic' of the *New Statesman* has very justly pointed out that, contrary to popular interpretation, there is excellent support for the advocate of non-violence in 'the story of a man who picks up a bundle of small cords and with this ferocious weapon drives a great temple courtyardful of tradesmen, herdsmen, and money-changers out into the street. Obviously, they went not because they were not powerful enough to resist him, but because they were shamed by the vigour of his personality and the truth of his words.'

support the fight but would give his sanction to the fiercest methods of prosecuting it.

To examine Christianity as it has been applied by some of those who have the word oftenest on their lips raises doubt as to whether the addition of the sentimentalized Jesus to Western theocracy has not hindered rather than helped progress, for the possession of an attractively benevolent figurehead seems in itself to afford a sense of moral satisfaction, and after a sufficiency of ritual observances has been performed, religion resolves itself into the game of 'finding the sanction' for doing precisely what one would have done in any case. The Churches supply the requisite formulae, the litanies and genuflections, the hard-and-fast lines of restriction as to certain petty details, which constitute a discipline. Discipline, if effective, must be repressive alike to reason and to spontaneous emotion. Within the framework of orthodoxy, one feels as cosy as a sheep in a fold; outside it, in one's daily life, one is what one would have been without it, but so much the worse for having surrendered integrity—for I do not see how it is possible to preserve integrity while subscribing verbally to propositions constantly refuted by one's acts, or by making a virtue of the kind of faith which is 'an illogical belief in the occurrence of the improbable.'

I will venture to recall a tiny incident in my childhood which made a profound impression on my outlook. At the age of eight I was a boarder in a convent school. One Sunday morning before Mass, the 'boarder's mother' noticed a small but conspicuous hole in my stocking. The dilemma was a painful one for her—whether to break the strict proscription against sewing on Sunday or to let one of her charges be seen looking slovenly; and as she decided to mend the stocking she gave vent to an anger quite out of proportion with the triviality of my offence, mentioning, among other matters, that the incident would be 'displeasing to Our Lord.' I remember very well how, as I stood listening to the sharp tirade, in which she blamed me for causing her to commit a sin, the absurdity of the accusation struck forcibly to my intelligence, and my reflection, clear and defined, was: 'Does she really think that Jesus is so silly?' With variations of the pronoun I have been asking the same question ever since.

It is, of course, unfair to blame the Churches for the silliness displayed by all their individual members. Though as a rule individuals reveal more intelligence than corporate bodies, there are exceptions. The College of Cardinals would probably take much the same view of the sin of mending a stocking on Sunday as I did. The Lambeth Conference would not applaud—at least not unanimously—the humour of the vicar who sent rat poison in response to a brother-clergyman's appeal for comforts for wounded German prisoners (and preached in his pulpit that it was 'the grossest perversion' to apply the teachings of Jesus and St Paul when dealing with Nazis). The dignitaries of the Free Presbyterian Churches might not feel perfectly comfortable about the refusal of a minister to baptize a child whose father, an elder, had gathered sheep knowing they were to be transported on a Sunday, and whose mother had attended a bazaar in aid of a hall where dancing was to be permitted.[1]

And even if the directors of church policy were as ridiculous as some of their followers cause them to appear, it might well be objected that to assail orthodoxy is to flog a dying horse, since the number of the orthodox is proportionately not large and is likely to go on diminishing. My complaint is not so much against orthodoxy, however, as against the degree to which sentimentality allows it to infect the manners of those who have no vestige of genuine belief in it, and to retain its undesirable grip on laws prescribed alike for those who are in sympathy with it and those who are passionately opposed to it.

Of all the legalisms that affect our everyday lives, none have so far-reaching an importance as those involved in matrimony. These, therefore, I shall take for my chief example of ecclesiastical intrusion into the law. I do not fail to anticipate the argument that as matrimony was in origin altogether a function of religion, the Church cannot be treated as an intruder upon that ground. To this it may be answered that, Church and State having once been indivisible, various hierarchies have in their time controlled, or sought to control, every phase of human activity. The process we call progress has consisted largely of successful attempts to shake off that enervating grasp which, when the Church had its way, was never relaxed from the compulsory baptism of the newly born infant to the burial of the anointed body in consecrated soil. It would be as logical to object to secular education as civil marriage : both were once equally unavailable. Education, though it has not yet cast off all its medieval fetters, has gradually ceased to be a clerical monopoly ; the first civil licences for marriage were issued in 1836, but the law continues to place a delusive sanctity before utility in dealing with conjugal difficulties, and our religious legislators have vigorously pitted themselves against reform, supported always by the sentimentality of an irresponsible public.

It would be pleasanter . . . it ought to be . . . it is. . . . Only a mental journey along these roads could have led to the conception of marriage which has given us the accepted system, a system definitely framed to make error irremediable. The vows that are exchanged in a church wedding service are such as it is hardly in human nature to keep. They are a fantasy of what love would be if it could go on as we think it will go on when we are at the height of an infatuation : the internal evidence suggests that they were composed by someone madly in love or living a life remote from any practical experience of an intimate sexual relationship. The heart's vicissitudes, the passions and repugnances of the body, remain bafflingly out of our control. To base a contract calling for the

[1] Instances gathered from the *Daily Mirror*, October 30th, 1944, and the *Yorkshire Evening News*, December 3rd, 1935.

highest degree of realism upon protestations which, if not mere empty ritual, are a manifestation either of beautiful delirium or stark ignorance is the outcome of a belief in magical dispensations. The nuptial ceremony was counted upon to work a miracle, to fuse two beings into one. Many legal principles still hinge upon this assumption.

The late Mr Justice McCardie, explaining the disabilities of a husband and a wife to sue each other for injuries,[1] remarked: 'The doctrine of unity gives rise to innumerable complexities. . . . There can be, I suppose, no doubt that theological considerations framed or deepened the common law doctrine of unity. As Professor Westermarck points out in his *History of Human Marriage*, it seems clear that the doctrine of the Western Church profoundly influenced the secular views of the countries in which she was established for so long a time. I find it difficult to see how the old and conventional doctrine of unity can be said to operate at the present day. There is, of course, no physical unity, save in the most limited and occasional sense. There is no mental unity in any just meaning of the word. . . . Upon the grave and delicate matter of spiritual unity it need only be pointed out that husband and wife may belong to different sects, or even to different creeds.' Yet, as he went on to show by a number of precedents, while for many purposes the maxim of the law that husband and wife are one person must be taken as a figure of speech, for other purposes it is understood *in its literal sense*. 'I hope,' he ended, 'that the day is not far distant when the vital and far-reaching relationship of husband and wife will receive the attention of Parliament. When that day comes, I trust that the present features of injustice will be removed, that the existing obscurities will be made clear, and that the great institution of marriage will gain a new dignity and a new strength through a wise and beneficent amendment of the law.'

Since this pronouncement, the law has been amended to the extent that a husband is no longer responsible for his wife's torts, and we are spared from reading those distressing verdicts (often delivered most reluctantly by the Bench) which compelled a man to pay damages and costs incurred by his wife for offences committed without his knowledge, or against his express wishes.[2]

The miraculous view of marriage assiduously promoted by the Church is less widely held than in the past, but it is still sufficiently unshaken to occasion much unhappiness. People may constantly be met with who seem to expect a wedding ceremony to bring about a total change in the character of one or both the parties, and who therefore risk, or encourage

[1] Gottliffe *v.* Edelston, 1930.

[2] Champions of traditional patterns, however, opposed even that very moderate departure from ancient usage. Thus in *Sex and Public Life* A. H. Henderson-Livesey's comment on the impending passage of the Act was: 'This Bill will not aid any decent man or woman; it will do two things only, it will help a contemptible skunk to evade what would still be a moral if not a legal liability, and it will enable a group of unmarried and unmarriageable females to record another "triumph".'

others to risk, matrimonial hazards which no one of thoroughly rational education would contemplate. It is not uncommon for impotent men to marry in the hope that lawful wedlock will somehow promote the virility that fails in illicit attempts!

When these ventures—and others of better promise—come to grief, and when that grief is brought into the law courts, ecclesiastical influence presents a series of antiquated obstacles to the dissolution of the unwholesome tie. It has been said a thousand times, and it must go on being said until the evil is at last redressed, that the Divorce Laws are essentially vindictive, aimed not at giving a fresh chance to persons who have made a mistake, but at punishing a guilty party.

Until very recently only one kind of guilt was recognized. Even now sexual intercourse is accounted so much the most important feature of married life that corporal infidelity gives grounds for divorce when the most extreme forms of incompatibility would be rejected. Miserable couples have been driven to the expedient of hiring a partner for a bogus adultery, thereby rendering themselves liable for prosecution on a criminal charge. For the more eagerly freedom is desired by both parties and the more both are willing to pave the way for it, the less chance there is that it will be granted, since the aim of punishment would not then be achieved.

The doctrine of collusion has been formulated expressly to provide against divorce by mutual consent. In every other contract made between two persons, so far as I am aware, mutual consent is a sufficient reason for abrogation. Marriage is 'protected' by conditions not applied to legal agreements in general, because it is 'the basis of national life' and involves considerations of a public nature.

It seems not to occur to the antagonists of reform that other nations having the same basis—which means no more than that they are made up of family units—have yet been able to revise their Divorce Laws without causing their social structure to collapse. One might suspect indeed from many references to marriage in public speeches and writings that it was something peculiarly English, and unknown elsewhere.[1]

Sir Henry McCardie, who was probably the most liberal-minded judge of our epoch and the one with least reverence for legal conventions (though his learning and knowledge of precedent were unsurpassed), more than once expressed his regret at being compelled to deal with divorce cases in a manner he could not think equitable. Of the doctrine of collusion he said:

'[It] is wide in its scope and comprehensive in its effects. In order to enforce the doctrine the vigilance of the Court will be aroused by slight circumstances and a rigorous scrutiny will follow. . . . Conduct will fall within this doctrine which, though permissible in ordinary

---

[1] See Appendix 17.

civil actions, is adverse to the principles on which the Divorce Court acts. . . . It is clear that collusion may exist not only when a false case is presented to the Court, but that it is equally possible even in a good case. . . . If the initiation of a divorce suit be procured or its conduct provided for by agreement (especially if abstention from defence be a term), this constitutes collusion, although it does not appear that any specific fact has been falsely dealt with or withheld.'

No Parliamentary common sense has been brought to bear on the doctrine of collusion since the time of the case he referred to, when the fact that a civilized husband and wife had resolved not to penalize each other either directly or indirectly was regarded as a sufficient reason for denying them the benefit which the law could confer. Vindictiveness is sometimes openly and always tacitly required by the Divorce Courts. In the suit he was trying when he spoke the words quoted above (Laidler *v*. Laidler, 1920), the judge held it as evidence of non-collusion that 'the wife has from first to last insisted on her right to costs against her husband,' thus indicating to future litigants that to forgo an advantage which might be obtained at the other person's expense is possibly to weaken one's case. This consideration may underlie some of those sordid claims for damages against a co-respondent which Mr Justice McCardie himself usually heard with manifest distaste.[1]

Besides collusion, there is a yet more serious stumbling-block in the disabilities arising from the doctrine of *compensatio criminis*—that is, the rule that a petitioner who is himself (or herself) guilty of adultery cannot secure matrimonial relief unless able to prove circumstances of strong mitigation—and in weighing up such circumstances the Court is more likely to see eye to eye with an assembly of bishops than with the ordinary run of private citizens. Here is a law which clearly envisaged divorce as an act of revenge at all times and took no cognizance whatever of the public morality it pretended to serve. Cases will be known to almost every normally worldly reader in which the last prospect of attaining domestic happiness has been withdrawn from both partners, and perhaps their children likewise, through a false move taken by one of them when under the stress of discovering the other's infidelity or worn down by the prolonged delays and anxieties of legal proceedings. The ramifications of cruelty growing from this one principle of a code which has always sought to placate the Church are more than the most energetic pen could describe.

'It may well be asked [said McCardie] whether the sum total of

---

[1] E.g. 'I often find it difficult to realize how a man of sensitive honour or of recognized rank can seek to recover financial solace for the dishonour of his wife's body.'—From *The Judicial Wisdom of Mr Justice McCardie*, edited by Albert Crew, Barrister-at-Law.

public morality is increased by refusing a divorce against a wife who has committed adultery because the petitioner husband has himself committed the same sin. The result of refusing the divorce is that each continues to live in adultery. The vital question is whether a refusal of divorce in such cases operates as a real deterrent for the prevention of matrimonial infidelity by others, and whether the amount of immorality which is prevented by the refusal outweighs the immorality which results from the refusal of decrees.'

Evidently that great lawyer felt the answer to the question to be unsatisfactory, for he added, giving his verdict in the case under review (a case in which the petitioner, while his wife was living with another man, had had relations with an otherwise 'respectable' young woman who was pregnant and whom he wished to marry):

'I am bound to administer the law as it is. Reform must come from Parliament. . . .

The result of refusing a decree in this suit may seem strange indeed. For if the wife alone had committed adultery, then the husband could at once have dissolved the marriage. Adultery is presumed to render further married life impossible. But inasmuch as the husband himself has here committed adultery also, and married life is therefore doubly impossible, the decree must, in accordance with existing law, be refused. The marriage must continue. I regret this result, but I must administer the law as it stands.'

We need go no further than the same authority for guidance on the almost equally obstructive dogma of condonation. 'It is,' he said, 'a doctrine established by the old Ecclesiastical Courts. The phrase does not occur in civil law. It was introduced into the English courts from the canon law.' In theory it means that a spouse who has once 'forgiven' a matrimonial offence has thereby waived his or her right to take proceedings in respect of it, which seems a sufficiently reasonable provision until we find that, while the law is ecclesiastical, the doctrine of condonation does not remotely resemble the Christian doctrine of forgiveness. It does not even, as the judge was obliged to explain on various occasions, resemble the lay doctrine of forgiveness. He was reduced to describing it as a doctrine 'peculiar in its origin, peculiar in its features, but perhaps most peculiar in its notion of forgiveness.' It is a technical term which, as sometimes interpreted, is merely one more impediment on a road so thorny that probably a majority of the unwisely married never venture upon it. A person risks being suspected of condoning who simply refrains from asperity, from rancorous sullenness, or from instantly and implacably shutting away the offending partner. To be quite certain of avoiding the presumption of forgiveness, any husband or wife who would seek legal freedom if marriage turned out a failure must cultivate from the first an attitude of demonstrative physical jealousy in one of its more primitive shapes.[1]

There are a hundred ways of wrecking friendship and marital comfort, all distinct from adultery, permanent desertion, incurable insanity, gross criminality, habitual drunkenness, or the one or two other extremely abnormal conditions which have at length been grudgingly conceded as grounds for dissolution; and by forcing those who would rescind their errors to bring one or more of these charges, common law and statutory law, based as we have seen upon canon law, are fostering dishonesty and what is commonly regarded as immorality on the part of the litigants [2] and a demoralizing sensationalism in the public.

There is no reason why what was good of canon law should not be kept in juristic use today if it happens to be still applicable, but where the moral codes of the Church no longer fit our conceptions of right and wrong, it is scandalous to continue to defer to them. The gravest aspect of the tyranny is that the same conditions as are laid down for those who have taken perfervid religious vows are imposed on others who have taken no vows at all—for the registrar's ceremony calls for none. The least that justice can do, if ecclesiastically guided divorce laws are retained in the Statute Book, is to ensure that they only operate against persons who have been rash enough to swear oaths in a church.

And since, without a revolution, the law is not likely to yield more than a step or two at a time, this might be an excellent method of reform —to have a separate and much more liberal jurisdiction for the granting of divorces after civil marriage. At first self-consciousness or the desire to make a traditionally romantic gesture would doubtless keep the proportion of couples deciding upon a church ceremony much the same as it is today, but by degrees, as experience proved their over-confidence, a more realistic attitude would almost certainly become general, except among the professed adherents of religious doctrine. These do not believe in the validity of divorce under any conditions and are therefore not likely to avail themselves of improved facilities. But by far the greater number of people who choose to get married in a church do so for various social and conventional reasons without any sincere and *permanent* convictions about monogamy. They do not take their vows

[1] Primitive jealousy has always been regarded as a pardonable and even praiseworthy emotion, at least for males, in whom an animal possessiveness is supposed to be romantic. I have pleasant recollections of a minor character described in Ouida's novel *Friendship* who, though a debauched wastrel, an unfaithful husband, a squanderer of his wife's money, a brute and a scoundrel, is of noble blood and has not yet sunk so low as to be a *cocu content*.

[2] 'In New York, where adultery is the only legal ground for absolute divorce, the National Divorce Reform League privately questioned some 500 recently divorced people and found that adultery was not the real cause of the broken marriage in at least 95 per cent. of cases. In less rigid states, "cruelty" or "desertion" are similarly used as ostensible, lying cloaks for the actual innocent facts—that two people couldn't make a go of it.'—An article on *Divorce by Mutual Consent* in the *Reader's Digest*, January 1939. Only a naïve sort of patriotism would reject the probability that secret investigation would reveal the same state of affairs in England.

literally any more than they take church services in general literally. They are a romantic relic, a sentimentally pleasing tradition.

'The present Divorce Law,' observed Evelyn Waugh some years ago, 'is a futile compromise. It is of no use to Christians [he means, of course, church communicants] because they cannot make use of it anyhow; it is a gross burden on the unbelievers. All we have is the beastly spectacle of a powerful section of the community fighting tooth and nail to prevent the other half enjoying something they do not themselves want.' Since this was written, Mr A. P. Herbert's famous Bill has slightly extended the legal grounds upon which relief is obtainable, but in other respects it is actually retrogressive, and I think that on the whole it conceded to the obstructionist bodies more than it ever got from them. The restriction against suing for divorce in the first three years of married life is likely to cause hardship more widespread, if perhaps less intense, than that involved in being tied to a partner mentally diseased. I do not know the comparative numbers of petitioners who, before the passage of the Act, sought divorce within three years after marriage and those who, since, have been suitors on the grounds of the partner's insanity, criminal convictions, etc.; but the first few years would not, in any case, afford a fair guide to the possible future average, because many actions will have been brought by husbands and wives whose troubles had been accumulating for a long while beforehand, when they had no means of legal redress. I fancy that, normally, marriages which prove unhappy at an early stage are more numerous than those which are destroyed through the pathological taint of one of the partners. Not infrequently the disasters overlap.

The enforced postponement of release is as illogical as any of the anomalies already touched upon. If divorce is wrong, it must be as wrong after three years as after two: if on the other hand it is, as the law admits, at times a right and a necessity, it may be as much so after one year as after twenty. Indeed, for all the imperfections of the law as it stood when Mr Herbert set to work on it, proceedings taken quickly and firmly did enable many ill-assorted couples to dissolve their bonds before the advent of children had complicated their problems: and if the fate of divorcees' children is as solemn a consideration as the orthodox allege, they ought not to oppose separation while these are still unborn.

Like so many other measures brought in to bolster up the 'sanctity' of marriage, the compulsory three-year union very positively encourages illicit relationships, for the majority of those who would otherwise have resorted to the law courts within that brief span of time are in the prime of youth and vigour and will not live celibate until joined in another wedlock.

Religions which claim to expound a 'Divine plan' for mankind have made a baneful contribution to systems of public policy and public morality. The codes which are built upon the virtues, failings, and expediencies of men are legalized as expressions of the will of God, and naturally they then tend to fossilize—to become a stony edifice which human beings are called upon to adapt themselves to, long after the standards that shaped it have vanished. God's will has always been represented as a static sort of decree. To say, 'The Divine plan has altered' or 'It was formerly misunderstood' might be to engender doubts.

So in an attempt to fit the man to the structure, instead of constantly reshaping the structure to fit man, pious authority has engaged in an age-long struggle with science to prevent the dissemination of ideas or the application of knowledge which might enable him to resist hypothetical 'laws of Nature' and 'designs of Providence.' The history of religious obscurantism in the past is long and discreditable : in the present day the spiritual descendants of the churchmen who contended against the various emancipations of the nineteenth century have been active in opposing not only more rational divorce but also a new legal and technical approach to the problems of abortion, sterilization, euthanasia,[1] and other possible avenues of social renovation; and such is their influence, through the sheer weight of tradition, that they are abetted by a large public which does not share any of their theological concepts.

So much for what is known as 'the law of the land.' In local government we see the Church most persistently at work in Sabbatarianism, a form of religiosity to which the Celtic and Anglo-Saxon races have been almost as much addicted as the Orientals. The entirely sound principle that people and animals compelled to work should have a regular and inviolable day of rest could not be upheld, it seems, without the assistance of superstition. The day which reason prescribed to be kept free for relaxation was 'put across' as the day celestial powers had ordained for church-guided holiness—a day in itself sacred and exalted. As rationalism has always been abhorrent to mankind organized in numbers, early in history the taboo-extolling aspects of the Sabbath took precedence of the utilitarian. The utilitarian were in some respects quite defeated, so laborious were the exactions of devotion, so strictly prohibited all the most healthful methods of recreation. And now, though the fanaticism which made Sunday a memory of dreariest gloom to most Victorians is in family life very rare, in civic life we still suffer a weekly pall to descend upon us.

I will not discuss the Sabbath suppressions in parts of Scotland where enthusiasm has been carried to its furthest extremes (even going as far as the cruelty and folly of leaving domestic animals unattended) : it is enough to mention only interferences we take for granted throughout England. Parks and 'show places' are often closed, and in children's

---

[1] I have conscientiously studied the case against the proposed reforms from books recommended by the League of National Life. It is chiefly a religious case. Religious arguments are greatly preponderant.

playgrounds one may see the swings and seesaws ludicrously, yet pathetically, chained up. On the only day when the majority is at leisure to benefit from them games are denied. Hotels, restaurants, and dance halls which could provide an alternative exercise and amusement in bad weather are obliged to leave their patrons to such other pastimes as they may be lucky enough to find. Theatres are not allowed to open, and only a very few provincial centres had followed London's example in licensing cinemas for Sunday performances before wartime exigencies caused a mild change in policy. Many where the attempt has been tried have fought a losing battle against the Sabbatarian societies.[1] Outside London hardly any museums or historical monuments can be visited. The shops are governed by a series of strangely inexplicable regulations which seem to be based on the principle that it is more godly to want luxuries, such as tobacco and chocolates, than necessities, such as cooking materials. The hours when drinking is permitted are curtailed. Nevertheless the pleasures of the public-house—which our licensing laws and our national temperament have combined to make so much more squalid than its counterparts abroad—are largely resorted to for solace by those whose circumstances or abilities do not qualify them to pass the whole day in homely avocations, in reading, or in worshipping.

The primary result of all this care for souls would appear to be an increased consumption of alcohol and a good deal of extra sexual activity —indulgences which are regarded as entertainments by millions who have never had enough leisure or privacy to be otherwise than pitifully opportunist. However, it must be conceded that, if the defenders of the Lord's Day (such they call themselves) had their way, even these occupations would be unavailable.

The extent to which Sunday observances are still forced upon us, and still generally accepted, gives striking evidence of the unreason of one section of public opinion, the unreality of another. The unreality lies in the fact, already touched upon, that most people do not believe, and when individually questioned do not pretend to believe, in the religious necessity of these observances, but only submit to them as a matter of policy or from want of courage to oppose. The unreason is to be found in the nature of the observances themselves even as practised systematically by those who are convinced that they are thus averting the wrath of God. The suspension of work is, as I have indicated, but a secondary consideration, and would be an irrational one in any case, since the attainability of rest is not limited to a particular day—though

---

[1] The Imperial Alliance for the Defence of Sunday organized a vigorous campaign some years ago to prevent Sunday open-air sports. They agitated indefatigably among Town Councillors, Justices of the Peace, etc., and their success is shown by the fact that in certain cases municipal authorities reversed a vote which had previously gone in favour of games. Such vacillations suggest timid capitulation rather than strong conviction.

The Lord's Day Observance Society is busy, at the time of writing, trying to make Sunday entertainments for troops unlawful.

whenever anyone gets a chance to write in the public press that Sunday laws should be revised, he is sure to be accused of wishing to keep people working seven days a week. Yet we have already many examples of the adjustments that can be made.

Let piety run to what lengths it may, there are tasks which must be accomplished by someone if we are to eat and drink and sleep in beds, if the helpless are to be tended, if ships are to remain in their courses, and communications not to be brought to a standstill every week. Sunday work goes on: Sunday oppressiveness is sheer taboo, as quaint and as incomprehensible to an outsider as the childish magic rites of South Sea Islanders are to us.[1]

I was once a guest in an old-fashioned country house where, on Sunday afternoon, my host and hostess began to teach me the game of Bezique. While we were thus engaged, the voices of the vicar and his wife were heard in the outer hall. My hostess looked round quite panic-stricken, for it was too late to hide the cards and the card-table. Then by a brilliant inspiration, as the footsteps neared our door, she whispered: 'Pretend to be playing Patience! I think Patience will be all right.' My host with a grin quickly drew his chair away from the table and took up a book, and as her sanctified visitors were ushered in, the lady of the house was heard to murmur: 'You put the red queen on the black king, like this. . . .'

Here we have in epitome the whole anachronism of pseudo-religious control. The vicar and his wife (assuming that the conclusions drawn about their views were not erroneous) have a notion that certain pieces of pasteboard are distasteful to the Creator of Heaven and earth. The vicar and his wife are not insane, but they are given to symbolism and they imagine their anthropomorphic God must be given to symbolism too. The cards are symbolical of a vice, and more so when two or three people make a reciprocal use of them than if the amusement is confined to one alone; and most of all so on a holy day. In their attitude we see conscientious unreason. The behaviour of the others, including myself, affords three distinct illustrations of that unreality which makes the value of any opinion on impersonal affairs so extraordinarily difficult to gauge. The hostess does not, exactly, share the vicar's convictions, but she approves of them; they have associations she reveres, and they fit in with her ideas of what should be a clergyman's character, so she is a willing hypocrite. The host thinks little of the matter, but he is accustomed to be obliging to his wife, the vicar, the vicar's wife, or anyone else with whom he is on good terms, and he therefore takes a fairly active part in the deception. I take a passive part against my will. I look upon the silly little situation as something which does harm to us all, but social considerations are overwhelmingly against my breaking out into a denunciation. So in our several ways we all play up to an empty convention, and it may well be that the vicar and his wife are playing up too

[1] See Appendix 18.

and would not cling to such puerile formulae if they did not think we expected it of them.

The parable has a wide and varied application. Little as I approve the persecution of ideas, however fatuous—and I may say I think the doctrine of Redemption by Blood as fatuous as any piece of voodooism recorded by Frazer—I could wish that all religious orthodoxy were abolished for a period of years, so that a new generation might have the chance of bringing a fresh and fearless vision to bear upon the meaning, if there is any, of man's place in the universe and the problems of his nature and his destiny. It would be necessary to make a temporary sacrifice even of things that are in themselves beautiful and valuable—to conceal the treasures of religious art, for example, which have been so efficient an instrument for 'solidifying' symbols and personifying abstractions; and certainly to introduce no one to the reading of the Bible until he attains maturity. It was almost a misfortune for the English-speaking people that, apart from the veneration accorded to this collection of ancient archives on religious grounds, a superb translation has placed it on a pinnacle as literature. Bibliolatry therefore has a double source—belief in 'the Book' as the Word of God, and literary snobbery.

The boy in *Of Human Bondage*, going through a phase of devoutness, applied himself to the Scriptures. He read 'without criticism, stories of cruelty, deceit, ingratitude, dishonesty, and low cunning. Actions which would have excited his horror in the life about him, in the reading passed through his mind without comment, because they were committed under the direct inspiration of God.' The same insensibility is often apparent in those whose scriptural enthusiasm is due not to godliness but to real or pretended literary appreciation. The appalling ethical standards expounded in parts of the Old Testament thus do not arouse the distaste which would have been their portion if they had made their appearance in any less fanatically admired work; and people will quote approvingly maxims and prophecies extracted from a context revolting in the lowness of its morality.

I do not think it would do any harm if the Bible were left unread and unquoted—supposing such oblivion could be achieved—for several decades so that it might be rediscovered without its aura of holiness or its intimidating reputation for matchless poetry. An appraisal made for the first time with detachment—a free departure from the old trite valuations—would do service to the cause of critical sincerity as well as morality, and meanwhile we should be given a respite from a vast number of clichés, tropes, and metaphors whose glories are worn threadbare. I would include even the New Testament in the embargo, being sure that the knowledge of psychology which it reveals, as well as its pathos and its splendour, would have infinitely more significance for readers approaching it without the interception of a thousand commentators, interpreters, prophetic cranks, and mawkish pietists.

It may be that after such an interim we should never again have religion as we have known it until now, religion which it is no libel, but if anything flattering, to show crystallized in the following passage from a proselytizing book:

'How is it with you, with your soul? It is well to remember that there is the deadly danger of perishing, that God, looking down from Heaven and seeing our hopeless position as helpless sinners, unable to save ourselves from our certain doom, in His love and pity made *a way of escape for us*, not a risky and dangerous one . . . but one which is easy to take and absolutely safe. For in having caused His Son to bear the curse and punishment of our sin upon the Cross, He is now justified in letting us off the eternal penalty which unforgiven sin entails, because its punishment which was ours has been borne by Another. At the same time He rewards us with the free gift of eternal life through simple faith, which is belief in His Word.' [1]

In this we have sentimentality resolved into its veriest elements—the simple explanation (involving certain fabricated complexities less troublesome than real ones) and the wish-fulfilling assumption (artificial sunlight which, however, is inevitably accompanied by shadows). All systems of personal salvation seem to the sceptical to thrive on these elements—though in some they are disguised rather more ingeniously.

'The chances are [said H. L. Mencken many years ago] that religion belongs to an extremely early stage of human development, and that its rapid decay in the world since the Reformation is evidence of a very genuine progress. Reduced to its logical essence, every religion now advocated in Christendom is simply the doctrine that there are higher powers, infinitely wise and virtuous, which take an active interest in the sordid everyday affairs of man, and not infrequently intervene in them. This doctrine is not purely romantic and *a priori*: it is based upon what is regarded by its subscribers as objective evidence. But it must be plain that the evidence tends to go to pieces as human knowledge widens—that is, appears massive and impressive in direct proportion as the individual impressed is ignorant. A few hundred years ago practically every phenomenon of nature was ascribed to superhuman intervention. The plague, for example, was caused by God's anger. So was war. So was lightning. Today no enlightened man believes anything of the kind. All these phenomena are seen to be but links in an endless chain of amoral causation. . . . Thus religion gradually loses its old objective authority, and becomes more and more a mere sentimentality.'

Sentimentality in this sense of the word—I read it as a feeble leaning upon tradition—cannot but entail a weak-minded acquiescence in any

---

[1] An M.S.O.C.A. pamphlet by Captain E. G. Carré.

ideas which have the look of coming from the 'right' source, and this in its turn demands an aptitude for deception both of the inward and the outward kind. 'Man becomes demoralized,' wrote Benjamin Constant, 'the moment he is possessed of a single thought which he is obliged perpetually to dissemble.' Modern analytical psychology has led to the same conclusion, thus expressed, from another angle, by a contemporary writer : [1] 'When we submit to a taboo in which we do not believe, or to a conventional prejudice which we do not share, then we may reasonably expect all the unhappiness and mental disorders that commonly result from cowardice.' It is an unhappiness authority does its best to impose upon us.

POSTSCRIPT

This war, like the last, has brought about a state of mind in which people are turning eagerly to the idea of a transcendent authority and a retributive destiny. The Churches are never slow to take advantage of the terror which makes the devil desire to become a monk. The Archbishops of Canterbury, York, and Wales have issued a plan which aims at making religious instruction the basis of school life. The plan provides that :

'A Christian education be given to all scholars in all schools (excepting children withdrawn by parents).

Religious knowledge and the imparting of it should count in the gaining of the teacher's certificate.

Inspections on religious teaching should be by H.M. inspectors and other authorized persons.

There should be worship by the whole school at beginning of the day.'

It is hard to imagine a more retrogressive measure than the adoption of these proposals, especially the second of the points quoted.

Another deplorable evidence of reaction is contained in a report about an Oxford debate during February 1941. When the Union declared on its agenda a motion that return to God through organized religion was essential to the reconstruction of the world after the war, influential representations were made to the Vice-Chancellor against debating on the subject at all, for fear the motion should be lost, and permission was finally granted on the almost unprecedented condition that the number of votes recorded on each side should not be made public. I hope it will one day seem very extraordinary that the authorities of a seat of learning should have considered such a piece of interference in any way relevant to their duties.

[1] Dr Harry Roberts, in a *New Statesman* review.

The imbecilities uttered by members of the House of Commons in attacking and defeating the Theatres and Music Halls (Sunday opening) Bill on April 1st, 1941, are less surprising.

The Lord's Day Magazine for the first quarter of 1945 records a new series of 'triumphs' in the suppression of Sunday entertainment, and promises a great new Sabbatarian crusade.[1]

As for the B.B.C., the amount of time it now devotes to direct and indirect religious propaganda seems to me to be a positive affront to licence-holders.

Unless those people who desire freedom from religious oppression should at last exert themselves in large numbers to contend against these ever-growing encroachments, a clamorous minority may soon impose its superstitions on the education and amusements of the whole community.

[1] It is gratifying to read that the London County Council Tribunal has 'turned a deaf ear to all appeals.'

The chief purpose of ancestors is to supply their descendants with warnings.

> *Feminine Fig Leaves:* DR C. WILLETT CUNNINGTON.

Emotion by rule is insincerity, and insincerity of emotion is of the essence of sentimentality.

> *Pamela's Daughters:* R. P. UTTER and G. B. NEEDHAM.

IF we wish to test the strength of tradition's influence on us, it is only necessary to imagine how we should regard any time-honoured institution if we had never heard of it before but were asked to consider it as a *new* custom, in the light of our ideas at their present stage of development. What reception, for instance, would be accorded to fox-hunting as an innovation—the great troop of horses, hounds, and men after one small animal, the ceremony of rubbing the freshly killed victim's blood on the face of a beginner, the ridiculous jargon ('pink' for 'scarlet,' taboo upon the use of such obvious words as 'dogs,' 'barking,' etc.) designed to give a feeling of exclusiveness like certain kinds of schoolboy slang, the damage to crops, the fantastic expensiveness? I fancy the question of cruelty would hardly need to be debated, so swiftly would the sport be condemned for stupidity. And can it be supposed that otter-hunting, beagling, and pig-sticking, not to speak of a large number of other ritualistic slaughterings, would seem more intelligent?

Thus approached, many features of our judicial procedure would fail to arouse the admiration we now profess for them. Many sex inequalities would surprise. Many social distinctions would prove entirely unacceptable. To give a man public rewards for the patriotic deeds of his grandfather would not strike us, if the idea were introduced suddenly, as any more sensible than to put him in prison for his grandfather's crimes.[1] Privileges obtained through being born sooner than one's brother would be judged grossly unfair.[2] Monarchy as a new theory would not excite the same response of highly emotional loyalty that springs from a very deep-rooted king-and-country orthodoxy. If we were not accustomed to the strange tradition of war, what scorn would be poured upon him who had the temerity to suggest so brutal and irrelevant an instrument

---

[1] See Appendix 19.
[2] Even in the eighteenth century, when the *claims* of primogeniture were seldom disputed, defence of the *principle* was anything but confident. All Paley could say in favour of it was that it had one public good effect : ' If the estate were divided equally amongst the sons, it would probably make them all idle ; whereas by the present rule of descent it makes only one so ; which is the less evil of the two.'—From *Political Philosophy*.

of policy, and how far from our thoughts would it be to choose for national and international heroes the men most expert in gambling with lives—that class of conquerors 'who have always been destroyers of civilization and the greatest pests in human history.'

The sentimentality which automatically supports tradition is, like most other forms of sentimentality, a compound product of the need to find things simple and the inclination to interpret them according to our wishes. Tradition provides a beaten track for minds which shrink from effort; while idealism, so often dismayed to contemplate the short-comings of the present, takes comfort from a persuasion that the past at least was worthy of emulation. Ritualism helps to give tradition a sort of tangibility, something the unimaginative find it easy to hold on to. It may also enable the traditionalist to perform self-sufficient gestures which leave him free to behave in a fashion completely at variance with his vaunted beliefs.

For example, the ritualistic practices by which men once signified, somewhat more intensively than now, their profound reverence for womanhood appear to have fulfilled all the requirements of their chivalry and exempted them from any necessity to attempt real kindness and courtesy; for it is a fact that when there have been most bowings and scrapings, most high-flown compliments and protective politenesses, then has the price of women been lowest in the labour market, then have their political and social rights been least regarded, and then has the law placed its 'favourite' under the heaviest disabilities.[1] To this day it will be found that men who tend to be pleasantly ceremonious with 'the ladies' are those who place the least value on the qualities and capacities of women; and travellers can hardly fail to observe that the further one goes from feminine emancipation—that is, from the practical proofs that women are respected—the more is theoretical respect likely to be displayed in picturesque formalities.

Religious history shows precisely the same trend, ritualism being so closely associated with a want of sincere feeling that in all revivalist movements it is deemed essential to discourage it.

In social life each epoch appears to have a typical ritualism of its own, ordering the pattern of certain basic relationships according to traditions selected to fit the taste of the time. The Elizabethans honoured an Italianate convention and went in for being lovers on a grand scale, running, if their literature is a fair guide, through an established gamut of sighing, adoring, raging, pining, and languishing, with assiduous application and, sometimes, decided artificiality, as we were meant to

[1] ' So great a favourite is the female sex in the laws of England,' said Blackstone, explaining that ' by marriage, the very being or legal existence of a woman is suspended, or at least it is incorporated into that of her husband under whose wing, protection and cover she performs everything.'

'This in plainer language,' comments Ray Strachey, in her history of the Women's Movement, ' meant that the property, earnings, the liberty, and even the conscience of a wife all belonged to her husband, as did also the children she might bear.'

infer from the forced passion of Romeo for Rosaline. After its phase of compulsory puritanism, the seventeenth century reacted to the other extreme and cultivated light and raffish gallantry, which must, when the heart was really moved, have been a difficult humour to sustain. The next great fashion, again an extreme recoil, raised feminine chastity to the loftiest pinnacle of all the virtues. By the middle of the eighteenth century it had become an obsession to both sexes, and with it, connected by links which are better understood now than they were then, grew a parallel obsession about filial duty. For many years the two stock themes of popular novels (which usually exhibit the code if not the conduct of their writers and eager readers) were the struggles of some pure girl to resist, at the cost of her life if need be, the tireless efforts of a seducer; and the sufferings of a daughter—very occasionally a son—whose happiness is completely surrendered to the will of a cruel or misguided father. Often, as in Richardson's *Clarissa*, persecuted virginity and parental harshness are more or less equally featured. Obedience to the will of the father, however glaringly unjust his demands, was always looked upon as meritorious. The relations between parent and child became at this time unprecedentedly emotional; indeed, a most maudlin emotionalism was admired in every aspect of domestic life, and novelists set the tone by introducing characters whose sensibilities were such that they were almost perpetually weeping.

In *The Beaux Stratagem*, written when the Restoration vogue for heartlessness still lingered, the hero receives the news of his elder brother's death with unfeigned joy and instantly takes advantage of his improved position to propose marriage. What the Men of Feeling born in a later day would have made of this callous opportunism we may easily imagine when we recall that they could scarcely harbour a thought of any tie of consanguinity with dry eyes. As for the nearest bonds, the filial and the matrimonial, to contemplate these was to give way to lachrymose sentiment at its most gushing.

'Whence these tears?' ask two authors who have made a penetrating enquiry into the eighteenth century's distilled emotions.[1] 'Why does the period known in the history of thought as the Age of Reason record itself in the history of the novel in terms of tearful hysteria that would disgrace a girl's boarding-school?' And their answer is: 'Because it *was* the Age of Reason.[2] . . . Since it cannot eradicate emotion it must govern it by rules. . . . Polite life is an art; if reality or intensity of emotion makes the artist unmindful, he fails. Form, which is mainly rational, prescribes occasions for feeling, its degrees of intensity, and manners of expression.'

---

[1] R. P. Utter and G. B. Needham in *Pamela's Daughters*, a study of fashions in heroines after Richardson's *Pamela*.

[2] 'Reason' is here used, I think, in the sense of 'Rationalization,' a word which, as I have already suggested, is truer to the intellectual character of the eighteenth century in general.

To show oneself moved by what was esteemed a proper object of sympathy was a rite—one which was, of course, practised much more dramatically and extravagantly in fiction than in real life. The various dues once paid, conventional people felt easier in following their inclinations, often palpably at odds with their code. For all their formal professions, the behaviour of Dr Johnson's contemporaries differed little from what ours would be in similar circumstances. Family quarrels were numerous, fathers were disobeyed, and lovely woman did not always take much trouble to preserve 'the virgin innocence which was her comfort and her glory, her brightest ornament and most valuable dowry.'[1]

Seldom have the favoured rituals been so completely a façade erected to conceal the shamefulness of reality as in the century that followed. It was a time when unctuous lip service to every noble and benevolent standard was coupled with a ruthless exploitation of the defenceless; when vigorous missionary work among the heathen was supported all too often by funds derived from mines, shops, farms, and factories where the sweated labour might have shocked savages; when verbal puritanism glossed over a disgusting system of vice and prostitution, and when the utterance of wishy-washy sentiments coincided with the acceptance of a thousand snobberies, cruelties, and meannesses. All this hypocrisy took conventional shapes and was therefore very simple if frequently rather irksome to sustain. It was a source of endless exasperation to reformers, because it made their task so much more difficult. The desire to stand well in one's own eyes and the eyes of the world by doing good was appeased with stereotyped gestures: the much-belauded 'Christian virtues' were expressed often enough in such shapes as Sunday-school classes for children who were half-clothed and underfed, Bible readings to the sick poor whose poverty and sickness were the product of a free charter to greed, subscriptions to one or two condescending charities, and a line of talk which irresistibly invited caricature from the satirists of the day.

Yet this sham goodness must be construed as a sign of progress, since the prestige of moral rectitude is always high when it can exact so great a tribute of hypocrisy. The misery of the nineteenth century was only worse than that of the eighteenth for the same reason that has made our own worst of all—namely, the fact that larger and larger masses are involved in every movement, their problems inevitably growing more entangled and the solutions cruder.

Now the practice of making motions of obeisance to an approved set of conventions—which I have somewhat loosely designated ritualism, having no nearer word—may in most cases be merely formal and therefore of small account in its influence on private behaviour, but if one should have the temerity to break away from it in public, or on any

[1] From Edward Cobden's sermon on chastity already quoted.

occasion which happens later to come into the public view, the offence will be as much reprobated by the mouthpieces of 'the social order,' as severely punished by the law, as if it were customary for all the rest of society to live up to its principles.

We do not need to go back to the eighteenth century to hear judges and advocates deal with sexual relations in terms which would lead the uninitiated to assume that chastity was always maintained inviolate except amongst a most depraved order of beings. Homosexuality, which has been medically recognized as a propensity inborn or acquired without volition through environmental factors, and which now meets with very general tolerance in the world at large, still evokes tirades of shuddering horror if it has the misfortune to be dragged into the murky light of courtrooms. (I recollect how at the trial of some young men who had been dressing up in women's clothes and conducting themselves in a manner ludicrous to normal people and consequently harmless, the Recorder observed that theirs was the one crime which was utterly unpardonable. Sentences much heavier than those commonly given for extreme cruelty were meted out to them.)

In real life, the life in which we are being ourselves, most of us are more or less ready to accept abortion as a means of escape from certain difficult situations: yet when the practitioner who makes this escape possible is brought into court—often to be condemned on the testimony of one who has had recourse to his services—the typical vocabulary of ritualistic indignation will be drawn upon to pronounce him guilty of a vile crime, an anti-social act shocking to all right-minded men and women. The public lets the stream of cant flow on with only a whisper of protest, the voice of the few who are striving for reform but are denied any rostrum from which they can convey an unbowdlerized version of their case to a sufficiently wide audience.

Pure cant constantly forms the basis of what is technically known as justice. Who would imagine, for instance, from our law of blasphemous libel that genuine reverence was so rare a phenomenon?[1] Who would deduce, when there is any legal discussion of obscenity or profanity, that quite reputable people are known at times to swear, to exchange bawdy jokes, to be amused at impropriety, and even to indulge in licentious pleasures?[2] Would it not rather appear from official and officious asseverations that such usages are confined to the lowest of the low? Do the ridiculous niggling restrictions of our licensing laws and betting laws and the solemn pomposity with which they are sometimes upheld convey any notion of the part which convivial drinking and mild gambling play in the enjoyments of people who are not dependent on public-houses for their rendezvous and on touting bookmakers for their 'flutter'?[3] Listening to the sanctimonious prophecies that sometimes issue from the lips of magistrates when young children are brought

[1] See Appendix 20.   [2] See Appendix 21.   [3] See Appendix 22.

before them, would any stranger to our habits be able to guess that petty pilfering, mischievous damage to property, and wanton naughtiness of every kind are common in early childhood (especially among the poor, whose families are often not well supervised or effectively occupied in leisure hours), and that a boy might be guilty of tiresome misdemeanours and yet grow to respectable manhood? [1]

Nor is it only where the law is administered that one perpetually meets with evidence of a curious double standard. In every sort of gathering which can exercise authority, great or trivial, direct or indirect, over an aspect of behaviour, it is startling to hear an opinion which is perfectly free from humbug, a sentiment which does not pander to some bogus and confused idealism. But, except to those whose ears and tongues through long perversion are attuned only to make-believe—and such is conspicuously the plight of many civic and religious dignitaries and most political personages—the shock is a pleasing and refreshing one. 'When a genuine passion speaks with strength and authority, false conceptions and formalities of propriety are put to silence.' Thus wrote Benjamin Constant, and the truth of the statement has been demonstrated with such success—wherever genuine passion is allowed to be heard—that every now and then cant changes its tone, trying to imitate the authentic voice of sincerity.

This double bluff has produced in recent years a great deal of hearty man-to-man oratory and ingeniously ingenuous journalism, and a horde of rough-hewn books described as human documents : it will be sustained until 'genuine passion' is seen to be breathing a different warmth, when the more adaptable publicists will begin to concoct their synthetic fervour after some new style.

That it *is* synthetic there is an easy means of discovering. If there is nothing fresh, nothing unanticipated in the substance of their adjurations, if there is not implied any appeal for reconsideration of existing values, if new forms and phrases are used only to disguise old systems and furbish up threadbare principles, then we may know we are witnessing the utterance of forged notes. For as long as the world contains widespread unhappiness, the truly honest man must question the established order, and must find it wanting. Not that honesty is always right in its conclusions, nor that it can infallibly detect flaws and falsenesses : the most far-seeing reformers have evinced strange blindnesses, the bravest have flinched from casting out every prejudice inculcated by a lifetime's training : but all who have spoken with the deep conviction which puts superficialities to shame have had something to say revealing, in its time, a daring novelty of outlook. And this statement I think as susceptible of proof as any which does not come within the range of the exact sciences.

It is my purpose in the ensuing chapter to take a bird's-eye view of some of the most intensively cultivated areas of sentimental belief, the

[1] See Appendix 23.

116

subjects which are particularly liable to be irrigated by rivers of cant, but first I must pause to explain the territory we are to skim over.

Bertrand Russell has divided the moral code into 'precepts . . . of three not sharply differentiated sorts: first, those which must be really obeyed on pain of general obloquy; secondly, those which must not be *openly* disobeyed; and thirdly, those which are regarded as counsels of perfection only to be obeyed by saints.' The prescriptions move from one category to another in a time sequence, the sin which would have made one an outcast yesterday being merely the action one is discreet about today and will probably commit without restriction at all tomorrow. A somewhat similar division applies in the sphere of tastes and sentiments, which have, of course, a close relation to prevailing morality: there are things it is imperative not to disparage unless one would be thought mad or deliberately subversive, and things one does not mock at in a very loud voice, and beyond these a range of freedom.

There is also a sort of lateral sliding-scale as well as the one that moves vertically (through time), codes both moral and aesthetic differing greatly in different classes. Among the younger fashionables, for instance, the Albert Memorial is an object to be smilingly admired, while older people, brought up in the period of reaction against Victorianism, are under a genuine aesthetic compulsion to deride it. Popular taste—that is, non-rebellious and unstudied taste—usually bows to the dicta of the elders, and many must have ridiculed the 'hideousness' of that entertaining monument who secretly wondered what was supposed to be wrong with it. (I belong to the generation which finds it difficult to see any merit in the typical art of the Edwardians, either the *nouveau* or 'ye olde' varieties, and it is very odd to reflect that my as yet unborn grandchildren, if they are modernists of their day, will almost certainly take pleasure in this epoch; yet the observation of psychological trends which I have recorded in my book on fashion [1] leaves me no room for doubt that it will be so.)

In the same manner, the personal qualities esteemed in one walk of life are disliked or despised in another. Feminine chastity, to use a hackneyed but pellucid example, is still, in churches and law courts, upheld as an essential of decency. The middle classes *forgive* unchastity as long as secrecy is attempted and moderation observed. In the fashionable section of the upper classes and among 'advanced' people in general, there is no demand for forgiveness; women are allowed scarcely less sexual freedom than men, and I have often been in company where to say 'My dear, she's a virgin!' was as much an unkind revelation, a piece of malicious gossip, as the contrary assertion would be in other circles. Thus we see the three standards all in operation simultaneously.

The popular moral code, out of which our ritual conduct grows, will tend to be a timid compromise between the rigid rules of orthodoxy as expounded by religious and professional bodies and a rather furtive

[1] *Pandora's Letter Box*, A Discourse on Fashionable Life.

willingness to make allowances for human nature, just as popular taste will be a compromise between what one ought to like and what one can't help liking. As I have explained in an earlier chapter, each member of the mass has, though perhaps less than half-consciously, what may be called a public and a private attitude to social questions. A tolerance of cant, indeed an enjoyment of it, may be coupled with a fairly clear-eyed view of persons and events observable at close quarters; but unluckily it is not his opinion of matters judged at close quarters that helps to form what is called public opinion.

Publicly approved idealism, for instance, decrees that children—alternatively, the kiddies, the little folks, the youngsters, etc.—are delightful and lovable, particularly when innocent. Private opinion admits freely of children personally known that they are merely incipient adults and sometimes sadly wanting in attractions, and, though their helplessness wakens a protective kindness and their ignorance of the world occasions endearing blunders, the absence of the tact, sympathy, and self-control that are only to be acquired through experience can render them highly unprepossessing as daily companions. If idealism bore the fruit of a real benevolence towards children, then its false assumptions might be worth maintaining, but the good-nature it engenders in those who try to flourish the popular standard is vague and often ridiculously mis-directed (I remember the sickly-sweet smile of a lady who said to me reprovingly: 'But we must always praise the little efforts of children, mustn't we?'), and it is characteristic of idealists that if disappointed they suffer a recoil which produces an intolerance as great as their former indulgence.

When we consider the dangers of conventional beliefs and the barrier they form against the salutary apprehension of reality, we cannot but ask ourselves whether they serve any end at all which it would not be neces-sary for a community bent upon further evolution to discard. Against the harm that springs from such rigidifications let us set the benefits we derive from them; not the doubtful benefits, such as the saving of thought, a commodity which does not grow more precious by disuse, and the shelving of personal responsibility, but the advantages that, superficially at least, appear indisputable. The more tangible sorts of ritualism will offer, naturally, the clearest illustrations.

I have noticed that when a small body of people meets for some specific business, if their gathering is disposed informally about a private room, the discussion will tend to be rambling, diffuse, and full of irrelev-ances. The moment, however, that they are formed into a committee and elect a chairman, who is seated apart behind a businesslike table, they begin to function with heightened efficiency. The very words 'Mr Chairman' seem to act as a control upon certain speakers, keeping them, if not to the point, at least nearer the point than they would otherwise have remained; occasioning a sifting of their ideas to exclude the purely personal. We see the same principle operating on a more elaborate scale in the procedure of the law courts. By separating the judge and advocates from the lay public in a very marked manner—wigs, gowns, respectful titles, antiquated ceremonial—an atmosphere is created in which it should be possible to achieve a measure of detachment. A judge who is referred to as 'his lordship' sheds more dignity upon the law than one addressed merely as Mr So-and-so; and though dignity should not be maintained at the cost of justice, few would deny that it is a desirable attribute in court-rooms.

The still richer rites and ceremonies observed, constantly or from time to time, by other orthodox institutions, Parliament, the churches, the armed forces, the older seats of learning, fulfil similar functions besides satisfying an almost universal love of pageantry.

But this meagre harvest of goods can be bought at too great a price. To speak both symbolically and literally, if committee etiquette promotes efficiency, prolonged experiences of it foster the dreary obstructiveness of the official mind, to which eventually procedure becomes infinitely more important than proceeding; a mind jealous of petty privilege, resenting everything which will not fit neatly into the old grooves of precedent, and tending to grow ever more unyielding and opaque until it resembles nothing so much as a blank wall. Again, the stylized decorum of a judicial trial may lend a dangerous illusion that prejudice has been discarded while, in reality, affording a screen behind which it is more insidiously powerful than ever. The personal judgments of Mr Jones, a contemporary gentleman vulnerable to criticism, might on many occasions be less sweeping than the legal judgments of that timeless de-humanized figure, Mr Justice Jones: and artificial dignity has all too often upheld laws a hundred years out of date.

Ancient customs retained for their picturesque charm or quaintness generally involve subservience to some equally anachronistic system of beliefs. An illustrated periodical [1] shows Professor Trevelyan becoming Master of Trinity College, Cambridge, at a ceremony, nearly four centuries old, which requires him to wait outside closed gates while his credentials are examined by the Fellows. It seems innocuous, delightful even, until we learn that this pleasing absurdity entails various pledges to observe the Protestant faith, support Royal Prerogative, and accept the Scriptures, conditions which ought not to be imposed upon a man of learning. Archaic vows reverberate through the celebrations of rites sanctified by historical association. The King at his Coronation takes an oath 'to maintain and preserve inviolably the Settlement of the Church of England, and the Doctrine, Worship, Discipline and Government thereof,' and to guard the privileges of the Bishops and Clergy—undertakings entered into when it was scarcely foreseen that the majority of British subjects would be non-Protestant and even non-Christian.

[1] *Picture Post*, December, 1940.

There is always a danger with traditional observances that their dignity will foster illusions of wisdom and lead to a vitiation of the critical faculties. I recollect a character of Aldous Huxley's remarking that an idea which seems dull to commonplace in one's native language takes on significance when expressed in Latin. 'A cracker motto in Latin sounds much weightier and truer than the same motto in English'—an effect due, of course, to the tradition which associates Latin with learning and with antique grandeur. The analogy will hold good of the thousand other deceptive formalities with which our judgment is bemused, from the time when we are first taught to pray by means of tedious reiterations or stand staring with reverent vacuity to the tune of the national anthem.

The difficulty is to learn how to relinquish the mouldering props of custom without discarding at the same time certain delicate restrictions and indefinable graces of approach which we ascribe to the sense of fitness. The work and conduct of the greatest artists, reformers, and innovators in general give proof, however, that the achievement, though sometimes costly and seldom consistently attempted, is by no means beyond the measure of possibility.

It is now almost my sole rule of life to clear myself of cants and formulas, as of poisonous Nessus shirts.

THOMAS CARLYLE, in a letter to his wife, 1835.

AS an example of an orthodoxy, apparently benign, actually harmful, I cited, in the preceding chapter, the sentimental attitude towards children, who are popularly credited with being always attractive and endearing, 'particularly when innocent.' Cant about the desirability of innocence in children is most vociferous somewhere near the lowest end of the lateral, or social, sliding scale, the upper classes being now quite alert to its dangers. The lower classes—excepting that section which, through the most sordid kind of poverty, has become amoral—fear the loss of innocence because, with them, sexual enlightenment is commonly achieved in very disagreeable ways: their ideas about sex tend to be dirty, and they naturally wish to defer the time when their children's minds shall be besmirched as theirs have been. In the middle classes, innocence is a charm which, on frankly sentimental grounds, it is thought a pity not to retain as long as possible: it causes children to make quaint and amusing remarks and to believe in fairy-tales, whereas accurate knowledge takes the pretty gloss off things.

Such must surely be the reasoning, if there is any reasoning at all, that actuates the strong resistance against proposals to include biological instruction in the ordinary school curriculum, the condemnation, sometimes violent, sometimes expressed only by a portentous head-shaking, of co-educational schools where there is no artificial sexual reticence,[1] and the newspaper or magazine contributions we may read from time to time deploring the precocity of the modern child and making wishful comparison to the advantage of the uninformed, deliberately deluded child of the recent past. (The precocity of the modern child has, of course, been deplored for many hundreds, if not thousands and tens of thousands of years.) I have even seen one newspaper article advocating in all seriousness a total return to the policy of obscurantism:

'Let Us, When Talking to Children,
GO BACK TO THE GOOSEBERRY BUSH
says Mrs W. R. Matthews, B.Sc.,
wife of the Dean of St. Paul's.[2]

---

[1] E.g. 'Lieutenant Commissioner' Flora Drummond of the Salvation Army was reported in 1939 to have denounced the co-educational system (apparently a product of Moscow and Communism) which, she said, was undermining the health of the nation, '. . . a determined cancer of filth that is out to destroy the constructive elements of this country. Our children are going out into the world and may meet those from these schools.' She asked her followers to write to their M.P.s about it.

[2] In what the *Sunday Dispatch*, March 10th, 1935, calls 'an authoritative view.' A longer extract will be found in Appendix 24.

... Why, why must we spread the facts of life before the eyes of the young in a clear, cold, north light, that is not what they look like when they are seen, as they should be, clothed in the sunshine of mutual love? Let us then start a movement. I will call it "Back to the gooseberry bush," and I shall expect all my followers to take an oath to give as little information as they truthfully can to the young and to leave the most mysterious things of life steeped in the awe and dignity which naturally belong to them.'

The simple, satisfying assumption that if children are not instructed by accredited elders no one is going to instruct them at all—that if sexual facts are not seen in a cold north light they will be seen in a sunshiny love-light—is one of the cruder manifestations of sentimentality. Those who, like the author, acquired their first knowledge of the human reproductive system from companions of twelve or thirteen will recollect how much awe and dignity then invested it!

The whimsy coyness of the English Bachelor of Science is evidently paralleled among the education authorities of the United States, where at intervals battles noisier than ours break out between the realistic and the idealistic factions. Ellsworth B. Buck of New York City's Board of Education tells of an attempt on the part of certain members to introduce sex instruction into high schools 'in the mild form of a study of mammalian reproduction. . . . They were turned down hard.' The junior high school principal who headed a special sub-committee on the subject reported that it was inadvisable 'for the school to shoulder the responsibility of shortening for these little ones their period of innocent childhood and of awakening in them an interest in a topic for which they are not ready.' The same report disclosed that a home for un-married mothers in that vicinity had been receiving an average of two girls a month from this principal's school!

'Of the 1347 illegitimate children whose births were recorded in New York City in 1934, about one in every fourteen was born to a girl of 16 years or less. . . . Talk of prolonging "the period of innocent childhood" begins to look frivolous against the reality of childhood years wrecked by ignorance. . . . Statistics of the Health Department show that from January to December 1938, 2388 cases of syphilis and gonorrhœa concerned children under 19. . . . Judging by New York City's Statistics, for each of the unmarried child-mothers one should apparently count something over three times the number of rapes and something like thirty cases of venereal disease.' [1]

That prolonged 'innocence' in England has any better outcome than in America is a proposition patriotic rather than logical. The situation improves, however, and we have at least to be thankful that the ban upon

[1] In the *American Mercury*, May 1939.

knowledge of important human functions now only extends to children —and that not universally—and adult women no longer come under it. It is not a great while since picturesque ignorance was regarded as an indispensable feminine attribute and mothers prided themselves on the genteel embarrassment of having to acquaint their daughters with the nature of matrimony on the wedding eve! An assiduous reader of nineteenth-century novels would not find it difficult to fill a volume with examples in the following style: 'Happy and charming I am sure you are' (the hero is addressing the heroine) 'only while you are innocent: for a knowledge of evil, even though it guard from a participation in it, leaves a stain on the purity of the female mind.' [1] Which is as much as to say that it is better to participate in evil through ignorance than to ward it off through knowledge: and such remains to this day the confused assessment of innocence-worshippers.

The cult of innocence has always been associated with the cult of modesty, involving an open or tacit belief in the indecency of the human body, and this too is strongest in the lower and middle classes. Those who are familiar with the sight of nearly naked male and female forms exposed to the sun in pleasure resorts favoured by the more or less leisured classes find it hard to imagine the outlook which results in men rejecting the offer of badly needed work rather than submit to examination by an elderly woman doctor [2] or in a child of five being salaciously jeered at by adults for running about on a beach without a swimming costume.[3]

Yet unfortunately it is the verdicts of such people as these, only slightly tempered by the judgments of a more wholesomely taught class, which are allowed to dictate our public rules and regulations. Policemen, town councillors, and petty officials in general, are seldom drawn from a very sophisticated milieu, and the higher authorities, hazily deferring to the double standard I have described, are inclined to play down to them. Moreover, the higher authorities are usually in advanced middle age or older, and are out of sympathy with recent changes in the point of view. So, although in private life the great majority of those who have troubled to give any thought to the question at all are agreed in deploring concealments that inevitably lead to prurience, the public code is often little better than mid-Victorian.

[1] Quoted by Dr C. W. Cunnington in *Feminine Attitudes in the Nineteenth Century*.

[2] 'Because they refused to be examined by a woman doctor a number of unemployed men lost the chance of jobs at a government depot in Lancashire.

'About 100 men between the ages of 35 and 57 were sent from employment exchanges in Oldham and Rochdale districts and at the depot were directed to attend for examination at the surgery of the local doctor.

'The first batch to attend found that the doctor was ill and his locum was an elderly woman practitioner. It was she who made the examinations.

'"When we heard that we should have to appear without any clothes on before a woman doctor many of us decided not to go on with the test," said one of the men, an unemployed cotton operative and ex-soldier.'—From the *News Chronicle*, May 3rd, 1940.

[3] An incident I witnessed in August 1940.

The purchase of Rodin's bronze 'The Kiss' for Stoke-on-Trent Art Gallery was opposed by a member of the City Council on the grounds that 'youths and girls would snigger at it; [1] an unpleasant indictment of adolescent education in Staffordshire. Sniggering youth was uppermost in the thoughts of those who clamoured, successfully, for the removal of two half-naked figures portraying Health and Beauty which had been designed for the Exhibition at Glasgow in 1938; and perhaps some such consideration affected that Mayor and Mayoress of Blackburn who leapt into celebrity a few years earlier by causing to be veiled with sheeting the statues of females which adorned the Town Hall; for they would hardly have claimed that these were demoralizing to themselves or their contemporaries.

Now if sniggerers had been primary objects of consideration in Florence and other Italian cities at any time during the last four hundred years, the streets and public buildings which are enriched by works of Donatello, Cellini, and Michelangelo would long ago have been shorn of their greatest glories, and sniggering, which is not a common habit among the children of Italy, whatever may be their failings, would have become the customary reaction to nudity. Other European nations have their own forms of prudery—particularly affecting female conduct —but the kind which manifests itself in a peculiar horror of nakedness and which consequently gives rise to a grinning and smirking attitude towards the body is, I am afraid, more likely to be found among British populations than elsewhere. That prudery is sentimental—an attempt to achieve self-protection by barrier, a veiling or shutting-away of facts which have been adjudged harmful—the reader cannot need to be reminded.

Incidentally, the conception of what is harmful is as unbalanced and blundering as one would expect from thoroughly muddled heads. On every side we are confronted with such anomalies as the law, of recent date, which forbids the vendors of contraceptives to introduce their wares to young people or to show contraceptive propaganda in their shop-windows, and which yet allows those windows to be filled with propaganda for sadism. It is well known that along with the rubber goods, trusses, and tonics for weak men so lavishly displayed in the neighbourhood of Leicester Square, certain types of books are invariably given prominence, and that among them will be found such titles as *The Pleasures of the Torture Chamber*, *The History of Flagellation*, *Bygone Punishments*, *The History of Torture in England*—works which cannot possibly have a legitimate market on premises devoted to the sale of hygienic paraphernalia. Restrictions have likewise been placed upon the admission of children to films like *Anna Karenina*, *Wuthering Heights*, and

[1] 'If photographs of it were exhibited for sale in shops the police would take action to have them withdrawn,' he assured the Council. It need hardly be said that he insisted, 'I'm no Puritan!'—Reported in the *Daily Mail*, February 1936.

Somerset Maugham's *Rain*—performances which might prove uncongenial but could not corrupt—while the news reels are free to show, in the most offensively vulgar manner, horrors capable of leaving a lifelong psychosis. Again, consideration for the morals of the young has caused many sincere works of art to be suppressed, but any youth can purchase across the counter at a newsagent's a periodical entirely devoted to the most perverse forms of fetishism, featuring in every issue letters (supposed to come from eager readers) describing the delights of a hundred dreary and silly practices, from watching young girls have their hair cut off to wearing some special kind of rubber mackintosh or high-heeled boot.[1]

. . . . . .

Ritual beliefs as to the nature of the proper and the improper are largely an outcome of chronology. The longevity of some practices protects them from question, the novelty of others stands for an imputation. I have referred to the exclusion of children from films unfolding an illicit love story. Yet the entertainment traditionally considered desirable for them even by strait-laced families, their annual pantomime, abounds in smutty innuendo and highly contagious vulgarities of speech and manner. The same material, if offered in a modern type of children's play, would seem an outrage.

Time is the essence of respectability. Indeed, any rebel, however derided or persecuted at the outset, who can live to be old will be found thereby to have acquired a sort of sanction, as a glance at the careers and reputations of Bernard Shaw, Mrs Besant, Havelock Ellis, Mahatma Gandhi, Mrs Emmeline Pankhurst, and George Lansbury will swiftly and amusingly show.[2] I have no doubt that if Isadora Duncan had survived till she was seventy, she could, without retracting anything she had ever said or done, have been accepted in impeccable society as a sweet and interesting old lady. D. H. Lawrence, had he not died so soon after the publication of *Lady Chatterley's Lover*, would ultimately have been able to bring out an unexpurgated sequel with the most reputable publisher in London.

Every man wishing to disseminate a revolutionary theory should strive to last until he wears the recognized emblems of decorum on his brow, white hair (or none), and furrows. There is no better way of removing his work from the underworld of objectionable ideas and gaining for it the prestige that will smooth the way for his disciples. The honour shed by time combines with other factors to make

---

[1] See Appendix 25.

[2] I have chosen these names because, with the possible exception of Mrs Pankhurst, their owners did not tone down their doctrines or become more conventional in behaviour as they reached old age. Mrs Besant, for one, increased in reckless individualism, yet had the satisfaction of homage where she had formerly been ostracized. Mrs Pankhurst unhappily did not live to see the statue of herself unveiled with the blessing of those who had formerly sent her, so repeatedly, to prison.

some very curious anomalies. Lewd *double-entendres* and anecdotes of smirking indecency are tolerated, or even eagerly collected, in circles which repudiate with angry disgust the theories of psycho-analysis and are genuinely shocked at the freedoms exercised by modern novelists. Sexual passion seems to them a fit subject to contemplate only when it is treated as a joke. This, I think, is due partly to the fact that a joke, being non-realistic, raises no problem, stirs no wincing emotions, and partly to the antiquated character of the themes which recur, handed down from one generation of gallant versifiers and raconteurs to another till we get back as far as Chaucer, and much further if we travel abroad.

In the same way, it is nearly always tacitly allowed that drunkenness and semi-drunkenness are humorous topics, while drug addiction is a morbid topic and would not be dealt with intimately in that 'wholesome' kind of play, film, or novel which is aimed at the taste of 'the plain man.' Comedians may lurch on to the stage hiccoughing and pretending to see double, and even a hero may have a hangover. The perpetual thirst attributed to the majority of robust adult males is still more fruitful of merriment than their sexual appetites. Whereas only Charlie Chaplin has been able to make the British and American public laugh at a man taking cocaine. Yet it is indisputable that the abuse of alcohol in these populations is immensely more widespread than the abuse of drugs, and the tragic consequences only seem less horrible because we are so thoroughly accustomed to them.

Here again I find that tolerance grows from the existence of a tradition. Our great orthodoxy of hospitality and conviviality, our ancient toasts and drinking-songs, our long association of beer with manly jollity and wine with elegant festivity, all combine to surround drink with an atmosphere of good humour; while drugs enter into the suspicious category of innovations—for, although they have perhaps been in use as long as fermented liquors, most of those that come to the notice of the lay public are of comparatively recent discovery and owe their existence to advances in analytical chemistry and medical anaesthesia. Time is not yet on their side. They are still 'against Nature.'

.   .   .   .

Nature is a word, always very loosely used, to which time has brought increasingly sentimental connotations. The decline of one superstition has encouraged the growth of another: God the Father has been dethroned from many simple hearts only to be replaced by Nature the Mother, an entity of strikingly similar characteristics, mingling benevolence with vindictiveness in quite the old familiar proportions. Nature has consciousness and makes rules and plans, and takes revenges. She is jealous and cannot bear interference. Her workmanship is perfect. Her desire for mastery is always overwhelming, and no one ever gets the upper hand of her for long.

Though everyone who lives what is called a civilized life must commit a hundred 'unnatural' acts a day, the mythical decrees of an imaginary Goddess are frequently alleged as the reason for opposing urgently needed social reforms, and even persons of quite sound intellect are sometimes so carried away by the poetical conception of a great, brooding, fecund, ingenious spirit, stern but loving, kind but inexorable of purpose, that they refuse to perceive how often the works of Nature—that is to say, effects which owe nothing to the touch of man—are botchy and ill-contrived, and how many animals have evolved at random, as it were, in the most blundering and groping manner. They are reluctant to acknowledge that the louse is Nature's creature no less than the lion: and they fastidiously close their eyes to the many clumsy, uncomfortable, and ugly aspects of mammal reproduction.

There is a wild fiction that 'natural' substances are invariably whole-some, and through some confusion which is not restricted to vegetarians, 'natural' means vegetable in preference to animal, and is especially thought to exclude mineral. We see on every side advertisements for medicines, cosmetics, and foodstuffs whose highest praise is that they are 'natural products,' implying that manufactured or blended products are noxious.[1] Numberless pills and potions are marketed with an assur-ance that they consist solely of 'vegetable matter,' as if strychnine, cocaine, and henbane did not, and as if mineral matter had no part in the composition of the human frame. Treatment by fasting and fruit juice, usually combined with special baths, massage, and colonic irrigations, is called a Nature Cure. I know it to be a good cure from several first-hand experiences, but it has always seemed to me quite as strongly opposed to the inclinations and habits of Nature as any of the cures of orthodox medicine.

The cult of Nature in the eighteenth century found its most acceptable expression in the rusticities of Greuze and Dresden china—flute-playing shepherds clad in satin and flowered brocade, and country wenches who could smell only of lavender: the twentieth-century version gives altogether tougher types, but they are hardly less meretricious. Satire has anatomized them and divided them into different schools, of which at least three are well established—the Crude Primitive or Visceral, the Wise Bucolic, and the Elfin Arcadian. The common feature is the substitution of Nature for the Victorian Providence, the conviction that lurking in the background there is a sort of She-who-must-be-obeyed—though nothing could show a wider disparity than their views of what her chief requirements are. According to the Primitives (who are *démodés* in the class which can afford to play with ideas when they are new but startling still to the patient rank and file), it is enough to obey the urgings of the abdomen and to despise cerebration: the Rustics

---

[1] This style of advertising suggests, I think, the same mentality as that which fits up factories to turn out 'Home-Made' bread, cakes, and sweetmeats.

think it superior to breed freely and live and die close to the soil: to the Arcadians it has been revealed as primary dogma that one must expose one's body to the sun and eat fruit. All these doctrines have proved beneficial to some of their disciples, but, like the discarded creeds of religion, they are rich in pleasing assumptions and short cuts. To the rational, Nature's thoughtful schemes for humanity are as much a flattering make-believe as God's.

The body has evolved with certain needs, some of which imperatively demand fulfilment, some of which can be fobbed off quite effectively with makeshifts. It will continue to evolve as long as it can adapt itself to the conditions which it encounters or creates. The stage of evolution at which man cut himself adrift irrevocably from the rest of the animal adventurers was when he learned to use tools, and these he can no longer discard without the suicide of his whole species. It may therefore be said that the one habit which is certainly natural to man is to be artificial.

The persistence of belief in an invisible omnipotent disciplinarian who can punish us or perform wonders for us is paralleled by many other survivals from an aboriginal phase of development. There are traces in all sentimental minds of the old superstition which regards pain as a sacrifice pleasing to some supernal power, and tremblingly fears pleasure.

The horror of drugs, which I have mentioned, ostensibly based on their dangers but in reality merely puritanical, is very widespread and results, on the one hand, in much unnecessary suffering and, on the other, in numerous cases of addiction, through morbid sense of guilt, through defiant reaction, or the hankering for sensational forbidden fruit.[1] Even the mildest analgesics and sedatives evoke disapproval in some quarters, and it is common to meet people who complain reiterantly of a headache or a bout of insomnia and mutely flourish their own merit because they refuse to be relieved. (There is also, of course, much self-deception aided by word-magic. A remedy will always have a better chance of appealing to the simple if it is labelled: 'Not a drug but a natural herbal compound,' words of precisely no meaning to anyone who knows what herbal compounds may contain.)

It would be pleasant if we were assured that all our pangs of bodily or mental anguish were purifying our souls and cancelling out our wrongdoings; and inasmuch as suffering enriches our understanding, or provides us with knowledge through which we can avoid occasions of greater suffering, we sometimes have reason to be grateful for it. But when we exert our private judgment instead of thinking in blurred clichés, we can hardly fail to notice that pain unduly intensified only brings about a state of self-absorption and that most characters would benefit greatly by a prolonged experience of happiness and success.

. . . .

[1] See Appendix 26.

Established religion in all ages and countries has fostered the wishful belief that affliction is salutary, because it is the business of prosperous Churches to support vested interests and maintain the *status quo* ; and by teaching that pains and sorrows of all kinds are an acceptable offering to Heaven, they have tried to allay discontent and keep the people doing what it was thought good for them to do. The State avails itself of the deeply implanted faith in resignation and sacrifice as major virtues to ensure the submission of the public to whatever miseries the ambitions or the stupidities of governments may involve them in. The 'No Cross, No Crown' of the church adherent becomes the 'We can take it' of the patriot left destitute through air raids,[1] and the 'Get on with it' of the overworked artisan who gives up in one day all the rights his predecessors struggled a hundred years for. There is no aspect of war more saddening in its implications than the pitiful vanity of skilfully flattered martyrs. In the words of Vera Brittain, writing in 1938 :

'Nothing could be more destructive of character and warping to vitality than a long course of abnegation and sacrifice. Were it not for this universal inertia of humble patient acceptance, the worst human evils—war, cruelty, poverty, the oppression of the penniless and the persecution of the weak—could be destroyed tomorrow. In the world as I have known it, I have come to recognize resignation as the deadliest of the seven deadly sins ; to see it as a positive menace to the civilization which only some tremendous renaissance of initiative can now rescue from doom.'[2]

Propaganda in favour of stoical endurance which must jest if it is not silent has now reached proportions of such ridiculous yet appalling effrontery, under the eager sponsorship of the popular press, that people actually have been called cowards for not being willing to expose themselves to the highest air-raid risks in the interests of their employers. The expression 'bomb dodger' is insanely used as a reproach. 'WE SHALL REMEMBER THE DODGERS' threatens a headline in the *Sunday Chronicle*, and the article which follows ingeniously consoles the luckless workers unable to get away from danger zones by promising revenge against those who infamously looked for safety : their jobs are to be closed to them on their return, they are to be covered with ignominy.[3] 'TUBE CUTHBERTS TOLD TO GO' shrills the *Daily Express*, triumphing in the brief success of its campaign to prevent able-bodied men from taking underground shelter. The spiteful epithet suggests

[1] '*THEY* CAN TAKE IT' says the front page of the *Sunday Pictorial* (October 20th, 1940) showing a photograph of two children ' bombed out of their homes.' The same day the papers announced that 694 children who evidently couldn't take it had been killed in the preceding month.

[2] From *Thrice A Stranger*.

[3] It is not to be supposed that the ' deserters ' who excite this contempt are men and women engaged on vital industries. These have had no option but to stay at their posts, refusal being liable to bring fines and imprisonment.

that a man of courage readily submits himself to nightly sleeplessness and the chances of perfectly futile death or mutilation. Furious readers expostulate against the *Picture Post's* photographs of homeless Londoners because the one used on the front page showed tearful eyes.[1] A Mrs Dunstan at West Didsbury thinks this 'a disgrace to the British civilians'; a Mr Mullock at Cowes says: 'We English always keep our chins up and shed our tears in private.' Somehow the old East Enders who weep openly when they think of the poor accumulated possessions of a lifetime lost do not count as English.

The balanced education of children, if it should ever be achieved, will teach them to weigh the value of renunciation. There are sacrifices that are useful and sensible inasmuch as the gain is greater than the loss, and there are sacrifices which are well-meant but destined to miscarry, and which, if not too foolishly or vaingloriously persisted in, are perhaps ennobling to those who make them. But self-abnegation for the mere sake of luxuriating in discomfort, and suffering borne so that one can boast one's fortitude with an air of jocular modesty, are symptoms of a most distasteful kind of hysteria, and a sensitive person will tend to avert his eyes from the embarrassing demonstration.

The exaltation of pain is always the measure of our wretchedness. We make a virtue of what we believe to be necessity. (Significantly, the chief symbol of Christianity is an instrument of torture.) It would be an immeasurable advance in the development of human affairs if pleasure, instead of being discredited, became the supreme standard of utility, and to *enjoy*, discriminatingly and without recoil, were recognized as a high and honourable aim, while a graceful appreciativeness would receive as many commendations as our present kind of civilization usually reserves for ostentatious and often pointless self-denial. Had it not been for men's feeble willingness to endure and to go on enduring, fruit of a lifetime's far from disinterested training, the grosser and cruder kinds of physical discomfort would probably in the last fifty years have been all but eliminated, and we should have entered upon a stage of evolution infinitely beyond the reach of those primarily occupied with trying 'to keep their chins up.'

. . . . . .

The puritanical distrust of pleasure gives rise to a somewhat confused attitude towards success. On the one hand, success induces respect because it is a manifestation of power which, if sufficiently publicized, can be tasted vicariously by all: on the other, it is associated, very frequently, with pleasure in its most seductive forms and it is thought to be a source of pride tempting to the gods. As sexuality, among those

[1] All these examples belong to October 1940. The flying bomb campaign of 1944 produced very similar manifestations, including all the weariful jocosities—such as 'doodlebugs' for bombs.

who have been brought up under puritan influences, is 'subject to the violent oscillation between craving and aversion,' [1] so the spectacle of other people's victories is subject to an oscillation between envying deference and a vague malevolence. If the successful are courted, they are also maligned; if their rise to greatness is acclaimed, a lapse into disfavour will nevertheless be noted with relish. A famous beauty is rapidly discovered to be 'going off,' an actor or author is generally reckoned to have done better work before meeting recognition, an assumption which, though occasionally true, is much oftener false. Clever gossip-writers know that the public loves celebrities to be portrayed with a faintly belittling touch, something to 'take them down a peg.' Stories in which prominent men or women are shown behaving with arrogance, utterances betraying their conceit, are always circulated with the utmost dispatch. Most of these anecdotes are untrue or cruelly misinterpreted, but they are perennially satisfying to the frustrated.

In one of the best chapters in *The Summing Up*, W. Somerset Maugham examines the good and ill effects of success without sentimentality: 'The common idea that success spoils people by making them vain, egotistic, self-complacent, is erroneous; on the contrary, it makes them, for the most part, humble, tolerant, and kind. Failure makes people bitter and cruel.'

The charge one most often hears brought against an eminent person is that he has behaved in an offhand way to old acquaintances, which is taken as a proof that success has gone to his head. What tends to be overlooked is, first, that an incipient celebrity is likely to have made a deeper impression on his acquaintances than they have made on him, leaving an inclination on their part to over-estimate the strength of former intimacy; and second, that even minor public figures may receive an amount of correspondence, of requests to do this or that, which it is quite literally impossible to cope with if private life and work are not to be abandoned altogether, and there have been very few successful men or women energetic enough to answer every irrelevant letter and accept every invitation to appear at uncongenial social functions. When people talk of a celebrity as 'unspoiled,' they nearly always mean that he suffers bores gladly—a kind of amiability, by the way, which is sometimes related not to modesty but to vanity.

Two small classes of successful people are, in some degree, exceptions to the rule of subterranean hostility; those who are hero-worshipped as potential saviours of a downtrodden or distraught following, and those whose connection with a section of the masses is peculiarly direct, so that the vicarious pleasure is acquired with unusual ease and there is a very close sense of identification. Into this latter category come persons otherwise not outstanding who display enviable physical courage and perform such feats as have been familiar in everybody's early day-

[1] I take the phrase from Gerald Heard's *Pain, Sex, and Time*.

dreams, and the 'self-made' celebrities who are diplomatic enough to retain, publicly at least, the tastes and manners of the people from whom they spring. Of these, Miss Gracie Fields was for some years the archetype, a living 'success story,' the embodiment of a working-girl's most dazzling fantasy. Yet even saviours, heroes, and proletarians who have reached 'the top of the tree' do not find their popularity quite beyond the caprice—which is to say, the strain of cruelty—that secretly enjoys seeing the idol totter.

. . . .

The same heritage of superstition which has encouraged us to replace a possessive anthropomorphic guardian called God by a possessive gynaemorphic guardian called Nature is also active in sustaining our primeval view of death. When I hear people drop their voices and talk reverently of some recently deceased individual whom they disliked and avoided when he was alive, I scarcely need an anthropologist to explain to me that they fear the spirit of the departed may do them some mischief and are anxious, in case it should be listening, to placate it.[1] The ridiculous precept *de mortuis nil nisi bonum* can have no other origin, and the motive generally alleged—that 'he is no longer here to defend himself'—could only carry conviction if it were *always* customary for those who are not in a position to defend themselves to be thus considerately regarded. But how seldom in life does absence bring immunity from criticism! The very fact that the ban upon frank discussion is limited to some years after demise proves the dishonesty of the excuse, for a man becomes progressively *more* unable to defend himself as friends too die and evidence is obliterated. Does not the gradual lifting of the embargo show that this fear of the dead is much more vivid when they are newly become spectres and may be supposed to linger about the earth retaining an interest in its affairs than when they have thoroughly settled down 'on the other side'?

Because of our wishful belief in personal survival, the act of dying, moreover, is invested with a consummate dignity and splendour as an act of translation. To be admitted to so great a mystery seems to purify the initiate, and more so when he relinquishes life in a sudden or spectacular manner than when the process is slow, tiresome, and attended by many humiliating symptoms of decay. The swift extinction of the vital flame naturally inspires greater awe than its gradual fizzling out, and the homage that consists in remembering virtues and forgetting faults is more likely to be paid to a man killed through catastrophe than one who has long endured some affliction. Aldous Huxley is perhaps putting the cart before the horse when he writes:[2] 'Our European admiration for

[1] Even this, however, is in the educated classes a 'double standard' attitude. Criticism of the dead will be very nearly unrestricted in private as long as it is uttered in a sympathetically regretful tone. It is on public and semi-public occasions that insincerity is obligatory.
[2] In *Ends and Means*.

military heroism and martyrdom has tended to make men believe that a good death is more important than a good life, and that a long course of folly and crime can be cancelled out by a single act of physical courage.'

Close investigation might demonstrate that it is not the prestige of militarism and martyrdom that makes us glorify the forms of death associated with them, but the prestige of death, impressively attained, that makes us glorify militarism and (even useless) martyrdom. They afford a means of bringing about the final metamorphosis rapidly, of saving us from decrepitude and 'the cruel dishonour of time.'

A man will be called a hero for dying catastrophically even when he has no volition in the matter and would obviously have avoided it if he could. 'FORTY HEROES FEARED DEAD IN PIT DISASTER,' the newspapers will tell us, or 'SEVENTY HEROES TRAPPED IN SUBMARINE.' There are certainly people who feel that every man capable of bearing the hardships and perils of an underground miner's life has something of the heroic in his quality, but this cannot be a general everyday opinion, or their rebellion against low wages and long hours would not so constantly have met with public rebuke. It takes death to make a miner a hero. Submarine crews, being seldom heard of except in connection with brave exploits, are given the title more readily, but it needs death to exalt seventy men out of seventy to the heroic level.

Death is not positively necessary in order that heroism shall be accorded full recognition, but it is preferable. It is, especially in the military or quasi-military sphere, the simplest and most idealistic arrangement. A man who is dead becomes a static figure, eternally heroic; a man who has the misfortune to be disabled and beggared may grow into a mere nuisance to the community. In 1937 the *Daily Mail* invited its readers to suggest ways of enticing more young men into the army, and published, among others, this reply:

'Abolish from the streets the great numbers of begging ex-Servicemen, wearing medals and giving, by their appearance, psychologically the worst impressions of an Army career to the young would-be recruits.'

Here was stated openly what many had secretly felt for years about the troublesome bemedalled fellows with missing limbs who played barrel organs or sold notepaper from door to door. Yet what difference was there between such redundant heroes and their comrades who had died? None except that their position in relation to the trajectory of a shell or bullet had been less uncompromising. But the names of the others were carved on Rolls of Honour, and it had been much easier to get people to subscribe towards costly memorials to celebrate their sacrifice than to raise money for the pressing needs of those who inconveniently continued to live. And this will probably be so again.

No reader who has reached the present chapter needs to be told why war memorials are usually of a romantic character. The human wreckage war leaves to be cleaned up fosters no sublime illusions and soon ceases to be moving.

While war still rages and we have to flog ourselves into waging it, its tragic victims are, of course, the objects of a boundless indignant sympathy—a sympathy amounting in some cases to frenzy. Thus Mr Beverley Nichols during the retreat of June 1940 wrote: 'An hour in the life of a single one of those men at Calais seems so much more important than the life of all the men of letters who ever lived.' [1] But, unlike some others in a similarly hysterical condition, he could foresee reaction and thoughtfully added: 'At least, that's how it seems to me just now.' When the shouting and the tumult die, needy warriors who have survived had better be as picturesque as Chelsea pensioners if they desire even a modest continuance of applause.

The religious view of death as a supernatural dispensation which changes a man instantly from whatever manner of human being he was to a noble enigma dovetails with an equally ancient belief in the resurrection of the body—a belief now, of course, only vestigial except among the few who are still able to take literally the astonishing Articles of Catholic and Protestant faith. The body when dead is treated with a veneration it frequently did not receive living, and in peacetime we have the pathetic spectacle of the poor spending their little substance upon funeral pomp; in wartime we are accustomed to the painful absurdity of encompassing the deaths of enemy soldiers at great cost of life and money and then burying them in a highly decorous and sometimes expensive fashion. [2] While the leaders of nations were preparing to smash up a new generation their conference-men were, I understand, busy getting assurances from one another that the cemeteries of the last war would not be defaced.

It will hardly be supposed by any reader of balanced judgment that I would advocate reverting to the practice of antiquity, when metaphysical concepts were still more primitive, and would have the bodies of enemies suffer public degradation, or that I do not mind what damage is done to cemeteries. There is a sense of fitness, quite distinct from superstition and sentimentality, which dictates that certain objects and effects shall not be dealt with on terms of immediate utility alone. The marvellous assemblage of instruments for perceiving and doing which is the mortal part of us, and perhaps all, cannot with fitness be used ignominiously even when it is no longer of service. Living or dead, the

---

[1] Mr Nichols proved his contempt for men of letters by publishing in the same *Sunday Chronicle* article a poem of his own composition which was largely a close echo of lines by Swinburne and others.

[2] When the cost of burying a German airman (approximately £10) was discussed by Bridlington Rural Council in December 1939, it was stated that double fees had been paid because the man was a non-resident in the district.

body demands respect; the difference between reason and sentimentality is that reason suggests the folly of paying more respect to a dead body than a living one.

The widely held fatalistic idea that death is a magical reward or punishment over which an invisible Providence exercises monopoly claims is doubtless the basis of those fatuous—and, it must be acknowledged, unpopular—laws that make suicide a crime and bid us prolong to the last possible hour the afflictions of the incurably diseased or totally disabled. The State frequently and extensively understudies Providence in terminating life, but never, except in the case of the lower animals, for the purpose of bringing relief to the sufferer. Those rights of extinction which are readily delegated to the hangman and the soldier are stringently withheld from the physician, an austerity which, it need hardly be said, is closely linked to the Puritan conception of pain as a highly desirable portion of human experience.

Yet it is by no means solely the value placed upon pain which actuates the postponement of release, for it has long been customary to soften the pangs of the dying as far as that can be done without bringing them nearer to death. Death itself is the forbidden achievement. Among nations whose established religions are still sillier than ours the prohibition against inflicting death extends even to animals and insects, and although the intention was perhaps originally humanitarian, it now results in nothing but horrible cruelty. Travellers in the East have told us how, because the Koran says 'the blood of an animal must not be shed,' pious men will work a lame horse till it drops and dies, an animal whose owner cannot afford to feed it will be slowly starved to death, and sick stray dogs whom nobody will kill wander about the garbage heaps carrying disease. Formerly, as is well known, the inhabitants of Stamboul, refusing to commit the sin of bloodshed, sent their stray dogs in hundreds to an island where there was nothing to eat and where they were assured of a slow death from neglect and hunger. In Egypt I was informed that one of the chief causes of the ophthalmic infections so common and so disastrous among babies was a germ-carrying fly which is—or was at that time—allowed to breed in unchecked millions because it would have been contrary to the literal interpretation of sacred law to kill it. The limits of sentimental simplification can be set no further.

As for suicide, here even the orthodox outlook is very evidently changing for the better. It was, in the past, coloured by an unmistakable savagery, of which we still occasionally see traces in the police courts, as here:

'Sentencing 45-year-old Frank McCulloch, of Liverpool, to one month's hard labour for attempting suicide, Sir Frederick Marquis

135

said: "If you are fool enough to pour poison down your throat you deserve to suffer." [1]

This sort of sentence has become fairly uncommon and would-be suicides are nowadays more often bound over; successful ones, to acquit them of crime, were generally found to be of Unsound Mind, until it was decided that the stigma of insanity was more painful to near relations than conviction for felony would be to the deceased, so a typical English compromise was effected and the verdict to be looked for in all but particularly exasperating cases is, 'Suicide while the balance of his (or her) mind was disturbed.'

The law is mildly administered, but it stands none the less in need of drastic revision. For one thing—and it is a very important one—in regard to Attempted Suicide, it plainly bears much harder upon the poor, who when they are ill from self-inflicted injury are taken to public institutions, than upon those whose friends or relations can call in the assistance of a private doctor not in the least likely to report the matter to the police. (Poor people, who have been starved of power, are also temperamentally inclined to draw attention to an attempt of this kind by making a gesture of it, which, partly owing to the nature of the means at their command, is not seldom ineffectual.)

It is a grave mistake, as many authorities have pointed out, to leave laws unrepealed which are no longer in accord with the beliefs of the administrators. Suicide may sometimes be folly, but the number of people who consider it a felony must be minutely small, and even if it were, punishment is absurd since it can hurt only the criminal who has failed to commit the crime.[2] The subject is scarcely appropriate in the present chapter, however, for it is one on which public opinion is by no means entirely sentimental.

. . . .

The great tradition of liberty might seem to deserve at least a chapter to itself, but it is only with reluctance and a premonition of weariness, both for myself and the reader, that I can bring myself to write of it at all. It is a tradition so steeped in humbug, so made over to cant, that there are contexts where the very mention of it produces, in one who likes words to relate to veridical experience, a wave of repulsion.

'First find your referent' should be an invariable rule for those who

[1] *News Chronicle* report, May 8th, 1939. The magistrate is now Lord Woolton. His pronouncement carries an echo of *The Chimes*: '"And if you attempt, desperately, and ungratefully, and impiously, and fraudulently attempt, to drown yourself, or hang yourself, I'll have no pity for you, for I have made up my mind to Put all suicide Down! If there is one thing," said the Alderman, with his self-satisfied smile, "on which I can be said to have made up my mind more than on another, it is to Put suicide Down. So don't try it on."'

[2] It might, I conceive, remain necessary to bring into court the surviving partner of a suicide pact, because undue influence may have been exercised, and there is always the remote possibility of an ingeniously disguised murder.

are about to discuss an abstraction. I suppose there is some state which philosophers could agree upon as relatively one of freedom, and I suppose that in some countries the people dwell in a nearer approach to that state than in others. The conditions must obviously be that one's needs are easily gratified, that one's obligations are few and light, and that any restriction placed upon speech and conduct shall be solely for the purpose of preventing fraudulence, cruelty, and oppression. By this definition, there have been no 'free countries' except perhaps some islands and remote interiors of benign climate and sparse population, not too highly organized; and freedom could prevail in these only so long as there was no invasion and no compulsion to defend against the risk of it. England, with its history of wars, religious monopolies, press gangs, political disfranchisements, sweated labour, rent ramps, repressive legislation,[1] commercially controlled newspapers, and, lately, general conscription, may appear as a sanctuary of freedom to eyes wearing those rosy glasses which obscure some objects and shed a glow on others: without this equipment, it will look no better and no worse than most other civilized countries. That is, our great men and women have usually upheld freedom, our small ones have often successfully opposed it.

'An age appears in history through its prominent individuals,' says Bertrand Russell,[2] 'and derives its apparent character from the character of these men.' Or, in the kindred words of Hamilton Fyfe,[3] 'What is called "national character" is the character imparted to a nation by its leading men. . . . Only upon a small proportion does this character have actual effect.' Our national reputation, in our own view and that of our friends, deserves to be enhanced by the deeds of brave individuals who endured persecution and sometimes martyrdom that we might be assured of certain rights. Our enemies are more likely to judge us by the equally English persecutors.

The author last quoted has some interesting passages on the enthronement of the tradition of freedom:

'Just about the time when Smollett was satirizing the French, Voltaire . . . was making fun of an English sailor, who was boasting of English liberty, although at that moment he was being carried off by a press-gang for forced service in the Navy. Freedom became the national deity and was worshipped, like other deities, with decent dissimulation by rulers, with unthinking acquiescence by the ruled.

Wordsworth wrote sonnets to it while the population was being reduced to a condition harder than that of slaves, Tennyson made rhymes about it at a period when another poet with clearer vision and purer sympathy called on her countrymen to heed "The Cry of the Children." The middle-class, enriched by slavery and the toil of

---

[1] E.g. on the consumption of alcoholic liquors, the marketing of produce, etc.
[2] In *Power*. [3] In *The Illusion of National Character*.

tiny hands, stroked their fat stomachs and declared England to be the finest country in the world. And the poor fools who had been liberated from the dominance of the King legend [the divine rights of royalty] rushed to put themselves under a delusion not less harmful.'

The delusion was that British subjects, more than any others, were dowered with a heritage of liberty and would brook no attack upon a boon so precious; almost anything in the nature of a change being interpreted by obstructive powers as an attack. Equivalent delusions, sporadic before the eighteenth century, were epidemic throughout Europe in the nineteenth, and have been strict articles of most nationalistic faiths ever since—not a discreditable doctrine, some may argue, for at least it denotes recognition of what is desirable. But it is to be remembered that the great reforms of history were not initiated or carried through by people who imagined we were *already* enjoying a sufficiency or near-sufficiency of liberty.

In my chapter on Demos and His Government I examined the popular belief that we have—or had before the war—free speech, free press, and free right of assembly. It will hardly be denied except by those who have never known what it is to rebel against any important part of the existing order that in practice this was largely a fiction, whatever the letter of the law may have been. (And, litigation being unpleasant and expensive, cases of suppression have been seldom fought out in the law courts. Besides, the most potent suppression is negative, and one cannot take an action against an editor for not printing certain opinions, or against the manager of a public hall for not letting it to certain organizations.) The propagandist of a cause deemed to be subversive will agree with Bernard Shaw that what 'the ordinary moral man' means by toleration is 'toleration of doctrines that he considers enlightened, and, by liberty, liberty to do what he considers right; that is, he does not mean toleration or liberty at all; for there is no need to tolerate what appears enlightened or to claim liberty to do what most people consider right.'

It is a particularly odious form of cant, and yet so prevalent that it excites little condemnation, to exult in a tradition of freedom, while profiting by the subjection of some class or race to which freedom is explicitly or implicitly denied. The much-praised Greek or Roman patriots vaunted their liberty while taking for granted the institution of slavery; they rationalized that freedom was for the free*born*. Englishmen who were making fortunes out of the slave trade from the sixteenth to the end of the eighteenth century were not without a keen patriotic appreciation of belonging to a country whose citizens never, never, never would be slaves. Queen Elizabeth, the monarch of the privileged race, owned shares in a slave-ship (named the *Jesus*). Such shareholders—Elizabethans, Carolines, and Georgians—justified their gains in various ways according to the ethics of the day. Some said that the negroes would have a chance of becoming Christians unattainable if they had been left at large on their own continent; some said that it was philanthropy to take them away because in Africa other negro tribes would have killed them.[1] Others argued that slavery was indeed a bad business but *someone* would surely go in for it if they didn't, and it might as well be them—a view often propounded by investors in modern enterprises of rather shady reputation.

In the Industrial Revolution, freedom, as I have had occasion to say before, was constantly evoked as a reason for denying bargaining power of any kind to a labouring class exploited to the limits of human endurance. The many acts framed during the first quarter of the century to prevent 'combination' among workmen were expressly aimed at leaving Englishmen their Heaven-bestowed freedom to make contracts as they pleased. Seldom has so much been heard about the Rights of Man, or such strange meanings been attributed to the words. Barbara and J. L. Hammond in their Life of Lord Shaftesbury even venture the theory that it was the love of liberty that kept little boys of seven and eight years of age at the vile trade of cleaning chimneys at least fifty years after the invention of mechanism able to do the work more efficiently— a disgrace, they remark, 'peculiar to the British Isles':

'Year after year children were bought and sold to a life of dirt and suffering, ended for many of them by a revolting form of cancer due directly to their occupation; year after year a child or two from the miserable number reached local notoriety by being suffocated in a flue; year after year persons otherwise kindly and humane continued to have their chimneys swept by children.

It is a strange story, and if we ask the reason why the practice continued, the answer must be sought in some curious "complex" connected with the Englishman's dislike of interference. The Englishman's home is his castle, and to dictate the method in which his chimneys should, or should not, be swept . . . meant an interference with private affairs.'

In about 1870, when the British proletariat had been relieved of its most insupportable burdens, the great Imperialistic ideal took on unprecedented vitality; we developed the resources of the possessions already in hand and looked for others. There began the series of episodes now known as the Scramble for Africa, in which England's predatory genius immensely outclassed that of France, Germany, Belgium, and

[1] In his *History of Dahomey*, 1799, Archibald Dalzel congratulated fellow slave-traffickers on 'saving so many unhappy negroes from the blood-stained altars of human sacrifice.' The unhappy negroes thus saved are estimated to have died in such numbers while being transported to salvation that only about half of each consignment survived to reward their benefactors.

Portugal, not to speak of the baffled Boers and Italians. From that time until this it has been customary for Englishmen who countenance the subjugation of hundreds of millions of persons with coloured skins to make liberty an even louder war-cry than it was before. It is true, of course, that the majority of these fond Imperialists have never been in any part of their Empire, or else have used one small corner and another as mere pleasure resorts, so that they have seen very little of the native and know nothing of the laws which govern him.

I will instance only South Africa, a country where I spent most of my youth, which I have revisited in maturity, and from which I constantly receive newspapers. I do not think it possible for anyone who has not lived in South Africa and studied its legislation to have any conception of the abasement of the negro there, the social and political disabilities under which he labours, the thinness of the pretence of native representation in local or national government (where there is any pretence at all), and the immense disparity between sentences meted out to natives and to white men for similar crimes; though it is fair to say that, bad as things appear still to be, judging by the South African press, they have been greatly improved in the last few years, owing to the efforts of reformers and the need for a counterblast to Nazi and Fascist propaganda.

It will perhaps carry more conviction than any personal reminiscence if I quote some opinions of the Hon. F. E. T. Krause, lately Judge-President of the Orange Free State, delivering a valedictory address to members of the Bar on his retirement. He is reported [1] to have declared that:

'fully 50 per cent. of the Union's statutory regulations [concerning natives] were *ultra vires* and illegal, that prison conditions in the Free State were "well-nigh unbelievable," cells in many cases being no better than barbarous cages, that the Native Pass Laws were an anachronism,[2] and that the Native Tax Law was uneconomic and unsound.

Our South African prison population [he said] is composed largely of natives, and the reason therefore is not far to seek. . . . It has been stated, upon good authority, that a raw native entering an urban area in search of work is fortunate if, within twenty-four hours, he remains out of prison for contravening some pass or municipal regulation.

Our Pass Laws . . . serve no social or useful purpose and have degenerated into an easy and convenient form of taxation for the native or his employer. . . . Our present system has the effect of making criminals of the natives. Their labour in prison is exploited because of its cheapness, and little is done to uplift their moral standard.'

---

[1] In *The Friend*, Bloemfontein, April 29th, 1938. Owing to the war, this retirement from the bench proved temporary. Dr Krause is not an Englishman but a Boer.
[2] See Appendix 27.

After paying tribute to the work of the Department of Native Affairs which was doing its best to remedy the abuses, Dr Krause continued :

'We should not send the native to prison for petty offences, and ample time should be allowed him to pay any fines that may be imposed, having regard to his meagre earning capacity due to the present restrictions and boycott placed upon his economic progress by our so-called White "policy"—a policy which is a negation of right and justice.'

He called for the abolition of the Native Tax Law as 'an act of mere justice.'

'The amount which the native pays to the State in comparison to what most Europeans contribute is iniquitous . . . especially in view of the fact that the average wage of natives in the Union is about £30 per annum. Colour prejudice so colours the vision of a large section of Europeans that they fail to realize and appreciate the fact that the native is economically the most valuable asset of the country, for without his cheap labour our industries, especially mining, would have to close down, farming operations would come to a standstill, and our domestic arrangements would suffer considerably.

No one is so foolish as to advocate social equality between Europeans and natives. The right, however, to develop upon civilized lines should not be withheld.'

He spoke of a disconcerting number of cattle thefts, for which farmers were demanding severer punishments :

'My advice to farm-labour employers is to pay their natives at least a living wage, provide them with decent and suitable quarters, and, most important, give them a ration of meat to satisfy the craving of their nature in this respect.[1] Brutal punishments do not act as deterrents and are futile in ultimate results.'[2]

Such an indictment, coming from so authoritative a quarter, might be expected to shatter the complacency of those who imagine that where the Union Jack is planted freedom and equity take root : but the true sentimentalist is impervious to evidence, which, in any case, seldom reaches him unadulterated. To the best of my knowledge, no word of the retiring Judge-President's momentous speech ever made its way to the English press, though space is always to be found for some picturesque

[1] See Appendix 28.
[2] Brutal punishments for stock thefts are, however, countenanced by a large number of South African judges and magistrates. At Newcastle, Cape Province, in August 1940, a farmer who had shot a native was fined £40 or four months' imprisonment, of which £20 or two months was suspended for one year subject to good behaviour. The provocation given by the native was that he had been convicted of a stock theft a year before, receiving a heavier sentence than the farmer who had attacked him with a gun.

expression of allegiance to the great white King by a native chieftain having no alternative. 'South African histories,' says J. E. S. Green, the historian of Rhodesia, 'are usually apologetics for the treatment of the native races.' Versions of current affairs are equally tendentious. The Boer rebellion during the last war, the strong and continued opposition to co-operation in this one, are movements quite unheard of by citizens who derive all their information from a press bent only on representing the Empire as one vast happy family.

Some curious little sidelights on the glorious liberties of black British subjects appear in the South African section of my cuttings-book. In several cities of the Union, for example, it is against the law for natives to walk on the pavements.[1] Hundreds of seemingly innocent practices lawful for what E. M. Forster called the pinko-grey races are unlawful for the beige or brown. A Durban report mentions a native from a rural area charged with 'carrying a stick more than 36 inches in length.'[2] The almost total abstention from alcohol demanded of the native population has stimulated a damaging criminal traffic in liquor and much drunkenness. (It is ironical to reflect that alcohol and firearms, first favourites of all the allurements introduced by white concession-hunters to black land-owners, are the two commodities most stringently denied them now.) The Pass Laws operate upon natives in a manner which appears to have been imitated by Hitler's executives in organizing the compulsory immigrations both of Reich citizens and inhabitants of conquered territories.

We are told—that is, the few who enquire are told—that such all but intolerable restraints are a necessity in view of industrial requirements and the temperament of the African negro, but it will be observed that this bogus realism is myopic and invariably ignores the ultimate outcome. In dismissing with a caution the native who had carried a walking-stick, the magistrate remarked that the prohibition of sticks had led to the carrying of knives. Enforced teetotalism[3] breeds the illicit liquor trade. The Pass Laws, together with the interdiction of Native trade unions, have been said to provoke gangsterdom and general demoralization.[4] One after another, each repressive law is discovered to contain a coiled spring.

Speaking on an India Bill in 1783, William Pitt declared: 'Necessity is the plea for every infringement of human freedom. It is the argument of tyrants; it is the creed of slaves.' It is the creed of slaves, but stealthily

[1] In East London (Cape Province), by a regulation of 1904, natives and Asiatics are forbidden to walk, stand, or congregate on pavements or sidewalks. In July 1938 someone wrote to the local press urging that the law be more rigidly enforced—'choke 'em off, sit on them, tell them to shut up or move on as occasion demands'—but I am glad to say the District Commandant replied that the police had other and more important things to do.

[2] In the South African *Sunday Times*, September 1940.

[3] Natives are allowed to drink only 'Kaffir beer,' and not even that except under numerous restrictions.

[4] See Appendix 29.

it wins more favour than the creed of free men to which it is customary to pay lip service : for there are psychological reasons why most people wish either to command or be commanded, and few are so harmoniously balanced as not to feel some glow of envy or respect for those who can impose their will on others. The world's idea of a great man is likely at all times to be a power-seeking man—one who will encroach upon the freedom of his fellows ; and an unscrupulous intriguer like Cecil Rhodes, who helped to plunge his country into two wars [1] and laid up an incalculable harvest of future trouble, will probably always have a better chance of becoming a national hero than an artist, inventor, healer, or reformer who has merely introduced new prospects of enjoyment or averted suffering. 'Greatness,' said Fielding, 'consists in bringing all manner of mischief upon Mankind, and Goodness in removing it from them.'

Addiction to Greatness usually goes with a tendency to grandiose abstractions—liberty and loyalty, honour and decency and the spirit of self-sacrifice, all flourishing impressively upon a verbal plane, with much the same degree of relationship to actual conduct as unicorns, gryphons, and sphinxes bear to actual animals. A man with an intense love of exactitude, for whom Greatness had no appeal, wrote to his future wife :

> 'Aren't you a little pretentious when you say you are perfectly free ? We are all slaves at least of our affections, slaves of the prejudices of those we love ; we must also earn our living. . . . The most painful thing is the concessions we are forced to make to prejudices of the society that surrounds us ; one makes them more or less often according to one's strength or weakness.' [2]

Marie Sklodovska was capable of perceiving that she had been using words without adequate sense ; it was a practice that, being strong, she rapidly abandoned. The little disciples of the Great will probably always prefer to talk and think nonsense.

[1] The conquest of the Matabele, whom he had defrauded, preceded the conquest of the Boers. J. E. S. Green's *Rhodes Goes North* gives a well-documented version of the transactions with Lobengula.

[2] From one of Pierre Curie's letters, 1894, quoted in *Madame Curie* by Eve Curie.

I in my own house am an emperor,
And will defend what's mine.
The Roman Actor: PHILIP MASSINGER.

ALL nations addicted to patriotism have some centripetal belief about which the sense of superiority can grow and gather. Ours is the tradition of sportsmanship. Few would have the courage, or the desire, to deny, in a public assembly, that this ineffable quality, though not exactly confined to the British Empire, is to be seen at its best in persons who own allegiance to the Union Jack. To win the approval of the masses, it is only necessary to remind them of their reputation for fair and decent dealing; and the editorial columns of the popular press therefore abound with praises of a national trait which, they tell us, is the admiration of the whole world.

Yet each member of the mass who reads with comfortable credulity, and sometimes thrilling pride, the well-worn journalistic flatteries [1] may find reported in the same paper actions of his compatriots in which no vestige of sportsmanship appears, actions of mean criminality, of treachery to benefactors, of cruelty to the helpless, of petty vindictiveness. Each member of the mass, secure in the orthodoxy of our unassailable fair play, is perfectly aware, and would readily admit in conversation, that there are among his own acquaintances individuals who cannot be trusted to act chivalrously, that in his time fellow-countrymen have let him down, taken advantage of him, played sly and cunning tricks upon himself or those known to him. In private he clearly recognizes that such conduct is to be expected from inferior Englishmen (not to speak of Welshmen, Ulstermen, Scots, Australians, and South Africans). In public he forgets it or, if constrained to refer to it, calls it un-English.

I turn over the pages of a few newspapers and I cannot but notice that various sorts of un-Englishness are occupying a startling amount of space. Here I see a picture labelled in big black letters 'This is a Photograph of a Licked Hun.' A smaller caption points out that the youth portrayed, a military prisoner of 1918, is hungry, exhausted, cowed, and ragged: and that there will be many more like him in the future. The reader is invited, by implication, to gloat. The gloating spirit, supposed to be so foreign to the British character, is, in fact, peculiarly in evidence. Here is an approving mention of a waitress who, seeing a German aeroplane sinking into the sea, remarks, 'Another nasty with wet feet!' Here is a crowd described as shouting and jeering as enemy aeroplanes crash down before their eyes. ('The thrill of a football match will never

[1] See Appendix 30.

144

be the same to these irrepressible enthusiasts,' says the jocular reporter.)
Here is a story to keep up our morale—I assume—about a German airman
of fifteen crying aloud for his mother as his parachute drops towards a
mob of Belgians waiting to lynch him. There is no limit to the number
of similar instances: they are the common daily fare—but especially the
Sunday fare—of nearly all the newspaper-reading population.

The certainty that Germans are gloating too does not make our own
blaring exultations more sportsmanlike, for surely it is of the essence of
sportsmanship rather to forgo an advantage than to use methods we think
despicable in our adversaries. Throughout all wars a controversy rages,
almost part of the din of battle, between those who wish to maintain a
few standards of magnanimity and honour, and those who readily
abandon themselves to insensate hatred. I look at my papers again and
see a letter from a Twickenham correspondent who says he will give up
contributing towards the Lifeboat Institution and the funds for soldiers'
comforts, and will urge all his friends to do the same, because he has read
of a lifeboat crew going out to pick up a German airman, and 'also of an
English soldier giving a drink and a cigarette to another of that breed.' [1]
I see a letter in a weekly paper (signed Officer Cadet K) expressing horror
because a Nazi pilot had been given a pint of beer before being handed
over to the authorities. 'Our job,' he says, 'is to hate these Germans
and exterminate as many as may be necessary to secure the foundations
of decency in a tottering world.' English sportsmanship, he thinks,
should be 'kept within the confines of sanity.' It should not be allowed
'to bring a nice friendly spirit into the war. Instead, we should hate, or
else not fight at all. . . . The whole tribe must be smashed and punished.'

The correspondent of a Leeds evening paper is even more uncompromising: 'Face to face with a dangerous wild beast one does not think
about "playing the game." . . . Let us take off the gloves of British
tradition. Let us go all out. Let us bite, kick, gouge, hit below the belt;
let us fight "all in."'

As if to show that we are doing this, the *Star* publishes a cartoon,
entitled *Serenade*,[2] which represents two smiling and singing airmen,
one labelled 'R.A.F.', the other 'U.S.A.A.F.', pursuing a terror-stricken
hausfrau (not a political personality dressed up, but a quite anonymous
stout and elderly woman, identifiable as German only by her swastika
badge). Each of the aviators is menacing her fleeing figure with a huge
black bomb, while they join, with balefully ironic gallantry, in the chorus
of Cole Porter's well-known song: 'No matter, darling, where you are,
we think of you—night and day.'

Nor is it only in relation to the enemy that so many Englishmen are

[1] In this case, the newspaper, the *Daily Mail*, September 6th, 1940, printed a note of
emphatic disagreement.
[2] In the issue of March 24th, 1944. It was signed Wyndham Robinson. In fairness to
members of the R.A.F. and U.S.A.A.F., I should mention that those to whom I showed it
were repelled.

willing to be un-English. The news columns of these same journals give us police court reports of cruel frauds practised upon the parents of soldiers named in casualty lists, and of a court-martial to deal with persistent thefts from the possessions of dead British airmen, and wholesale robbery by soldiers charged with the care of friendly aliens. There are records, greatly minimized in sections of the press, of the usual profiteering and battening upon necessity: and, several times repeated, the familiar tale of the conscientious objector who wins with difficulty from a Bench of Government officials the right to remain exempt from military service as long as he keeps his present employment, and is then triumphantly sacked by his employer.[1]

It may be argued that it is as unfair to judge people by their delirious ravings in wartime as to condemn the utterances of a patient in a high fever. But even in peacetime, affairs of public concern may often be seen in retrospect to have been conducted in a most un-English fashion. I will not go back to such far-away violations of the gentlemanly code as may be found in the archives of days when the slave trade was respectable, when the Established Church was busy imposing political and other disabilities upon non-members, and when citizens found it funny to throw disgusting missiles at men in the pillory—though these phases of development have their place in our tradition. The more recent history of Feminine Emancipation, Trade Unionism, or the nineteenth-century practice of Empire Building in other people's countries, provides an immense mass of evidence that, when gain is promised or vested interest threatened, the rules of fair play, as expounded in our public schools, have seldom been strictly observed.[2] Sentimental loyalism forbids us to admit in the aggregate the facts which singly would only be disputed by ignoramuses.

Though in a group of educated men these facts could be presented without exciting any feeling that there ought to be patriotic denials, the moment the same gathering approached the dimensions of a crowd, the public attitude would be assumed like a garment—a cloak, as indeed it is —and we may imagine what reception would be accorded to any speech which should be couched as frankly as the foregoing paragraphs, written for the judgment of the individual! In a trice almost every listener would have adjusted his mind to cant.

Without cant there would be little sustenance for the oblique self-flatteries which are popularly known as loyalty. To have given blind loyalty the dignity of a virtue and made it a feature of almost every type of education from earliest infancy is among the greatest of the many wrongs mankind inflicts upon itself. It is a tragedy, but not a mystery:

[1] The worst offenders here appear to be town councils, education authorities, and large corporations; employers whose personal contact with the employed is probably slight, and who thus find it the more easy to be 'public-spirited.'
[2] See Appendix 31.

loyalty upholds authority, and that is a very sufficient reason for establishing it as a principle.

The baby in the nursery is told that it is right to love its father and mother and wrong not to. (This lesson is so firmly inculcated that not to be able to love one parent or the other is generally to contract a sense of guilt said to have profound consequences in later life.) The explanation offered for this demand upon his emotions is not that his parents are kind—for he knows it is 'right' to love them whether they are kind or not—but simply that they are his own, his family, part of his endowment from Providence, which he is encouraged to be thankful for as, vaguely or glowingly, superior to the endowments of others.

Dutiful love is bound up with dutiful faith, and faith facilitates obedience. When beliefs about the veneration a child owes to a father were very much more irrational than they are today—for there has been a marked advance—no juvenile reading-book was complete without the idiotic poem about the boy who stood on a burning deck and went on standing there until he was burned to death because his father had told him to wait and had subsequently perished. The moral was that, even in desperate straits, it was noble to subdue reason in favour of obedience —*blind* obedience, blind loyalty's favourite offspring. Casabianca is *démodé*, but the young are still taught to glory vicariously in such incidents as the Charge of the Light Brigade, a truly dreadful example. The intelligence of any child not mentally deficient must grope towards the idea that it might have been more admirable if, instead of committing mass suicide, some of those unfortunate men had had the strength of mind to protest, 'Look here, someone has blundered.' But if he hints at this obvious alternative he will, of course, be told it would have been mutiny, and that, as society is organized, there must be some classes of people who understand that it's theirs not to reason why, theirs but to do or die; otherwise everything would be confusion. I suppose the docile child and also the one who himself has an ambition to command quietly accept this verdict and time will confirm it for them; but a few gradually discover that society must be wretchedly organized if large groups of people exist who are expressly required not to use their brains.

I am not refusing to recognize a real loyalty of love besides a loyalty of falling into line. Our trouble is that we have so little emotional integrity, not many of us know the difference between feelings that are spontaneous and those generated by a fear of being left outside the fold. The loyalties most loudly acclaimed are usually an inextricable mixture of love and self-love, our loftiest sentiments being more often due to egotism, or strongly adulterated with egotism, than our forefathers suspected. We love the things that are *ours*; that is a natural bent of the affections, which are drawn towards the familiar. We also feel the things that are ours are hallowed and must be honoured and upheld at the expense, if necessary, of the things that are not ours, and even at times to the exclusion of criticism. Such a conviction is rooted in vanity, and in any highly evolved order of society would be reprobated as a childishness of the most unlovable kind.

'Every rational and civilized man [says Leonard Woolf] is aware that not very far below the surface of his mind there lurks a savage, primitive instinct of self-glorification. One's own family, house, village, country, nation, school, university are all *felt* to be in some way superior to those of other people. Reason, if it be used, teaches us that the feeling must be a delusion and superstition. Even the most patriotic can hardly believe that every family is superior to every other family and every tribe or nation superior to every other tribe or nation, yet this must follow from the logic of this kind of patriotism which requires that Mr Jones believe in the superiority of the Jones family, Mr Smith in that of the Smith family, an Etonian in that of Eton, a Harrovian in that of Harrow, a German in that of the German nation, and a Peruvian in that of the Peruvian nation. When I notice the following facts: (1) that I have an instinctive feeling of superiority to Herr Schmidt because I was born of English parents in Kensington and he was born of German parents in Berlin; (2) that Herr Schmidt has an instinctive feeling of superiority to me because he was born in Berlin of German parents and I was born in Kensington of English parents; (3) that our mutual feeling of superiority would have been just the same if I had been born in Berlin and he had been born in Kensington—when I notice these three facts, I am reluctantly forced to conclude that our belief in superiority is a mutual delusion.

Savage society accepts and encourages this delusion; its institutions are built upon it, and it is the very fabric of politics and social relations.'[1]

In his addiction to this particular form of vainglory—through which, with an affectation of modesty, conceit is transferred from oneself to one's background—the product of modern education is far more assiduous than his counterpart in the Dark Ages. At least religion then strove to be universal while, if the rodomontades put into the mouths of knights by the chroniclers of chivalry are to be relied upon, boasting was permitted to be personal and brazen and did not always pose as a disinterested allegiance to exalted objects.

To distinguish the elements of true loyalty, which can only engender good, from those of sentimental loyalty, which nourishes bitter rivalries and all the evils that grow from defensive vanity, is often a difficult, sometimes an impossible task, but a broad rule may be laid down that sentimental loyalty attaches itself to institutions rather than individuals, or to individuals when they are primarily the representatives of institutions, whereas rational loyalty can only be given to those who are respected or loved for *their personal qualities personally experienced.*

[1] From *Quack, Quack!*

148

There are necessarily great numbers of borderline cases. What are we to say, for instance, of family loyalty? On which side of the line must that be placed? To answer so delicate a question accurately would obviously require a full knowledge of the circumstances in each separate case. The honouring of one's father and one's mother is doubtless very often based on respect for their characters and pleasure in their company, and may be as spontaneous as the emotion inspired by friendships one has delightedly chosen. On the other hand, there are parents who command loyalty only because they represent the institution of the Family and because their children believe it would be 'unnatural' not to love them. Then, again, there are others whose effect is to evoke a subtle mixture of conventional sentiments and genuine ones.

To some extent it *is* 'natural' to love our parents. We have an opportunity of getting to know them so extremely intimately, and at close quarters nearly everyone's character has some endearing features. Equally, at close quarters nearly everyone's character has some very tiresome features, and that is why most people who live a family life oscillate perpetually between affection and irritation. The affection, however, is there—genuine affection based on personal qualities—and therefore family loyalty should not be put by and large into the sentimental category.

That category contains (as I have never given the reader any opportunity of forgetting) the beliefs which are founded upon simplification and idealization. We approach it with more certainty in the deliberately manufactured loyalty of the schoolboy, though even this may consist of many ingredients so closely blended that it would be hopeless to attempt to measure them. We may fairly assume, I think, a large proportion of that egotism we have touched upon which will make him wish to glorify the place he himself is associated with. Then, there is the logical preference for a familiar little world. Then, submission—often quite unconscious—to the numerous authorities who have told him that it is proper to be loyal, and also a desire to stand well with his companions. And probably, among these and two or three elements which I overlook, some real attachment to certain teachers, pupils, and pleasant objects; parts of the routine, games, or congenial learning.

That attachment constitutes by far the most valuable part of his loyalty, but it would not by itself result in a general principle of honouring and upholding. Without sentimental training the schoolboy would merely support those aspects of his school which he happened to admire, and no others. His attitude towards it might be much the same as towards the hotel where, in later life, he will go year by year for holidays. The fact that he enjoys the food and is fond of various people he meets there would not—unless he were exceptionally silly—make him feel an obligation to defend it passionately against someone who should truthfully

149

complain that the service was slow and the hall porter uncivil. He might be slightly annoyed to be reminded of defects in an otherwise praise-worthy establishment, but he would hardly say: 'What a cad to go round letting down the hotel!' It would be nice for the hôteliers if they could get *esprit de corps* accepted as a convention among their patrons, but it would not be very good for the hotels.

Because it saves effort and promotes obedience, young people from remotest times have had their 'characters formed' by being trained to suspend their faculty of judgment; indeed, it is a method which used to be carried very much further in the past than now, and far more brutally. Whether the character so attained is likely to be worth having when one has got it is a matter of opinion; but as far as the critical faculty is concerned, it is obvious that only the fittest can survive, and even those not wholly without damage. Private judgment is a serious nuisance when the intricate individual is commanded to submerge himself in the simple mass: it becomes imperative, almost, to refrain from critical thought. That is why men of genius, who find this compulsion exceptionally painful, have so seldom been able to tell us anything satisfactory about their schooldays.

Not that I fail to perceive a certain improvement. Irrational devotion may be even more commended than formerly, but its manifestations are at any rate less raucous. A hundred years ago, Eton and Harrow boys used to feel in duty bound to fight one another with fists on all possible occasions, and after the annual cricket match there was a battle which often resulted in bloodshed and permanent injury. One would be naïve to interpret such pugnacity as a symptom of loyalty, but the honour of the school afforded a *pretext*. It was the sacred mission of Harrovians to prove that Etonians were cads, while Eton had to be upheld by the humiliation of Harrow. There is a particular danger with sentimental loyalties that they may easily be made the excuse for acts of sheer self-gratification. History bristles with disgraceful examples—affairs like the bombardment of Canton and the sacking of the Summer Palace in Peking, the Fashoda incident and the Jameson Raid; all sorts of un-justifiable claim-stakings and punitive expeditions. The loyalty of the schoolboy was regarded as an excellent preparation for the loyalty of the flag-planting adventurer who was to succeed later on in combining glory with profit. The great periods of British expansion had for heroes patriotic buccaneers. Their consummate type is displayed at its best and worst by Rudyard Kipling, from whose poem *Loot* I quote, with shame, a few all too revealing lines:

Now remember when you're 'acking round a gilded Burma god
That 'is eyes is very often precious stones;
An' if you treat a nigger to a dose o' cleaning-rod
'E's like to show you everything 'e owns.
When 'e won't prodooce no more, pour some water on the floor

Where you 'ear it answer 'ollow to the boot
    (*Cornet:* Toot! Toot!)—
When the ground begins to sink, shove your baynick down the chink,
An' you're sure to touch the—
    (*Chorus*) Loo! loo! Lulu! Loot! loot! loot!
        Ow the loot!...

When from 'ouse to 'ouse you're 'unting, you must always work in pairs—
    It 'alves the gain, but safer you will find—
For a single man gets bottled on them twisty-wisty stairs,
    An' a woman comes and clobs 'im from be'ind.
When you've turned 'em inside out, an' it seems beyond a doubt
    As if there weren't enough to dust a flute
    (*Cornet:* Toot! Toot!)
Before you sling your 'ook, at the 'ousetops take a look,
    For it's underneath the tiles they 'ide the loot.
    (*Chorus*) Ow the loot!...

The spirit of the patriotic pirate extended upward from the private soldier to the politician. In *The Illusion of National Character* Hamilton Fyfe instances among many others Edward Dicey, active against the Home Rule movement, 'who not only favoured the use of violence to prevent the Irish from obtaining a quarter of the independence they possess today, but proclaimed the doctrine that any territory his country wanted should be seized by force of arms.'

'In every part of the world where British interests are at stake I am in favour of advancing those interests even at the cost of war. The only qualification I admit is the country we desire to annex or take under our protection should be calculated to confer a tangible advantage upon the British Empire.'

Satiety toned down the harsh accents of overt greed (how high-minded we have since been in condemning them!), but genteeler echoes still occasionally remind us that patriotism is one of those loyalties which do not function *in vacuo*. Admiral Mark Kerr, C.B., M.V.O., straight-forwardly tells us the point of it:

'Patriotism implies the placing of the good of one's country before one's own personal interests. It is an investment that pays a good dividend, which is what many people fail to realize.... Those countries that have more patriotism than others will also lead in the race for world prosperity.

The education of children in patriotism is an absolute necessity, and the need for it should be taught in all schools. This fact has been shown in the history of Japan, which country gives the lead to the world in the unselfishness of its children and people.'[1]

---

[1] From *What is Patriotism?* edited by N. P. Macdonald.

151

Now the education of children in indiscriminating patriotism has without doubt paid good dividends via the Stock Exchange, but in other respects it has proved an inexpressible calamity. Discriminating patriotism can be expressed in loyalty only to those compatriots, places, and qualities which one has known and respected. I, to give a personal illustration, have always been loyal to the British Museum, to Kew Gardens, and to the Georgian architecture in Bath. I have never been loyal to Peacehaven, or the slums of Liverpool, or the vulgar financial opportunism which did not need the assistance of bombs to destroy some of the best buildings in London, or the tasteless negligence which allowed Oxford to be disfigured and disturbed by industry. I incline to be loyal to the Post Office, but I am bitterly disloyal to English middle-class cooking. I have a particular loyalty to St. Paul's Cathedral, but I am unreliable in my view of British jurisprudence. I would defend E. M. Forster, Beatrice Lillie, and Margot Fonteyn, but I would not defend Beverley Nichols, Lord Reith, or Mr Duff Cooper. I ought perhaps to mention that I am also loyal to the Uffizi Gallery, the works of Palladio at Vicenza, the climate of the South of France, to Athens seen from the Acropolis, and to the voices and faces of certain American film stars.

I do not feel that it is unpatriotic to pay homage to a number of different countries at once—or rather to a number of things in them—or to pick and choose the objects and institutions I revere in my own. Nothing (I hope) would induce me to honour the Englishmen who have littered the countryside with hideous advertisements, and the ones who join Sabbatarian societies, or the promoters of football pools, or the financiers who for years before the war ran armament factories to make dividends and bonuses of 30 and 40 and 50 per cent. and talked noble-sounding stuff about patriotism at their Annual General Meetings.

It might be argued that I have only catalogued a selection of my own likes and dislikes, and that, although I am entitled to uphold these in the bosom of my country as in the bosom of my family, loyalty implies submission to a wider standard of judgment; so that, pick and choose as I may in my private capacity, as a citizen I must help to present to the outside world a solid front. That sets up something of a problem. Different people and different parties of people in England think different things even about international affairs. In helping to present this solid front, with whom must I throw in my lot?

With the majority, I may be told; but the opinions of the majority are very difficult to find out and also very changeable, as the Duke of Windsor could tell us, and Mr Neville Chamberlain must have learned. The majority does, in a certain limited sense, however, elect a government, and I suppose it is behind this that I am, with some tens of millions of others, to toe the line. True-blue loyalty thus always serves the useful purpose of making the way smooth for the authorities . . . an excellent purpose if the authorities are good and incapable of error; an unfortunate one if they should be grasping, dishonest, or merely muddle-headed.

For many years before 1914 the most important governments in Europe were all three, and loyalty cost millions of individuals an untold amount of physical and mental anguish besides inspiring them to commit some exceedingly disagreeable deeds. The inhabitants of one country after another were wrought up to present a solid front under the impression that they were Defending Right against Might, or Making the World Safe for Democracy, or winning for Germany her Place in the Sun: and all they were actually doing was reaping the harvest of generations of shady statesmanship and sowing the seeds of the next war. I think it is now self-evident that it would have been a good thing, a gloriously good thing, if reckless and stupid rulers had *not* been able to rely on the obedience of their loyal peoples.

It happens that political memoirs have supplied in my life the need that might otherwise have been filled by horrifying detective stories. The histories of sordid greed and mean manœuvrings, of secret treaties which virtually nullified what had been pledged in open treaties, of financial dodges for taking advantage of the so-called 'backward' races, of cunning methods of playing off one country against another, apparently satisfy some craving similar to that which is generally assuaged with villainies devised by E. Phillips Oppenheim, Dorothy Sayers, or A. E. W. Mason. But the worst of it is, the statesmen were not villains, nothing so obvious and so comparatively easy to cope with. The appalling transactions in question were carried out by diplomats who were the flower of gentility under the instructions of governments consisting for the most part of quite humane and moral persons. Unhappily, humane and moral persons often follow strangely inhuman and unmoral courses when they are acting as governments: they get detached, it seems, from the sense of private responsibility, and besides, there are the nicenesses of diplomatic language to cloud over plans and policies which, stated bluntly, would appeal only to gangsters.

Wonderful disguises of terminology made nastiness seem noble and grand, and the rulers knew they could count on astutely nourished loyalty even when they were visibly incompetent and, moreover, had been elected without a pretence of popular suffrage. In some countries, like Russia, there was no semblance of democracy; in others, like France and most of the British Empire, the system of representation was incomplete and excluded whole immense sections of the populace [1]—all females, for instance, or all natives. There were everywhere privileged classes and powerful vested interests, and the people were ignorant and fed with propaganda. Surely their inexacting fidelity was a great disaster for the world! The statesmen knew, consciously or unconsciously, that

[1] In any case, the ambassadors and other emissaries who help to shape and work out foreign policy are seldom known to the public, and almost never subject to election.

they were dealing with masses who had been intensively trained to regard narrow national loyalism and its corollary, obedience, as a resplendent virtue; they knew it was not necessary to present a full explanation, a just, sensible, and sufficient cause, for there was a tradition that 'your country's cause' must always be right; and they knew, too, that they would not be called upon to answer for mistakes, because there was another tradition that it was in itself a beautiful thing to be sacrificed for your country.

'By school and university, by church and press, by cinema and politics, the same nationalist education, whose shades only vary in the different countries according to cultural traditions and secondary politico-economic conditions, is drummed into the youth and working-classes. As soon as any tension arises in the relations between one country and another, all powers available are brought into play to encourage the masses to sacrifice themselves blindly for the national defence: *dulce et decorum est pro patria mori !*' [1]

It is sweet and seemly to die for one's country. . . . The Horatian tag is constantly quoted, as many have pointed out, without inclusion of the lines which follow, 'Mors et fugacem persequitur virum,' etc., which is to say that, as death does not spare the fugitive, one had better face it boldly, being once on the battle-field. In an earlier ode, Horace admits that he himself had preferred the fugitive's risk and, at the rout of Philippi, after 'dishonourably' dropping his shield, had taken flight; thus keeping himself intact to produce the famous *dulce et decorum* verses and others more delightful.

(Incidentally, there could hardly be a more perfect example of 'protection by barrier' than the illusion almost universal when dangers of a kind traditionally associated with valour are to be braved, that the issue will be simple Life-or-Death. Though death is spoken of as the supreme sacrifice, and perhaps when we are face to face with it the instinct of self-preservation makes any other fate seem preferable, healthy people are usually convinced that they would rather die than suffer the ugliest and most disabling kinds of injury. Therefore, in times of acute peril, the grimmer possibilities are quietly thrust into the background and the patriot is urged to be willing to die, which is comparatively easy, and encouraged to forget that he may only be disfigured, crippled, or left with a permanently damaged nervous system. Indeed, he hardly needs encouraging, so eagerly does the mind exclude what it does not wish to harbour.) [2]

[1] From *The Conquest of Violence* by Bartholomew de Ligt.

[2] The chances of being seriously injured in an air raid are about three times greater than the chances of being killed outright, yet the I-can-but-die tone is still commonly taken by those who remain in dangerous areas. A parallel idealization exalts the soldier as one ready to die for his country, which, of course, can only benefit—if it benefits at all—by his killing for it.

One cannot but conclude that leaders might be inclined to act more prudently if they were doubtful whether they could unite the people, whether their slogans would evoke any emotion, whether their treacly euphemisms would not begin to provoke nausea. But now, as in 1914, when flags are brandished at us, and words of power intoned, critical judgment is regarded as almost a shameful thing and the spirit of sense-less acquiescence is exalted. Here is an extract from a speech made by Sir William Young Darling, District Commissioner for South-Eastern Scotland,[1] appealing—three days before a sudden Cabinet shuffle—for perfect trust in the leadership of Britain's war effort. 'The needs of the moment,' he said, 'were discipline by the civilian population and readiness to accept and obey orders. If criticism reached a serious stage, the responsible Government would also reach a stage when it would become timorous about taking action. *War was a business of 99 per cent. of blunder and confusion. If the people of this country, at every blunder, every misfortune, were going to raise criticism, they wholly misunderstood the nature of war.*'

This plea for loyal tolerance of unlimited folly and error wakes echoes of many wars lost or prolonged or madly undertaken. Mr Vulliamy's grim history of the Crimea alone contains enough illustrations to make criticism of every public policy seem a duty. Before the advent of that critical and (some thought) carping spirit, Florence Nightingale, hospitals from which only a few emerged alive were loyally described by Sir Strafford Canning as having no defects: he suggested that the money collected in England for the wounded should be spent on building a Protestant church in Constantinople. The head of the medical department wrote to the principal Medical Officer, Dr Hall, and asked him, almost in so many words, to prove his loyalty to it (the Department) by sending him every kind of information likely to establish a character for it which would silence the tiresome enquirers who complained about the death-rate. Dr Hall was knighted. Under his administration 13,568 more men died in hospital than were killed in action.[2]

A thousand equally incompetent officials were protected by the patriotic nature of their services from any of the tests of efficiency which would have been applied to factory foremen, or civilian doctors, account-ants, and lawyers, and the whole war was the upshot of almost un-believable ineptitude. Hardly anyone now knows how we came to fight it. Hardly anyone later will be able to unravel the imbroglio of 1914. The various human herds rallied, as they had been taught was proper, to flags and proud phrases and pictures of kings in uniform.

[1] Reported in the *News Chronicle*, October 2nd, 1940.
[2] Dr Hall disapproved of anaesthetics. He said: 'The smart use of the knife is a powerful stimulant, and it is much better to hear a man bawl lustily than to see him sink silently to the grave.' He failed to observe that his patients were doing both. His outlook has every-thing in common with that of certain government officials and publicists of our own time who have talked as if bombing were a tonic for the populace.

All that was necessary was to adjust the tempo and the pitch of the propaganda.

But it is difficult, some readers may protest, to convey full explanations to large masses of uneducated and half-educated people. If you want anything done, you must reduce the situation to a simple formula or two.

And so we touch the very spring of our worst miseries. The wider the field of operations, the more complex will be the questions involved, and yet the more they must be simplified to arouse a response from the constantly enlarging masses. Moreover, the spheres of sentimental attachment are continually extended. Once a Welshman had only to be faithful to Wales: now he must be ready to offer himself up for whatever the statesmen in power may consider to be the interests of England, Scotland, and possibly Ireland, not to speak of Afghanistan, Tanganyika, Tasmania, and British Honduras, and also, owing to alliances, Cochin-China, Senegal, Sumatra, and the Philippines.

Nothing could be more ironical than that the identification of interests which should increase the well-being of mankind turns out so detrimental to it. The men who have succeeded in uniting small kingdoms and been hailed as benefactors were sometimes actuated by genuinely noble motives, but mass-imbecility is so enormous that on balance the evil consequences have far outweighed the good. The wars between petty states were less terrible than the wars between great ones. Germany divided into Bavaria, Wurtembourg, Coburg, Brunswick, and so on, was not afflicted with the furious ambition that drove a united Germany on to the cataclysms of the twentieth century. And Italy certainly appears to have managed rather more pleasantly before Garibaldi.[1] The abolition of frontiers which was meant to bring peace only augmented sentiments of racialism or nationalism and promoted bigger wars.

Frontiers must be abolished—that is what most persons likely to be reading such a book as this will take for granted—but only because they are a dangerous nuisance, not for the aggrandizement of the men who perform the act of abolishing, not to enable feeble creatures to compensate themselves for weakness and deficiency by imagining themselves part-owners of a great territory, not to enlarge the realm of undiscriminating loyalty. In the beginning it was only, I assume, the family that could make claims on one's allegiance; then the tribe, then the little nation, then the great nation, next the empire. If such expansions amplified the field of sympathy, the gain to humanity would obviously

[1] That perfect absence of provincial flatness which one has noticed gratefully in cities like Venice, Florence, and Milan is due, I think, to their having been, until very recently, capitals in their own right. The dreariness of the English provinces is possibly because London has stood as the one unchallenged capital so long. And now Edinburgh has declined from its pre-Union integrity and is getting the atmosphere of a secondary place; and so no doubt will Florence and Venice. I have stood on some balcony in Verona where Garibaldi told the crowd that he brought them 'Rome or Death'—no choice at all as it turned out.

be immense, but since the strength derived from union is taken to mean brute strength, the casting down of petty national barriers is succeeded only by the formation of 'solid fronts.'

We should be educated to hate solid fronts and despise them, to know that they cannot exist where taste and reason and intelligence are valued, and that loyalty is to be deplored, not admired, unless it is based on something better than a combination of vanity, self-interest, timidity, and mental laziness—the four prime factors of the herd instinct. Indeed, no loyalty can be commendable but that which grows naturally out of affection and the sense of honour and the sense of fitness.

I cannot supply infallible referents for those terms, but I think it will be apparent to one who has read thus far that the sense of honour here intended is rational and can therefore only be expressed in honourable actions. It has nothing to do with the self-glorifying, duel-fighting, chastity-obsessed code which was called honour by our ancestors and still sometimes passes for such in the law courts. It could not, in fact, be reduced to any code at all, because it must be free to adjust itself to the variations of circumstance which can so profoundly modify problems of right and wrong.

Each of us must judge for himself from the strength of his affection how he can best uphold something he loves, and the sense of fitness—if he allows it to function—will tell him whether the instruments within his reach are honourable or otherwise. There is no one outside ourselves who can do that. But the right kind of training in youth would aim at giving us the adroitness to pick our own way through private and public muddles, and would at least try to make us impervious to catchwords and scornful of the primitive idolatries by which 'our country' is held in veneration as the object of our highest earthly devotion while the human beings who comprise it are to be ready to immolate themselves in millions. Certainly there would be no attempt to inculcate loyalties requiring suspension of judgment for their application. Not that we would be excused from honouring our obligations, but it would be an axiom that we can only contract obligations through our own agency. We have a duty, for instance, to be loyal to our children because it was through our wish, or fault, or folly, that they exist; but we have not, automatically, any duty to the geographical territory in which we happen to be born, though it is evident that through affection, interest, or a form of altruism, we might be willing to undertake responsibilities, and in that case we should be expected to fulfil them.

Patriotism would not be encouraged to become a nuisance. Plainly we owe it to our neighbours to conduct ourselves decently towards them, but that duty is the perfectly reasonable non-sentimental one of courtesy and kindliness and does not exact any suppression of the critical faculties. We owe as much as this to all neighbours wherever we might find ourselves, and the responsibility laid on us is no higher in the case of our own country than any other, though the *opportunities* are likely to be wider.

All the training of all the psychologists and philosophers in being would probably not redeem us from an inclination to exalt first and foremost the things that belong to ourselves, but if we were taught to know this emotion for what it is, the results need not be very disastrous. We should then be ready to say: 'This adherence to my own real or abstract possessions depends on a mixture of self-importance, conservatism, and so forth, and is a normal feeling but not in the least a noble one, and I must be on my guard in case it should lead me to do any injustice to the belongings and the feelings of other people.' With such precautions loyalty would, even at its silliest, be fairly innocuous.

Without them it is liable to develop strange connotations. A few years ago there was a serious upheaval at Dartmoor. A number of the convicts rebelled against their living conditions and attacked the warders; others refused to join the mutiny and came to the warders' assistance. These prisoners were described in some of the newspapers, and, I believe, by counsel, as having been loyal to the prison.

When the Home Guard was first formed, as the Local Defence Volunteers, many stories of feverish zeal were told in the press. For example: 'A man in the Doncaster area, too old to join . . . unslung his ancient "blunderbuss" from its resting-place on the wall and offered it instead. From the condition of the old "Carron" . . . the result of a shot might be infinitely more harmful to the shooter than his intended victim.' This, commented the *Yorkshire Evening News* [1] with unconscious irony, was typical of the spirit in which Doncaster was rallying to the call.

I do not know which is more objectionable—flattering the loyalty of the slave or encouraging the loyalty of the fool.

The press, of course, makes it its special business to do both, and the National Person, once typified by John Bull, has now become that miserable nonentity, the Little Man, the Plain Man, John Citizen, Mr Everyman, the Man-in-the-Street. John Bull, whose occasional appearance in cartoons is now a mere sentimental anachronism (presented in the same spirit which gives us Ye Olde Englyshe Gyfte Shoppe and Ye Tudor Lounge), might have been overfed and somewhat arrogant, but he was supposed to boast a stolid common sense, an independence, a resoluteness in defying unjust authority which could not but command respect. The Little Man is notable chiefly for his submissiveness, the way he falls into line, the way he can 'take' whatever burden is thrust upon him.

The reason for the changing fashion in imagery is palpable. John Bull was created a hero when those in power needed the support chiefly of squires and farmers, who were bluffed into believing they resembled this sturdy patriot and doing as they were told he would do. And out of

[1] On May 18th, 1940.

deference for tradition he was retained as a popular symbol long after he had ceased to be even speciously representative. Today the potentates must get and keep the approval of immense classes which formerly had no political rights and no means of uniting to make any demands. These millions have been taught to read; they buy advertised goods, they vote for advertised men; they have become worth humouring. The press, acting on behalf of the vested interests concerned, has evolved a complete technique of humouring them. The methods may be studied in Denys Thompson's useful little book, *Between the Lines* or How to Read a Newspaper.

Dull and insignificant readers everywhere, labouring all their lives under a multitude of disadvantages, are subtly made to feel that to be dull and insignificant is a merit, that Little Men who will do whatever they are ordered—with the right to grumble slightly as a harmless safety-valve—are the salt of the earth. A hundred clever lines of humbug are exploited to carry the message that it's absolutely grand to be one of the ordinary folk just going unassumingly about their daily jobs, not knowing anything much, not analysing anything very deeply, but somehow capable nevertheless of exercising an acute judgment whenever it is required of them.

It is the modern version of being content with that station in life to which it has pleased God to call us: but the press has taken the place of the Church as the drover of the flocks, and its method is not to exhort and command, but to coax, to cajole, to suggest that the status of a sheep is wonderful. 'TAKE A BOW HERE, JOHN CITIZEN,' says an approving headline when a Ministry of Information speaker in Bradford tells a meeting that 'plain John Citizen is the finest person in the world,' a statement which has no meaning at all unless it means that a citizen who is 'plain'—i.e. undistinguished—is automatically finer than a citizen who has some claim to attention. Such utterances are always well received, for the bulk of an audience will usually be plain rather than colourful, while distinguished persons are apt to feel indulgent towards the rank and file plodding thanklessly on so far behind them, and even to sentimentalize about their virtues. The cult of the Little Man has never wanted for encouragement from the big men.

An example of this idealizing tendency is the long-standing fashion among critics who both serve and direct popular taste to ascribe the appeal of that extremely sympathetic actor, Charlie Chaplin, to his presenting us with an incarnation of the Little Man in all his pathos and lovable absurdity—an identification almost sure to please both nondescript little men themselves and those who pay them verbal homage. But a cool glance at the picaresque material with which Chaplin always works and the striking eccentricity of his handling will surely demonstrate that the claim is far-fetched. His universality depends on something greater than typifying mediocrity. In any case, the mediocre have no interest in seeing themselves typified, but have always sought entertainment in the bizarre, the romantic, the sensational.[1] That is why the wider the circulation of a newspaper, the more it will give prominence to news of murderers, millionaires, adventurers, society leaders, royal personages. It may flatter Mr Everyman but it does not feature him, except in a very limited sense.

It is interesting, incidentally, to see that even the physical deficiencies of that ignoble being receive an implied compliment. The Little Man, whether he figures in comic strips or in patriotic cartoons, is depicted as really undersized and unquestionably Plain. The *Sunday Chronicle*, when conscription was new, ran a series of illustrated jokes about a militiaman and his girl friend, intended evidently to help in popularizing general military service. 'He' was a stunted youth of repulsive appearance, while 'she' was portrayed as comparatively attractive and standing head and shoulders taller, which, in pre-Little-Man days, was regarded as an unsuitable grouping. (Though in a sense a tribute to the superior charms of women—for both were meant to be typical—it was also a dismal reminder of their lower status, since it seemed that the unprepossessing young man was thought quite fittingly paired off with a girl who completely outclassed him : and that, of course, was true to life.)

It is questionable whether the practice, in editorial and 'feature' columns, of making mentally and physically inferior people feel satisfied with themselves as they are is more, or less, pernicious than the entirely different technique used in preparing advertising copy. Here the principle is to 'glamourize' a few conventional types—dear old granny, mother and child, the young bride, the enamoured sweethearts, etc.—and persuade members of the public that by eating this, by smoking that, by wearing the other, they will be entering into the same class as these desirable people. Perhaps on the whole it is better to encourage aspiration, even to meretricious standards, than to glorify littleness.

A wartime issue of the *Sunday Pictorial* [2] gave nearly a page of space to a poem *Just An Englishman* . . . by Ernest Collyer. 'This,' it announced, 'is a poem you will read and admire.' It was illustrated by the silhouette of a soldier holding his rifle with bayonet fixed, and also by an immense

[1] Roger Dataller has written a Nelson Discussion Book, *The Plain Man and the Novel*, purporting to show the outlook of that dreary person, whom he represents as thinking : 'Why not let up for a while on glamour girls and playboys of Mayfair and give the more "ordinary" people a chance?' Nothing could be further from the truth of commonplace taste, as the author himself shows in his succeeding chapters. Ordinary characters in fiction are only acceptable when they are found in extraordinary circumstances. Books about ordinary people doing ordinary things, like R. C. Sherriff's *Fortnight in September*, are found very dull by dull readers. I remember the surprised indignation of some servants who had obeyed a recommendation to see Emil Jannings in his finest film, *The Last Laugh*, and had discovered that it was only a tame story about a hall porter. The equivalents of glamour girls and Mayfair playboys, under whatever modish name—coquette, belle, beau, rake, fashionable philanderer—have always been an alluring subject to the unprivileged, and there is no reason to suppose that psychology has suddenly changed or will do so.

[2] April 21st, 1940.

cannon and some clouds. It began with the statement that 'No-one knows but a no-one, what a no-one has to be, No-one cares what a no-one knows, for no-one knows—but he,' and after more to this effect went on :

> Troubles cling to a no-one ;
> Sorrows check his pride,
> Could anyone know but a no-one
> What goes on inside ?

The tone then changes from a whine to a snarl :

> But here is a text from a no-one—
> A text that is plain to see—
> It's the no-ones that make the some-ones,
> Else the some-ones could never be !

And after a further admonition we learn :

> It's the no-ones who mould tomorrow's world,
> By the sweat from an unknown brow,
> England depends on unknown hands—
> Would you call them no-ones now ?

Self-glorification is commonly taught to wear the guise of self-abnegation during wars, though not always as inanely as this. I offer it as a tragi-comic little pendant to the grandiloquent assurances of civic leaders, the exhortations of industrialists, and the blandishments of leader writers, all answering much the same purpose as the barkings and manœuvrings of a shepherd's dog.

> Britain has had enough of this modern conception of feminism. It
> has probably done more to cause the present war than any other factor.
> Ever since the last war feminine influence has weakened our manhood,
> created pacifism, opposed conscription, usurped men in industry, and
> taken the guts out of the British Parliamentary system.
>
> Letter signed 'Realist!', *News Chronicle*, May 17th, 1940.

OUR survey of irrational territories cannot pretend to even a sketchy
comprehensiveness until we have taken the measure of unreason
between the sexes. In tracing my own rough chart of this well-trodden
ground it may seem that I lose sight of my purpose of displaying sentimentality. I am assuming, however, that the reader by this time will be
very well able to distinguish the elements for himself, and they will
seldom be absent from the various credos which are now to be
considered.

I have spoken of our having public and private attitudes. Excepting
perhaps religion, there is nothing in which the difference between these
attitudes is likely to be so marked as in what men feel and what they
profess to feel towards women, and nothing, again excepting religion,
in which the effects of the duality have been more unhappy. A concrete
illustration will give us our starting-point. Let us guess something of the
state of mind of a man who is listening to an after-dinner speaker, a
pattern of eloquence in the mayoral style, propose the toast of The Ladies.
He hears with facile responsiveness the honeyed clichés—'lovely woman
. . . a delightful subject . . . indebted to her for all that is comforting
and gracious . . . the charms and attractions of the opposite sex . . .
mother and wife, the most beautiful words in the language. . . .' He
exclaims 'Hear, hear!' and glows warmly with vague reverence. He
knows that all women are not lovely, that all do not inspire gallantry,
and that his own mother and wife, to name no others, are far from
perfect as characters. He can see that the lady on his left is a scraggy
creature whose charms and attractions have never been up to much, and
the lady on his right reminds him painfully of an aunt-by-marriage who
cheated at Bridge and was something of a family skeleton. He would be
aware, if he were to think about it, that he could not apply any of the
speaker's compliments to Mrs A——, that vigorous and sarcastic woman
who deliberately made him look small at the Committee meeting, or
Miss B——, the noisy, fast young person who is having such a bad
influence on his niece, or Mrs C——, the dirty and slovenly charwoman
who stole the bottle of whisky. Precisely where and who the captivating
ladies are whose praises are being sung so unctuously he would be at a

loss to say; nevertheless it gives him a sense of well-doing to show that he approves the wholesale commendation.

And, I may be asked, what harm in that? The harm is this, that although his personal relations with women are hardly affected at all by his public attitude towards them, his non-personal relations with them—his political and professional relations—may be affected very radically indeed. 'The Ladies-God-bless-'em' were the most serious obstacle that was ever opposed to the emancipation of women. The Ladies—those lovable grown-up children, fascinating but fickle, soft and clinging and full of pretty wiles, endlessly chattering and running up dress bills and daintily maligning one another, yet so useful in the home, so comforting in cases of pain and anguish—what could they want with having money of their own and being educated and mixing themselves in the gross affairs of the world? Ray Strachey, in her admirable history of the Women's Movement (*The Cause*), sums up thus the professed reaction of men towards the mid-Victorian struggle for female education:

'Not that they feared the competition of women; far from it. What they feared was the effect upon women of the rough jostling with men in the intellectual world. They feared that it would for ever destroy that special and peculiar bloom which they regarded as women's greatest charm, and take away that valuable, intangible "superiority" of women which they now appeared so unaccountably to be disregarding. Women were, and must be, kept as creatures apart, sheltered from the harsher forms of arithmetic, as from the discoveries of medical science, and not allowed to contaminate themselves, even though they wished to do so. They might indeed have a better education than they had hitherto been allowed; it would keep them happy, and would doubtless do them good. But it must stop short of being quite the real thing, for that would be dangerous and unsexing.'

In the affairs of women, the reckoning of a hundred years has shown a bold and wonderful advance towards sanity, but we are still liable to stumble against débris left over from the Victorian and Edwardian battle-grounds. It is worth while to glance at that débris and consider its origin.

Whatever unrecognized sexual motives and jealous desire for monopoly may have been the true mainspring of anti-feminism, the motives *alleged* were until lately nearly always religious. God had set the limits of feminine activity, and to wish to extend them was profane. In an early Debate on Women's Suffrage (1870) a Member rose and remarked, without, as far as we know, exciting any audible amusement: 'Man in the beginning was ordained to rule over woman, and this is an Eternal decree which we have no right and no power to alter.' Women who sought to curry favour with men, or who were obsessed with an implanted masochism, fully concurred in the doctrine of God-ordained dependence. Hannah More had looked upon the mere mention of women's rights as wickedness:

'... Among the innovations of this innovating period the imposing term of *rights* has been produced to sanctify the claims of our female pretenders, with a view not only to rekindle in the minds of women a presumptuous vanity dishonourable to their sex, but ... to excite in their hearts an impious discontent with the post which God has assigned to them in the world.'

That 'post' was described very knowingly by various contemporary or near-contemporary authorities. For example, an anonymous magazine writer:

'The peculiar province of Woman is to tend with patient assiduity around the bed of sickness; to watch the feeble steps of infancy; to communicate to the young the elements of knowledge, and bless with their smiles those of their friends who are declining in the vale of tears.'[1]

A now forgotten divine named Fordyce took a slightly less depressing view, but was very much opposed to rights:

'Women were manifestly intended to be the mothers and formers of a rational and immortal offspring; to be a kind of softer companions, who, by nameless delightful sympathies and endearments, might improve our pleasures and soothe our pains; to lighten the load of domestic cares, and by that means leave us more at leisure for rougher labours and severer studies; and finally, to spread a certain grace and embellishment over human life. To wish to degrade them from so honourable a station indicates a mixture of ignorance, grossness, and barbarity.'

Washington Irving was equally certain that he knew the intentions of the Almighty:

'... It is beautifully ordered by Providence, that woman, who is the mere dependent and ornament of man in his happier hours, should be his stay and solace when smitten with sudden calamity; winding herself into the rugged recesses of his nature, tenderly supporting the drooping head, and binding up the broken heart.'

In 1857 the *Saturday Review*, troubled by women's insistence upon a right to earn their living if they did not marry, asked why they were not satisfied to become domestic servants, since these 'fulfil both essentials of woman's being; they are supported by and they minister to the comfort of men. . . . Nature has not provided one too many.'

The tussle over the Divorce Bill, also in the Fifties (the Bill which

[1] Quoted in Dr C. Willett Cunnington's *Feminine Attitudes in the Nineteenth Century*.

enabled women for the first time to seek dissolution of marriage, though under great disadvantages as compared with men), produced another spate of homiletic utterances on the duty decreed in Heaven for women. Ray Strachey quotes from a pamphlet discrediting the Bill: 'Some loose notions have been thrown out of women's intellectual equality with men and of their consequently equal right to all the advantages of society . . . these are speculative, extravagant, and almost unnatural opinions.'

The specifically feminine work of instructing the young and minister-ing to the afflicted was to be performed intuitively. No training, no technical qualifications, were allowed to be necessary for it, and all attempts to acquire a scientific groundwork were discountenanced. Even Frederick Maurice, who, as one of the founders of Queen's College, had been a courageous pioneer of female education, felt obliged to record his disapproval when Miss Blackwell won notoriety by coming from America with a medical degree. 'The more pains we men take to call forth and employ the faculties which belong characteristically to each sex,' he said, addressing an audience of lady students, 'the less it will be intruding upon the province which, not the conventions of the world, but the will of God, has assigned to the other.' [1]

With the decline of authoritarian religion from about the Seventies onward, arguments based upon the wishes of God confided to the Clergy began to sound somewhat unconvincing, and in their place were advanced biological and what we should now call psychological reasons for keeping women in subjection. It was very damaging to the cause of Women's Suffrage when, in 1889, a group of eminent ladies, including Mrs Humphry Ward and Mrs Sidney Webb, who had both supported women's demand for education, signed 'a solemn protest' to the effect that: 'We believe the emancipating process has now reached the limits fixed by the physical constitution of women. . . .'

I have touched obliquely in a later chapter on the supposed biological disabilities. The psychological hinge upon the long-standing conviction that women, much more than men, are enslaved by the need for affection and are consequently incapable of attaining the detachment requisite for dealing with large-scale extra-domestic affairs. In the words of Wash-ington Irving—words which have been paralleled in many writings of more recent date and greater scientific pretensions:

'Man is the creature of interest and ambition. His nature leads him forth into the struggle and bustle of the world. Love is but the em-bellishment of his early life, or a song piped in the intervals of the acts. He seeks for fame, for fortune, for a space in the world's thought, and dominion over his fellow-men. But a woman's whole life is the history

---

[1] It is only fair to mention that Maurice changed his views later, and supported the agitation to admit women to the medical profession.

of the affections. The heart is her world: it is there her ambition strives for empire: it is there her avarice seeks for hidden treasures. She sends forth her sympathies on adventure; she embarks her soul in the traffick of affection; and if shipwrecked her case is hopeless— for it is a bankruptcy of the heart.'

And in another passage by the same author: 'Her lot is to be wooed and won; and if unhappy in her love, her heart is like some fortress that has been captured, and sacked and abandoned, and left desolate.' The fickleness gaily attributed to 'the Ladies' is oddly at variance with the unfailing constancy which belongs only to 'Woman'—'in her almost an unavoidable virtue,' as one connoisseur has expressed it—but idealizers never find it troublesome to hold several opinions separately which, taken together, make nonsense.

It was always considered that a woman's propensity to become the victim of her own devotion—a propensity in itself unctuously exaggerated by men—was inborn and ineradicable, and few seem to have realized that, given a different upbringing and a wider horizon, females might not prove much more liable than males to suffer from lifelong emotional derangements. Everyone saw that man's social freedom was the reason for his comparative emotional freedom ('Man may range the Court, Camp, Church, the Vessel, and the Mart' . . . and so forth), but it was revolutionary to perceive that emancipation might provide a similar release for women. The people who believed that the children of the lower orders went to work at six years old because they chose to,[1] found no difficulty in persuading themselves that woman was kept in subjection because subjection was her natural element.

'Her temperament,' said one optimistic apologist,[2] '*must* be one which can be *satisfied with sameness*, else there would be no fitness between the being and its circumstances.'

Florence Nightingale, in the impassioned protest written before she found a stern peace of mind in the Crimea,[3] expressed bitterly her scorn for that complacency which could suppose all circumstances apt for those who endured them:

'Why have women passion, intellect, moral activity—these three— and a place in society where no one of the three can be exercised? Men say that God punishes for complaining. No, but men are angry with misery. They are irritated with women for not being happy. . . .'

The family, she cries angrily, is 'too narrow a field for the development

---

[1] Dr Cunnington quotes this typical opinion from a ladies' magazine in 1843: 'The system of *levelling* which is now so much the rage must in the end overturn the whole state of society. . . . Because the children and labourers in coal-mines endure many hardships (of their own choosing, as they are not compelled to that employment), does that render it a crime for a nobleman who owns a colliery to give a fancy-ball?'

[2] An anonymous contributor to *Fragments on Women*, c. 1830.

[3] *Cassandra*, published posthumously.

of an immortal spirit.' And 'people rail against men for choosing a woman "for her face"—why, what else do they see?' Novels, she thought, were popular with women because the heroines were so often dowered with independence—'alone in the world'—which gave them a potent fascination for readers who had been brought up on the doctrine, perpetually reiterated, that 'in whatever situation in life a woman is placed, from her cradle to her grave, a spirit of obedience and submission, pliability of temper, and humility of mind are required from her.' [1]

Now the notions about female limitations which Florence Nightingale fought against and did so much to overthrow are a long way from being demolished. Though the view of woman as a creature framed exclusively for domesticity is no longer extant, the complementary view, that she has by nature a much greater hunger for affection than men, a more insistent kind of amatory appetite, and a proneness to cherish fixations, remains in very general acceptance. Periodicals and newspaper columns for feminine consumption are edited on the time-honoured principle that the one sex must for ever be struggling to master the art of pleasing though affecting to be passive while the other sits back, sultanwise, to be amused or bored, though affecting to be active. The Ladies, as portrayed above, have been supplanted in certain aspects of our ritual belief only by The Women—The Women of Clare Boothe's successful comedy, as dependent as their grandmothers but more spirited, predatory as well as parasitic.

There are also other aspects of being female very ingeniously brought to the fore in wartime, when we are deluged with cant about the comradeship of splendid girls standing shoulder to shoulder with their menfolk; but brave and fine as it sounds, it amounts to little more than a new way of stating the proposition that the true woman is the faithful supporter of man in all his enterprises, and especially loyal when those enterprises are dangerous. In point of fact, the women's armies are chiefly used to do dull and menial jobs for the men's armies. A reputed feminist, Miss Eleanor F. Rathbone, has stated in print that we must no longer talk of women's rights—'except one of them: the right of women to give their lives for their country,' and that 'the lives of a dozen average women just now are worth less to the country than one efficient soldier or male key worker and so should be proportionately more freely risked.' [2] So much for equality.

The promoters of public entertainment, who are usually male, have a firm conviction that women will not take pleasure in any play or film unless it abounds in 'love interest.' The result is that a sexual 'angle' is constantly given to stories where it is totally inappropriate, with no effect as far as I can see but to exasperate all but the most uncritical people of both sexes. How often have I heard women, even those for

[1] The last quotation is from the preface to *The Young Lady's Book*, 1829.
[2] From an article in the *New Statesman*, July 1940.

whose palates in particular this sickly fare is concocted, complain with disgust about a syrupy love story thrust into some context where it is fatuously misplaced! Who that can be interested in the adventures of African explorers at all needs to believe, to get full entertainment value, that Stanley persisted in his search for Livingstone because he was urged on by the memory of a sweet young girl who had attracted him at Zanzibar? Who can find the history of the Suez Canal more engrossing because Lesseps is depicted as carrying out the scheme for love of a lady? Does anyone, normally incapable of appreciating Bell's career as an inventor, grow suddenly attentive when he is shown as an ardent lover and husband acting under the influence of a pretty wife?

When one asks executives of the film industry why a love story will be dragged in to delay the action of wholly masculine adventure tales, one is invariably told that it is done for the sake of 'the women,' whose psychology exacts romantic treatments of every subject. My own observation is that these pictures frequently fall between two stools, giving little satisfaction to anyone, or succeeding, if they do succeed, *in spite* of the very features which are believed to make them popular. If it be argued that the directors of screen and stage enterprises must know their own business best, I can only reply that, as most of them have failures which outnumber their triumphs, it would appear to be open to question. It is certain, in any case, that many conventions meet with tolerance, not because they gratify current taste, but because they are well established and an alternative is seldom offered.

No doubt the generalizations which produce these affronts to our intelligence contained a good measure of truth when the sphere of women was the narrowest possible and they hung slavishly on the favour of men for every privilege. No doubt they contain a little truth today, chiefly apparent in women who have been bred up to the old ideas and who have not enjoyed the full fruits of our (as yet very incomplete) equality of opportunity. In others there is, I think, merely a diminishing residue of the traditional tendencies, often more feigned than real. That one sex consists of yearning, clinging, and devoted creatures is a conception flattering to the other and therefore not readily to be relinquished by them: many women, to give men what they are said to want, pretend to feminine weaknesses from which they secretly derive amusement. Men likewise are known to emphasize their so-called masculine traits in the presence of women, sometimes assuming pugnacity, sexual vigour, and the will to dominate beyond the degree that comes naturally to them.

Even comparatively dispassionate critics will propound doctrines about women that are primarily wishful. Thus Dr Renier declares with airy assurance:

'Whatever one school of anthropologists may tell us about the private life of anthropoid apes, man is polygamous, woman mono-gamous. This is in accordance with the scheme of Nature. The male can fructify many wombs, while the female is slowly fulfilling the laborious process of gestation and parturition for which she needed the assistance of only one male. Messalinas are exceptions.[1] A woman needs only one partner, and even her love for him is soon eclipsed by that which is inspired by her offspring. Mated English-women are therefore as a rule contented.'

I am aware that it is only my word against Dr Renier's, but, besides being female myself, I have enjoyed the intimate confidence of what is probably an uncommonly large number of women in circumstances very propitious for candour, and I have excellent reasons for believing that the theory outlined above is a work of hopeful masculine imagination. It is my experience that, whatever the 'scheme of Nature' may be—my sex has never been foremost in professing to understand the designs of abstract entities—if it includes any demand for monogamous content-ment on the part of women, it is a scheme which has gone agley. Women, scarcely less than men (and that little only a heritage of long-standing repressions), seek the stimulus of novelty in sexual relationships and seem to lose heart and purpose unless their vanity is buttressed from time to time by new admiration.

When female chastity was the most belauded of the virtues and severe social penalties attached to the loss of it, women were compelled to disguise their polygamous hankerings, and the majority probably suc-ceeded in concealing even from themselves the cause of the unrest which they often diverted into highly regrettable channels.[2] So strong indeed was the taboo upon corporal infidelity that it gave rise to a taboo upon pleasure. The amorous and insatiable nymphs who had inspired Restora-tion poetry were looked upon as a disreputable crew in the eighteenth century, and by the beginning of the nineteenth, erotic desire was thought wholly impossible in a respectable member of the softer sex. 'It was her duty, as a wife,' says Dr Cunnington,[3] 'to love her husband, but it was her duty as a lady to do so without passion. . . . Contemporary medical works state that the existence of such feelings in a woman was to be regarded as abnormal.' Miss Stella Browne instances Acton, one of the leaders of British medicine, who wrote that to attribute sexual feelings to ladies was 'a vile aspersion,' and termed them lascivious

[1] The implied suggestion that any woman not monogamous is a Messalina is one more example of that excessive language which is habitually used to present uncertain arguments.

[2] In Chapter XI will be found a mention of the ritual whipping of children which en-grossed numerous correspondents of *The Englishwoman's Domestic Magazine* and other feminine periodicals of the Victorian era. It hardly needs psycho-analysis to suggest that the incompleteness of their sexual lives had warped the character of these mothers of large families.

[3] *Feminine Attitudes in the Nineteenth Century.*

if they experienced sexual desire 'even in the embrace of their husbands.'

One of the most commendable discoveries of the twentieth century is that sharp lines of demarcation between masculine and feminine characteristics are as artificial and almost as fruitful of evil as the lines which divide territories on maps. Among the many differences which surely prove, on investigation, to be legendary are these contrasting rôles assigned to male and female passion, that of men being urgent, direct, and rapidly burned out, that of women more diffused, more pervasive, and very much more adhesive. I am inclined to deny even the plausible hypothesis—approved by Dr Renier and so many others— that women readily deflect to children the love which does not meet with adequate response from husbands. That such a transference some-times does take place is obvious, but that it would be an acceptable solution to one who had opportunities of further sexual fulfilment is quite out of keeping with what I have seen and known of womankind.

There is, I fancy, a good deal of exaggeration about the extent to which the maternal function can be turned into a compensation and a substitute for other enjoyments. Men try to have it both ways, first pleasing them-selves with the fantasy of arousing the most dog-like fidelity in beings to whose happiness they are indispensably necessary, then excusing their own philanderings by an assumption that these faithful mates can turn to their children for consolation.

Besides the theory of the searchingness and tenacity of female love there are various associated tenets, such as that women, being in keen competition for the attentions of men, have a spontaneous hostility towards each other, that, owing to jealousy and small-mindedness, their friendships are precarious, that they are disposed to reserve all their charm for the opposite sex, and so forth. There was perhaps a time when these ancient articles of faith had more truth in them than could coolly and fairly be maintained today, but I suspect that they have always been largely fictitious. I am not in the least concerned to whitewash women, who have often subscribed to these fables themselves and helped to keep them in circulation—being prone, like men, to take the correctness of established reputations, including their own, for granted: my purpose is solely to encourage a re-assessment of as many stale and hackneyed beliefs as the reader can bring himself to examine.

My own researches lead me to the conclusion that the inferior members of *both* sexes are given to jealous depreciation of one another, and that neither sex has the monopoly of the virtues that make friendship durable and social intercourse pleasant.

Differences there certainly must be, psychological as well as physical, but that these have ever been definitively charted and analysed is an igno-rant delusion, and many that are most generally received as self-evident appear to be due to engrafted custom rather than ingrained character.[1] Custom, for example, gives men the initiative in their dealings with women, and there is still a loss of prestige and possibly even of self-respect when a woman betrays her emotions without going through the prescribed postures of being 'wooed and won.' Yet even here we seem to be in a state of transition. In a great many new films the woman who shamelessly pursues the man she desires, once a stock subject for derision, has been a popular heroine, and there is little doubt that film themes influence conduct. In this case it is as well that they should, for the male prerogative of the first advance, which must have been a source of much unhappiness, is pure convention and does not correspond to anything radical in the disposition of either sex. A female human being is not essentially passive, coy, retiring; males are not essentially ardent and dominating.

To balance the privilege of initiative, men shoulder the burden of responsibility. It is a white man's burden—one which the bearers have long seemed resolved to endure in spite of the appeals, protests, and determined ingratitude of the beneficiaries. Our law and social usages are still, in ways more numerous than first appears, framed on the principle that women require masculine countenance and support and are morally as weak in relation to men as children in relation to adults.[2]

In the economic sphere the dogma that the protective breadwinners were of one sex, the protected home-keepers of the other, brought about the dowry system under which the protectors frequently lived on and sometimes squandered away the money of the protected, and the disqualification of a guarded woman, a *feme covert*, from owning even the money she might save or earn; while today it leads to such remarkable exactions as an inferior standard of pay for female labour, the presumption being that men will have dependants, women none. The grievances of women in national services and well-organized industries have often been ventilated, and have perhaps distracted attention from the yet greater inequalities which exist in the obscurer kinds of employment. If I prefer a manservant to a maid, he will not only get a bigger wage but will probably have better outings and shorter hours. If I require a typist or secretary, I shall naturally look for a woman since I know she is likely to be as efficient as a man and that she will take a lower salary. Although in 'big business' men take care to occupy most of the executive posts, it is usual, embarking on small private ventures, to choose for assistants those whom long tradition makes more diligent and less exigent. Thus the financial disadvantage imposed on one sex acts to the detriment of

[1] Even the pre-1914 conclusions, supported by abundant statistics, of such a painstaking piece of research work as Havelock Ellis's *Man and Woman* have grown somewhat obsolete in only a few decades of changing standards. How much more so the many assumptions which never had a scientific basis !
[2] See Appendix 32.

the other, which, with few exceptions, has always failed to see that the low wage rates of women are a perpetual cause of unemployment among men.

These anachronistic practices have a way of injuring those whom they would seemingly benefit. The survival, for instance, of that piece of etiquette which decreed that a man should pay for any entertainment shared with ladies was superficially a favour to them, actually a severe injustice, as it occasioned many embarrassments, placed them under disabilities in making social contacts, and could destroy prospects of intimacy with men perhaps attractive and desirable in every respect but the most extraneous. The rule is moribund but far from extinct. A young man's consciousness that he cannot pay a taxi fare may still stand between him and a new-budding friendship; acquaintance is often only to be pursued by means of invitations which the one party cannot afford, the other is not privileged to extend; and, among conventional people at least, a sense of discomfort generally makes itself felt whenever the accustomed monetary relationship is overturned.

All these nuisances and numberless others which I leave the reader to explore alone are a legacy from times when constantly recurring pregnancies imposed on women a measure of real biological dependence, intensified by their being regarded as property: but a substantial period of freedom from this condition has enabled us to see very clearly that dependency is not, as was formerly believed, an integral part of the feminine psychology, while to be masculine by no means certifies a love of responsibility. Everyone knows families in which the dominant figure, the organizer and planner, is a woman; and if there has seldom been a successful ménage with the wife as sole provider, this may well be because it is hard to sustain good-humouredly a situation the world regards as ignominious.

We have broken down the ridiculous verbalism that once made us suffer any distortion of our true tastes and aspirations rather than be called 'unladylike' or 'unwomanly.' It is to be expected that men will ultimately outgrow their terror of the label 'unmanly' with its misleading suggestion that there are proven standards of absolute maleness, and its implicit condemnation of qualities admittedly excellent in themselves. When this happy state of affairs comes about, men and women will follow their natural bent undeterred by fear of mockery, and our descendants will see without surprise households in which the parts supposed until recently to have been assigned by God or Nature will be effectually reversed.

Not until then will women be able to exercise the one right which has necessarily been withheld from them—the right to put creative work first if they are so inclined, even when they have no place of business but their own homes. Miss Vera Brittain's lamentation on this theme (in *Thrice A Stranger*) must have been echoed by every

reader who, while engaged in non-domestic labour whether for liveli-
hood or love, has tried to breast the never-ebbing tide of minor
domestic exigencies:

'Only those who appreciate the different qualities of work produced
by complete and by partial concentration can ever estimate the extent
to which women's performances suffer from constant small interrup-
tions and petty, time-wasting tasks. The triumphant enquirers who
put their hackneyed question: "Why have we never had a woman
Shakespeare, Michelangelo, Rembrandt, or Beethoven?" need look
no further than the ill-adjusted burdens of the average household for
their answer.[1]

. . . As long as I can remember, I have craved for the privilege—
accepted as a matter of course by the masculine world—of a life
organized to fit the needs of my work, instead of one constantly
requisitioned by miscellaneous external claims to which my work has
perforce to adapt itself. . . .

For all the political feminist triumphs of the past two decades, men
alone remain able to satisfy their biological impulses without partially
ruining their intellectual accomplishments. This sex monopoly of
balanced human development will probably continue until a generation arises with sufficient courage, generosity and sense of justice to
repudiate the prevailing assumption upon which most marriages are
based.'

It is a sorry reflection on human ethics that the self-imposed calamity
of war, rather than a wave of generosity and justice, has so far produced
the occasions for raising the status of women.[2] Before the conflagration
of 1914 nothing aroused more resentment—and that 'nothing' must be
taken almost literally—than any suggestion that a woman of talent should
be free to pursue a career on masculine terms. The ability of the Brontës
to bake puddings or make beds and Jane Austen's unrebellious life in
the bosom of her family were continually adduced as proof that it was
right for gifted females to place their womanly duties before ambition
and to be willing, if necessary, to leave their gifts altogether unrealized.
Ambition was not immoral, but it must always be subject to the claims
of the household.

It was the need for women as labourers and artisans rather than any
sudden impulse towards equity that produced the amazing *volte face*
which, in 1916, inspired a once keen opponent of the Suffrage Movement
to announce: 'There are still, unfortunately, villages to be found where

---

[1] See Appendix 33.
[2] The relatively subtle changes introduced by the Napoleonic wars deserve more attention
than they receive, and the spectacular incursion of women into the Crimea has naturally
eclipsed the tale of their further progress through more diffused efforts in the Franco-
Prussian conflict.

the women have become imbued with the idea that their place is the home. That idea must be met and combated.'[1]

The present war is also yielding its crop of emancipations, but they take, I feel, a peculiarly misguided course. The least admirable features of males are being aped, even to their ill-designed clothes (numerous clumsy details of which are emulated in the uniform of women's armies), their intemperate conviviality, and their approval of violence. One can only hope it will be seen, when the fever has abated, that parity of rights is not at all the same thing as parity of habits, and that if one sex must be imitated by the other, it is time it were the one whose vanities take a decorative shape, and whose follies are by comparison innocuous.

Our slavery to verbal forms is probably, as Stuart Chase suggests, the main source of the evil here as in so many other instances of misdirection:

'For centuries the concepts associated with the words "masculine" and "feminine" hindered the education of both sexes. . . . Into this extreme differentiation . . . the words about "equality" swept like a fresh wind. Many men gave up with a sigh of relief the attitude of protecting women. Many girls and women struggled against bio-logical limitations to surpass their husbands in money-making. The pendulum is still swaying between the artificially contrasted rôles of the sexes and the artificially identified rôles that succeeded them. If "equality" had not befuddled us, we might have analysed the real differences and developed them to enrich the lives of both men and women.'

It is not too late to correct the distorted balance, but I believe that, if the pendulum swings much further towards the masculinization of women, humanity will stand in peril of total destruction—not through their refusal to bear children, a danger which has always been grossly exaggerated, but through the ever-increasing scale and scope of warfare.[2]

Until we reached the unhappy theme I leave here, this chapter was confined to the inspection of fashions which are obsolescent. It was, so to speak, a map of streets which, though still inhabited, are known to be condemned and whose breaking up is only a matter of time. Among the decaying ideas which men are most reluctant to demolish is one which has lately become quite strikingly untenable; namely, that their own sex remains young much longer than the other and, in any case, can continue to be attractive even in advanced maturity. At a supper-table in a night-club I once listened to two men exchanging jocular

[1] Mr Walter Long, in a speech on the Land Army. The quotation is from *The Cause*, where we learn that at the end of the First Great War there was a strenuous and partly success-ful attempt to wrest back from women their hard-won gains. Although the able-bodied male population had been diminished by millions, ' public opinion assumed that all women could still be supported by men, and that if they went on working it was from a sort of deliberate wickedness. . . . Employers were implored to turn them out as passionately as they had been implored to employ them.'

[2] See Appendix 34.

comments, tinged with indignation, on a stout but frivolously dressed matron who was dancing delightedly with a partner some years younger than herself. It happened that her scathing critics were both themselves elderly, and that one of them, fat, bald, and upwards of fifty, was paying gallant attentions to a member of our party nearly thirty years his junior. It seemed to me remarkable that they should have supposed themselves immune from the laws by which they wished to govern the lady and should have failed to perceive that their power to obtain the companionship of young women was almost wholly an economic one.

For it is a melancholy fact that, with very rare exceptions, ageing men are not more alluring to women than ageing women are to men, and those who find it easy to have sexual adventures late in life are usually gifted with money, celebrity, or influence that can be made to serve the person whose favours are sought. From time immemorial men, consciously or unconsciously, have exploited these assets, once possessed by only a fractional minority of women : yet though there is no rivalry, the greed of privilege arouses in them a real repugnance when they see women able to use the same expedients.

As for the actual retention of youth, there is no doubt that the conditions of domestic and industrial life before the twentieth century ensured a premature deterioration for women in general, but nowadays on every side they may be found successfully taking pains to preserve their looks and their resilience, while men, sure of perennial desirability, do little or nothing to improve on Nature, and sink easily into the rut of middle age. Among married couples of approximately equal years I constantly find the wife giving a much more youthful impression than the husband, and I do not know of many elderly men in public life who keep up as good an appearance as their female contemporaries.

Yet it must be acknowledged that, for all their negligence, men still enjoy an advantage. Women are obliged to maintain very much higher standards to be sure of pleasing, whereas men of the most inferior mental and physical attributes need never want for company as long as their means and position enable them to dispense hospitality—women still being tacitly debarred from many forms of entertainment unless escorted. The process of financial and social evolution, however, may eventually reduce the temptations which girls are now under to admit attentions which, if taste only were consulted, would be swiftly rejected, and men of all ages will learn that their charms are not as durable or as independent of external aid as they have been led to imagine.

When it is no longer possible to acquire by direct or indirect purchase the flatteries of youth, middle-aged men may cease to be contemptuous of middle-aged women, and the hungry and undignified pursuit of youth for its own sake will become a pathetic aberration as odd to the people of the future as the once-frequent marriages between senile men and girls in their teens now seem to us.

Thank God my character has now been cleared. I am the mother of four fine sons and have never done anything wrong in my life.

> Woman's statement to a *News of the World* reporter after a case at Lancaster Assizes, January 1940.

With tears streaming down her cheeks Mrs E—— T—— explained that she had lost four children in the raid. Another son was still in hospital. Mrs T—— told the Queen: 'I don't mind losing what I have lost so long as we win the war.'

> *News Chronicle* report of a Royal visit to a raided area, Nov. 1940.

I WAS recently startled by a curious headline, 'MOTHER WINS HISTORIC HORSERACE.' My inductive faculties are slow and I did not instantaneously discover that the lady in question was the owner, not the understudy, of a horse. Even when that ray had dawned, the word 'mother' surprised me, for I could not perceive that it added to the interest of the matter sufficiently to warrant large black type. At first I conjectured that the headline writer was providing a little extra news value for those who still find it remarkable in a mother to do anything beyond bearing children and looking after them, but in a moment I reflected that it is a very long time since women began to achieve victories outside their homes, and other headlines began to flit through my memory:

'MOTHER OF EIGHT TORTURED BY POISON PEN.'
'MOTHER OF SIX TELLS COURT STORY OF ARMED BURGLAR.'

Apparently the idea of Mother lends 'human interest' to a newspaper report, and Mother of Eight, it may be, is thought to lend eight times as much interest. At any rate, when the children exceed three or four, great stress is laid on their number. This 'human interest,' I now conclude, depends upon a certain sympathetic attraction which the name of *Mother* is likely to have for the reader. A Mother is automatically held to be *Good*.

I will revert to the Sentimentality Formula: 'It would be pleasanter. . . . It ought to be. . . . It is.' Never is the application of this more clearly to be seen than in the popular view of motherhood. Psycho-analysts may account for the impassioned idealization of the maternal character by various remarkable theories of infantile eroticism, not all, I dare say, deserving the mockery they sometimes incur; but for my part, I find the tendency too obvious in its sources to need recondite explanations. It is greatly to be desired that those who bring forth children and have power over their health and happiness should be worthy of so important a charge: that they *are* worthy is a wish-fulfilling belief very readily attained. Parents, and especially mothers—whose goodness is more essential to children's welfare than that of fathers [1]—are thought to be somehow sanctified by their office. In times when a personal God was credited with having worked out a plan for each of his creatures, this sanctification could be assumed on religious grounds. Today there is an optimistic feeling that, though parenthood may often be an accident, Nature provides instincts ennobling to human beings when the accident befalls them. The dismal records of the N.S.P.C.C. cannot, apparently, do much to shake a faith which is founded upon wishes.

Yet it is true that artificial respect for parents does diminish a little with each generation. In the days when priest-given law allowed a man to regard his family as his absolute property, and even encouraged him to slaughter one or other as a thank-offering, how little could anyone have foreseen the code under which a child might be removed from a father's custody! It has taken some thousands of years, however, to travel from that primitive darkness to this primitive light, and I fear it will take at least some hundreds more to destroy illusionism about parenthood altogether.

We do not, of course, come across much of it in private life. In their private capacity, individuals are well accustomed to disregard the sacred status of other individuals, and to offer criticisms and, when occasion arises, protests. But public opinion—the synthetic generalized opinion we bring to bear on public institutions—usually maintains archaic standards and resents their modification by reformers. There is a great disparity between our judgments of situations we know and have seen developing and our judgments of similar situations occurring among those who are strangers to us. Things seen at a distance have simple deluding outlines, and it happens that laws and the conduct of institutions are prescribed by the distant view. People not disciplined in independent thinking vaguely respect what they have been taught to respect, and do not realize that in private life they are constantly guided by a more flexible standard. Thus though in practice it may often be admitted that this child or that would be better off away from its parents, in theory a kind of magical affinity is presupposed to unite infants to those who are accountable for their existence.

This is not the view, needless to say, that represents what is called enlightened opinion; it represents public opinion, which has only a remote connection with what private people are thinking. We are not to be guided by the extent to which a popular view finds utterance, for people who judge with their emotions tend to be considerably more vocal than those who reason. They are less tolerant and have the habit

[1] It is interesting to see how, while the law vested autocratic power in the father, it was towards him that sentimental adulation was chiefly directed.

of expressing their indignation forcibly, of making a fuss, in fact; whereas their opponents all too often maintain a contemptuous silence, feeling that logical argument will be useless. Then there is that vast class of middle-grade minds which are quite capable of working out a problem sensibly if left to themselves, but which have not strength to resist importunate influences, and so are subdued by the noisy outcry of the emotionalists. Their verdict goes to make up the weight of public opinion, but it would have swung in the other direction if other influences had been more pressing. (To catch these middle-grade minds, the rationalists have only to become more vocal than the emotionalists, but, unfortunately, tradition and authority and, above all, the press nearly always support the emotionalist, and that adds enormously to his power.)

From time to time reason does gain a victory in spite of everything, but seldom without a struggle most exhausting to the energies of its supporters. The debates leading up to the passing of any progressive law we now take for granted—say the Abolition, or the first Factory Acts, or the Married Women's Property Bill—contain astonishing passages. Superficially it might not appear that the arguments for retaining the slave-trade or battening on child labour could be sentimental, but, when analysed, they will be seen to belong unmistakably to that category. Quotations given earlier will have recalled to the reader how every attempt to regulate the horrible conditions under which the Victorian artisan laboured for his pittance was described as an unwarrantable interference with man's sacred right to dispose of his services by free contract. Here is a casuistry designed to appeal wholly to sentiment. The idea of a sacred right to a certain freedom stirs emotions which may quite obscure the fact that the freedom is non-existent. The right itself may be equally fictitious, but if you can make people believe in it—make them believe, particularly, that it is being threatened—you can generally produce a very powerful reflex.

Sacred rights are inclined to coincide with legal rights. Man provides his own possessiveness first with a divine charter, then with a legal one. Though the law, I am glad to admit, improves. A hundred years ago, who, for instance, would have questioned the celebrated Mr Dionne's right to do with his own family precisely as he desired? As it was, when he signed a contract for the exhibition of his newly-born quintuplets in the World's Fair, Chicago, the Canadian Government did question, and because it very sensibly ignored public opinion, the children, who would probably have died, were given a most favourable start.

It may be considered by some that the public unreason which was displayed so strikingly as to parental claims over these infants [1] is not actually a sound illustration. Parents who could produce five children at once probably seemed to have special claims—to be inspired with the

[1] See Appendix 35.

178

very quintessence of parental magic. The public, I may be reminded, is not always on the father's or mother's side. Sometimes police protection has to be given to a parent found guilty of cruelty.

I acknowledge that disgust of cruelty—the grossest forms of cruelty—is a stronger emotion now than respect for parental rights. Public opinion advances. Often it moves much faster than the law: that depends, perhaps, on where the influential private voices first began to be heard. But it is obviously still a very long way behind what is being thought by reasonable individuals.

Though it is part of the case for individualism that individuals do not all hold the same views—not even the views that are said to be held by 'every right-thinking person' and 'every decent-thinking man or woman'—there must of necessity be a certain number of common factors in the opinions of people who are following the path of reason. Two at least seem to have become axiomatic. First, the belief that those who would be undesirable as parents should be discouraged from having children. Second, that, where there is a necessity to choose, the rights of the child should rank higher than the rights of the parent.

Here I imagine a protest: 'But these principles are accepted everywhere—not only among your conscientious rationalists!' Unhappily refutation is only too easy. The controversies of the last few years over the birth-rate, abortion, contraception, and the decreased size of families supply depressing evidence of the passion with which sentimentalists will fight to preserve the *status quo* of their grandfathers and the widespread influence they still maintain, to the detriment of education, hygiene, and the standard of living.

Not that they positively advocate the begetting of children by unsuitable people. They merely refuse altogether to recognize unsuitability. How else can one interpret it when, in spite of all objections on the grounds of poverty and physical and mental deficiency, anybody and everybody is urged to produce large families? My books of cuttings show an assortment of diatribes by priests, professors, and politicans railing against those who fail to maintain the birth-rate.

Here is a popular Roman Catholic preacher who, forgetting that his Kingdom is supposed to be elsewhere, laments the declining strength of 'what has been the strongest nation in Europe. One does not like the phrase cannon fodder,' he confesses, 'but the power of self-defence and Empire defence is so steadily dwindling that England will inevitably lose its place in the world.' A professor of physiology announces: 'The Government must follow the example of the dictators and teach that it is a national duty for parents to have three or four children and disgraceful not to.' A Member of Parliament proclaims that there is 'nothing more dreadful than the propaganda of contraceptionists. A British workman with his two arms could produce enough to feed ten children, but if he only had two children, what right had he to three meals a day ? The justification and spur to a full day's work was a father's children round a father's table.'

In the years before the second Great War, when all these utterances and a thousand others like them were made, unemployment was widespread, millions lived in slums, millions were undernourished, and there were schemes in progress for helping the families of the destitute to emigrate to countries which might be better able to support them.[1] A number of mothers and fathers in the desperation of poverty killed one or more of their children.

The practice of urging people to breed irrespective of their eligibility may seem cynical rather than sentimental, especially when there is an express demand for 'cannon fodder'; yet it is, in fact, based upon a series of idealizations, such as that life is always a boon, that God will provide, that parenthood is a sacred thing, and so forth.

Although the birth-rate alarmists want children for political reasons and not because they take a romantic view of parenthood, nevertheless it is by the romantic view that they justify themselves. For it is not to be suspected that all these worthy gentlemen are entirely indifferent to whether children when born have any decent chance in life or not— indifferent to malnutrition, overcrowding, bad heredity, incompetent upbringing, and all the other potential evils. If they looked such a state of affairs in the face, it is most unlikely that they would still make an undiscriminating appeal for more babies. Clearly they deceive themselves with rosy visions—visions of the British working man spurred on to constant healthful effort by the sight of his ten merry children round his well-provided table, and a general vague idea, culled from the Bible and supported by a normal instinct, that procreation is good.

There would be difficulties, no doubt, in giving poverty official recognition as an obstacle to begetting families. It would seem like inflicting a double hardship, letting people be poor and then asking them to refrain from procreation because they are poor. But positively to demand the presentation to the State of children for whom no adequate subsistence is available seems to me the grossest kind of impertinence.

In the admission of forms of unfitness other than poverty, particularly disease and mental defectiveness, there has been some advance. Some advance, but not nearly sufficient to warrant an assumption that the advanced principles are accepted everywhere. Mountainous barriers have to be climbed by social workers who specialize in contraception. There is feverish opposition to the movement for sterilizing the unfit,

[1] E.g. this *Yorkshire Evening News* report of an emigration in 1936: ' Only seven years old, but with no prospect in life. This was the plight of three little children who, with 25 others from the Tyneside area, all under the age of 14, emigrated from Liverpool to start a new life 6000 miles from their homes.
' All are the sons and daughters of unemployed people who could not afford to keep them and feared they will be doomed to poverty if they remained on Tyneside. . . . The Government contributes towards the travelling expenses.'

and the faint prospects of legalized abortion are condemned in arguments reminiscent of the Middle Ages.[1]

Look where we will, the reactionaries still hold most of the fort. Private opinion operating upon situations individually known would be very largely against them. Public opinion we can only divine from the simple incontrovertible fact that undesirable parents are *not* discouraged from producing children.

As for the other premise which I took to be an axiom among rational thinkers—that the rights of the child are greater than the rights of the parent—we have moved a vast distance in the last hundred years. Those eighteenth-century philosophers who were so fond of expounding the duty of everybody to everybody else would be struck speechless with amazement at the extent of the change. Consider Paley on the proper conduct of children 'after they have attained to manhood, and have left their father's family':

'In this state of the relation, the duty to parents is simply the duty of gratitude. . . . It will show itself in compliance with the will of the parents however contrary to the child's own taste and judgment, provided it be neither criminal, nor totally inconsistent with his happiness; in a constant endeavour to promote their enjoyments, prevent their wishes, and soften their anxieties, in small matters as well as in great; in assisting them in their business; in contributing to their support, ease or better accommodation, when their circumstances require it; in affording them their company, in preference to more amusing engagements; in waiting upon their sickness or decrepitude; in bearing with the infirmities of their health or temper, with the peevishness and complaints, the unfashionable, the negligent, austere manners, and offensive habits, which often attend upon advanced years: for where must old age find indulgence, if it do not meet with it in the piety and partiality of children?'[2]

Growing old must have had many consolations when you knew it was your children's undisputed duty to put up with all the bad habits you might care to develop. We can gauge how highly such reckless filial piety was esteemed from the immense number of eighteenth-century novels whose plot hinges upon the immolation of a virtuous child upon the altar of a parent's vanity, ambition, or caprice. The Victorians continued, though with a little more flexibility, to build domestic relations upon the same set of ideas. The sacrifice of one's happiness to a parent was looked upon as a quite admirable career; for a daughter at any rate.

[1] One of the most active anti-eugenic bodies is the League of National Life which professes to stand for: (1) the physical and moral health of the individual; (2) the welfare and safety of the home, the nation, and the Empire; (3) the national tradition of reverence for marriage and parenthood and the truth as taught by science and religion.

[2] From *Political Philosophy*, 1785.

There has been a decided improvement in ethic, notably among the more fortunate classes. It coincides in time with the rise of the Women's Movement, which curtailed the autocratic power of fathers. Gratitude for being born is no longer cultivated as a first principle. In theory people recognize—rather dimly—that to beget life, it may be accidentally or unwillingly, is not invariably to confer an obligation, and that one is only entitled to as much gratitude from one's children as one earns. But this liberal outlook does not always influence conduct as profoundly as might be assumed. In practice, reliance on 'parental magic' is still widespread, especially on the part of fathers and mothers. Those who are idiotic or unscrupulous are allowed abundant opportunity for wrecking their children's lives. The rights of the child may be acknowledged, but they are not protected except when the violation has been so extreme that protection comes almost too late.

This is a position which cannot be remedied without a certain encroachment upon family life. And so we come up against that primary article of sentimental faith, the sanctity of the home—a fine phrase which has licensed a world of misery. The evil that can be done by giving family life a sacred status must be patent to everyone capable of using his brain at all, and yet how immensely unpopular any measure has always been which tries to set limits to a man's power in his own house.

A *man's* power . . . the man of the house . . . an Englishman's home . . . the principle of power appears to be masculine. I think it not unlikely that, now the law gives rights to women too, we should find much more tolerance of legislation affecting the family. It is men, always, who put up the most vigorous resistance when it comes to defending sacred rights. They take their stand upon the love of liberty—the very key-word of sentimental idealization—but the real psychological need is rather for power. Perhaps it is because men have such a little liberty that they so dearly treasure power. Women, it may be argued, have even less liberty; but the power-seeking method of redress is a masculine one. That there exist many power-loving women it would be fatuous to deny, but on the whole the feminine impulse will be to look for compensation through the affections. Their tyrannies are thus less obvious, and in some respects less harmful.

My reader, to whom I assign a somewhat protestant rôle, may here take up the thread and give it a sharp pull: 'Well, what's to be done about it all? We're agreed that parenthood isn't sacred, and that home life isn't sacred, and that a belief in their sanctity may have evil consequences. The question is—what remedy? A communal existence with perpetual examinations and inspections? It doesn't sound very tempting. One can't wonder that the public doesn't show any signs of aspiring to it. Surely we ought to have one little place on earth where we can be private by legal right?'

To this I assent with more enthusiasm than may have been expected.

Privacy is essential to living as an individual, and should not be the expensive luxury which most people find it. I am saddened to contemplate even the growing numbers who live in flats, because I so detest, on their behalf, the inevitable restrictions. I want them to be able to keep dogs and cats if they choose, to be undisturbed by their neighbours' noises, to play music when it suits them, which may be later than eleven at night or earlier than eight in the morning, to move in spacious surroundings with their own kind of order and disorder, their own possessions around them, and room for more than basic necessities, room for a certain amount of nonsense. It seems to me a tragedy that so many tens of thousands of families are cooped up in little box-like apartments where every half-foot of space is precious and must be utilized as carefully as in the cabins of a ship. I feel, perhaps irrationally, that such cramped bodies must harbour cramped minds. And since I should be the last person to settle down in a State where the private household was superseded, naturally I hope no such State will ever come into being.

What is required is that the right to have a private household—a private household which includes children—should be granted only to those who are fit for it. Marriage should be treated essentially as a licence to procreate. It is sentimentality run mad to give this licence, as we do now, to people who are clearly unable to beget sound children, or to bring them up successfully if they did.

Reproduction, admittedly, can only be controlled in a negative sense. That is to say, unsound stock can often be weeded out in advance, but sound stock cannot be guaranteed—though very evidently the chances of soundness will be much greater when there is fair promise. (Contrary to a widespread superstition, good-looking parents seldom produce plain children, nor intellectual parents stupid ones.) But bad upbringing damages more human beings, in my opinion, than are ever marred by bad heredity, and it is this danger which most urgently requires attention.

Ignorant people, themselves the victims of ignorance, are everywhere despoiling the health and future happiness of children in their care. Warping fears are implanted, there is a thoughtless half-jocular propagation of lies; an ugly outlook tending in particular to exalt violence is taught almost deliberately, and the use of reason is discouraged because the parent is too lazy or too foolish to explain himself and demands an unquestioning obedience: while, on the physical side, errors arising from prejudice and want of knowledge result in defects never to be outgrown.

It is a fact that many parents, especially in country districts, refuse to allow their young children to have dental treatment. A case has come under my own notice where a girl in her teens, needing one or two fillings in otherwise excellent front teeth, was advised by her mother to 'have them all out' as it would be so much less trouble in the long run; and I am told by more than one dentist that this attitude is not uncommon among the classes bred, through no fault of their own, to low standards.

183

This is but one of many ways in which permanent injury may be inflicted by those whose 'mother love' is vulgarly regarded as an infallible guide.

'I believe,' observes Mr Beverley Nichols, 'that the longer a man lives, and the more he learns, the more he will realize that his mother was the wisest woman he will ever meet.'[1] Which is tantamount to saying not merely that every mother is wise, but that every mother is wiser than every other mother. Samples of maternal wisdom may be freely garnered in the newspapers and will sometimes take such shapes as the following. Mrs B—— had three children evacuated from London to a Lincolnshire village. She paid them a visit after six weeks to see how they were faring, and her youngest, aged five, failed to recognize her. 'He looked at her,' so the reporter tells us, and cried, 'You're not my mummy,' and ran to the woman who was caring for him. Then his mother noticed that, by a strange coincidence, his hostess resembled her, being of the same build and complexion, and wearing similar glasses; the child called her 'Mummy.'

'I'm going to bring my children back,' said the real mother to a *Sunday Chronicle* reporter.[2] 'I would sooner my baby were with me in all sorts of air raids than that he wouldn't know me when I go to see him.' The love that is prepared to destroy its object rather than lose possession of it to another does not call forth the same reproval in a mother as in a friend, and the story was presumably told for its sentimental appeal to other parents.

I spoke of the implanting of fears. Everyone who has had to do with unimaginative and coarse-grained persons in any walk of life knows how indiscriminately they will use fear as an instrument of policy or even of gaining a moment's amusement at the child's expense. There is the bogyman who will catch him if he gets out of bed, the policeman who will be fetched to take him away if he is naughty, the supernatural power which will play mean little tricks of every kind upon him, down to making his features 'stay like that' if he should be discovered pulling faces. When I was five or six years old, a servant, who has probably since had children of her own, informed me that the wax dummies which were then a conspicuous feature of many shop windows were corpses taken from their graves and painted up.[3] I have obtained from a nurse employed in the children's ward of a hospital pitiful data as to the extent to which dread of the doctors, the operating theatre, and the routine

---

[1] *Sunday Chronicle*, March 24th, 1940.   [2] October 15th, 1939.

[3] On September 11th, 1939, the newspapers reported that a crowd of women holiday-makers, *many of them accompanied by children*, broke through a cordon to get a closer view of bodies which had been submerged for three months in the *Thetis*. Children are always to be found among the morbid sight-seers who congregate about the scene of a murder. They also form a large proportion of the attendance at Tussaud's very frightening Chamber of Horrors, which I believe they are not allowed to enter without an adult. The want of protectiveness which allows these self-scarifying excursions is another characteristic of parents of inferior mentality.

afflicts newly admitted children whose heads have been filled at home with terrifying rubbish.[1]

The fears so recklessly engendered do not long persist in their original form and are therefore thought to be trivial: yet their influence upon the mental make-up is actually profound. Mistrust of a hostile world is succeeded by mistrust of the liars who made it appear so. The resulting uncertainty plays no small part in creating those various defiant, self-assertive, self-compensating impulses whose devastating effects are to be seen all about us.

I spoke also of the exaltation of violence. Here I will touch upon only one aspect of it, the disgusting abuse of corporal punishment which cannot but remain a feature of much home life while uninstructed, uncontrolled, and in some cases perverted individuals are allowed to beget and bring up children as they please. Those who have been more humanely nurtured may well have difficulty in realizing the enormous extent to which physical assault is still sanctioned as a mode of admonition.[2]

I myself once had occasion—much to my own discontent—to make a series of observations which convinced me that the English child is reared very largely by the capricious administration of blows and slaps. I spent a month writing for some hours daily in Kew Gardens, and my attention was soon unwillingly drawn to the number of parents or persons acting *in loco parentis* who were threatening to hit their charges, generally on very trivial provocation.

The warnings varied from the mildly expletive ('You come here or I'll give you a good smack!') to the wildly explosive ('You stop that or I'll knock your head off!'), while the sinister suggestive ('You wait! You just wait till I get hold of you!') also became drearily familiar to my ears. That the children in most cases took little notice of these menaces is an extra proof of the silliness of their adult guardians. Sometimes a child could be seen running away from a hot and flustered mother or nurse, who was usually outstripped with indignity. It was customary, very naturally, for the young people to address one another in terms exactly similar to those favoured by their seniors, a habit which did not much increase their attractiveness.

I think that I have few illusions about the dispositions of children. Like Copperfield's Mrs Crupp, I'm a mother myself. I am also an aunt, a sister, and a daughter, and I know the appalling strain which an active and irrepressible child can lay upon the shoulders of those responsible for it; but both from my own experience and that of better authorities I have learned that a régime of threats, whether likely to be acted upon or used as mere vituperation, is fraught with serious dangers for nerves and personality, and that it is perfectly possible to attain reasonable control without resorting to any such measures.

If it be objected that these are the measures which have been employed

---

[1] See Appendix 36.   [2] See Appendix 37.

in the government of children from earliest recorded time, I can only reply that the wickedness and folly of mankind make it very apparent. It is high time we publicly acknowledged the failure of the old, facile, and haphazard practices and attempted at last to see what can be done by allowing the privilege of initiating a family only to those who are deemed likely not to degrade it, and by taking steps to secure that it is not, in fact, degraded.

Although to breed rationally has been the dream of eugenists in all countries for a long period, the experiment has never anywhere, as far as I can learn, been tried upon a scale of sufficiently revealing magnitude. Certainly the problem is a very complex one, and it becomes still more so when we try to work out a method not merely of restricting undesirable procreation but also of regulating to some extent the influences of home life. I have heard it argued that, even if we succeeded in getting the eugenic principle adopted, even if sterilization and abortion were legalized to prevent the worst types from reproducing themselves, and all the preliminary steps were taken to ensure a better average heredity, there would still be many bad parents, since neither intelligence tests nor blood tests nor any other tests at present known to science will reveal in advance whether a person is going to develop some vice or form domestic habits that will make it harmful to live with him. This is beyond question true; yet though there would still be many bad parents there would be considerably fewer than there are now; and if we only undertook those reforms which were bound to work perfectly and universally, what laws should we have to protect any creature, child, adult, or animal?

Possibly, until human nature has become less unpredictable, it will be necessary to organize some occasional supervision of every young child's living conditions, with power to alter them. There are readers who will flinch from such a prospect, haunted by the sanctity of the home and the fear of losing what little personal liberty has not already been destroyed. No one could resent more passionately than I the onslaughts upon freedom which have overwhelmed us in the last few years, but I cannot think that purely social reform is in the same category with political oppression.

There has hardly ever been an important piece of legislation which did not infringe personal liberty. In comparison with infringements, enfranchisements have been almost negligible. And though the classes concerned have at first grumbled and groaned and prophesied the end of all privacy, the compulsions are soon so taken for granted that no one remembers how irksome they once seemed. Such hackneyed examples as the indignation aroused by the first census, the first levy of income tax, and the first Acts providing for the inspection of workshops, will afford us an adequate reminder. If factories are inspected why should homes be exempt, being, as they are, the workshops where human beings are turned out? No one any longer complains because schools are liable to inspection. Yet a hundred years ago there were numbers who, on the principle of freedom, would have defended Mr Squeers's right to treat his pupils as he pleased.

I believe emphatically that parents are in general the best people to bring up their children, for they are, after all, *likely* to love them and to try to give them the best chance possible; and even the injuries they do them are inadvertent and nearly always through ignorance rather than ill-will. This fact should, however, facilitate, not hamper, the building-up of a new system. Good parents will have nothing to fear from investigation, and ignorant ones, if they are well disposed, will ultimately be glad of enlightenment. True, the surveillance of authorities might be a nuisance, but so is the gas-meter man, the window-cleaner, and the assessor of the rates. To prevent only a little of the suffering which sometimes comes to light in the police courts, most of us would be willing to endure far greater inconveniences. And what I envisage would only be a periodical enquiry, not a daily interference.

It will be asked, if there is to be a standard of parental fitness how are the tests to be devised? Who and what will be the examining body? What will be their methods? How shall we deal with the possibilities of abuse? I am not daunted by those questions. Difficulties of that sort are always raised before reforms of magnitude, and sometimes very properly. Yet if the reformers are given scope, ways and means are found. The terrible abuses which are predicted seldom, if ever, come to pass; and a standard is worked out which is inclined to be too low rather than too restrictive.

But, unfortunately, all that psychologists and sociologists working in concert might accomplish for the betterment of the species must continue to be a matter of tentative suggestion while there looms before us an objection greater than any I have so far anticipated—that is, poverty. We cannot dictate living conditions to people who have not the means to realize them, and unless we are prepared to offer some better alternative than such as have recently been exposed, it will not be much good planning to remove children from unsuitable homes, except when the need is desperate. As long as poverty remains, the eugenist must direct most of his efforts into the channels of sterilization, legalized abortion, and greater proficiency in contraception.

These may bring about an immense reduction of the population, but, as Havelock Ellis effectively showed, the quality of small populations tends to be high. The excellence of a people, or even its security, does not lie in its numbers. Florence in the fifteenth century produced a blaze of peerless genius and the influence of its art and learning was beyond calculation; yet it was no size at all compared with Liverpool, or Chicago, or a quite small modern city like Johannesburg. As for security, anyone who should seek to prove that the most populous nation has always been the most secure would be flying in the face of history.

The motives underlying the desire for numerical strength have never been noble. The Victorians were anxious to keep up a cheap and abundant supply of labour: their descendants want man-power for political reasons. A sentimental habit of mind allows them to talk as if it were babies they delighted in, or as if they cherished large populations from the sheer love of crowds.

I am aware that much of the opposition to controlled reproduction comes not from professed nationalist patriots, but from the Churches, taking their stand upon the will of God and the sacredness of human life. But the Churches cannot make any convincing claim to be detached from secular ambition, and it is noteworthy that those which have raised the loudest voice against eugenics have been the feeblest in their condemnation of mass slaughter in warfare. The most powerful religious sects have never, in fact, explicitly forbidden their members to take part in killing and maiming for State purposes: far otherwise. The 'will of God' likewise fails to persuade, since there is no logical reason for believing God's will to be frustrated by the death of unformed creatures in the womb and not frustrated by the death of fully formed creatures on the gallows or the battle-field.

Along with those who feel a political need of man-power, and those who presuppose the indignation of the Deity, the genetic reformers are confronted with a group of curious faddists—invariably of the male sex and of strongly anti-Feminist tendency—who seem to take a grim pleasure in the idea of a woman as a child-bearing vessel obliged to exercise her function whether she will or not, and who dwell with manifest relish upon her enslavement to the processes of gestation and parturition—processes they would like to be able to regard as inescapable. This attitude is correlated, no doubt, to a thwarted longing for sexual domination, and perhaps has some part even in the propogenitive anxieties of priests and politicians.

Finally, interference with Nature is resisted on medical grounds; but it is to be remarked that these objections are always put forward by persons who oppose reform on one of the grounds already described, and they have a peculiarly 'cooked-up' flavour. Statistics are quoted, for instance, of the complications and morbid conditions known to follow artificial abortion, but no mention is made of the severe disorders which frequently result from childbirth. By an ingenious use of half-truths, the impression is conveyed that abortion is fraught with more perilous consequences than normally completed pregnancy.

I am concerned here with abortion only as a means, plainly a secondary means, less desirable than birth-control, of preventing the advent of children for whom nothing in life promises fair. Within the limits set by that end—that is to say, dissociating the topic from its significance to the supporters of women's social and personal rights—I venture some discussion of it in this chapter.

No one has advocated indiscriminate breeding with a more reckless and ruthless ardour than Captain Anthony Ludovici,[1] and no one, under the guise of sturdy realism, has adduced so many childishly irrational arguments. I will quote one or two of them from his essay against the legalization of abortion,[2] so that the reader may judge what the genuine realist is up against.

The case he builds up stands or falls on the premise that abortion inevitably produces grave physical and temperamental damage while normal parturition is thoroughly health-promoting, joy-giving, and psychologically necessary. When he meets with any evidence which conflicts with this theory he tosses it briefly and angrily aside. Thus he disposes of the figures of ordinary maternal mortality and invalidism by the suggestion, made without credentials, that they are partly due to previous histories of criminal abortion, and reiterantly insists that pain and risk in childbirth are abnormal, although they are irrefutably the lot of most women. With typical sentimental idealization he throws out nostalgic allusions to a state of nature (which has never existed since written records began) in which labour and delivery are altogether pleasurable.[3] 'Imagine,' he says, 'another state, in which the function of parturition was the delight it should be (and often is today, in spite of everything the masculinized population may say); imagine a state in which . . . the parturient female was the emblem of the Joy of Life . . . and you would find aesthetes like Goethe laughed at, birth-controllers reviled as jealous puritans, and doctors who advise anaesthetics for child-birth stigmatized as the ascetic killjoys of the age.' We may well imagine such a state, for none is traceable in the world of reality. However, Ludovici has created an agreeable fantasy of the past (he speaks of 'restoring' the experience of 'pleasantness in childbearing') and urges us to make maternity less painful by making it 'more generally normal,' whatever that may mean. 'The solution,' he insists, 'cannot be more anaesthetics. The solution is the normalizing of a natural function.' How this undefined aim is to be achieved remains totally obscure.

In the course of eulogizing the feminine mission of fecundity, and stigmatizing as deficient and masculinoid the women who do not lavishly

[1] Captain A. H. Henderson-Livesey, author of several fervent anti-Feminist books, runs him a close second.

[2] In *Abortion* by F. W. Stella Browne, A. M. Ludovici, and Harry Roberts.

[3] This most egregious piece of illusionism has been elaborated by him in a book called *The Truth About Childbirth*, published in 1937. Dr Harry Roberts, in a *New Statesman* review of it, commented: 'I have been present at the birth of several thousand babies, and my heart is still not sufficiently hardened, and my instinctive sympathy not sufficiently atrophied, to enable me to share Captain Ludovici's vicarious delight in the pleasures of parturition.'

Speaking as a woman who has endured these 'pleasures,' I can only regret that Captain Ludovici's delight in them *is* vicarious. Few of us would begrudge him the first-hand experience.

fulfil it (though he is equally severe on 'the recruitment to motherhood every year of thousands of degenerate women who have no business to become parous,' so it is very difficult to please him), he rejects one after another the various pleas that have been made for legality of abortion under certain conditions, and there is not one single instance in which he admits or even mentions the rights of the child who is to be brought into the world by a reluctant—often desperately reluctant—mother. His reasoning is always after the patterns that follow. Dame Louise McIlroy had proposed legalized intervention 'in the case of females pregnant as a result of criminal assault, and also in those not infrequent cases when young girls, just after reaching puberty, were the victims of incest.' Ludovici retorts:

> 'The girl who has been raped, incestuously or otherwise, has obviously been grievously wronged. But do we not do her a further injury if we make her risk her life, and more certainly her health, or as certainly her sexual desires and feelings, by interrupting her pregnancy? Surely the merciful course is to leave her as little damaged as possible, and this can be achieved only by letting her terminate her pregnancy while affording her all the comforts and protection we can.'

It will be noticed that there is no reference whatever to the predicament of a child born of an adolescent mother, the product of incest, and presumably in the poverty-stricken circumstances which are the likely nursery of rape and incest. This is one of the anti-abortion fanatic's favourite entrenchments—to ignore the fact that when pregnancy comes to term, for good or evil, happiness or misery, a new and sentient creature enters the world. Another is a gross exaggeration of the dangers of abortion, as may be seen in each passage cited. Yet another is the supposition that a woman's sexual desires are impaired by it, which is a very clever piece of propaganda for winning male support.

Here is the Ludovici answer to an American authority, Dr A. J. Rongy, who had suggested that, among others, women deserted by their husbands might be allowed legal abortion:

> '. . . A woman deserted by her husband surely does not deserve—unless the desertion was her fault—to be punished for her unenviable plight! Both she and her child may be desirable members of the community. Even if, for a while, she become a burden, it may be one society is glad to shoulder, and justified in shouldering. Why risk killing her, or risk more certainly making a permanent invalid of her, or a creature devoid of sexual feeling and incapable of sexual pleasure?'

This shows us not only the usual wanton over-statement of risk and under-statement of the economic problem, but also the writer's habit of brushing aside as irrelevant the woman's own preference. Thus, to Dr Rongy's appeal on behalf of women widowed while pregnant he replies that 'to demand abortion for such cases would be both heartless and frivolous,' as if the operation were to be forced upon persons without choice or initiative. Monetary difficulties he deals with in the most summary fashion, waving away with scorn but without alternative suggestion the plea that abortion might be available to a woman who, having several children already, conceives another which cannot be provided for. His only admission of the economic hardships involved in unlimited begetting [1] is contained and dismissed in this sentence:

> 'We should ponder the desirability of subsidizing or endowing indigent motherhood, but only in those cases which give reasonable hope . . . that the offspring will be an asset to the nation.'

What is to happen to the offspring *not* likely to be an asset to the nation, and yet brought into being because the Ludovicites have succeeded in discouraging birth-control and preventing legal abortion, we are never told.

It would be unjust to take a theorist so eccentric as a representative of the popular view on procreation, but since he has on his side all the laws which ostensibly reveal the state of the nation's conscience, it is not inappropriate to show with what arguments he defends the position. Public sympathy is actually, I believe, in favour of reformed legislation, as we had an opportunity of learning at the trial in which Mr Aleck Bourne, the eminent surgeon, was very gratifyingly acquitted for performing an operation upon a girl of fifteen who had been raped. But here as in other cases where we may presume that majority opinion is correctly interpreted by the press, the mother's welfare alone is subject to question, and the plight of the child who might have come into being at so unspeakable a disadvantage is the last aspect ever to be considered. The sentimental eye seems unable to look so far.

A pregnancy brought to term is often regarded, we are led to think, as Nature's vengeance on women who are wicked enough to wish to be childless, and upon the panic-stricken cowards who are determined not to endure the pangs of giving birth and the society butterflies who refuse to miss a Season. (I have good reason to believe that the two types last named are extremely fictitious, though the writers of the opposition make great play with them.) Dr A. J. Cronin probably spoke with the authentic voice of the muddle-headed man-in-the-street in an article written when the judgment referred to above was one of the topics of the day.[2] While approving heartily of Mr Bourne's acquittal and bidding welcome to some new law that should provide for surgical interference

---

[1] It should be borne in mind that he opposes contraception as we llas abortion and advocates very early marriages.

[2] In the *Sunday Chronicle*, July 24th, 1938.

in similar hard cases, he is very chary of admitting any undue latitude for fear of 'a whole sequence of unhappy consequences.'

'It is not fully realized [he says] how many women there are who for selfish or neurotic reasons object to bearing children. They represent a vast and ever-growing army. A detestable, self-indulgent, unnatural brigade!

When I was in medical practice one of the many staggering facts I had to face was the number of these women who came and begged to be relieved of their incubus of approaching motherhood. They simply wanted to be rid of their baby—to secure that they were prepared to do anything, pay anything, and risk anything.'

And, as if gestation were an end in itself and the awaited baby were a doll without feeling or future, he deplores the possible emergence of legislation allowing these neurotics, these 'self-indulgent, unnatural' creatures, to avoid motherhood! Motherhood, apparently, is to be a punishment for their wickedness, inflicted at the child's expense. Or does Dr Cronin treasure the consoling faith that the female character undergoes a complete metamorphosis when baby fingers cling and the soft tendrils of baby hair wind their way round a mother's heartstrings?

It would be dishonest in me not to acknowledge that women who think themselves indifferent to children and contemplate maternity in the most pessimistic mood often turn out to be proud, loving, and efficient mothers when accident brings them to that condition. But here is no change of character, no sudden conversion from unscrupulous selfishness to domesticated benevolence. The needful instincts were merely dormant and required awakening. Positive defects of temperament such as would justify the use of Dr Cronin's strong epithets will not be charmed away by the unwilling attainment of a family. That is one of the great wish-fulfilling myths.

It belongs to the trilogy which includes the very widely held belief that large families are always happier and better brought up than small ones, and the persuasion that a woman's destiny is only to be fulfilled by frequent experiences of maternity, all other forms of self-expression being unappeasing makeshifts. Dr C. Willett Cunnington, whose painstaking studies of the feminine mentality make an admirable counterblast to the cocksure assumptions of the Ludovici school, has dealt with both these delusions, so congenial to fertility-worshippers.

Of the Victorian habit of perennial breeding which kept families numerically strong despite an immense death-rate, he concludes that it 'produced a mass of psychological morbidity.'

'In the first place it led to a grandiose conception of "the family" and its ramifications into first and second cousins, with an exclusive family conceit. In the second, there was no privacy for the individual who was surrounded by family quarrels, jealousies, and favouritisms inevitable in such an establishment. Always there was at least one condemned as the inferior in looks or brains, while the youngest was branded for life. The amount of "inferiority complex" created by these conditions must have been enormous. A further aspect were those unwholesome alliances between brother and favourite sister, with distortion of the normal instincts. Always there was that nameless creature "Mother's right hand," the unmarriageable daughter, whose fate was to nurse her ageing parents into their tomb, and then retire to Leamington as a decayed gentlewoman. The big family, in fact, was a breeding ground for disharmony, narrowness of outlook and perpetuating family faults, kinks and defects of character, for it encouraged imitative habits and checked originality.' [1]

Dr Cunnington has made a most minute and exhaustive research into the habits and outlook of the Victorian woman, and I could wish that those who put so many of our so-called 'modern ills' down to the decreasing importance of the family background would take the trouble to examine his findings. On the subject of childbearing and rearing as the one effective means of satisfying woman's spiritual, sexual, or animal needs, he strikes out a bold pioneering line of scepticism.

'Maternity is apt to narrow the mental horizon and blunt the finer qualities of the mind. . . . Periods of huge birth-rates were distinguished for cruelty to children and indifference to the sufferings of animals. The improvement in those respects coincided precisely with the decline in the birth-rate, as though women were only then able to appreciate the sufferings of others.

An extraordinary feature of modern life is the widespread interest in schemes to reduce this suffering . . . and this change has been largely the product of the feminine mind acting on the social fabric. If in some measure this valuable social force is to be expended in other directions, such as the purely domestic, humanitarianism is likely to be to that extent impoverished. A reduction in her domestic ties has enabled a woman's imagination to travel beyond the four walls which used to confine it. No woman was so narrow in her outlook and so indifferent to impersonal matters as the mother of a large family. She must, of course, be distinguished from the mother whose family is small enough not to be all-absorbing; it must be small enough to permit the mother as well as the children to develop. The mind of the typical Victorian mother ceased to grow after an early stage in her married life. . . . She settled down to interminable breeding in a kind of mental lethargy. At forty-five she had acquired the physique and mentality of a dear old lady.' [2]

---

[1] From *Feminine Attitudes in the Nineteenth Century*
[2] From *Feminine Fig Leaves*.

It was this prematurely ageing matron, idealistically represented as a sweet and placid influence, more often fretful, bigoted, petty and capricious, ignorant even on her own ground, and darkly, dismally ignorant on any ground outside it, who had in charge the tender and responsive minds of such infants as survived her early care. The results were as bad as might, with better scientific knowledge, have been expected. If any reader doubts the nastiness of customary 'motherly' methods in the days when women had no alternative but 'to go on producing noble Britons'[1] as and when Nature imposed that service, let him look through *The Englishwoman's Domestic Magazine* for the early Seventies, where he may follow a correspondence on the beating of children which will inspire his miserable wonder. Here month after month the guardians of the nursery compared notes on flagellation—the best means of inflicting it, the degree to which punishment could be supported, the ritual of penitence before and after, the various shapes in which humiliation might be heaped upon the young offender, until, reading at this date, we half suppose we have got hold of some horrible publication for perverts and degenerates, and can scarcely believe the writers were generally the loving mothers of large families—women who, according to Ludovici, knew a more complete degree of normal sexual satisfaction than many have tasted in this birth-repressing age.

Captain Henderson-Livesey in an anti-Feminist tract, *Sex in Public Life*, points out scornfully that female reformers and politicians have contributed very little to the birth-rate. This is precisely Dr Cunnington's case. If these women had been contributing to the birth-rate (that is, on anything like the old pre-contraception scale) they would not have been contributing to the cause of social reform. The captain's sneer must therefore fall very flat except among those few who feel that Florence Nightingale could have been more creditably employed bringing up ten children, possibly of the most mediocre capacities, than in advancing the general well-being of humanity; that Elizabeth Garrett Anderson was not as worthy a citizen as one who, summoned before a court[2] to account for the condition of a little boy found to be 'unwanted, isolated, and neglected,' announced by way of disclaimer that she was the mother of seventeen.

There was a time, no doubt, when the accepted standard of values would have obliged all but the boldest to insist that the mother of seventeen had indeed fulfilled a higher mission; since it was universally agreed that a woman was created by the Almighty for the purpose of bringing forth children who, if female, were created by the Almighty for the purpose of bringing forth children; and so on to the end of the world. The quality of the children was not of primary consequence. Number

---

[1] Thus Dr A. C. Haddon described the ' duty ' of my sex in a letter to the *British Medical Journal*, January 1935.

[2] At Liverpool, June 1939.

was what earned approval. Numbers were needed, for nearly half of those who were born did not live beyond childhood, and there were the busy labour markets to be replenished, the multiplying colonies to be peopled with masterful white men, and a new class of rich families eager to be built up into great ones through the careers and alliances of their members. Where formerly to breed had been looked upon with resignation as woman's unavoidable portion, a destiny sometimes agreeable and sometimes unfortunate, with Industrial Revolution and Imperial Expansion there was inculcated by subtle propaganda a new pride of office, a romantic, idealistic attitude undreamed of in the days when to keep *down* the population had seemed a vital problem. Motherhood was, so to speak, 'glamourized.' The mother was flattered into believing herself sacrosanct, a bogus chivalry paid deference to her, sweet pathetic legends began to envelop her, maudlin songs and poems were her tribute.

When the Women's Movement began to assume proportions rather alarming to its opponents, this glorified Mother-figure was used to shame the Feminists and to keep from their ranks great numbers of potential supporters who were taught to believe that only those unfit for the sacred duties of maternity could possibly treasure extra-domestic ambitions. And today, though every circumstance has changed irrevocably, we are encumbered with relics of the old illusionism.[1]

It is still the official doctrine of the Church and State that to breed largely is a praiseworthy activity, and as far as the ministrations of these guardians are concerned, children are allowed to be born to poverty, dirt, and disease with as little check upon their arrival as existed a hundred years ago. And yet, now as in the past, extremely big families show a much higher proportionate rate of mortality than is found in those of moderate size, and news items of the type that follows are uncommon only in so far as immense families are, mercifully, uncommon.

'Twentieth child of Mrs J—— McA—— . . . baby J—— McA——, a 4½-months' child, is described as a wonder. When she was born on January 16 she weighed 13 oz., and was only 8 in. long, with a head as small as a hen's egg. . . .

She lives in a clothes-basket wrapped in cotton-wool, with hot water in a lemonade bottle to keep her warm.

Of Mrs McA——'s previous children, eight are living.'[2]

Of nineteen children born before the 'wonder' in question, eleven died; the general quality of the breed may be guessed at; and this in a period when, as Miss F. W. Stella Browne has written[3]: 'The control of reproduction . . . is as much a part of our heritage and our achievement

[1] See Appendix 38.
[2] From *Reynolds News*, February 8th, 1942.
[3] In her essay on *The Right to Abortion*.

as the use of fire, articulate speech, agriculture, mechanical transport, sanitation.' That it is not accepted as such is one of our major sentimental tragedies.

I will anticipate one last and very customary objection. 'Is it not possible that, by this control of reproduction, you may be preventing the advent of a Hogarth, a Byron, an Emily Brontë, or a Dickens? None of these creatures of genius was born in promising circumstances. All might have been debarred from entering the world had the means and moral support been available.' I see the answer thus: It is true we might waste, and do waste now, some prospects of valuable human material, but the most reckless squanderings of man are as nothing to the habitual and inescapable squanderings of Nature. For every child conceived, the germ of life has been scattered a millionfold. Who can say the seed that travelled swiftest to the womb has not outstripped thousands otherwise far superior, yet destined to come to nothing? To produce children under unfavourable conditions on the remote offchance that one of them may prove indispensable to mankind is to imitate the wastefulness of Nature at a cost which that insensate creative force has not to pay.

In any case, *extreme* poverty, ill-health, or family discord is so rarely to be found as part of the early background of great men and women that one may safely assume greatness is not likely to survive it. If we disregard the sensational anecdotes which, in a wonder-loving world, gain easy currency, and apply ourselves to careful biography, we shall find that the heredity of the highest types is seldom remarkable for its badness. It betrays a childlike ignorance to suppose that geniuses are begotten by people so evidently diseased in mind or body as, for instance, to be fit subjects for sterilization. Though it is true that notable parents have often developed infirmities that have made their children's lives miserable, yet I cannot recollect that any one of them was ever confirmed in vice, transmissible disease, or criminality at the time when the brilliant offspring was begotten—that is to say, that any one of them would have been restrained, in a more advanced social order, from begetting. Compulsory genetic control will never, I fancy, err on the side of exclusiveness.

In reading what I have written to this point and trying to draw together, in my own mind at least, the somewhat rambling threads of the discussion, I cannot but come to the conclusion that in this matter of the ethics of procreation feminine opinion is for very good practical reasons less confused, less cluttered up with pseudo-religious and patriotic nonsense, than the opinion which is characteristically masculine. Women are too closely in touch with the realities of birth and breeding to go on cherishing, now that they have achieved a certain degree of independence, the illusions natural to males. Men, whose impulse to get children may be carried into effect with ease and pleasure and, generally speaking, a comparatively small degree of disturbance in the results, have justified their reproductive activities—since the growth of a conscience towards women—by the maternal mythology at which we have briefly glanced, coupled with such political or religious beliefs as seemed expedient. And while they have wrangled over this mythology and these creeds, driven by economic necessity to admit a problem, women have made controlled reproduction a *fait accompli*—often a bad, risky, illegal *fait accompli*, but a contribution nevertheless to the future : that future when, in Miss Stella Browne's encouraging words, 'children will be welcomed and created as achievements, and not flung into life with fear and anger as disastrous accidents.'

It is officially estimated that upwards of 100,000 illegal abortions are performed in England annually. I should suppose the real number to be enormously greater. One cannot but echo Dr Cunnington's *cri de cœur* : 'What a mercy all these felonies are not discovered. For if we had to accommodate that number of fresh convicts every year the overcrowding of our prisons would become inconvenient.' Unfortunately, the women with spirit and ingenuity to defy anachronistic law are often of the type whose posterity we can ill spare, while persons of the lowest mentality burden the race with human dross and are taught to believe that the country owes them a debt of gratitude. And it is an easy belief for feeble intellects, a flattering and reassuring belief which assorts well with others favoured by tradition. A mother is loving and kind. Children bring happiness. God sends children into the world. A large population gives strength and security. . . . So run the simple and idealistic legends. We must not interfere with Nature. We have no right to deny life, even to the unborn. . . . Life is precious. Life is sacred. Life once conceived must be allowed to burgeon, no matter how bedraggled the blossom or how bitter the fruit. . . . War, not contraception, is Nature's pruning-hook.

... Strongly entwisted with human nature is the desire of exercising
power, however that power be gained or given. Let us pity it in others,
and despise it in ourselves.

DR JOHNSON, in a letter to 'Queeney' Thrale.

THE timidity with which the less candid and less gifted cling to 'the
formalities of propriety,' and a propriety which, as a rule, is not
rational but purely arbitrary, is especially apparent in the little use that
is made of the social sciences—sciences concerned with the investigation
of the human species, individually and in groups, in conformity and in
rebellion, in normality and in alienation. It is an axiomatic characteristic
of conventional minds to desire fixed and defined outlines, to dislike
subtleties and changefulnesses. Thus there is always a fear of handling
the mutable fabric of present reality, and a marked preference for academic
analyses.

Until very little more than a hundred years ago our native language
and literature were not deemed worthy of any place in the school curriculum, while several hours of daily study were devoted to Greek and
Latin. The case of psychology is analogous. A mild disdain similar to
that which was once felt for modern languages as an educational subject
is now shed on the attempt, still looked upon as slightly eccentric, to
take human motives and behaviour seriously. It has only recently ceased
to be a disreputable thing to examine men objectively; that is, in themselves and not in relation to a set of rules they are expected to conform to.

The late Professor McDougall, a pioneer who in his prime was both
brilliant and balanced—which is what cannot be said of all his confrères
—frequently called attention to the neglect of the great potentialities of
this youthful science, neglect amounting, in his opinion, to a 'positive
contempt.' Such a state of affairs is obviously in some measure to be
attributed to the extravagances and naïvetés of the most widely known
theories (widely known only because they *are* extravagant),[1] but mainly
perhaps it is due to an unavoidable deficiency, the want of an agreed body
of psychological doctrine:

'In many of the sciences it is possible for a single worker to make
a discovery, and to establish it by evidence so clear and decisive that
the new truth is at once accepted by all his colleagues and by the public
in general. In psychology this is not possible; every observation is
capable of widely different interpretations, between which only experts
can decide; and in the absence of any consensus of opinion among

[1] See Appendix 39.

them, the public must continue to oscillate vaguely, likely to be inflated by each new wind of doctrine, seeking in vain any established principles of human nature which it may confidently apply to the urgent problems of daily living.' [1]

While we may sympathize with the dilemma of the psychologist, who can only gain the confidence of the lay public—so necessary for the extension of his practical work—by ceasing to dispute with rival theorists and joining them to present a solid front, yet it is in many respects very desirable that no such solid front should be presented, for there can scarcely be a worse hindrance to the genuine progress of a science than the establishment of an orthodoxy. But though the various branches of psychology cannot, by the nature of their material, provide us with unvarying scales of measurement and precise gauges for ascertaining the effects of causes, though it may be a long time before they are able to give a guidance that is unerring, they are certainly in a stage of advancement worthy of better opportunities than have so far been opened to them.

In his plea for the extension of sociological research work and more effective recognition of its findings,[2] Raymond B. Fosdick, President, at the time of writing, of the Rockefeller Foundation, speaks of 'the extraordinary contrast between our willingness to make any change whatever in our physical environment that convenience and well-being may prescribe, and our obstinate determination to leave unaltered as far as we can our relations both to the world and to each other. We eagerly apply to our methods of living the conclusions of the natural sciences; we scorn to apply the conclusions of the social sciences.'

Here tradition is upheld by extremely strong unacknowledged emotions springing from instincts which have been warped in striving to fit them to the demands of society. (The evidence is good enough, I think, to enable us to accept this premise without laying ourselves open to a charge of facile assumption.) The instinct of fear, the instinct of sexual desire, the instinct to win approval, all expressed fairly openly in a primitive stage of development, appear, when they are associated with shame and subjected to a long course of concealment, to generate a covert feeling of inferiority or insecurity, or both, which the subject seeks to assuage by the exercise of power; directly when he believes himself strong enough, vicariously when he is weak.

That there is in mankind a hunger for power which is in itself instinctive and would be an active agent in human affairs even if there were no repression of other instincts is doubtless true. Bertrand Russell's celebrated thesis surveys the question from this angle: 'The fundamental

---

[1] From McDougall's *Psycho-Analysis and Social Psychology*. It is hardly necessary to say that when the writer speaks of 'the public' in this context, he means the learned or at least the aspiring public, the remainder having little interest in psychological doctrines, and no interest at all in applying them to the 'problems of daily living.'
[2] *The Old Savage in the New Civilization.*

concept in social science is Power in the same sense in which Energy is the fundamental concept in physics.' Nothing that he says, however, rules out the probability that the appetite would take a healthier turn if it were not usually vitiated by errors of education.

I have spoken of 'the instinct to win approval,' and I pause to allow that many psychologists would regard this as a loose figure of speech. The desire for appreciation is, in their view, only accessory to sexual desire —the one instinct which, some of them would say, is properly so-called. Nevertheless, I believe there is an intuitive eagerness to find favour quite dissociated from sexual impulsion—probably more closely allied to some aspect of the herd instinct, the need for the warmth and support of one's fellows—which we may see at its simplest when children are showing off before their elders. But from infancy candid boastings and blatant methods of attracting notice are snubbed, often very cruelly, with the result that they give place to ruses; false modesty accompanied by subtle 'fishing for compliments,' elaborate pretences of indifference, arrogant defiance, etc. Most adults are afflicted with vanity in some such contorted shape.

Fear, like egotism, is also accustomed to be driven to subterfuge. Dr G. F. Morton, from his long experience as an educator, has written an erudite book on the fear-suppressing tradition.[1] The evils of sexual concealment have, he points out, been accorded a disproportionate amount of emphasis: the evils of habitually concealing fear are everywhere under-estimated:

'The gospel according to the Freudian seems to be that fear is never repressed, but that sexuality always is; that sex is regarded with reproach, but fear with benignant tolerance. Every schoolboy knows better than this. . . . It is high time that schoolmasters proclaimed from the house-tops that with the average healthy boy sex has the lesser reproach and fear has the greater. . . . Rivers gives whole-hearted support to this position. "From infancy the influence of parents and teachers is directed to bring about the repression of any manifestation of fear," and "Owing to the way in which the society to which we belong . . . looks upon fear, its occurrence . . . arouses other emotions, and especially that of shame, which greatly enhance the strain to which fear is primarily due."'

Linked with society's demand that we hide our fears is the prescription that we should be stoical in bearing pain, and even tiny children walking at large for the first time are taught to be 'brave' and cry as little as possible when they hurt themselves. In school life, to be afraid of pain is a disgrace, to bear it stolidly is creditable. We know from many adult reminiscences of childish unhappiness what ordeals hinge upon this ancient standard, and it does not always require abstruse study to perceive

[1] *Childhood's Fears.*

their later ill effects. 'Experience of cruelty and unfriendliness,' says Bertrand Russell,[1] 'may operate in either direction: with those who are easily frightened it produces the wish to escape observation, while bolder spirits are stimulated to seek positions in which they can inflict cruelties rather than suffer them.'

However the passion for power may be generated—whether spontaneously or through the struggle to dam other instincts—its manifestations are easy enough to recognize. Nationally it reveals itself in imperialism, militarism, power politics, fanatical worship of leaders,[2] and so forth. Privately we see it in numerous kinds of acquisitiveness, in the longing to organize other people's lives which frequently takes a benevolent shape, in the enjoyment of 'being in the know' which promotes gossip and scandal, in amatory conquests for the mere sake of the victory, in being waited upon and sought after, in mortifying selected victims, and in a thousand and one other fashions, some amiable, some detestable.

In civic affairs, direct and indirect gratification of the will to power is demonstrated by the abuse of bureaucratic methods and the enforcement of obsolete, niggling, and unnecessary laws, by harsh penal codes maintained despite evidence of their uselessness, repression for repression's sake in the education of children, persecution of uncongenial opinions, emphasis on exclusive class distinctions, masculine attempts to renew the subjugation of women, and attempts of both sexes to make the pleasures and pastimes of others unlawful. The list will admit of limitless extension.

I do not suggest that the power principle is solely responsible for all these public nuisances: that would be a crude over-simplification. Other factors undeniably operate—fear of change, want of courage to oppose, ignorance and misinformation. But that persons who actively uphold or initiate policies such as I have briefly touched upon are primarily induced by an inward despotism, and that this in its turn may originate in certain fears and longings partially or wholly repressed since childhood, I take to be a well-established case.

Foremost among the detestable products of that early injury, though it is so nearly universal that it is still widely taken for granted as natural and commendable, is the tendency to find satisfaction in the idea of punishment. A vein of cruelty is easily rationalized into something praiseworthy by the mental processes that simplify and idealize. We are soon persuaded that punishment must not only deter the offender from committing the same crime again, but also others from following his example. Hence, when currently accepted penology was even

[1] In *Power: A New Social Analysis.*
[2] I fancy this is a psychosis which may more reasonably be attributed to a vicarious appreciation of power, similar to that experienced by readers of boys' serial stories in which the hero achieves amazing deeds in the face of tremendous odds, than to buried memories of joining one's brothers in loving, hating, and ultimately killing and eating a 'violent primal father'; which seems to be the explanation offered in Freud's *Totem and Taboo.*

simpler and more idealistic than it is today, it was matter for civic pride that offenders were submitted publicly to lingering torments, and anyone who ventured to question the value of this proceeding was looked upon as defective in moral judgment or an unpractical dreamer. And though the taste for premeditated brutality is greatly diminished, suffering inflicted self-righteously still affords such compensation for past and present thwartings that proofs of its futility are seldom heard with patience. Reforms based upon the abolition or modification of penalties are usually undertaken more charily than any others except those aimed at the abolition of war (which happens to involve the same emotions).

'Is there anything more revolting,' I heard Professor John Hilton ask, 'than blood-thirstiness masquerading under the guise of outraged virtue and a desire for justice?' The fury of a large section of the public against the Bill to do away with judicial flogging inclined one to answer with an unhesitating 'No.'

Remembering the demonstrations in favour of flogging, the vivid interest aroused by the Debate (which commanded an immensely bigger attendance than any other part of the Criminal Justice Bill, or most other Bills for that matter), the heated speeches and newspaper correspondence, the heavy flogging sentences meted out shortly before the Bill was passed, as if certain judges were having their last fling, the haste with which wartime conditions were seized upon as an excuse to overthrow the findings of an expert committee of enquiry and retain the cat-o'-nine-tails after all—remembering that amazing outburst of emotionalism, I think it probable that it will be used by our posterity as one of their most telling pictures of a neurotic age.

It is true that corporal punishment existed in the past and was ordered with very much less compunction than modern judges feel; the difference was that hardly anyone had ever questioned its utility. Scientific investigation of such a subject was so unheard-of, effects were so generally assumed from immediate appearances, that it was really possible even for thoroughly humane people with no streak of sadism at all to believe that flogging and birching assisted the cause of morality. Sadism there certainly was, and a great deal of it, as naval and military records make clear; but not everyone who approved the infliction of physical pain was inspired by a warped hunger for power.

Today, however, there is a vast body of authoritative evidence that physical pain does not cure the particular vices for which it is, so to speak, the popular specific. We have it on the word of a government-appointed committee—seldom a revolutionary sort of body—which examined every record of judicial flogging over a period of fifty years; we have the exposure, by clear statistics, of the widely accepted fallacy of 'crime waves' being stemmed by flogging sentences and criminals who have once had the lash never committing the same offence again; we have also the example of countries where such punishments have long been obsolete and where the incidence of ruffianism has yet been strikingly low. In short, emotional grounds are now the only grounds upon which a well-informed person can be an advocate of flagellation.

The morbidity which in a greater or less degree affects almost the entire populace reached its fever pitch at the Women Conservatives' Conference in May 1939, when two thousand five hundred women (minus about a dozen who were in opposition) worked themselves up to what seems to have been a frenzy on being asked to vote for a Resolution 'deploring those sections of the Criminal Justice Bill which seek to abolish corporal punishment.' Inspired by a well-known fox-hunting maiden lady who was much concerned with sexual offences against girls and children, the vast gathering, so it is stated by numerous eye-witnesses, became wildly excited, howled, jeered, and hooted at the one or two speakers who had the courage to appeal for a fair trial of the Bill's provisions, and rose to their feet stamping and shouting. Descriptions of the scene carry a reminiscence of the intoxicated behaviour of the mob at public executions in the last century, when the hangman's name would be chanted in a delirium of sado-masochism: 'Calcroft, he's the man.'

With only one or two exceptions, the million-sale newspapers, doubtless pandering to the known proclivities of their readers—for whose titillation the flogging of the 'Mayfair men' a little while before had been exploited by every ingenious device of sensationalism [1]—reported the uproar with visible approbation: headlines such as 'WOMEN DEMAND FLOGGING FOR BRUTES' gave the keynote. But the *News Chronicle* published an article of strong condemnation by the late Professor Hilton, who pointed out that:

'Persons who have given their minds and hearts and lives not to the hunting of foxes but to studying how to diminish the causes of these attacks on women and children, how to treat those who display a proneness to sexual violence . . . have been coming with one accord to the conclusion, based on deep knowledge and wide experience, that the flogging of sexual offenders is not only in itself for the most part a brainless brutality, in that many of them are mentally afflicted and need treatment rather than punishment; but that instead of providing a deterrent it excites depraved passions and in so doing actually creates criminals.'

The incident at the Women's Conference, he wrote, gave 'an appalling glimpse of the lusts which lurk below the surface in all of us; of the animal unreason, which can, in a moment of mass hysteria, supplant the judgment that is the noble prerogative of humankind.'

---

[1] One of the journals which attempts to make up for the absence of other entertainments on the Sabbath devoted two full centre pages to discussion of the punishment in store, with a 'life-size' picture of the 'cat' across the breadth of them.

Professor Hilton's protest induced so many readers to write letters that in a second article on the same subject he observed: 'The mere mention of flogging excites passions in a most disturbing way. . . . An interesting feature of the angry criticism is that not a single one of my critics had grasped what my argument was. It was evident that as soon as they discovered I was against flogging they ceased to take anything more in.' Sir John Anderson was similarly unwilling to subjugate feeling to the impartial inferences of science, and one of his first acts on becoming Home Secretary was to shelve the Bill which had been passed by Parliament and carry the penal code backwards as far as he could, actually extending the number of offences for which corporal punishment may be administered.[1] 'BLACK-OUT BRUTES TO BE FLOGGED' the headlines announced triumphantly, just as if the long enquiry had never taken place and its careful findings had never been debated. All the results of experience and research went for nothing in the face of that abysmal appetite for ritual torture.

It is regrettable indeed that it is not called torture instead of corporal punishment, since dislike of the word would have tended to make people ashamed of the thing. 'The "cat" is the only deterrent for your class of crime,' says a learned judge, in strange ignorance both of human nature and ascertainable facts. If he would force himself to say instead 'Torture is the only deterrent,' he might apprehend something of the anachronism.

'But I am glad to realize,' commented Mr Justice McCardie on one of the occasions when he reluctantly upheld what he felt was an archaic law, 'that the views of the Judges may slowly change with the times on questions of public policy.' Or in the less circumscribed words of Dr Cunnington, 'The judicial mind has moved forward and is now only a century or so behind the times.' The judges of Great Britain are worthy of respect for their independence, their striking freedom from corruption, and their competence in stating and administering the law as it exists: on the other hand, they have never as a class been in the vanguard of progressive movements, nor have they given much countenance to new legislation designed to curtail their own powers. And having been subject to the same repressions and lessons in evasion which scarcely any child could escape forty, fifty, or sixty years ago, when they were in their tutelage, their rationalized prejudices will be only—through training —a little less inveterate than if they had followed other walks of life.

When even persons of superior mental attainments are victims of deceiving emotions, we may imagine that the stupid and unthinking—

[1] It must be mentioned to his credit, however, that very shortly after taking office he refused to confirm a decision of visiting magistrates that a Liverpool prisoner who had assaulted a warder should receive 12 strokes with the 'cat' besides 28 days' solitary confinement, 15 days' special diet, and a forfeiture of remission marks and earnings.

The man had already been flogged three times for attacks upon warders, which suggests the absurdity of retaining flogging as a 'deterrent' even for prison offences.

an immeasurably larger class—find a very real gratification in the panoply of legal retribution, the more so as few among them have ever had the equipment, physical, economic, or intellectual, for wielding much power through direct and personal channels.

Dr Renier, the Dutch scholar who examined us with such courteous detachment in *The English: Are They Human?*, found that, for a people which considers itself enlightened, our addiction to punishment, and especially the death penalty, was singularly tenacious and out of keeping with the spirit of the times.[1] 'The nation loves its executioners,' he says, 'and experiences a thrill of self-righteous satisfaction at the news of each artificial extinction of human life.' The self-righteous part of the satisfaction is at times permitted to become the thinnest of veneers. Sensation-hunters who leave their homes before dawn to stand outside the prison where someone is about to be hanged belong, like the parties which hired windows for a good view of public executions a hundred years ago, to a rowdy and dissipated rather than to an ostentatiously respectable set. I have seen a photograph of the waiting crowd on the morning when Dr Ruxton was hanged in 1936 which it would take the combined skill of Hogarth and Dickens to reproduce in any other medium, so terrifying was the concentration of laughing, leering, jeering, hideous faces, intoxicated with malevolence.

I have no regrets for the dispatch of Dr Ruxton: I find it easy to be glad that a man capable of the repulsive actions he performed is dead and done with, and I think it better for his own sake, though he might not see eye to eye with me in this, that he should die rather than drag out a useless life in prison. But if I go to the trouble of taking the long view, both backwards and forwards, I get, first, a difficult, imperfect glimpse of factors that may have conspired to instil into this man the raging jealousy and crazy fear so clearly indicated by his crimes, and then an inkling—remembering the newspaper gloatings and the assembly outside the prison—of the harm the community suffers by having power-compensation impulses played up to in this deleterious manner: and I feel we cannot afford to be sentimental about the murderer. Unless his death can be accomplished without the morbid ritual of gallows, black caps, and condemned cells, and without publicity—which, although troublesome, happens to be a safeguard we cannot dispense with—it is preferable that a dangerous man should exist under perpetual restraint.

'A life for a life' is wishful, over-simple reckoning. The penalty of suspending a culprit by the neck is, as Dr Renier tells us, degrading alike to those who apply it and those who tolerate it. As a deterrent it is futile, since 'the murderer . . . either imagines he will be able to hide his action and escape punishment, or else acts under the influence of a passion which blinds him to the consequences of his crime.' As an act

[1] The book was first published early in 1931. Since then many countries have put the clock back.

of justice, it fails to convince, for there is hardly anyone nowadays so naïve as to believe that murder is always and absolutely the worst offence that can be committed against society, and most people's memories would not have to stray far to capture instances of crimes which seem more loathsome than killing. Killing, in fact, being periodically urged upon us as a noble duty, and being at all times held before us as an act which a man who loves his country will be eager to perform at the request of the Government in power, it is hard to feel that abhorrence towards it which criminal law is built upon. We cannot be surprised that murder is 'glamourized' in novels and dramas, and that the crook who will draw a gun seems a more admirable character than the sneak-thief who bereaves nobody.

Canon Maynard Smith, an author of detective stories, is reported to have told the Stroud Rotary Club some years ago that 'as far as he could make out, the fiction of the present day was divided into books dealing with adultery and with murder. He was sure they would agree that to read books on murder was by far the more healthy and laudable pursuit.'

The curious standard of morality implied in this is widely approved, and must in some measure be due to the enforcement of the capital penalty, which lends a murderer the 'heroic' quality of one willing to risk his life. I doubt very much whether, unless invasion has already produced more than superficial changes, Danes and Hollanders have any idea that it is more creditable to be interested in illicit killing than illicit love.

It is generally accepted and frequently stated (in this country) that our legal system is a pattern for the whole world, and I dare say many of Dr Renier's readers were surprised and pained by his reiterant comments on its harshness.

> 'The thought [he says] that the criminal may be a victim of society or of circumstance, that society has obligations towards him as well as a right to protect itself from him, is almost absent from the judicial mind, and altogether from public consciousness. English law is still a *lex talionis*, even if the principle of an eye for an eye is not carried out to its final consequences. *Any act of grace, such as one of those rare occurrences when a man is sent to a criminal lunatic asylum instead of to the gallows, is sure to raise a storm of protest in one or another section of the community.* . . . If it be true that the accused person is not treated as one who has to prove his innocence, but as one whose guilt remains to be proved, it is not the less a fact that, once found guilty, the prisoner as often as not receives a heavier sentence than in most other countries.'

The passage I have italicized reveals an attitude equally evident in respect of offences which are less than capital. The zest for punishment makes any suggestion of a criminal's non-responsibility, however well supported by medical observers, extremely unattractive to court officials and still more so to the public at large. The reluctance of lawyers to throw off the old obsession of deliberate sin is lighted from various angles by the following examples.

In January 1940 an actively religious woman of fifty pleaded guilty to writing what are known as 'poison pen' letters making a gratuitous allegation of incest between two brothers and a sister. The Old Bailey Recorder reproved her scathingly: 'It may be that you are suffering from what nowadays is incomprehensibly called a complex. If that is so, it is something you can and must overcome, otherwise you will spend some time in prison. . . . You ought to be ashamed of yourself.'

This is a milder version of a remark made some years earlier when a valet was tried at the Central Criminal Court for demanding money with menaces from the wife of a Cabinet Minister. He was sentenced to three years' penal servitude, and the Recorder (according to *The Times*) addressed him thus: 'I think you are mad, and so does Dr Grierson, and if you are, you will be sent to Broadmoor for the rest of your life, or until you recover. We cannot allow this sort of thing. The lives of public men are not going to be rendered more difficult than they are by nuisances like you.' I do not know whether the would-be blackmailer was sane or insane; in either case he was probably a highly exasperating character. My only concern is with the Recorder's unwillingness to grasp that a man who is literally mad is the victim of disease and that it is futile to rebuke him for it.

More recently—in April 1940—a man aged twenty-nine, who had been several times in prison for housebreaking and similar crimes, made an earnest plea before being sentenced. 'Why do they not treat people psychologically and with medicine? All they do is to lock men up in cells and leave them to their own thoughts.' 'When you broke into the house,' said the Recorder, giving him three years' penal servitude, 'you didn't break in psychologically; you went in through the window.' As this is the same Recorder who found it 'incomprehensible' that a mental entanglement should be called a complex, or perhaps that it should exist at all, it is not astonishing that he is unaware of the meaning of the word 'psychological' and seems to confuse it with 'psychic.'

Once again, I am not venturing any opinion as to the justness or otherwise of the man's punishment. It may one day seem as curious that a criminal should have begged in vain for psychological treatment as that an insane person should formerly have had no ministrations but whipping and semi-starvation in a dark cell. On the other hand, I know very well that thieves, blackmailers, procurers, drug pedlars, kidnappers, receivers, and the rest of society's outlaws, are much easier to deal with in theory than in practice, and though the laziness, egoism, and insensitiveness which are among the causes of crime may be deformities as involuntary on the part of the sufferer as a wry neck or a club foot, they render him extremely unprepossessing to normal individuals. This repugnance makes it hard to behave equably towards the anti-social. But it was once fully as hard to be equable towards the insane, and is not very easy still for those who are in close contact with them.

For reasons which are far from mysterious, there are no forms of anti-social action which excite more vindictive indignation than those due to some kind of sexual hypertrophy. The anonymous author of *English Justice* explaining that offences against the person, such as assault, are usually treated much more leniently than offences against property, makes an exception in cases of a sexual nature.[1] 'In these the justices tend not only to be unduly severe in dealing with men who are fitter for the hospital than the dock, but also to convict on insufficient evidence. . . . As a rule, it may be taken that if a man has only once been convicted of an offence such as indecent exposure, there has been a miscarriage of justice. I have known of a man with over fifty convictions for this offence.'

In the Home Office *Report on the Psychological Treatment of Crime*, one reads with unhappiness such passages as the following:

'Case LVII Aged 36. Indecent exposure. Twelve months' imprisonment. . . . He was an example of the chronic exhibitionist. . . . His penal record was appalling not only from the point of view of the frequency of the offence but also as it seemed entirely pointless, serving neither a punitive, preventative, or isolable purpose.'

The peculiar satisfaction which many neurotics obtain from phallic exposure is largely due to the knowledge that they are exciting sensations of shock and amazement. It is unlikely that Greek athletes, accustomed to appear naked at public performances, would have derived amusement from the surreptitious display of their genital organs to young women, or that the young women themselves, to whom representations of naked men were familiar from childhood, would have been seized with trembling terror at the sight. 'Put it away! I've seen hundreds!' said a lady who had been a hospital nurse on encountering a doubly misguided exhibitionist. I can well believe that the smile faded from his face as he obeyed: two or three more such errors might have removed all the fascination from his vice.

It is unfortunate when children are drawn into this kind of disagreeableness, but it would be less so if sex were rationally regarded by parents and nurses. When adults shrink from something as a bogy, children will naturally find it more frightening still. A girl who could tell her father and mother about some absurd and unaccountable piece of sexual behaviour without throwing them into paroxysms of dark resentment would be in little danger of developing a trauma.

I speak from some experience of youthful reactions towards adult sexualities. Children are involved in them much oftener than is generally

[1] See Appendix 40.

suspected; only a small proportion of the offences committed are ever brought to light, since in all but a very few homes and schools such matters are invested by the elders with an air which begets shyness and nervous confusion; and an unpleasant incident will be hidden in an obscure kind of shame and horror. It is upon this secretiveness that lecherous old men and ill-balanced adolescents—the most typical offenders —depend for immunity from troublesome consequences. What is required is not more punishment for the guilty, but less murky mystery for the innocent, less salacious modesty and idealized ignorance.

But if our traditions and our self-compensating impulses support foolish and ruthless methods of dealing with sexual excess, what are we to say of our legal attitude towards inversion? It is probable that every reader of this book will have among his acquaintance at least one homo-sexual who is a useful and agreeable member of the community and whose desires are centred only on people of approximately his own tendency, doing no injury to anyone. The squalid seductions and assaults which lead to criminal prosecution, the association that appears to exist between homosexual propensities and dishonesty, are often directly traceable to the suppressions and distortions demanded by society and the ignominy always heaped upon the abnormal in low life.

Nor is it in low life only that Biblical morality prevails. The social scientists themselves, except for a few pioneers whose iconoclasms have been reckless, are too much inclined to accept, without adequately sub-mitting them to dispassionate criticism, beliefs, customs, ancient taboos which are deplorable in men and women of technical attainments such as ours. Thus in the Government Blue Book already mentioned,[1] Dr W. Norwood East and Dr W. H. de Hubert, two practitioners who have had great opportunities of prison work, are untroubled, it appears, by any intellectual scruple in publishing the ensuing comment on the prospects of curing criminal sadists or masochists:

'Treatment of these conditions presents profound difficulties and real dangers. . . . It is not unusual to see a man who shows by slight difficulty in adjustment to sexual or social life, or by psychoneurotic reaction, that his drives are not in harmony or completely adjusted to his environment. Very little investigation may show that these difficulties are dependent upon strong homosexual interests of which he is not properly aware at the present. Clearly, clumsy therapy, with no idea of a practical goal, may remove from him minor difficulties, at the same time presenting him with the major problem of strong, conscious homosexual feeling with which he may be totally unable to deal. There is no question here but that the last state is infinitely worse than the first. . . .'

Here we have an implied suggestion that sadism, of which some

[1] *Report on the Psychological Treatment of Crime.*

disgusting instances are given, is preferable to recognized homosexuality, that a craving to maim and torment is a 'minor difficulty' compared with vices which long tradition more explicitly condemns. And certainly most judges and magistrates seem to concur in this opinion.

In October 1940 a scientific research worker, aged forty-four, a man of creditable career, was prosecuted for attempting to commit an offence with an R.A.F. mechanic of twenty-five, who did not deny his willing-ness. Medical evidence as to the older man's mental condition (he had been to a nursing home for special treatment, having developed 'an inordinate affection' for the other) was discounted by Mr Justice Croom-Johnson, who referred with contempt to 'all this modern jargon of inhibitions.' Complacently ignoring the labours of three generations of psychological investigators, he launched into the well-worn commina-tions: 'Both of you have admitted an attempt to commit a loathsome, abominable and serious crime. You must be punished for conduct which cannot be tolerated.' The older man was given eighteen months' hard labour, the younger nine months' and a lecture on disgracing an honourable uniform while his fellows were saving the country from disaster.

What end is served by this prosecution and this punishment? How is the cause of morality supported by the nasty means of securing evidence and the attendant scandal? If, as was said, the scientist's married life had been broken up by his passion for the mechanic who had worked in his laboratory, was it to be mended by sending him to prison? And was the alleged disgrace to the uniform of the R.A.F. expunged by wide-spread publicity? Is there, in short, any room for doubt that the pursuit of this class of crime is linked with the pursuit of vindictive power for its own sake, an association none the less unwholesome because it is unconscious?

Oscar Wilde, like many men whose wit and gaiety give them an air of light-mindedness, frequently expressed himself on social questions with a flash of clearest common sense. Himself destined to be the saddest of all martyrs to the passion for punishment, he spoke of it thus:[1]

'As one reads history, not in the expurgated editions written for schoolboys and passmen, but in the original authorities of each time, one is absolutely sickened, not by the crimes that the wicked have committed, but by the punishments that the good have inflicted; and the community is infinitely more brutalized by the habitual employment of punishment than it is by the occasional occurrence of crimes. It obviously follows that the more punishment is inflicted the more crime is produced; and most modern legislation has clearly recognized this, and has made it its task to diminish punishment as far as it thinks it can. Wherever it has really diminished it, the

[1] In *The Soul of Man under Socialism*.

results have always been extremely good. The less punishment the less crime.'

.   .   .   .

The punishment of nations can be shown by the clearest historical evidence to be even less effective as a deterrent than the punishment of individuals. Its underlying motives are largely the same. It is another and still more heady means of assuaging the unhealthy thirst of the *amour-propre*.[1] The problem of war has been closely studied, especially in the last three or four decades, and various causes assigned to the recurrence of the hideous phenomenon. The verdict of the past, that it is God's retribution for sin—retribution falling upon guilty and innocent alike in the true Jehovah manner—has been abandoned by all but a few weak intellects, and an economic theory is now in favour. I am in accord with those who see war mainly as a psychological problem, and in this the economic problem is comprised. For, whatever intricacies have evolved to obscure the underlying facts, the greed and envy which beget aggression are certainly symptoms of power starvation, and the passion for property, which has been described as the most difficult of all passions to civilize, is fundamentally a passion for power. The economic diseases of the social order are, as it were, the complications of a psychological malady.

We hear a great deal about the will to peace of the common people and the reluctance with which they fight the wars thrust upon them by evil rulers. This I believe to be an illusion comforting to those who wish to think well of the human race. Wars, if they do not drag on too long, are generally popular. Hero-worship has always been bestowed on conquerors rather than peaceful benefactors, and I cannot recollect that any dictator ever seized and held authority without a sustained appeal to combative instincts. Not that these are always in the ascendant. There are periods when men of the dictator mentality are at a discount, when peace is valued with more than lip service and pacific doctrines are sympathetically, even enthusiastically, received: but such phases will be found, as a rule, to correspond with the years of exhaustion after defeat and satiety after conquest, and have seldom lasted even so long as a generation except in countries where living conditions and social customs have permitted the development of an anti-militant tradition; that is to say, where malnutrition, physical or mental, in childhood is less acute and adult self-compensating impulses therefore take milder shapes.

[1] It should be borne in mind of the present war that the Germans believe it to be punitive against Britain just as the British believe it to be punitive against Germany. Those who imagine that any war is begun for frankly aggressive purposes over-estimate human honesty. The highly provocative doctrines of the Hitler régime were always represented to the German people as a means of keeping the peace of Europe. That they have culminated in war is supposed to be due to British injustice and arrogance.

'The supposed economic causes of war,' says Bertrand Russell,[1] 'except in the case of certain capitalistic enterprises, are in the nature of a rationalization: people wish to fight, and they therefore persuade themselves that it is in their interest to do so. The important question, then, is the psychological one—"Why do people wish to fight?"'

To answer in terms of the self-compensation theory alone is to make the thing too simple. There are, of course, a great many other factors, not directly traceable to the power-hungers of the people who actually do the fighting but only to those of the men who make the wars. For example, the intrigues of statesmen, who, as we have since learned, played so nefarious a part in the cataclysm of 1914, the exigencies of the armaments industry which thrives upon international fears and suspicions,[2] the disregard for truth shown by a sensation-mongering press, and the mysterious complexities of commerce and finance.

As to the warriors themselves, their mingled emotions are described thus by G. Lowes Dickinson in his fantasia *The Magic Flute*: 'As they came together and marched, a new mood took hold of them. Something there was of adventure, for they were young; something of consecration, for they were generous; some vanity, for the women and old men praised them for their courage and their looks; for the weaker, much relief, for they had put themselves under direction; for the worser, much delight, that they could give the rein to their passions.' We know now that women, who participate more actively in each successive war, are moved by sentiments which do not appear to be in any way different from those of males.

But the most active participation in war by no means implies the strongest expression of the will to power. On the contrary, the pugnacity of non-combatants is so widely recognized as to have become almost proverbial, and the hatred that desires to smash, crush, and grind down the enemy seems to intensify in demonstrable ratio to one's distance from the scene of action, or the unlikelihood of one's being called upon to bear arms.

This, I fancy, is why, in every recent war, civilian clergymen have led the way in exhortation to violence—if we exempt publicists whose specific task it is to keep animosity alert. Thus, under the headline

[1] In *Power*.
[2] The exposures of what is often known as the arms racket have been nearly as numerous as they are ineffectual. *Merchants of Death* by H. C. Engelbrecht and F. C. Hanighen, a sensationally named but very calmly documented work, gives some extraordinary evidence of our perpetual danger from the necessity of making lethal weapons pay dividends. The Royal Commission Report on *The Private Manufacture of and Trading in Arms* (1936) is also worth reading, though it is more remarkable for its evasions than its disclosures: but it contains interesting appendices, including reference to notorious cases, and presents, quite incidentally, specimens of the self-justifications used by profit-making armament manufacturers. In 1944 a new work on the same theme was published, *Death Pays a Dividend*, by Fenner Brockway and Frederic Mullally. It disclosed the dividend in cold figures.

'WIPE OUT ALL GERMANS,' the *Daily Mail* [1] quotes the Rev. C. W. Whipp, Vicar of a parish in Leicester, as saying (in his church magazine) :

'There should be no R.A.F. pilot returning home because he cannot find a military objective for his bombs. The orders ought to be "Wipe them out." These German devils (that is the only word one can use) come over our cities and turn their machine-guns on women and children.

All I hope is that the R.A.F. will grow stronger and stronger and go over and smash Germany to smithereens.

A minister of the Gospel, perhaps, ought not to indulge in sentiments like these. I go further, I say frankly that, if I could, I would wipe Germany off the map.'

Wiping large countries off maps is a maniacal gesture frequently performed by fevered imaginations in wartime. Possibly if the suggestion of another minister of the Gospel were adopted,[2] and a 'Parsons' Battalion' were formed consisting entirely of Christian clergymen 'who believe in fighting for righteousness,' the senseless gibbering rage of some divines —deprived of the solace of prophesying hellfire—might be cooled down. The soldier on active service, by merely feeling himself to be part of the mighty war machine, the dynamo, probably has his power-impulses to some extent gratified, and, except in the heat of battle, experiences few sensations of ferocious longing to destroy. The same applies to those civilians who are engaged in war-work involving animal energy and personal risk. But passive suffering and vicarious sacrifice beget a much more virulent type of emotion.

After the first air attacks on London, demands for the total annihilation of German cities and merciless bombing of Rome poured into the newspaper offices—though perhaps they were not so numerous in relation to correspondence giving the opposite view as editorial selection made it appear—and the letters, as far as can be judged, were seldom the work of those in possession of any real and direct power to injure the enemy. I give one or two representative specimens from a copious collection :

'WIPE TOWN OUT'

'Sir,—The present policy of systematic bombing of important military objectives in Germany is the right one. But could not a portion of our bomber force be released one night from these duties, and be sent out to bomb one German town completely off the map ?

Tell the Germans that we intend to do it first, and after it is done

---

[1] September 5th, 1940. The Vicar's remarks were written before the bombing of London.
[2] In a letter to the *News Chronicle*, February 6th, 1941.

let them know by leaflet and wireless that such and such a town is
no more. "West Country," Bristol.'[1]

'RAZE BERLIN'

'SIR,—We should call on Berlin to evacuate its women and children
in, say, 24 hours; then, with our growing air ascendancy, we should
level that accursed city to the ground.

Then and then only will Hitler and his Godless hordes understand.
GERALD B. G——, Hampshire.'[2]

These letters illustrate with praiseworthy neatness something of the
sort of fantasy which goes on in the minds of men ruled by emotion.
Both writers, in humanely suggesting that the enemy should be given
notice of the intention of our Air Force, are apparently assured that there
would be neither defence nor retaliation in kind—and this at a time
when, according to the Prime Minister, the Germans 'had it in their
power to drop three or four tons of bombs on us for every ton we could
send to Germany in return.' Both desire to release destructive energy
for its own sake, but have convinced themselves that good would come
of it without troubling to enquire why or how. The implicit assumption
is that the Germans would react quite differently from ourselves to the
razing of a city, and that, while our resistance is stiffened by atrocity,
theirs would be broken at once. Such reasoning as this, if it can be called
reasoning, is the basis on which all great armaments are piled up and
all wars fought.[3] It recalls us to glance again into the great abyss between
our academic knowledge of psychology and any vestige of an intention
to apply it in the conduct of public affairs.

We know that in real life—that is, individual life, when we are accepting responsibility for our own actions and frequently seeing their immediate effects—we are able, in calm moments, to recognize that behaviour which offends us in other people is likely to offend other people
in us. It is true that this perception is far more sensitive in some than in
others. Those in whom it is very dull go through a whole lifetime
antagonizing acquaintances by their want of tact and blundering into
quarrels, while sensitiveness is the foundation of diplomacy and social
success. Such books as Dale Carnegie's famous *How to Win Friends and
Influence People* consist, quite properly, of little more than an attempt
to make their readers acquire the habit of 'putting themselves in the other
person's place.' Couched in loftier language, this is one of the official
doctrines of the Church which is supposed to follow Jesus Christ, who
committed the precept unforgettably to his disciples.

But in international affairs the effects of behaving towards others as
we should emphatically resent their behaving towards us are persistently
ignored and there is a general preference for attacking every problem

[1] From the correspondence column of the *Daily Mail*, September 13th, 1940.
[2] *Ibid.*   [3] See Appendix 41.

in the way that might be chosen by badly brought-up children.[1] To help our children to become endurable adults, we teach them—not, it must be acknowledged, by very far-sighted methods—to refrain from seeking to get their own way through lying and tale-telling, threatening, bragging, and blustering; we discourage them from the most self-stultifying forms of make-believe, only to relapse when we enter the precincts of the Political Madhouse into every vice and weakness we despise in private relations.

Consider, for example, the sneaking and eavesdropping of the system of international espionage financed by governments and almost universally countenanced by the people, in peace as well as in war. The secret agent—so named in the country he works for; the spy if he is an alien—is undoubtedly a necessary adjunct of the sovereign State, aggressive or defensive, and the records of his activities that emerge from official censorship are in themselves a powerful indictment of national sovereignty. The organized propaganda which emanates from each country's Ministries is still more pernicious. In his widely read but little regarded book, *Falsehood in War-Time*, Lord Ponsonby draws an analogy to point the calamitous distinction between public and private moral codes, picturing rival country houses in which the butlers are bribed to convey information about guests, to listen at keyholes, and to tap telephones.

'... When a great match, say a cricket match, which excites the whole district, is played between them, those who are not present are given false reports of the game to make them think the side they favour is winning, the other side is accused of cheating and foul play, and scandalous reports are circulated about the head of the family and the hideous goings on in the other house.

All this, of course, is very mild and there would be no specially dire consequences if people did behave in such an inconceivably caddish, low, and underhand way, except that they would at once be expelled from decent society.

But between nations, where the consequences are vital, where the destiny of countries and provinces hangs in the balance, the lives and fortunes of millions are affected and civilization itself is menaced, the most upright men honestly believe that there is no depth of duplicity to which they may not legitimately stoop.'

The hypnotics and stimulants thrust upon the public by the State may be concocted quite cynically after the fashion assumed by Sidney Rogerson in his *Propaganda in the Next War* [2] (and incidentally by Herr Hitler

[1] Mr Cyril Scott, in *Man is My Theme*, has drawn an amusing and impressive parallel, more sustained than anything I can attempt here, between the conduct of children at their worst and adults in wartime.

[2] Published in 1936 as part of a series edited by Captain Liddell Hart. The author speaks of the modern State as 'a highly nervous organism for whose stability and concentration both the hypnotics and the stimulants of propaganda are increasingly needed.'

in *Mein Kampf*) or devised in all sincerity by men like the 1914 H. G. Wells, who describes himself as having had 'a rash and eager confidence' in the good faith of the Foreign Office and War Office and becoming, on that account, merely an unwitting decoy, 'just as T. E. Lawrence . . . was used all unawares as a decoy for the Arabs'; [1] but a habit-forming drug is equally toxic whether it is administered by a deluding physican or a deluded one.

I am here, however, concerned only with the appalling *wrongheadedness* of the traditional technique of menace and counter-menace.

Academically speaking, we know that in a personal quarrel, boasts, threats, and gibes will produce but one reaction from any less than saintly opponent who has the least power to retaliate, and that is to intensify his anger and goad him on to show us what he can do; and though when we lose our tempers we also lose our heads, those of us who call ourselves civilized are seldom long in recoiling from a course that so visibly defeats its own object. Yet in warfare public spokesmen will go on for years taunting and jeering and daring their adversaries to do their worst, utterly incapable of realizing that such measures have precisely the same effect upon the enemy as similar derision from the enemy has upon themselves. So much is this the accepted and admired attitude that I found it surprising and refreshing to see Captain Liddell Hart, in the full limelight of a *News Chronicle* article, attributing Hitler's Western offensive (May 1940) not to a desperate gambler's throw, due to the imminence of economic collapse in Germany—the popular explanation at the time —but at least partially to the 'psychological effect of the Allied statesmen's refusal to consider his earlier peace moves, combined with their constant declaration that our victory is certain. The feeling "I'll show you" is one of the most common human incentives to drastic action.'

The Kaiser's alleged scorn for Britain's 'contemptible little Army' (a phrase which is now known to have been apocryphal) [2] was invaluable in stimulating the determination of the British soldier to prove what a mighty force he represented: it must not be imagined that our opprobrious terms for the German soldier did anything but prolong the war.

And so little have we learned, that both sides are at the same imbecile game all over again. We freely quote the sneers of the German leaders and their bombast about invincibility, well able to perceive that we are spurred on to fresh exertions by their braggadocio, but it does not seem to occur to any publicist that the Germans respond in the same manner to our own vapourings.

Newspapers have actually boasted with triumphant headlines the fact that their promises of retribution have been quoted in Germany. Un-

---

[1] The quoted words are from Wells's *Experiment in Autobiography*.

[2] This most subtle and successful of all propaganda inventions in the last war was exposed by General Sir F. Maurice in 1925. The false attribution, however, still persisted in most of the obituary notices which appeared on the Kaiser's death. By this time it had again become the fashion to blame him for the whole catastrophe of 1914.

aware of the impending collapse of France, the writer who calls himself 'Augur' addressed a gathering of commercial and civic leaders, sponsored by a Yorkshire journal, and made a statement to the effect that:

> 'After the war, Britain and France would impose peace. There would be such a chaos in Germany that no possibility of a "peace conference" could exist and 25,000 Allied warplanes would direct the settlement of Europe.'

This ranting came to the notice of Dr Goebbels' Department and was broadcast as 'a demonstration of the sinister war aims of the Allies,' and, with a surrender of judgment to passion which ought to be extraordinary but is regrettably almost universal, the Yorkshire newspaper crowed jubilantly: '"AUGUR" MAKES DR GOEBBELS THINK.' Dr Goebbels' thoughts were probably fraught with gratitude for so excellent a piece of anti-British propaganda supplied by an Englishman. Personages in much higher places have continued to feed the flames during all the ensuing years.

That bravado is often made to look ridiculous by the subsequent course of events is a consideration which appears to have no weight with the Bombastes Furiosos of the press and platform, whose comfort-loving memories quickly draw a veil over whatever might be humiliating to recall. Indeed, the more intense the illusionism, the greater the supposed patriotism. Victory must be taken for granted, all advantages on the one side magnified, all on the other minimized; to question the policies of the executive is to be guilty of 'defeatism'; to prophesy a disaster which comes to pass is practically tantamount to having caused it. Belief in word-magic is never so apparent as during hostilities.

If it be argued that this insistence upon having faith in faith helped to win the last war in spite of notorious muddling and a number of incompetent generals, I reply with firmness that, on the contrary, it brought us near to losing it. The Germans and their allies indulged in an entirely similar practice of word-magic and did lose. Nations at war, in short, have always been loud in self-praise and vehement in self-assurance, and yet every battle which was not a draw must have left the prolocutors of one side to eat their words—only, of course, they never do eat them.

I append a few sad little illustrations of contemporary rodomontade:

'INTO BATTLE WITH A SONG'

This was one of the sub-headings to an English report of Marshal Smigly-Rydz's address to the people of Warsaw on the verge of their 1939 ordeal. Urging them to take the unexampled opportunity of showing their patriotism, the Marshal—who was soon to hurry from his country—pointed out that 'to abandon Warsaw at this hour will be looked upon as an act of cowardice. . . . If Polish soldiers can see around them calm countenances and smiling women and know that the blessing of the people goes with them then they will enter the battle with a happy song.'

Here we have a sort of idealization comparable with those archiepiscopal utterances in which the unlikely symbol of modern warfare is always 'the Sword.' Going into battle against bombs, tanks, and machine-guns 'with a happy song' was a feat the Marshal was at least realist enough not to attempt in his own person.

In February 1940 M. de Kerillis wrote in *L'Epoque* that France and Britain should immediately discuss and prepare treaties of victory. 'The struggle will end only when Germany has been decisively beaten, if necessary by the sacrifice of our last sailor, our last soldier, our last shilling.' What sort of victory a country may be said to enjoy when left in so terrible a state of ruin—a condition presumably worse than that of the vanquished since it is desolation *à outrance*—it is not necessary to envisage, since such oratory always proves to be the emptiest of rhetoric.

Here is an example of fanfaronade from a private propagandist, a lady who had been exasperated by a reference in the American Magazine *Life* [1] to certain out-of-date equipment used by the British Army. She wrote to the editor:

'One Englishman armed with antiquated weapons or only with the weapons of his own courage and determination is worth more than the whole Nazi might of tanks, sub-machine-guns and the rest. . . .

It is difficult to explain the universal feeling that defeat is impossible. . . . We just know that we can't be whacked because we would rather die first. . . . We laugh at everything: even death. The kids here look upon war as an exciting sort of game. It's fun to be evacuated, fun to wake up in the middle of the night and go to the shelter in the garden, fun to realize that this is the "pictures" come to life when the searchlights and anti-aircraft guns go into action . . . fun to be rationed and carrying gas masks "just like a soldier."

America has done us a great service by giving us the expression "So what?" It may well become the national motto. So what? Our turn will come. . . .

MABEL S——, Liverpool.'

Whether this patriot went on inanely saying 'So what?' when the children whom she described as having such an immense amount of fun proved vulnerable to high explosives, whether she is still fatuously laughing at death, we cannot know, but I think it may be doubted that so inveterate a fantasist has been of much practical use to her fellow-citizens in Liverpool.

Surrender to pleasing illusion naturally demands strong precautions against encounter with potentially disturbing influences. Many protests

[1] July 1940.

218

have been sent to the press against our being allowed to know the enemy's interpretation of current events. Here is one from the *News Review* : [1]

'Few newspapers would dream of printing conflicting views which might be expressed by a competitor.

Why, then, do so many of these press organs print on one page glowing accounts of the R.A.F.'s glorious activities against the enemy and then, on another, promptly proceed to take the gilt off the ginger-bread by printing the lying German versions ?

E. D. W——.'

'Too much ginger causes gripes' is the editor's comment ; but I fancy he under-estimates the digestions of those who have trained themselves to desire almost no other sustenance than gilded sweetmeats.

A Leeds correspondent pleads [2] for some means of preventing British listeners from hearing the broadcasts of 'Lord Haw-Haw.' He has been finding that interspersed with their lies is some truth, and cannot help wondering 'which was true and which was lie.' Anxious to spare himself and all his compatriots the distress of having to use judgment, he implores the authorities to take some measures.[3]

The need of bolstering up courage and at the same time keeping nerves alert, primed for exertion, may demand belief in propositions which contradict each other. The country is more firmly united than ever country was before, but it is seething with Fifth Column activity. Britain is strong and invincible and can't fail to win, but her defences have been neglected for years. And so on. Often the same page of a newspaper, or even the same article, will contain assertions which cancel each other out.

A sensational Sunday paper, after contrasting the woman's-place-is-in-the-kitchen philosophy of Nazism with the equality existing between woman and man in England, was indiscreet—and untruthful—enough to inform its readers that many of the German parachute soldiers who landed in Holland and Belgium had turned out to be women. The B.B.C., though it has a sober air, is not irreproachably clear-headed. An announcer in the same series of news items remarked that bombers over London the night before had been obliged by bad conditions to drop their bombs indiscriminately, and that they had chosen hospitals for 'their targets' as usual.

The wiseacre already referred to as 'Augur' unconsciously provides in one of his articles (April 1940) the paradox of a united Britain which is full of 'a host of pacifists, Germanophiles, League of Nations enthusiasts,

---

[1] October 10th, 1940.   [2] In the *Yorkshire Evening News*, January 30th, 1940.
[3] He might have saved his ink, for 'Lord Haw-Haw' is defeated, and not so much by obstinate unbelief as by the menacing disagreeableness of his voice and his scornful statements. Dr Goebbels is not above the weakness of most propagandists—i.e. drawing the psychological line at the borders of one's own country—and he failed to realize that the tones which might find chinks in the English armour must not threaten.

non-resisters and moral improvers' backed by the agents of Berlin and Moscow; a righteous Britain including in its population a multitude of 'cranks, fools, perverts and cowards,' all behaving subversively.

To maintain high courage a nation in arms must have faith in its ultimate invincibility, but on the other hand it gives moral satisfaction to suppose that it has had a war thrust upon it for which, in its innocence, it was all but entirely unprepared. The legend of Britain's unpreparedness in 1914 has been quite refuted by high authorities, but the idea that we achieved victory with all the odds against us is too delightful to be easily abandoned.[1] If Britain was not adequately armed in 1939, it was not due to any parsimony in voting money for purposes of armament, for statistics show expenditure over a period of many years at the highest level ever reached or dreamed of in peacetime,[2] and such knowledgeable statesmen as Earl Lloyd George have declared our disarmament a fiction: but this fiction is kept up assiduously by constant public repining against our want of foresight, even while the columns expounding military affairs may contain such a reassurance as this:

'The German air staff know that our bombers can outpace their fighters: that our training of pilots and crews is superior because we have been at it without a gap since 1919 whereas they only began in 1934. . . .'[3]

The *News Review* in a cheering article on Imperial strength[4] reminds us that this country has been 'extraordinarily lucky at playing the war game, for of all the world's Powers it has done most scrapping.' The writer calculated that 56 per cent. of Britain's long history had been spent at war, against 50 per cent. for France, 46 per cent. for Russia, 36 per cent. for Italy, and 28 per cent. for Germany. For a race which is most earnestly believed by its members to be more than commonly peace-loving, this, if true, is a startling record, and hardly supports the idea of our being taken unawares in one war after another.[5]

The illusion of innocence is not, of course, peculiar to England, but, as Colonel W. Trotter has stressed in his *Instincts of the Herd in Peace and War*, is common to all belligerents, each side defending its cause 'with arguments perfectly convincing to itself, and wholly without effect on the enemy. . . . The sense of rectitude,' says this author, 'is in fact and manifestly a product of mere belligerency, and one which a nation may

---

[1] See Appendix 42.

[2] In the year 1913-1914 (the most heavily armed year in history up to that period), £77,000,000 were spent on National Defence. The *average* figure from 1924 to 1935 was £112,000,000 per annum. From that time onwards the estimates rose in unparalleled leaps and bounds.

[3] *Yorkshire Evening News*, October 3rd, 1941.   [4] September 19th, 1940.

[5] Dr Renier, to confirm his observation that the English have a naturally martial character, points out that, between 1849 and 1900, the British Government in India engaged in 110 wars and expeditions, of which 64 took place between 1878 and 1898.—From *The English : Are They Human?*

confidently expect to possess, no matter how nefarious its objects may ultimately appear to be in the eyes of general justice. The fact that such a sense of rectitude is a universal and inevitable accompaniment of war, and as strong in a predatory and criminal belligerent as in a generally pacific one, gives us a convenient measure of the extent to which prejudice must prevail in warfare.'

This assurance of perfect non-responsibility makes it easy to work up a loathing which becomes progressively more merciless as increasing suffering seems to cry for vengeance. The enemy, generally personified in a group of cunning homicidal maniacs,[1] carries such a load of guilt as to extinguish pity. Towards the business of destroying representatives of so vile a régime there will be, in some cases, an attitude of righteous and apparently calm implacability, in others, a zestful determination enlivened by sardonic humour. Both these aspects of wrath are exploited to the full by everyone who sails on the wind of public sympathy, from music-hall singers to Cabinet Ministers. An example of the cult of implacability is contained in the following headlines for a *Sunday Chronicle* article :

'POLISH ACE FLIER SWEARS VENGEANCE ON HITLER
He Never Smiles Until He Bombs!'

The story which follows tells how this pilot, known to his companions as the Man-Who-Never-Smiles and The Man Hitler Fears, would sit for hours, day after day, 'always with the same bitter, unsmiling face,' never joking, never being amused, until orders came for his squadron to undertake a bombing raid, when he would spring to his feet, his face lit up with a terrifying smile—'a smile,' as the reporter rather imaginatively phrases it, 'that the Nazis fear.'

But this sort of story does not go down as well as the more facetious exhortations to vindictiveness : the Englishman has a strong sense of the ridiculous and cannot take the enemy quite as seriously as the more romantic Poles.

'POP 'EM AS THEY DROP!' is the headline for some paragraphs of advice to the Home Guard on dealing with parachutists. The invading soldier, having been shot (or 'popped'), should not be picked up but pinned to the earth with a bayonet. That is the counsel of the Lord Mayor of Cardiff. On the same date, Lord Donegall, writing his usual page in the *Sunday Dispatch*,[2] is full of fun about the bloodthirstiness of readers' suggestions on the same theme ; they come as a 'pleasant surprise' to him ; they unveil 'a streak of savagery' which he would like Goebbels to know about. There is amusing banter about plunging invading troops in scalding water or stabbing them with bread-knives ('They mostly have a saw edge. . . . You want to start with the knife level with your

---

[1] See Appendix 43.   [2] February 16th, 1941.

thigh. The blade goes into the small of the back in an upward direction.
. . . That's the way the Finns did it and, believe me, they knew their
stuff'). Citizens are longing for a crack at the first German they see,
and everything is very jolly and in the spirit of hanging out one's washing
on the Siegfried Line.

And here is another grim trifle for the social historian of the future:

'FASHION DOG-FIGHT

A Bournemouth milliner is displaying new season's models named
Hurricane, Spitfire, and Defiant. There is also a Messerschmitt model
composed of narrow strips of black felt shot (to pieces) with holes
of varying sizes and shapes. The Messerschmitt model is not displayed
on a stand, but lies on the ground in a collapsed heap.' [1]

But, contrary to a widely held opinion, the tone of these incitements
and exultings is not nearly so cruel as in the last war.[2] We have learned
something about sadism and its motives in the interim, enough to penetrate even to the intelligence of patriotic journalists. I have seen no lower
depth of brutality reached in the press than the quotation of a remark
supposed to have been made by a woman in an air-raid shelter—and
meant to show how splendidly Londoners were 'taking it'—to the effect
that she could bear anything that was happening here as long as she knew
'their' women and children were suffering too. What disgusts is not
that a terrified creature should have uttered such words, but that a crusader
for Christian civilization should have cited them as an indication of typical
British bravery.

Statements of this nature have a way of looking odd to the point of
incredibility when the passions that inspire them have subsided. So too
does the reasoning by which people tormented with anger justify their
actions or buoy up their hopes.

'WINTER BRINGS LONGER NIGHTS FOR R.A.F. TO BOMB
GERMANY.' Will anyone believe, in a few years, that this headline
was actually printed and that the article which followed took no account,
by word or implication, of the fact that winter was also bringing longer
nights for the Luftwaffe to bomb England, which was being done very
painstakingly at this time? It is such infatuation as this on both sides
which makes war possible—and, incidentally, which gives to out-of-date
newspapers their almost unbearable quality of the pathetic-ridiculous.' [3]

'Athens, that immortal city, had its first air raid warning last night.
[This from a leading article.] Can we doubt that the bombs will

---

[1] From the *Daily Mail*, September 12th, 1940.
[2] F. A. Hornibrook in *Without Reserve*, a book largely composed of 1914-1918 reminiscences, gives a considerable dossier of examples, but they are too horrible to be quoted here.
No sentiments so monstrous are being publicly admitted at the present time. Atrocity
stories have also been toned down.
[3] See Appendices 44 and 45.

follow soon? And if Athens, with all her meaning to civilization, with all her ancient beauty, is to be bombed by the modern barbarians, need we stay our hand a moment longer over the bombing of Rome?'

I do not know by what rationalization the writer of this piece of mock-logic gives a virtuous colour to what seems to me sheer destructive mania. He may take his stand on the old eye-for-an-eye doctrine, now identified with the simple two-blacks-one-white theory; to mutilate the Sistine Chapel would somehow make damage to the Acropolis more bearable. A similar notion actuates the woman whose sufferings are sweetened by knowing that people as innocent as herself ('women and *children*') are on the rack in Germany. But the would-be devastator of Rome is even more insensate, for what he wants to smash up s the heritage of the world, as dearly treasured by many of his compatriots as by the Italians themselves, and this he shows he realized by his reference to 'the meaning' of Athens. But more probably he has sought refuge in an argument based upon the customary *a priori* assumption that an opponent's psychological processes will always be the exact antithesis of our own, and that the frightfulness which strengthens *our* will to resistance will immediately cause *him* to collapse, so that to bomb Rome becomes a matter of great military importance. There exists also a third possibility—that he assumes the Italian people are pre-eminently gifted with aesthetic and historical appreciation and would on that account alone possess little fortitude to risk the sacrifice of their noblest city. And such appears to have been the case.

It is curious indeed to see how, while our propaganda makes the enemy out to be infinitely worse than ourselves, our policies may imply that he is better. Our blockade of countries victimized by Germany, for instance, has been excused on the grounds that if the people involved should be hungry, Germany must arrange to feed them, which is to credit Germany with being more compassionate than we are; and is incidentally a very odd way of trying to gain the confidence and esteem of these nations without whose co-operation victory is a phantasm.

Most of the muddled ratiocinations and errors of psychological judgment I have illustrated are palpably related to the impotence, bewilderment, or frustration which expresses itself in day-dreams of power. Such percussive longings are at their most intensely vivid and direct in a subject who has some particular long-standing grievance to torment himself with, and before the outbreak of a new war hardened our attitude and blinded our understanding it was generally recognized that defeat in 1918 and all its subsequent humiliations had engendered in large numbers of Germans exactly the frame of mind in which a philosophy of ruthless masterful activity was certain to prove congenial. Hitler himself was the better able to supply that philosophy and to put behind it the driving force which pressed it even upon the unwilling, because he had been starved of power, humbled and disconcerted, and the brooding desire for compensation seems to have been in his case exceptionally intense.

It is the virtual certainty that defeat will have in the future repercussions akin to those it has always had in the past that makes mere 'victory' so unfit to be an end in itself. So expert an authority as Liddell Hart, one of the very few war technicians who has recognized the importance of considering what may be going on in the mind of one's adversaries before, during, and after a war, has questioned whether, even in 1918, the Allies' desire to end the war with victory 'did not bring them more loss than gain, both immediate and ultimate'? He points out that the true scientist of war must extend his studies to the state of peace after war:

'In weighing the advantages of "victory," he has to take account of the ultimate effect of the extra moral and economic loss suffered in reaching it. Also, of the way it may tend to sow the seeds of a further crop of wars. The time to draw attention to these factors is before war comes, since the conservation of energy and preservation of sanity are as difficult in war-crazed democracies as in glory-thirsting dictators.'[1]

But even before war has broken out, if its clouds have once become visible on the horizon, it is of little use to preach the poignant lessons of history. In the words of Dr William Brown, the eminent psychologist[2]:

'As soon as the war atmosphere is created, as soon as, or even before, the enemy is identified, a pugnacious feeling, uncontrollable by reason or prudence or compassion, develops in the vast majority of human beings. They may know intellectually that the situation is preposterous. . . . Indeed, the psychologist would say that if we want to prevent war the first thing we must do is to discover in our own minds what it is that makes for war.'

And so we return to our main argument. I believe that, if as much trouble were taken to disseminate a comprehension of our emotional reflexes as at present goes to whip up fear, hatred, and vanity, large-scale war would rapidly become an impossibility; and this even if only one 'Great Power' were psychologically educated, for, since it would neither provoke nor respond in the customary senseless manner to provocation, the successive steps that never fail to end in débacle would not be trodden. Those policies by which nations (i.e. national leaders) recurringly drive one another first to suspicion, then to fear, then to fury, would naturally find no place in the programme of statesmen answerable to unsentimental electors, who would see the risks too clearly to purchase any advantage at a cost ultimately so great: while, being on guard against all the usual

[1] From *The Defence of Britain*, 1939.
[2] In an article in *The Times*, February 1939.

224

dangerous reactions to supposed threats against their interests (and having, in fact, a radically different conception of what national interests are), the representatives of an enlightened Great Power would refuse to be drawn into compromising situations—arms races, competing alliances, the building of tariff walls, etc.

The hunger for power which until now has commonly been revealed in the love of dominion, the pride of wealth and rulership, or the mere vain symbols of such ascendancy, could assuredly be taught to appease itself with healthier food. International co-operation would take the place of international rivalry, for desire would lead towards grandeur rather than direct and indirect self-aggrandizement, and the dominion striven for would be dominion over the causes of misery, disease, premature death, poverty, and ignorance.

Much more than can be immediately realized has already been achieved through collaboration, but while nationalism is esteemed a glowing virtue and internationalism actually excites vehement condemnation, the prospects for world comity are by no means inspiriting.[1]

The passionate clinging to national sovereignty, with its inseparable corollary of power politics, is likely to remain an obstruction to every continuous line of progress as long as the nation and the State afford the chief means by which asthenic, repressed, much-thwarted men and women—in our present civilization ordinary men and women—can glorify themselves and the herds with which they shelter. What is required is a wholly new type of education and upbringing which will impart, ingeniously but not dishonestly, the sense of personal worth and benevolent potency.

Bertrand Russell, a pioneer who has braved much obloquy to change educational ideals, said in an essay [2] explaining the creed which was the residue of a long lifetime's research: 'If we are fit to profit fully by our new-won mastery over nature, we must acquire a more lordly psychology; instead of the cringing and resentful terror of the slave, we must learn to feel the calm dignity of the master.'

The cringing and resentful terror of the slave—it is this which produces so many of the grandiose gestures and bombastic mouthings by which we persuade ourselves of our courage and greatness when in reality we are only committing mean crimes. And while most of us build delusion upon delusion, an army of panders and prostitutes is cashing in; the advertisers who urge us to drink this, smoke that, and wear the other for our country's sake; the wire-pullers of the markets who manipulate scarcities; the little parasites who write fancy jolly songs about soldiering and bombing and the fun of it all; the journalists who accept orders to work up public sentiment in accordance with the policies of the men at the back of the newspapers. They at least have taken the trouble to learn a little about how the mind works.

[1] See Appendix 46.   [2] In *I Believe*, by various authors.

> I have ever hated all nations, professions and communities, and all my
> love is towards individuals; for instance, I hate the tribe of lawyers,
> but I love Councillor Such-a-One and Judge Such-a-One; principally
> I hate and detest that animal called man, although I heartily love John,
> Peter, Thomas and so forth.
>
> DEAN SWIFT, in a letter to Alexander Pope.

I ONCE heard an eminent psychologist give a lecture on the power of suggestion in which he mentioned by way of illustration that business men and women converging towards a suburban station to catch an accustomed train will quicken their pace at the sight of someone hurrying even when they know they are not behind time. A lady in the audience afterwards remarked that she had often noticed this suggestibility, but, being impervious to it herself, when she saw others beginning to hurry she always walked more *slowly*.

This is an analogy of the state of mind of many who think themselves unswayed by public opinion. They imagine they are proving their freedom from susceptibility by exactly reversing the view of the ordinary sentimental man, making fun of everything he respects and upholding everything he reprehends; thus showing us sentimentality standing on its head, a tiring and tiresome performance which does nothing to bring it nearer to reason.

Because it is commonplace to over-estimate the happiness of childhood, the inverted sentimentalist represents childhood as the grimmest and most painful phase of human experience: because uncritical taste demands stories of success and happy endings, he will not concede literary merit except to the representation of failure and frustration: because there is a great deal of silliness about animals, he persuades himself that cruelty has a primitive beauty, a pagan splendour, and makes heroes of bullfighters and trappers: because most people too easily assume that natural ties and socially approved relationships are what it is thought they ought to be, the inverted sentimentalist is always ready to believe that they are what they certainly ought not to be. He has a cultivated antipathy to whatever the world at large might expect him to admire; he is incapable of a dispassionate approach to anything that is popularly acclaimed, and studiously conceals his feelings when they would be likely to meet with the approbation of the majority. 'Never shall it be said that I obliged my Father,' cries the noble Youth in *Love and Freindship*, Jane Austen's skit on false sensibility. 'Never shall it be said that we performed any act the common herd would applaud,' is the tacit challenge of those who feel that by this resolution alone they have constituted themselves into an *élite*.

It is not by such easy means that the critical faculties are sustained. No short cut, no arterial way, is to be trusted when it comes to intellectual processes. To follow the herd or to walk in the precisely opposite direction, neither course is likely to lead to a very distinguished goal. The pathways of the honest mind are often craggy and tortuous, dim and solitary, but it is only by these that we can reach those spacious clearings and higher levels of consciousness where we find our sole hope of any future for humanity other than painful and ignominious extinction.

But what inducement is there to travel by these lonely private roads when the main road, Right or Left, is so exceedingly convenient ? The upbringing of most of us ensures that we shall grow to maturity with languid, timorous, and slovenly minds, shunning exertion, blustering to hide our uncertainties, aspiring after nothing but reassurances : how can we counter the effects of such appalling training ? Or must we abandon ourselves to the certainty that they can never be countered at all—that there is no other training we are capable of responding to ?

'In spite of his new weapons and of his increased powers [says Raymond Fosdick], man himself remains as he was and always has been—irrational, impulsive, emotional, inherently conservative to change, bound by customs and traditions which he will not analyse, the victim of age-old conventions and prejudices. Except for a certain urbanity, the good nature and good temper of the herd, modern man is probably not far removed from his palaeolithic ancestors. Kept normally in control by the pressure of social institutions, he is easily tempted to throw off the restraint, and all that is cruel and credulous or destructive in his inheritance wells up like a fountain of wine to intoxicate him. . . . All that is base and brutal in mankind is glorified and sanctified.' [1]

In the still more pungent words Lowes Dickinson puts into the mouth of Candide [2]:

'. . . "One thing is certain, that men's opinions about what is true are always changing, whether in religion, or morals, or science. On the other hand, they continue to live always in the same way. From which I conclude that their opinions about truth do not influence their lives, which are determined, like those of the other animals, by their passions." . . .

"You do not think, then [Tamino asks], that man improves with time ?"

"Why should he ? The other animals do not, and history does not suggest that man does. He does indeed acquire new arts and instruments, but whatever his tools, he is always, where we come upon his

---

[1] From *The Old Savage in the New Civilization*.
[2] In *The Magic Flute*.

traces, what we find him now, a liar, a traitor, a coward, a bully, a drunkard, a thief, a hypocrite, a fanatic and a fool.'''

Our armaments, our wars, our State coercions, our organized propaganda, our intoxications of rage, our ignoble religions—all will bear out this pessimistic view of *man*, but *men* perhaps are not quite so incorrigible. Detached from the mass and free in some measure to act without reference to its opinions, they are no such terrifying monsters, but, on the contrary, friendly, well-meaning, and even brave and unselfish. The aim of everyone who has ever cared about the ultimate fate of humanity, and not merely the immediate fate of some government, monarchy, or artificially bounded nation, has always been and must always be to promote a personal sense of values in the individual. The very salvation of the human race—not simply its well-being but its actual survival—would appear to depend upon its entering a new stage of evolution in which it will throw off the last vestiges of the stultifying herd instinct and begin to learn what can be done with the magnificent instruments of reason when they are no longer kept subservient to Stone Age appetites.

Individualism has a bad name in this epoch of relapse into tribal hordes: we are told, for instance, that the individualistic philosophy of the Bentham School produced unbridled greedy competition, exploitation of labour, and a general lowering of standards for all who could be victimized. But anyone whose historical evidences go back further than the nineteenth century will know such a theory to be based on oversimplification. The abominations of the Industrial Revolution were, like the abominations of modern warfare, an outcome of the fact that man's technical progress has always outstripped his progress in the sphere of personal relations. The poor had been exploited cruelly in many an era before the Benthamites existed,[1] and all that they did was to provide some arguments which could be turned to account by those who were already irretrievably bent upon a certain course. What educated person can seriously suppose that, without the Utilitarians, there would have been fair wages, control of profits, or abnegation of self-interest? And who but propagandists and their dupes would venture to assert that the freedom of the money markets is a true expression of what great teachers have meant by the freedom of the individual?

The opponents of individualism are invariably, in my experience, State-worshippers of one kind or another—that is to say, persons who wield or hope to wield power through State agencies, or whose debile drifting characters make them glad to give themselves up to external control; and persons so feeble-minded that they shrink from the com-

[1] I recommend Dr Dorothy Marshall's *The English Poor in the Eighteenth Century* for the perusal of those who believe that all was idyllic rusticity before the harnessing of steam power.

plexity of reality and seize gratefully upon the simplicity of abstraction, or so muddle-headed that they exalt the machinery which is or might be useful for performing certain functions above the public for whose benefit those functions are to be performed—as if one should treat the kitchen range as Moloch and be willing to use the occupants of the house for fuel.

Mankind is being immolated to glorify States; and States are nothing but governments and their instruments; and governments are nothing but committees of fallible men and women. In other words, mankind is being immolated, willingly, eagerly immolated, to save the faces and serve the ambitions of a few who, if they were seen without the panoply and mystery of State-symbolism to support them, might not inspire one family to sacrifice so much as a night's sleep.

Yet the fears and weaknesses which make the majority ready to throw off personal initiative and run in droves are no longer inherent in the human mode of existence—as, presumably, they were when men were still contending naked with the untamed forces of Nature—but are now merely neuroses deliberately or ignorantly fostered by our herdsmen and the little animals who bark for them. And the evil does not end with the follies and brutalities directly traceable to collective unreason. 'There is a sense,' says Dr J. A. Hadfield,[1] 'in which the herd instinct is responsible for most nervous ills, since repression of the instincts is largely due to the conventions and injunctions of the herd.' Dr André Joussain's book on the psychology of the masses provides abundant data for this verdict. Following a passage in which he explains how a man's 'intimate ego' must always differ from his 'social ego,' he writes:

'It is by a duality of this kind that one often sees political representatives vote against their own declared opinions and belie their private conversations by their public acts. . . . A similar duality, however unequally marked, is found in each of us when our métier and environment call for acts, attitudes, and language different from those we commit or adopt as private men.'

This want of integrity can only engender conflict, alike in those who agree to the necessity and those who refuse to acknowledge it. 'It is a question,' wrote Oscar Wilde, 'whether we have ever seen the full expression of a personality, except on the imaginative plane of art. In action we never have. . . . Most personalities have been obliged to be rebels. Half their strength has been wasted in friction. Byron's personality, for instance, was terribly wasted in its battle with the stupidity and hypocrisy and Philistinism of the English. Such battles do not always intensify strength; they often exaggerate weakness.' Nor is it, of course, only the English whose stupidity and hypocrisy fray the nerves

---

[1] In *Psychology and Morals.*

of those who will not conform: crowds and masses everywhere are passionately addicted to cant—though the English have perhaps excelled by their fervour of sexual intolerance.

Wilde believed that individualism would be achieved through social-ism. The socialist movement was at that time young, ardent, and sufficiently unpopular to attract only sincere, devoted spirits, but he was shrewd enough to perceive the dangers that might develop:

> '. . . No Authoritarian Socialism will do—for while under the present system a very large number of people can lead lives of a certain amount of freedom and expression and happiness, under an Industrial-barrack system, or a system of economic tyranny, nobody would be able to have any freedom at all. It is to be regretted that a portion of our community should be practically in slavery, but to propose to solve the problem by enslaving the entire community is childish.'

We have seen such childishness in one guise and another carried to the utmost extreme of infatuation in our time, and surely when the present crisis in frenzy is over, there will be some—perhaps an appreciable number—who will see that the herd must either be resolved into its individual elements and given courage to use reason, or rush to its final descent bearing with it in the desperate stampede even the aloof and unwilling.

The demobilization, intellectually speaking, of the masses would not in the least impair what exists of helpful co-operation and fellow-feeling. Individuals can, in fact, collaborate far more efficiently than mobs. Work of precision can only be done by large numbers together when they have been drilled and disciplined to the exclusion of initiative, and it is hardly open to dispute that all the major co-operative achievements which as yet stand to the credit of our species are the product of unique intelligences and have been carried out through the efforts of subordinates endowed with a high sense of personal responsibility.

What the greatest of these achievements are is a matter upon which agreement might not be easily reached: my own first choice would be the international postal service, a miraculous complex of organization in which the herd instinct and its tributary, strong nationalistic or racial sentiment, have played little part. The same may be said of the code of the high seas, which enjoins upon the seafaring men of every country the duty of going to the rescue of any others who send a distress signal, irrespective of the flag they fly. In wartime, naturally, such manifesta-tions of human sympathy and nobility suffer a grave setback, for the drovers then use every device of ingenuity to make us herd-conscious, to release the panic terror and anger that isolate one foolish flock from another. But even in that tragic condition, men whom disaster brings into relief—airmen who fall helpless into 'enemy' territory, sailors who cling to spars in icy seas—are sometimes able to find kindness, so brittle are communal hatreds, so strong the persistence of sanity in people who have a moment's freedom from the weight of public animus.

How is this freedom to become a permanent state? How, since collective emotion is so deleterious, are men to be taught to resist the powerful contagion? I confess I see little hope for those who have already formed the habit of surrender. The present generation is probably, with few exceptions, a lost one. Redemption lies with the children of the future. For them experimenters who do not flinch from the long view will devise—indeed are even now devising and in some cases practising—systems of education which, unless the entire basis of modern psychology is fallacious, will immensely fortify the pupil against the dread of separateness. Such education must begin in earliest infancy and will be planned to encourage the freest use of reason, to build up confidence and restrain suggestibility. It need hardly be said that it will absolutely renounce the weapon of fear: not that there is the remotest likelihood, in a world so full of painful and alarming potentialities, of eliminating fear altogether, but the unsentimental parent or teacher will refuse to further his own immediate convenience by adding manufactured anxieties to those so lavishly supplied in the natural course.

So far there is nothing very revolutionary in my proposals. They are agreed in principle by all educators who have not sacrificed their science to some reason-defying religion of Church or State, and if they are not extensively carried out, that is because the requisite patience and intelligence are not to be consistently found in adults who themselves have to struggle against the effect of bad training. But as we proceed from the nursery to the school we enter upon altogether more controversial territory. To the anti-sentimentalist there is almost nothing that seems right about school education, yet here tradition holds such fortresses that the boldest may well hesitate to challenge their strength. That education is worse than useless when it teaches chiefly respect for orthodoxy is not generally denied, but the number of orthodoxies thus supported is scarcely realized, so many are accepted unconsciously as articles of a creed which it is perilous to question.

To deprecate, for instance, the 'ideals' instilled, with the best intentions, into each new generation of school-children is to cause discomfort even among those who readily acknowledge that the formal curriculum needs revision. Blind faith and futile self-sacrifice are still, at least by implication, exalted; a critical attitude towards approved objects of veneration is solemnly discountenanced; the boy is taught a stale old code of chivalry, the girl has been set free from the tradition of coy humility only to emulate the boy in the smug virtues of so-called sportsmanship. And just as a bad photographer will take his sitters a little out of focus so as to give them a fictitious glamour, so the bad pedagogue presents the 'facts of life' enveloped in a specious romantic haze.[1]

The prevalence of rank humbug, which is idealism in a state of decomposition, is so general in conventional schools that education for nine children out of ten is a mere brain-softening process. King-worshipping humbug, which, when the god refused to be imprisoned on the pedestal, gave rise to the ludicrous fantasy of those historical events known as 'the Abdication' and yet was not discarded; humbug of stereotyped prayers and hymns without relevance to the situation or emotions of the singers,[2] bringing about an early destruction of any religious feeling which can possibly cohere with conduct, antiquated humbug about glory and goodness and obedience and modesty and morals and a hundred other abstractions of debatable meaning—such is the fabric of ideas presented to the abused intelligence of youth. Of what use is it to teach reasoning processes by grammatical analysis, algebra, and problems of geometry if the next lesson is to be full of discredited metaphysical senselessness?

While pious fictions ensure mental debility, fear is allowed to remain a source of shame and strain, and the sensitive child is at a great disadvantage beside one who can appear stoical—perhaps at the cost of a permanently warped character in both. Ordinary high spirits are most injuriously suppressed. 'Much entertainment and some instruction,' says G. F. Morton wryly,[3] 'can be gained on looking through the pages

---

[1] Some years ago a newspaper ran a correspondence on the pictures most suitable for a boy's room. The following complete list of nine exemplifies the widespread feeling that youth should be nurtured on romanticized versions of bravery and holiness:

> *A Knight's Prayer*, by J. M. March.
> *The Vigil*, by J. Pettie, R.A.
> *Faithful Unto Death*, by Sir E. J. Poynter, R.A.
> *Suivez Moi*, and *Go Ye Into All the World*, both by Eugene Burnand.
> *The Heavenly Pilot*, by Harold Copping.
> *The Shepherd Boy*, by Lenbach.
> *The Boy*, by K. Wilkowski.
> *Happy Days*, by Eugene Iverd.

It is really hard to imagine a more sickly collection or one of less artistic merit. That a boy might derive some benefit simply from good works of art seems to have been one of the last ideas to occur to contributors.

[2] Brought up as a Roman Catholic, I recollect well my discomfort in having to utter such an unlikely promise as the following, from a hymn of repentance:

> 'Oh, pardon me, Jesus! Thy mercy I implore.
> I shall never more offend thee, no, never more.'

Or the extravagant untruthfulness of this statement to the Virgin Mary:

> 'I think of thee and what thou art,
> And I keep saying in my heart
> "Immaculate! Immaculate!"'

The hymn-books of most orthodox Churches are rich in asseverations which it is fatuous to expect whole congregations to sing with sincerity. Such empty formalities are the pathway to active hypocrisy.

[3] In *Childhood's Fears*.

of the Detention Book of any Secondary School. As reasons for half-hours with the Drill-Sergeant may be found the following: Laughing, Smiling, Humming, Making uncouth noises, Rudeness, Shouting out, Playing the fool, Squirting water, Writing nonsense, Striking a boy, etc. In a period of time covering just two months the writer found that 25 per cent. of the punishments were given for talking, 19 per cent. for inattention, and 13 per cent. for forgetting.'

It is both ridiculous and infamous that this sort of flattening-out process is permitted to continue, and that the natural and, in most cases, healthy propensities of childhood are actually, midway through the twentieth century, persecuted and punished. Disciplinarians often insist that the persecution was formerly much more ruthless without our forefathers being any the worse for it. The argument only holds good for those who believe that our forefathers were *not* the worse, that the adult part of the human race has hitherto been almost wholly admirable: others, who take a less complacent view, are bound to doubt the efficacy of the old order. It is quite true that great individuals have emerged from a discipline far severer than our own. The reason, I think, is that persons of first-rate mental equipment develop an increased resistance through contending with attempts at suppression; but though in a number of instances moral courage seems to gather force from the struggle, in many more it grows defiant and spends itself in mere eccentricity. We are no more justified in ill-using children on the offchance of bringing out rare qualities than we should be in shooting people in the street because we may conceivably be saving some of them from living burdensome lives.

I have heard a story told more than once as evidence of the ultimate beneficence of hard training to which I give precisely the opposite interpretation. Dr Keate, a late-Georgian headmaster of Eton, was notorious for what we should now call sadistic floggings. He was in the habit of caning boys quite indiscriminately, and on one day publicly flogged eighty without regard to their guilt or innocence. It was reported by W. E. Gladstone that, at an Etonian dinner in 1841, Keate was cheered with the wildest enthusiasm by a company which consisted almost wholly of men he had once mercilessly birched. The old boys, says Gladstone (without *arrière-pensée*), were hardly able to keep their seats and the cheering rose in wave upon wave.

Now I find this anecdote singularly disgusting. I trace Dr Keate's ovation not to the old boys' sense of the benefits he had conferred, but to several other sources none of which is creditable to him or them. First, there is the sado-masochism which the public school régime of that time so ignorantly engendered [1]; second, the weak-minded tendency

---

[1] If any reader can still doubt the evil potentialities of corporal punishment as usually administered, let him put himself to the trouble of reading a Georgian or Victorian book on Flagellation, or even a few back numbers of *London Life*. (See Appendix 25.)

to idealize the past, exaggerating its happiness and glossing over its defects; third, the vanity which makes adults settled in life believe that the methods by which such excellent persons as themselves were brought up must, after all, have been good methods; and last, the ubiquitous herd instinct which will set members of a crowd off cheering with very little volition.[1] I do not think that Shelley would have cheered, or any other of Eton's finest pupils, or that their emotions towards that incompetent and maladjusted man could have been, at best, warmer than pity.

There is a constant gradual abatement of the old harshnesses, and each century finds it perceptibly easier for children to enjoy the pleasure and relief of self-expression (the very name of which may be observed to have an annoying and disturbing effect upon reactionaries). Irrational detractors of our own time choose to ignore the often ferocious repressiveness of the nineteenth century, the legal brutalities of the eighteenth when children of the unprotected classes were chastised for trivial offences with a severity we should now think grossly excessive for adults, and the terrible penal code of the seventeenth under which homeless and unfriended boys in their early teens were publicly hanged for deviations that today would excite compassion. The diminution of punishment is always succeeded by a proportionate expansion of sensitiveness and sympathy in the generation which reaps the benefit, so that now we have arrived at a stage where, among families of good breeding, adult cruelties and bullyings are largely impersonal, inflicted from the distance as it were, and even the juvenile self-compensating impulses are not what they were. It is no longer normal, for example, for children wilfully to torment animals, and old men's tales of ordeals at the hands of schoolfellows are far more harrowing than similar anecdotes from their sons and grandsons.

When personal violence is relinquished altogether as an instrument which public opinion can ever be imagined to endorse—when no man acting in a public capacity will dare to give it sanction whatever his private opinions or practices—then we may hope that *im*personal violence will begin to seem equally contemptible. Though less demoralizing to the character of the agent, and perhaps the sufferer, it usually does infinitely more material damage. The decline of physical fear will not by itself produce firm, independent, energetic minds, for there is also moral pressure which is often stronger, but it will go a certain very necessary part of the way.

Of scholastic subjects, by far the most important in its influence on the future outlook of the child is probably history, and this has for a long time been attacked as hopelessly destitute of the impartiality and sense of

---

[1] The Mass Observation report of Coronation Day contains various admissions of the following type: ' The most stirring incident was the unreasonably (so it seemed) fervent cheering I felt compelled to give with the others to the King and Queen on their return.'

proportion which alone could render it useful as information or valuable as mental training. 'I believe,' said Mr H. G. Wells in one of several diatribes against teaching methods,[1] 'that the crazy combative patriotism that plainly threatens to destroy civilization today is very largely begotten by the schoolmaster and the schoolmistress in their history lessons. They take the growing mind at a naturally barbaric phase and they inflame and fix its barbarism. I think we underrate the formative effect of this per-petual reiteration of how *we* won, how *our* Empire grew, and how relatively splendid we have been in every department of life. We are blinded by habit and custom to the way it infects these growing minds with the chronic and nearly incurable disease of national egotism.'

(A trifling but not irrelevant item may be used for illustration—a book bearing the imprint of a preparatory school for girls in which the first page I opened contained the following statement: 'With Scotland and Ireland to help her, England was great enough to save Europe from Napoleon, and to win the mastery of the seas. Now for a hundred years the power of the nation has been slowly rising until today our British Isles have nearly fifty million loyal people in them, and beyond these islands our flag flies over the lives and homes of hundreds of millions of the human race.' Of the Crown it says: 'It is the personal symbol of the highest office any man can hold in this world, for it invests him with the solemn lordship of one quarter of the human race.' Of the Empire: 'We cannot imagine the time when the world will cease to talk of the British Empire. . . . Our flag flies over regions Caesar never knew. Long before the world talked of the League of Nations, the British Empire had made one of its own. . . . We have carried the blessings of civilization to every continent. We have borne the heat and burden of the day to scatter freedom like the mustard seed that covers the earth. We have a Dominion which rules over more of America than the United States. We have a matchless Empire in Asia. We have a whole continent to call our own in Southern Seas. . . . What harvests our Empire builders have prepared for us! What riches they opened up for their vast pos-terity!' 'The great ruling race of the world'—thus the author, writing in 1937, describes us to his child-readers. I cannot see that we are in a sound position for mocking the nonsense of 'Aryan' education in Germany while such egregious stuff is presented to an English schoolgirl.)

Mr Wells's own theory of historical instruction, which is to begin with 'simple descriptive anthropology,' to go on to trace the growth of primordial communities, and so on, seems to me to be both uninviting and based on a mistaken principle, and the children I have known who were started on these lines have complained of the ineffable boredom of it and the longing to get on to a stage where they would hear some-thing of recognizable personalities. I agree with his strictures on 'making

[1] A paper on *The Informative Content of Education* delivered to the British Association, September 1937.

an important subject of the criminal history of royalty and . . . the border bickerings of England, France, Scotland, Ireland and Wales; Bannockburn, Flodden, Crécy and Agincourt'; and on the Bible's 'wild exaggeration of the importance of Palestine'; but I think it would be possible to contrive a form of history in which the process of human development could be studied through the lives of individuals of real, not accidental, significance, and this would mean beginning in a well-documented age.

The selection of these subjects would certainly be a matter of difficulty and dispute, but at the worst could hardly produce such distorted results as the quite arbitrary system of concentrating upon kings and statesmen. The names and reigns of monarchs do afford a clumsy means of fixing events into periods, but we might well look for some less haphazard and more convenient grouping. It is a curious reflection that, by our present arrangement, a child must get the impression that Queen Victoria was the most distinguished person in the so-called Victorian Age, that George III was a greater eighteenth-century figure than Dr Johnson, and that the dreary intrigues of the Court of Louis XIV are better worth knowing about than the life-work of Pascal.

The elements of history as they are and so far always have been taught, with their simplification of motives and idealized versions of national buccaneering, are wholly sentimental and constitute a most serious obstacle to the attainment of adult mental capacity.

A tendency to glorify the past, to imagine that all which is sufficiently remote was on a nobler scale and of a richer quality than recent times can show, is, as I have pointed out in earlier chapters, very common even in persons of superior intellectual gifts, and much to be deprecated. It is coupled with another tendency—fanatical respect for the utterances of the Great and a belief that these have some sort of mystical sanctity and are practically expressions of Law. Somerset Maugham makes one of the characters in *Of Human Bondage* remark: 'Reverence for what somebody said is a stultifying quality. There's a damned sight too much reverence in the world!' Sentimental reverence, like sentimental loyalty, is usually compounded of muddleheadedness (allowing belief in utterances which contradict one another) and illusions—like pieces of old china—more dearly cherished because they are frangible.

Besides a new kind of history, I would have taught some rudiments of psychology, so that the child shall learn something about normal human reactions to various recognizable stimuli, will be fortified against meretricious propaganda, and, above all, will have some notion of distinguishing reason from rationalization. The dual purpose even of elementary schooling should be to impart such practical knowledge as may, directly or indirectly, be of service to the pupil, and to assist him in an honest co-ordination of reason and feeling, or an honest admission that they cannot on every occasion be co-ordinated. To take the rationalizing tendency at an early stage and at least study what chances there are of overcoming it cannot be considered outside the province of education.

The vitality of the old daemonic conceptions of sin and virtue, good and evil, in despite of their rejection by modern philosophy, is really a very pathetic evidence of the craving to cling to absolute standards.[1] But education is—or should be—a science, and it is one of its essential functions to probe and question, and, if necessary, to expose the falsity of beliefs based on needs and wishes.

Without the props of superstition, the yard-sticks of established moral codes, the boundaries of sacrosanct traditions, greater demands will be made upon the thinking capacity of both teacher and pupil; that is precisely what should be aimed at. Young people wanting in spiritual courage will no doubt continue to huddle together seeking conviction and security within petty limits, but they will not be praised for it and held up as patterns to be copied, and their number will tend to diminish as the temptation to be gregarious (using the word in its original Latin sense) grows easier to resist.

The old Jesuit motto 'Give me a child for the first seven years and you can do what you please with him after' coincides identically with the findings of certain modern psychologists. While I would not go as far as to say that after the age of seven a child's fundamental characteristics and outlook are fully fixed for good or ill, I think it probable that the main lines of development are completely laid a long while before the attainment of adulthood, and that the most important part of the training for individual responsibility will be accomplished in infancy and schooldays. I therefore abstain from discussion of education in its later stages, suggesting only that it will set a value on many qualities which today are regarded as a handicap and will endeavour to correct others which now receive commendation.

I write optimistically in the future tense, but I am only too well aware that it would be more prudent to use the conditional. Even as I assemble my groping notions of what the future might be, I see plans being laid which, if successful, will bring about the ultimate demolition of all that seems to me to make the prospects of humanity endurable. In one country after another National Youth Movements are being formed or mooted, the aims of which are to cultivate the herd instinct under such

[1] Even Dr G. F. Morton of the Leeds Boys' Modern School, by comparison an enlightened headmaster, writing on *Childhood's Fears* constantly refers to masturbation among adolescents as 'secret vice,' a perfectly mid-Victorian piece of terminology. He quotes with approbation testimony given to the National Birth-Rate Commission on the superiority of English boys over Indians, who marry early, and the French, who do not sublimate their sexual drives, because they (the English) postpone their sexual experience with the aid of cricket and football till they are fully adult; as if it were a finally established scientific fact that postponement of sexual experience promotes absolute virtue. It is at least arguable —and it has been very impressively argued—that this compulsory 'sublimation' is the cause of much that is distasteful in later conduct.

names as 'the team spirit,' 'the inspiration of leadership,' and 'the sense of direction,' to foster self-glorification in the guise of patriotic ardour, to satisfy the thwarted will to power by demonstrations of mass strength and the manipulation of competitive and combative impulses, to encourage suggestibility by every device known to the national advertising agents, to substitute the motives of the State for the motives of the man, and to set at naught the separate tastes, fancies, desires, repinings, impetuosities, fastidiousnesses, by which alone human beings are beautiful.

I am told that the nation-wide organization of youth will serve the good purpose of levelling class distinctions and raising the physical standards of young people accustomed to be ill-housed and undernourished. I feel somewhat dubious of this highly artificial method of levelling class distinctions. My own observation of enforced companionship between persons of extremely different social status is that each presently longs to return to his own environment, more than ever convinced of the distastefulness of the other. And I question whether in order to provide food, fresh air, and some opportunities of exercise for the young, it is necessary to influence their politics and to impose on them a ready-made code of ethics.

My only hope—and it is but a fragile one—is that, if these degrading Movements assume the immense proportions threatened, and all or almost all adolescents are to be drilled and regimented, there will be generated so strenuous a reaction in favour of freedom and privacy as must bring nearer the final disintegration of the masses.

The writer is daily more and more convinced that the cause, for which he
pleads, is that of Humanity and Justice . . . and if we descend to lower
motives, of a Shrewd Practical Policy—not less.

Rhymed Plea for Tolerance: JOHN KENYON, 1839.

THIS book, by an endeavour to diagnose the maladies of the vulgar
heart, has inevitably grown into a plea for independent judgment
based upon the tests of intellectual enquiry. The validity of these tests
has been denied even by persons of considerable mental vigour, largely
because our inadequate and misused language seldom differentiates
between *reason* and *pretext*. The jesting assertion that our most significant
actions have two reasons, 'the real reason and a good reason,' depends
both for its wit and its fundamental truth on the fact that 'a good reason'
usually only means a pretext: and many who think they are attacking
rationalism are in fact attacking rationalization. There are other—
slightly overlapping—grounds of objection (apart from those of the
deliberately sentimental, reason's avowed enemies) which sometimes
carry an air of plausibility. They are admirably crystallized in some lines
from Robert Bridges' *Testament of Beauty*. After a recommendation to
respect 'the general commonsense of man,' we read:

> . . . Tho' common opinion may be assent in error
> ther is little or none accord in philosophic thought:
> this picklock Reason is still a-fumbling at the wards,
> bragging to unlock the door of stern Reality.
> Ask what is reasonable! See how time and clime
> conform mind more than body in their environment;
> what then and there was Reason, is here and now absurd;
> what now I chance to approve, may be or become to others
> strange and unpalatable. . . .

Here are three ever-recurring criticisms. The first suggests—what
great numbers of people seriously believe—that it is better to agree in
supporting a fallacy than not to have reached agreement at all; the
second, that inflated claims are made for reason, as to its power of displaying the 'real' nature of things; the third, that our ideas of truths
based on rationality change with time, place, and circumstance.

As for the first, that philosophers dispute amongst themselves proves
nothing worse than that there is much still to be learned about the
universe, and is no more a condemnation of their researches than a dispute
among physicians is a condemnation of the study of medicine. Enlightenment is more likely to be achieved through diversity of opinion than
through 'assent in error.'

The second premise would only be sound if it were true that reason's votaries boast of having discovered, or being about to discover, the secrets of Reality. Such claims are, in fact, made by none but sentimentalists, whose specific habit it is to offer concise and comforting explanations of the will of God, the destiny of man, and the whole earthly and heavenly scheme. Intellectual integrity (without which, I reiterate, a man is not a rationalist but a rationalizer) is more likely to produce agnosticism than bragging certainty.

Last, there is the criticism directed against the shifting character of reasoned judgment. But it is no sound disparagement of objective deliberation to say that it may countenance new verdicts under new conditions and hold what is sensible at one time to be absurd at another. Rather, that is its highest praise—that it indulges in no simplifications, assumes no absolute truths, no unchanging universals, but is prepared for the labour of making new evaluations as often as may be necessary in the light of unfolding knowledge.

Probably, however, there is some verbal confusion here, and what the poet calls reasoning should more correctly be named pretext-making, for it is the motives *assigned* to taste and conduct, rather than the motives which afterwards reveal themselves, that undergo such striking changes in different times and places. The disparity between the motives we fabricate and those which later appear is something which our own memories, when we use them searchingly, will not infrequently teach us. Thus, after a quarrel, we may hear an honest person say: 'I suppose I wouldn't have taken offence so easily, but I was upset at the time about something else'—an admission that the anger which once seemed righteous was partly actuated by the desire for an emotional vent. And again, when a love affair has been long ended and its pain and pleasure are over, it is common enough to come to the realization that the irresistible, incomparable charms which tempted us to so many follies were largely a fiction begotten in our own minds by vanity, pique, loneliness, curiosity, or the pressure of sexual need.

(Not that I think the phenomenon of passionate love owes as much to a simple biological urge as some psychologists insist. Apart from other mysteries of this alternately rapturous and agonizing state, it is difficult to see why the human animal should experience emotion so immeasurably greater than is required for reproductive purposes—which, in fact, are often thwarted by the fixations of love. It is true that the biological methods of Nature are notorious for wastefulness and excess, but they are not framed to defeat their own ends. Yet it is by no means unusual for people in love to squander what might have been fecund years, unable to break themselves of a longing fixed solely upon someone who cannot or will not fulfil Nature's hypothetical intention. To interpret love as a mere mating impulse seems to me, in short, as irrational as the 'twin soul' theory.)

The possession of a good intellect does not ensure that there will be no false assignment of motives. On the contrary, men of marked cerebral ability have often been the worst self-deceivers of all, having the most skill in finding pretexts. This is particularly evident in what they have said and written and obviously believed, while emotion was in the ascendant, about war, many of those who have composed brilliant pleas for pacifism in peacetime being equally ingenious—and certainly more effective—in their pleas for the support of war in wartime. In fact, the wartime defection of the intellectuals from their customary peacetime positions has earned a special designation: *Le Trahison des Clercs.*[1]

It is said that in the First Great War ninety-three German professors signed a manifesto stating their reasons—their 'good reasons'—for believing the cause of the Central Powers to be virtuous and just: we know that equivalent demonstrations were made by learned men on the Allied side to assert the opposite view. One group or other *must* have been wrong; both might be wrong, but both could not have been right. We can only conclude, therefore, that the reasoning of the erring ones was impure and a betrayal of their rational pretensions. Mr. H. G. Wells, one of the most ardent propagandists for fighting at the time, has pronounced that the Great War was 'an All Fools' War.'

In the years of recoil after the years of violence a very large number of intellectuals made full confession of self-delusion, and I have heard some express regret and even amazement at having been so carried away with deceitful emotion—like men who have been in love and come to their senses. But we do not speak of being 'in hate.'

It is useless, then, to place reliance on the wisdom of the intelligentsia. The intellectual, as Leonard Woolf (himself now something of a recusant) has pointed out in an eloquent passage,[2] is, like the politician, a weak human being not far removed from the animal and the savage:

'. . . From the moment of his birth he is taught to regard the shadow of shadows as reality and to accept the nightmares of dead savages and old wives' tales as absolute truths; he is the easy prey of his own and other people's instincts and emotions. It is not therefore surprising that the conduct of intellectuals should have persistently fallen below the intellectual ideal. They have continually and usually honestly betrayed their faith. They have accepted quackery and denied reason, hated with the haters, burnt witches and hunted scape-goats; they have often sold their souls together with truth and civilization for a handful of silver or a ribbon to stick in their coats. And they did this, according to their lights and to the standard of contemporary social morality, honestly. They were in the cave where everyone knows that it is only the shadows which are real, where one has to earn a living, where it is terrifying to be outside the smell and warmth of the herd, and where patriotism is more than enough.'

---

[1] See Appendix 47.   [2] From *Quack, Quack!*

We are obliged to depend upon the intellectual research worker for *information* as to those facts we ourselves have no means of investigating, and for the truth of which his probity may be the only guarantee, but to place implicit confidence in his *judgments* is to lean on a reed that may break at a crucial moment; yet this is not to condemn the intellectual method, only its misuse under the stress of emotional influences. From scholars and scientists we can learn the processes of analysis, we can copy the habit of criticism, and catch glimpses, occasionally prolonged, of a dispassionate manner of approach. All this is of immense value. But when we commit ourselves wholly to the guidance of other people's reasoning, we are renouncing our own and submerging our individual voices in the bleatings of the herd. A sheep is not the less a sheep because he is driven by a scientific shepherd.

Much has been written about the past and future evolution of man, and in the realization that we have reached a stage where all of us—at least all who are educated—can acknowledge that man is indeed evolving and is not a degenerate, fallen from the glory of having been God's image, there lies some solace: for we may hope that our divergent faculties, the instinctive and the later-developed rational, may yet be correlated—'the bridge,' as the *Testament of Beauty* has it, 'which all men who can see the abyss have reasonably and instinctively desired to build.' That the generality of men have grown better, more altruistic, more honourable, and more moral, I think must be perceived by anyone whose readings about the past are not confined to retrospective idealizations; that mankind has grown worse is a destructive illusion, conjured up by the grievous fact that he has created an environment over which he has no control. World wars, poverty amidst abundance, the oppression of the labourer, the meanness and squalor of the industrial city, these are not the outcome of wickedness but of ignorance and vulgarity.

Ignorance can be enlightened, vulgarity will be dispelled, when the tastes and vanities of crowds are no longer pandered to. Unless these vital purposes can be achieved, the final desolation will be such as no eloquence can figure.

The struggle before us is a hard one and the sentimentalist will not be equal to it. Our ills are not to be cured by pretending that they do not exist, or that they exist in order to ennoble our characters. Their remedy depends upon knowledge of reality; and knowledge cannot be won except by readiness to sacrifice the immediate ease of mind which, so far, all but a few men have preferred to truth.

Tradition cherished for its own sake must be discarded even though we relinquish with it some picturesque ceremonies and stirring pageantry; institutions honoured only because they are old must be allowed to crumble; ritualism is not to be tolerated unless the rites have some utilitarian value beyond mere impressiveness. High-sounding abstractions will be avoided by speakers and writers who wish to be taken seriously. The very language, to be made a reliable medium of communication, must undergo radical changes of structure and usage.

I do not think that these changes will involve the loss of much that will leave us the poorer for beauty, though some beautiful legacies of the past may become more obscure and remote in their meaning. These better parts of our inheritance will be evoked again and again by traditionalists as an argument for clinging to the leading-strings of the old order, but such pretexts will not sound very convincing from those who have boasted their fortitude in risking the annihilation, in warfare, of civilization's noblest treasures. Unless man is to be himself annihilated, the past, which has been much more terrible than beautiful, must be hewn down to make way for the future.

And—most difficult and uninviting condition of all—the movements by which these mighty changes are to be accomplished must be gradual. The rapid, decisive, and spectacular overthrow of conservatism would be no true victory. Coercion is self-frustrating. 'The whole structure of society rests upon habit. With the new organization must therefore grow the new habit that is to support it. To precipitate organic change is merely to court reaction. That is the lesson of all revolution.' Thus speaks the Socialist in *A Modern Symposium*, and the trend of events since 1905, when it was written, gives us no reason for supposing that he would find it necessary to revise his words today.

Ruthlessness is the sentimentalist's instrument, for sentimentality, with its impatience of subtleties and rosy-spectacled myopia, makes us not soft but hard. Our passions have striven long and vainly to force the doors that stand between mankind and happiness. Reason at least is fumbling at the lock.

APPENDICES

APPENDIX 1

NUMEROUS experiments have been made which reveal the physical superiority of the well-nourished upper classes. For example, Dr H. Bathurst Norman described in the *Lancet*, August 1939, the result of comparative tests carried out with 500 public school boys and a homogeneous group of secondary school boys in Durham, when very exhaustive measurements were made of height, weight, and strength. 'There are,' the doctor stated, 'significant differences. At each year between the ages of 14 and 18 a boy of the first group, public school, is approximately 16 lb. heavier and 3 in. taller than a boy of the second group, secondary school. His lumbar pull is 30 lb. greater. The difference noted in height is shown to be chiefly a difference in the length of leg. A record of the ratio of weight to height shows a greater weight per unit of height in the public school group.'

A similar report was made by Dr Spence in 1940 after a comparative study of 125 Newcastle children drawn from the poorest class and the same number from families of more than adequate means. Approximately 50 per cent. of the poor children were of lower and frailer stature; 80 per cent. of them were suffering from the effects of anaemia, which was not found at all among the well-to-do.

Intelligence tests are equally positive, demonstrating that children from more comfortable homes are quicker of understanding and better informed. In his book, *Mental Tests*, Dr Ballard, the eminent authority on educational psychology, records the observations he made in 49 schools, of which 10 were in the poorest districts of London and 9 in 'good residential areas': 'The results show that both boys and girls in good neighbourhoods are about 6 months . . . in advance of the average; and in poor neighbourhoods the boys are 3 months behind and the girls 6 months. Thus for the extreme type of home we found a difference of 9 months for the boys and 12 months for the girls. A girl of 8 in Dulwich can read as well as a girl of 9 in Bermondsey.'

APPENDIX 2

The ill-usage of children lies not merely in the ready blows and explosive outbursts which are naturally common where families live together in the most irritating proximity, but also in many practices of less spectacular disagreeableness. I was once in the women's ward of a public hospital when, for some reason I cannot recollect, a little girl recovering from burns was brought in, lying in a cot. This child kept up a disturbing appeal for a visit from her mother, and first one exasperated patient, then another, assured her that her mother was coming for certain that afternoon. I enquired aside from a nurse whether this was true, and was told quite casually, 'No, they only say it to keep her quiet.' I was very much surprised that everyone present tacitly or volubly acquiesced in this shockingly unkind deception, which I do not think any well-bred group of women would have tolerated. I have since noticed that the children of the poor are compelled to harden themselves to many forms of mental cruelty, of which the above is a fair example.

APPENDIX 3

The privacy and social freedom enjoyed by the members of better-class families (almost irrespective nowadays of sex) are so established that many perhaps do not fully realize the existence of a sphere in which no one but the head of the house owns a latchkey, and young people are kept, as far as can be, under perpetual surveillance, while fathers still forbid their grown-up daughters to use face powder or to come in later than a certain early hour.

The war has disturbed the domestic pattern, but not to give liberty, only to substitute one form of ownership for another. Some change may certainly be looked for after demobilization, but such an upheaval is more likely to disrupt family life than to lead to the amelioration of its bad features. The prospect of living in highly organized herds rather than families which some post-war planners seem to find so inspiring must be deeply depressing to one who believes that privacy is the first essential of an improved standard.

APPENDIX 4

The following passages from *Tory M.P.*, Simon Haxey's careful dissection of the British Constitution, tell briefly how matters stood with our native subjects in 1939:

'The British House of Commons is elected only by the people of Great Britain, and it is for this reason that many people believe that its power and activities are largely confined to Great Britain.

In fact, the people of Britain are only a minor part of the population ruled by the British or *Imperial* Parliament. But as only the population of Great Britain is directly represented in the British Parliament, it is a *democratic* body for only a small part of the population over which it rules. The white minority of the Empire's population numbers only 70,000,000, of whom about 30,000,000 have their own Parliaments in the Dominions. Over 430,000,000 people are ruled by the British or Imperial Parliament, and have no representatives at Westminster, play no part in deciding the composition of this body which decides their destinies, and are unable by any legal or constitutional methods to change its policy.[1]

. . . The only form of direct representation of our Empire in the House of Commons is the representation of Boards of Directors of profit-seeking companies. . . .'

Bad as political conditions are, however, the conditions of life and labour

---

[1] In figures easier to grasp, out of every fourteen British subjects abroad only one has democratic rights.

which they sustain are yet more distressing, and make the equivalent evils in Great Britain seem quite negligible by contrast. They have much in common with the state of affairs prevailing here in the days when Shaftesbury (then Lord Ashley) sorrowfully indicted human cupidity: 'Over a large surface of the industrial community, man has been regarded as an animal, and that an animal of not the highest order; his loftiest faculties, when not prostrate, are perverted, and his lowest exclusively devoted to the manufacture of wealth.'

Add to this, if we apply it to our Colonial drudges, that insult is heaped upon injury by a colour bar which sets the silliest and meanest member of a white race above the most intelligent native, and it must be agreed that democracy, in Mr Streit's sense of the term, does not appear to have penetrated very far into the British Empire. Perhaps it has not penetrated very far into America either.

APPENDIX 5

The most serious aspect of the tacit censorship is the suppression or distortion of any news which reflects discreditably upon the conduct of the British Empire. Immense financial interests being involved, the whole endeavour has been—in the huge sections of the press to which I refer—to stress the unity and well-being of 'our' people overseas, and to keep the ruling race as ignorant as possible of conditions which might make some of its members question the pure benevolence of empire-builders. During the years between the great wars, recurring industrial troubles led to some investigation of the bondage enforced upon native populations of Colonies yielding a rich revenue to shareholders here. It was unusual in the English newspapers for these revelations to be given more than a brief paragraph, placed where it was likely to attract little notice. Those who receive any journals direct from troubled parts of our Dominions must share my astonishment at the extent to which Englishmen remain unaware of the real state of affairs, and are even able to believe sincerely that native welfare is the prime consideration of those who rule under the British flag.

News of disaffection is minimized or garbled. It was interesting, for instance, to see how, at the beginning of the present war, offers of help from comparatively unimportant Indian princes were given all the prominence of large headlines, while many papers barely announced the protests of the Indian Congress, so much greater in numbers and influence. Constant disturbances in South Africa in the first year were all but ignored.

The constraint exercised by advertisers is venial only by comparison, and tolerable only because we have never known anything better. According to Professor A. J. Clarkson in a monograph published by *Fact*, about one-sixth of the advertising space in the popular press is normally occupied by advertisements of patent medicines: in the lower-grade weeklies the proportion is about a third. One may imagine how much chance there is of any unbiased presentment to the public of knowledge which might affect the consumption of home remedies.

Beauty preparations, beer, spirits, and tobacco are further classes of goods which, through their enormous advertisement assignment, lay an embargo upon frank discussion.

APPENDIX 6

The passage cited is by Raymond B. Fosdick in *The Old Savage in the New Civilization*. This book contains some of the results of intelligence tests given to the American Army in 1917-1918, the first time in history, I believe, that such an enquiry was ever attempted on a large scale. Of the white soldiers, 30 per cent. were found to be illiterate or nearly illiterate, while 66⅔ per cent. did not attain the 'minimum capacity necessary to carry on the so-called paper work of the army—that is, making reports and keeping files. Out of all those millions of drafted men just a third had ability to carry on this by no means laborious type of mental work.'

The soundness of the tests, even in that early phase of their development, was confirmed by the way in which the findings of the newly appointed examiners tallied with the opinions independently recorded by officers who knew the men.

It is improbable that in the matter of basic intelligence Great Britain was then, or is now, superior to America. When the much fuller statistics of recent years are published, the level will doubtless be found to have improved all round, though not sufficiently to warrant universal suffrage.

APPENDIX 7

I believe that cities and rural districts might be divided up into companies of about fifty voters, all of whom should be personally known to one another. From this personal knowledge each company would elect a member. The leaders of fifty of these Minor Groups would compose a Major Group whose business it would be to work together for the welfare of their locality and who would be able to discuss questions of public importance, not in the shallow generalizing terms which are customary when great masses have to be appealed to, but with some attention to their intricacy. This committee would, in due course, elect one representative, and the representatives of forty Major Groups would constitute a District Council, superseding the present means of local government. Each man or woman chosen for office would be, under ideal conditions, the ablest of fifty, who in their turn were the ablest of 2500; and even allowing for errors of judgment, it is probable that the selected persons would have talents above the average, since no Major Group would wish to be represented by an incompetent spokesman, and direct contact would allow the members to form a fairly accurate estimate of one another's qualities.

The District Councillors would likewise elect a leader—who would not be eligible for that office, however, without having had his fitness confirmed by some such Public Service Examination as I have already touched upon—and the leaders of ten District Councils, mustered in convenient geographical areas, would be known as a Regional Committee, and would represent a million electors, having arrived at their high position in every case by a progress through closely knit groups and not by clamouring for the suffrages of an ill-organized mass. Each Regional Committee would send its best intellect to Parliament, which would consist of as many members as there are millions willing to be governed from Westminster.

Instead of the cumbersome and amorphous body which shapes our policies today, arrayed in vestiges of outworn codes and rituals like an Early-Victorian railway carriage wearing the useless relics of a stage-coach past, we should then have a compact and cohesive organism, a group answerable to a series of lesser groups, each representing the will of a gathering of electors well acquainted with one another and not numerically large enough to succumb to mass-emotion. Technical committees, concerned with transport, major industries, etc., would work conjointly with Parliament while remaining detached from its structure.

The scheme perhaps slightly resembles the Soviets of Russia, which, as originally planned, gave promise of a great sociological advance. But since the whole principle is to oppose collectivism or any form of dictatorship, it is obvious that it cannot be compatible with Sovietism of the post-Lenin epoch.

A difficulty to be surmounted is the method of establishing the basic Minor Groups, which, if they were arranged according to a topographical plan, would present something of a jig-saw puzzle to the organizers. The necessity of passing an intelligence test, apart from any other condition which might be demanded, would cause the percentage of qualified voters to vary greatly from district to district or even from street to street, so that a thousand inhabitants of a bad residential area might only yield as many persons fit to have a voice in civic affairs as five hundred in a better locality. Such inequalities might be expected to adjust themselves gradually with the raising of standards for many at present deprived of opportunity by grinding want, and with the levelling down of the immensely higher birth-rate which now distinguishes the lower classes from those accustomed to take more care for their posterity. Fifty sensible electors could, in any case, do as much for the well-being of their region as a far greater number where every kind of moron is given the franchise.

Fluctuations in the size of Groups would be unavoidable, even under the most perfect conditions, as new individuals grew eligible for admission and others fell away. The membership of each Group might be allowed a variation of—say— five above or below the round number of fifty. Thus, provided the average of fifty was maintained, vacancies could be kept open pending the arrival of expected members, or places in a full-sized Group could be found for a few newcomers. In each area there should also be a certain number of Transitional Groups, consisting solely of those who, for one reason or another, could not be placed at once in the appropriate permanent section. To these a greater numerical latitude could be granted, though there should always be a bias against large-scale assemblies, with the peculiar temptation they hold out to lazy minds to submerge themselves and sink into irresponsibility. In fact, it may well be considered that even fifty is too big a number to remain quite free from the foolish and evil propensities of the crowd. Many might reckon twenty or thirty a safer maximum. I need hardly say the figures I have suggested are tentative and only intended for illustration.

APPENDIX 8

The author of *The Tyranny of Words* is particularly well fitted to deal with the language muddle of political economy, for he is a professional economist. He gives the following illustration of a pronouncement acceptable to readers of financial reviews:

'Reflation is an alternative to inflation. When the Central Banks are in the strategic position of manipulating credit it is quite possible—see the action of the Danzig Kronbank in 1934—by employing sundry well-known techniques such as the inversion of the rediscount rate, and the hazardous but conclusive open-market operations, to bring about an upward movement in values which reacts unfavourably on speculative activities, tends to thaw frozen assets in the commodity exchanges, implements stock movements, attracts gold from abroad, revivifies the climate of opinion, and so arrests the vicious spiral.'

There is not, says Mr Chase, 'an atom of meaning in the entire statement. Not one scintilla of sense.' He wrote it himself. Presumably the students of high finance grow hypnotized by phrases which sound so pregnant and run over them as a sort of incantation, ceasing to look for meaning. I found how far this was possible when I read aloud to someone a book on the chemistry of precious stones—a subject I am not educated to understand. The sonorous words, the pleasing associations of ideas from the knowledge that sapphires, rubies, emeralds, and aquamarines were being analysed, and my confidence in the writer's authority, had such an effect that I must have persuaded myself I was following the sense, and suddenly discovered with laughter how little I had made of it.

APPENDIX 9

In 1885, to prove his statement that, in London's underworld, parents were able with perfect impunity to sell young children for prostitution, Stead, aided by Salvation Army officials, arranged a transaction whereby he paid £5 for a girl of thirteen with the professed purpose of sending her into a brothel, the bargain being at that time legally defensible. Although the girl was, in fact, most carefully protected, Stead and his helpers were arrested in a storm of moral indignation and were convicted on a quibble, namely, that the negotiations, to be lawful, should have been entered into with the child's father, not her mother!

As the direct result of the publicity which at last broke upon a subject considered too shocking to refer to, the law was drastically amended. Among other changes, the age of consent was raised from thirteen to sixteen, procuring was made a criminal offence, and children could be transferred to the custody of guardians appointed by the court. The passage of the various Acts which followed did much to dispel that mephitic darkness which had previously enveloped all sexual activities.

APPENDIX 10

I recollect an article by the late James Douglas in the *Sunday Express* in which he commented indignantly on a young lady who had been sued—and had paid damages—for casting a slur upon a most respectable young man (he subsequently went to prison as one of the notorious 'Mayfair men'). It was Mr Douglas's contention that a nice girl of eighteen would not know the meaning of syphilis, much less mention it.

The Victorians certainly held the same view and applied it not only to young ladies but to married women, with the result, according to some medical critics, that many of them were infected with syphilis or gonorrhoea without being aware of it. Embarrassing symptoms were treated with home remedies in prudish secrecy and a condition of invalidism would develop which was confused with other forms of ill-health then prevalent, no measures, of course, being taken against the transmission of the evil effects to children. Nor must it be assumed that the policy of taboo is no longer observed rigidly enough to produce similar squalid tragedies today. I have been allowed the opportunity of making enquiries into cases where I am satisfied the disease was contracted in the first place through sheer ignorance that any risk was being taken, the girls concerned having grown up under the impression that such afflictions were reserved for beings obviously low, degraded, and promiscuous; and where symptoms were neglected until a late stage in the belief that they could not possibly refer to anything so unlikely.

Though improved, the attitude of the medical profession itself and its subsidiary profession of nursing is by no means always scientific on this unlucky subject. A doctor, knowing that a female patient has contracted gonorrhoea from her husband, will sometimes conceal the nature of the complaint from her, thus risking, it seems to me, the hazard that she might not persist in treatment, or might not sufficiently appreciate the necessity of sexual abstinence: while nurses not infrequently adopt a manner of thinly veiled disgust towards venereal cases.

A nurse once informed me that an ex-patient of hers, a well-known local character whom I perfectly recognized from description, was suffering from what she whisperingly called 'a dirty disease.' I was shocked by her professional misconduct in imparting the fact, but still more by the reactionary view her words and tone implied.

I do not think there is much hope for the conquest of this bogy until we realize how much of its strength it derives from emotional prejudice, and set out to vanquish the prejudice not less than the disease.

APPENDIX II

Here is a curtailed sample from the *Sunday Chronicle*, December 31st, 1939. Under the headline, 'PILOT SINKS U-BOAT BETWEEN THE SOUP AND COFFEE,' a young officer is reported as telling his exploit in these words:

'I fancied Fritz must be somewhere near. And then we spotted him. He was on the surface all right. That moonlight was a godsend!

At 5000 feet I shut off engines and went into a deep dive. All unsuspecting, Fritz was entertaining himself.

I swear I heard a gramophone. It seemed a pity in a way—but there was that convoy!

Fritz got scared and began to make ready for a crash dive. . . . The moonlight made him an excellent target. I put my machine into a climb all out, swung, dived again. . . . One bomb registered a direct hit on the whale-back of the foredeck, bursting beautifully. Another grazed the conning tower, exploded, rocked the U-boat, and lifted Fritz out of the water.

He was in his death-throes, like a harpooned whale, keel uppermost, and floundering.

I had no more bombs, so I started back for home, signalling a chance-met destroyer *en route*. The destroyer hurried to the spot, but there were no survivors—only wreckage, oil, and scum.

Returning after an absence of little more than an hour, the mess servants had failed to keep my coffee hot. But it didn't take long to warm it up.'

There are several different kinds of word-magic displayed in this interesting passage. The light touch makes the frightful activities involved seem innocuous, almost engaging, and the whimsicality of the coffee warmed up for the man who had just, in dutiful pursuance of his profession, killed seventy or eighty human beings, contributes to the air of *bonhomie*. The personification of the U-boat itself and the description of its 'death-throes' as if it had been alive, enables thought to hedge away from the young sailors under orders, some of them perhaps as amiable as the aviator himself, who were literally in their death-throes as the result of his lethal skill.

The submarine, if not disposed of, would, of course, have been responsible for the destruction of even more lives, and all in the same cheerfully detached spirit on the part of its commander and crew as was shown by the bombing pilot. (For although each side likes to accuse the other of fighting with savagery and blood-lust, in point of fact those emotions, in their crude forms, seem to be rare in men whose weapons are machines, and the crews of the U-boats are found, by those acquainted with them as prisoners, to be very similar to their counterparts in other races.)

APPENDIX 12

Among the words 'tainted with gentility' which Fowler in *Modern English Usage* bids us avoid are many which we could only lose at the cost of having to invent others to replace them. He objects to 'carafe' for 'water-bottle,' 'chiropodist' for 'corn-cutter,' 'couch' for 'sofa,' 'recreation' for 'amusement,' and 'stomach' for 'belly.' But a carafe is a bottle of a particular sort; a chiropodist does much more than cut corns and would rightly object to being known only for that accomplishment; a couch is not the same piece of furniture as a sofa; recreation, when it is amusement, is a special kind of amusement; and the stomach is not the belly, as a simple diagram will show, nor is 'belly' what Fowler calls 'the ordinary natural word that first suggests itself to the mind' when one speaks of 'stomach.' Sickness appears to be felt in the stomach, hunger possibly in the belly, but it would be tiresome to have to work out anatomically the precise area of discomfort (or comfort) in order not to use a euphemism.

I offer this interposition because the cause of verbal accuracy cannot but suffer from the pedantic robustnesses which some of the self-consciously anti-prudish, anti-squeamish school endeavour to thrust upon us. Professor Fowler faintly recalls rather than represents the philologists in question.

Polish post-1918 maraudings have been allowed to lapse into a convenient oblivion. Extracts from a speech delivered in March 1925 by Mr Lloyd George in Parliament may prove a slight corrective to the views of those who were reading only contemporary newspapers in August and September 1939:

'The Eastern frontiers are throbbing with trouble from the Bosphorus to the Baltic. Every European frontier is marked in red, but the frontiers of Central and Eastern Europe are a deeper red than any.

There is none of these borderlines that has not been fought over for centuries. There is not a tract of territory in regard to which any country cannot claim precedents for saying that it belonged to them at one time, and there have been conquests and re-conquests.

There is a tangle of races and a general inextricable mix-up, as anyone knows who has ever been trying to decide whether a particular territory ought to belong to Czecho-Slovakia or Poland, or Hungary or Rumania or Yugoslavia.

There you have questions of racial pride and racial and religious antagonism. There is no mix-up of races, records, and religions like it outside Gehenna. . . .

The worst of all is Poland. . . . Alsace-Lorraine provoked a war in Europe. Poland has five Alsace-Lorraines—Eastern Galicia, White Russia, Vilna, the Corridor, Silesia—she is not satisfied and she now wants to add a sixth, Danzig. . . .

Do you [the Government] deny that Poland annexed Vilna in spite of the protests of the League of Nations, annexed Galicia in spite of the protests of the Supreme Council, that she has annexed part of White Russia, where the majority of the population is Russian, beyond the ethnographical line drawn by the Supreme Council?

Do you say the decision in Upper Silesia is one which you would be prepared to go to war in order to maintain? . . .

With regard to Danzig, you know perfectly well that Poland is persisting . . . in spite of the ruling of the British Commissioner who represents the League of Nations, and it has now been referred again for consideration. But she did not accept the decision. . . .

[There follow references to "the policy which the French, one Government after another, have pressed upon us—an attempt to engage us with the whole of our strength in supporting the *status quo* not merely upon the West but upon the East as well!"]

A free hand has been given to Poland. What is the result? This is the real menace to European peace. It is no use shutting our eyes to this fact.

The real menace to European peace is the fact that out of 27,000,000 people in Poland, 9,000,000 are there by force of arms—Russians, Lithuanians, Ukrainians, and Germans—most of them there in spite of the protest of the League of Nations and of the Supreme Council.

Does anyone imagine that that is going to be accepted by Russia and by Germany once they are restored in power? And when that moment comes, what is our position?

I do hope that whatever happens in the way of arbitration we are not going to base arbitration upon those explosive treaties in the East of Europe, and the acceptance of these annexations, which would be fatal. . . .'

Mr Lloyd George prophesied well. We did accept the annexations, we did ultimately engage to support an unsatisfactory *status quo*, and the result was 'fatal.'

APPENDIX 14

I give a compact illustration from the *New Statesman*, January 6th, 1940. The writer, surprised and dismayed at the extreme repressiveness of the measures then being taken by the French Government against political opponents, yet casts about for a charitable explanation and produces this:

'. . . The first thing for us in England is to understand the reasons for the French reaction. It must be remembered that whereas Britain has always emphasized liberty and meant by liberty, most of all, the rights of minorities, the French have emphasized equality and stressed rather the constitutional rights of the majority to use its full legal powers against a dissident minority. In exercising what they regard as the rights of a sovereign people over the minority, the French do not feel that they have surrendered their democracy.'

In plainer words, the English favour liberty to preserve the rights of minorities, the French favour equality to destroy the rights of minorities! It is a curious interpretation of equality. I find it pleasing to imagine what this particular Critic's indignation would have been if any German had excused the suppression of dissenters on the same grounds. The sovereign people's legal power to take a short way with other sovereign people would then have been recognized for the absurd verbiage that it is.

APPENDIX 15

At least one Indignant Ratepayer did attain the moral courage necessary to prosecute a church for bell-ringing (Soltan *v.* de Held, 1851), but the judge ruled against him, holding that though a peal of bells might be 'an extreme nuisance and perhaps an intolerable nuisance' to a person in their immediate vicinity, yet to anyone who lived at a distance they were likely to be a 'positive pleasure,' and therefore they could not be regarded as a public nuisance. The plaintiff, to obtain an injunction, must show that he had sustained some special damage over and above that inflicted on the community at large.

As society, at the best of times, shows little sympathy for the sleepless, it is not to be supposed that a spa patient, claiming the special damage of broken rest, would carry much weight against an abbey (though if all who grumbled had courage to complain, they would make a formidable party). That the noise can be torture to the nerves of the sensitive is evident from the case of a friend of mine who left a hospital at her own risk dangerously early after a major operation because she could not endure the frequent ringing of church bells and striking of a church clock in the vicinity.

Here are extracts from some of the speeches:

'We reverently commit our cause to God. . . . With God's help we shall prevail. May He bless and keep us.'
(The King.)

'Now may God bless you all and may He defend the right.'
(Mr Chamberlain, then Prime Minister.)

'I bid you all . . . to be of good heart, and God be with you.'
(The Leader of the Labour Opposition.)

'. . . With a firm reliance on the protection of Divine Providence.'
(The Leader of the Liberal Opposition.)

The Churches in all the belligerent countries were, needless to say, busy with supplications and thanks for services rendered:

'The mere act of prayer, rising above all the changes and chances of the struggle, to God who is our Refuge and our Strength will be a source of inward calmness, steadiness, and courage.'
(A united utterance from the Archbishop of Canterbury, the Moderator of the Church of Scotland, and the Moderator of the Evangelical Free Churches.)

'We thank God that He gave a speedy victory to our arms. . . . We thank Him that injustice, centuries old, has been broken down through His grace.'
(German Spiritual Councils Proclamation on the conquest of Poland.)

The legislators of France and Poland committed themselves dramatically to supernatural agencies: and Herr Hitler was not behindhand:

'I only wish that God Almighty, who has blessed our arms, may enlighten other nations.'

It was amusing to see the rage with which some English people learned that he also had flung himself before the Invisible Throne. Yet his opposition to religion had been strictly confined to certain orthodoxies, and there was no logical reason why he should leave to other statesmen the monopoly of superstition.

APPENDIX 17

An article by Sir Seymour Hicks supplies a typical example of patriotic faith. 'Marriage,' he says, 'is the home tie that has bound our country so securely.' Presumably, since all other countries have an equivalent home tie, it is to this that we owe the present happy security of the world. 'All decent men and women are proud of the reverence in which they hold the sanctity of marriage,' he goes on. And: 'Marriage is the greatest earthly gift vouchsafed to man. Life and death are but its twin servitors, the one a welcome the other a farewell.'

It is seldom that any discussion of marriage finds its way into a daily paper which is not an emotional effusion on these lines. Even the weeklies have to take their courage in both hands, so to speak, when a contributor treats coolly and soberly of domestic relations. I have kept the correspondence elicited by an article in the *New Statesman*, June 26th, 1937, in which Dr Harry Roberts attacked conventional ideas about monogamy and appealed for a kind of matrimony free from dog-in-the-manger possessiveness, winding up with these words:

'The increasing economic independence of women and the increasing use of contraceptive measures are removing the last excuses for that artificial jealousy whose roots lie not in love but in fear. I believe that the only sound foundations for a worthy and continuous marriage are love (preferably with a history of passion behind it), true freedom, absolute candour, a complete altruistic and mutual respect, a desire for mutual understanding, and an intellectual, aesthetic, and spiritual capacity for attaining it.'

A member of Parliament, Mr J. A. Leckie, the Liberal representative of Walsall, wrote immediately from the House of Commons to enter what he called a strong protest against a 'disgracefully low view of marriage and the family.' He considered it a tragedy that ideas of this nature should be 'propagated so brazenly,' and refused to believe (emotionalists are adept at refusing to believe) that they were held 'by more than a comparatively few [*sic*] in a limited category.' He ended:

'After all, this is a Christian country, and ideas that strike at the root of marriage and the home are not suitable for your pages, however advanced. You yourself carry a tremendous responsibility in disseminating these repulsive views.'

Unfortunately such vituperative protestants never feel it necessary to explain the grounds on which we are asked to assume that they are right and all who think differently, wrong and wicked. My personal belief is that frankly avowed physical infidelity usually results, sooner or later, in the disruption of the union, and that Dr Roberts's views, though lofty rather than repulsive, portray an ideal beyond reach in our present stage of development.

APPENDIX 18

In 1939 I wrote an article for the *News Chronicle*, pointing out, in terms far more moderate and conciliatory than I have used here, some of the evils of Sunday idleness enforced upon people who need and deserve recreation. (It is noteworthy that this article had first been commissioned by another national daily, which on second thoughts decided that it might give offence to readers.) Its publication brought me several abusive letters which left me in no doubt whatever as to the superstitious character of the Sunday defenders' beliefs. Here are some extracts from the almost frenzied denunciation of a Scottish minister with a parish in London:

'Dear Madam,—I consider it my clear and definite duty, as an ordained minister of religion, to write to you relative to the Heaven-provoking, God-defying article . . . written by you in today's issue of the *News Chronicle*. It is very obvious, judging by the satanic note of that article, that you are as ignorant of the purpose God had in view in creating you . . . as if you had been born and brought up in the outlandish haunts of benighted Heathendom. . . .

You should pray to God, in the name of His eternal Son, Jesus Christ, the only Saviour of the world, that He should savingly and supernaturally enlighten your sin-darkened mind, by His Word and Spirit. Should that article by you have been composed in the very bowels of Hell, it could not have expressed more gratifyingly the heart of the Devil. I am consequently as convinced, before God, as I am of my own personal existence and identity that, failing repentance towards God and faith unfeigned in the Lord Jesus Christ (the only Saviour of sinners), that article will yet cost you your immortal rational soul. Failing evangelical repentance, you can anticipate as your most appropriate epitaph "And in Hell she lifted up her eyes, being in torments."

People of your devilish sentiments relative to the Lord's holy Day are the greatest possible curse to any nation or generation. . . . If the question were asked to what does the British race owe its greatness since the Reformation, the true answer must logically, scripturally, and inevitably be to the scriptural observance of the Christian Sabbath. Your article and those of other unconscious propagandists of Hell are thus fertile instruments in the hand of the Devil in destroying the very foundations of our national character.

It is very evident to all right thinking men and women that God has a controversy with our nation and generation, and I am fully convinced that national Sabbath desecration, such as you advocate in your cursed damnable article, is the main ground of that controversy on the part of the Most High, together with such sins as Romanism, betting and gambling, and general religious indifference and apathy. Those, therefore, in this country and other countries who practise Sabbath desecration . . . are responsible for wringing judgments from the Hand of God upon their nation and generation. They are the people who are bringing the roar of Hitler's and Mussolini's death-dealing bombing aeroplanes nearer and nearer to our shores. As it is written in the Word of God, "Shall I not be avenged on such a nation as this?" And again, "The nation and kingdom that will not serve Thee shall perish, yea, those nations shall be utterly wasted." The history of God's providential dealings with the rebellious great nations of antiquity is ample proof of the eternal veracity of the foregoing Biblical statement.

When there is today such uncertainty about the international situation my way of knowing whether a crisis is inevitably approaching is not by considering the views of this statesman or that, but by observing the increasing Heaven-challenging opening of more and more cinemas in London, and the increased activity in opening more and more golf courses in Scotland. . . . The God-forsaken brutish men and women guilty of these damnable activities on the Sabbath are the real bloodthirsty murderers of women and children, and I charge you before God, as a fellow-traveller to His Judgment seat, as guilty through your article of that unspeakable damnable crime.

Are you really so besotted and blinded by sin as that you imagine that an infinitely wise and intelligent God had no higher purpose in view in bestowing rationality upon mankind than that men, women and children should spend their lives eating, drinking and making merry, not only for six days of the week, but also on the Lord's Day, according to their own will, pleasure and inclination. . . .

I have now warned and admonished you, faithfully and conscientiously, and if you repent of your sins towards God and believe in the Lord Jesus Christ,

256

you are eternally saved, but, if not, you shall be eternally damned.—I am, yours faithfully, (Rev.) J. P. MacQ——.'

It is curious to reflect that the views expressed in this interesting document, which, but for a few words, might have been written in the seventeenth century, are those which gain consideration from many civic authorities to this day when they are laying down regulations for Sunday observances.

Incidentally, we see hinted at above a new kind of fortune-telling akin to ichthyomancy, pyromancy, ornithomancy, etc., which had their day in earlier civilizations. Divination by the opening of cinemas may become known to the grammarians of the future as kinematomancy; divination by Sunday golf offers a knottier problem.

APPENDIX 19

England does not draw the line at a grandfather. The deeds of a great-great-uncle may also be profitably honoured. Thus, in February 1940, Mr J. Davidson, a Labour M.P., suggested (vainly) that 'in the interests of national economy' the pension which has been paid to the Nelson family since 1806 should be investigated, together with certain other large-scale pensions. The present Lord Nelson receives £5000 a year for the naval victories of his great-grandfather's brother. So far about £800,000 has been paid, chiefly to the Admiral's collateral descendants.

Hereditary pensions reached such proportions in the last century that a Select Committee was appointed to enquire into them. It is, of course, a difficult matter to know when to stop paying moneys which have been solemnly, if rashly, promised in perpetuity. Would that governments were more often as reliable in keeping pledges!

APPENDIX 20

In January 1940 a middle-aged man was sentenced at Jersey Assizes to a month's imprisonment for carrying on his person a photograph of himself in bathing trunks which he had touched up to turn into a representation of Christ crucified. When he handed his passport to the Chief Aliens Officer at Jersey to get an exit permit, the picture was found in it and he was reported, in a transport of religious zeal (what other motive could there have been?), to the police, who, in a transport of religious zeal, brought him before the various legal functionaries, who, likewise in transports of religious zeal, gave him a prison sentence. This was afterwards rescinded at the instance of persons who would seem to have studied the actual teachings of Christ as presented in the New Testament.

The proceedings and newspaper reports impress a straightforward mind as being a more efficacious way of 'publishing a blasphemous libel'—the crime with which the accused was charged—than the possession of a silly photograph folded in a passport.

Much has been written of ritual prudery both here and in America, and in such books as *To the Pure*, A study of Obscenity and the Censor, by Morris Ernst and William Seagle, *Lars Porsena* or The Future of Swearing, by Robert Graves, and *It Isn't Done*, Taboo among the British Islanders, by Archibald Lyall, interesting analyses will be found which make it superfluous for me to seek new illustrations. The author last named tells us of police witnesses, asked to repeat exactly what the prisoner said, still referring unsmilingly to 'Big B' and 'Little B,' 'just as if they were lulling the magistrates to sleep with the tale of little Goldilocks.' He quotes the following *Sunday Express* report of a dialogue at Marlborough Street in July 1930, where the magistrate 'sternly rebuked' a stockbroker who had admitted uttering the word 'bloody':

> '"Are you in the habit of using expressions of that sort—you, a gentleman in an honourable profession?" asked Mr Mead.
>
> "No, but I did because the thing warranted it," retorted Mr H——.
>
> "Nothing warrants foul language from a gentleman," commented Mr Mead.
>
> "It is in a lot of books and a lot of plays," said Mr H——.
>
> "What's that to do with it?" demanded Mr Mead. "Do you take your conduct from books and plays?"

This is the more extraordinary inasmuch as 'bloody' was at the height of its career as an expletive at the time, and stockbrokers, though their profession is 'honourable,' have never enjoyed the reputation of being purer in speech than other men.

APPENDIX 22

The hypocritical attitude taken by a large number of magistrates towards licensing and gambling offences is pictured by the well-known lawyer who signs himself 'Solicitor' in his book *English Justice*:

> 'It is common to hear a magistrate, who is notoriously in the habit of betting on the principal races and of playing cards for money, sternly rebuking some unfortunate lad who has been caught playing pitch and toss or having a game of cards under the shelter of a pit mound. Similarly, one of the strictest justices in the administration of the licensing laws that I have known was in the habit, just before the bar at his club closed, of ordering two whiskies and sodas, which he would place beside him for future consumption.'

The licensing and betting laws are the principal peace-time instruments for creating artificial crime—that is to say, offences which are harmless in the light of reason but criminal in the Courts of Summary Jurisdiction. They are also, I have long contended, potent in stimulating the very vices they are intended to eradicate. Moreover, in order that artificial crime may be detected (since the public does not readily co-operate with the police when its sympathies are on the other side), it is often subject to artificial provocation; and so we have those unedifying cases in which policemen put on plain clothes to seduce publicans, bookmakers, and club proprietors into breaking the law.

Artificial crime, being powerless to stir genuine moral feeling, frequently takes on a risible complexion, injurious to the dignity of the law. The authority above quoted mentions a case in which a publican was fined £5 at Bradford City Police Court for supplying more beer than was asked for:

'Mr J. B. Willis (prosecuting) said that a man leaving defendant's shop with a jug of beer was stopped by the police. The man said he had ordered a pint of old and a pint of mild beer at defendant's shop. The police took the man back to the shop, and when the beer was measured it was found to amount to two pints and a third of a pint. It should have measured only two pints.'

The validity of this asinine prosecution did not depend upon some decayed and obsolete statute but on a Licensing Act of 1921. 'Can anyone believe,' writes 'Solicitor,' 'that there is any reason for such a law other than that mania for issuing orders and forbidding this, that, and the other that was one of the consequences of the war?' (He was referring, of course, to the war of 1914–1918. The present conflict bids fair to produce a far richer crop of mysterious prohibitions than its precursor.)

APPENDIX 23

There are, of course, many magistrates and policemen who are extremely good-natured with children, and the separate Juvenile Court has greatly improved the delinquent child's position. But, despite recent attempts to rejuvenate the Bench, magistrates are still likely to be between sixty and eighty years of age, and, as the author of English Justice points out, 'old men tend to be cruel, for definite psychological reasons. They do not all become cruel, of course, for many men and women remain young by retaining interest and sympathy, and others deliberately guard against the tendency they know to exist. But, generally speaking, the older the magistrate the more merciless he or she is. Everyone who is familiar with the police courts must know the veteran who never misses an opportunity of advising the father of some trembling lad to "take him home and give him a good thrashing."'

Two boys, both aged ten, were brought before Biggleswade Juvenile Court in February 1940 for stealing an electric torch and a pocket diary from a car. The Chairman, who was just sixty-two years older than the children, asked their fathers to

Give them a good thrashing with a razor strop or belt.
Put them to bed.
Give them only bread and water for 12 or 14 hours.

A fortnight before, this gentleman's daughter, a teacher of psychology, had put it to him that he was wrong to have ordered the birching of two other juvenile criminals, and this appears to have been his answer. When questioned by a reporter as to what his daughter expected him to have done, he rejoined: 'Tickle them under the chin and kiss them, I suppose.' It is very typical of the strategy of people who take pleasure in the misuse of power to cast ridicule on their opponents by attributing to them far-fetched suggestions which they never made.

'The action we took a fortnight ago has had its effect,' he told the journalist, perhaps rather prematurely. 'I think we are too sloppy in these days.'

He would have found many sympathizers on the Bench, and one at least, it is possible to suppose, at Liverpool Juvenile Court, where, in sentencing two boys, aged eleven and thirteen, to be birched for pilfering from cubicles at the public baths, the Chairman said: 'I think it is a contemptible, mean theft and you deserve horse-whipping. Birching has not been inflicted in Liverpool for many years and we have an opportunity today of inflicting it.' 'Opportunity at last!' was V. S. Pritchett's comment. But this occurred in 1937, and perhaps Liverpool has since reverted to its former more adult methods.

APPENDIX 24

Mrs Matthews' article is such a rich specimen of sentimentality at its most drivelling that further quotation is irresistible:

'The gooseberry bush—what does it mean to this generation?

A prickly bush with fruit, sometimes green, sometimes red, hard in May and soft in August.

But to the middle-aged and those older still what a different significance!

It was a home of miracles, for had we not ourselves, a little while before we could remember anything, emerged from beneath its branches.

"But where does a baby come from, Mamma?" "Oh, from underneath a gooseberry bush, my dear."

It is true we never saw the process, but we believed it, for had not one older and wiser than ourselves told us?

Can I, I wonder, persuade the young mothers of today that there was any virtue in the story, any wisdom in a return, if not to the gooseberry bush, at least to the mystery we used to feel surrounded it?

I doubt it. We have all become so inured to the sight of the nursery linoleum littered with the raw facts of life that an attempt to wrap any of them up would seem to resemble the Victorian's attempt to conceal the legs of the table.

But perhaps after all I may gain courage to attempt it from this very illustration, for only last week a Piccadilly furnishing shop told me that it was becoming fashionable to cover a table with a decent cloth down to its very feet. . . .

It is true that familiarity with the facts of life has helped us to meet them without fear, but surely that is not because we have been made more courageous, but because the adventure of union with another human being has been robbed of its greatness and made a common thing.'

The idea that sexual intercourse is a great adventure only if the participants are inexperienced and ignorant is a very curious one, and certainly entirely fallacious.

The war has not, up to the time of my writing this, deprived a certain class of newsvendor of such profits as may be made from the sales of the periodical in question. I append a much abridged selection of material in a Christmas number.

Under the heading, 'Our Special Christmas Correspondence Section, Written and Illustrated by Our Readers,' we have letters to the editor on the following subjects:

The 'strange fascination' of one-legged women, with a detailed catalogue of a collection of crutches.

The confidences of a lady who signs herself Madame Highboot, and who informs the editor, 'I like passers-by to notice my boots and high heels. . . . At home I wear the highest heels I can stand on, and when outdoors I never wear heels less than 5 in. high.'

The hobby of a correspondent who collects (and induces the editor to print) photographs of feet clad in high-heeled shoes and of a South African soldier wearing lady's button boots.

The merits of old-fashioned cotton underwear.

A lengthy and emotional account, supposed to come from a young man, of how he watched his sister's hair being cut off.

The description by a companion-chauffeur of the uniform his employer likes him to wear—tight corsets, spike-toed boots, a starched collar 3 inches high, and so forth.

The attractiveness of transparent rubber capes.

The pleasures of tight-lacing.

The devotion of a girl aged sixteen to an aunt aged twenty-four, who makes her wear tight corsets and 4½-inch heels. ('She is very beautiful. I am very fond of her and wouldn't dream of going out with a boy even if she permitted. . . . Aunt loves dressing me up.')

The charm of female wrestlers, especially when they inflict pain on males.

Flagellation applied to persons who are harnessed like horses.

A request that someone may send a photograph of 'a human pony in full harness . . . and one of the dominant sex's victims imprisoned in corsets and knee-length boots.'

Transvestism.

The corporal punishment of children.

These letters, tricked out with lingering salaciousness, have a most striking affinity in style. One might almost think they were written in the office as propaganda for neurosis. If anything can be said to answer to the famous definition of obscenity—that which has a tendency 'to deprave and corrupt those whose minds are open to such immoral influences'—it is this miserable rubbish which is allowed unimpeded circulation in the country which forbade Havelock Ellis to publish a scientific treatise on the same topics.

It is so generally taken for granted that the rigours of the law against the sale of certain drugs are a successful means of protecting the community, that it came as a refreshing shock to me, one day in 1936, to hear Professor John Hilton giving a wireless talk[1] in which he questioned whether these constantly multiplying legal measures had not, like so many other laws, done a great deal to promote the evils they were intended to redress. He pointed out that every time you pass a law that something shall not be made, or sold, or used except for what are called legitimate purposes, and every time you impose severe penalties on anyone breaking that law, you are making the illicit manufacture of the article and illicit traffic in the article more and more profitable to anyone who is not afraid of risks.

Such powders as heroin and cocaine, he said, lawfully costing £1 to £3 an ounce (and even that is an artificially high price inflated by the legal proscriptions), are peddled unlawfully at from £50 to £150 an ounce, profits which offer the underworld an irresistible temptation to create addicts. He referred to the days when, as a mill mechanic, it was his practice to use cocaine in taking painful specks of grit out of the eyes of fellow-workmen and he was able to buy a tablespoonful for threepence, enough to last six months:

'I was regarded then, with my cocaine flakes in my waistcoat pocket, as a God-sent benefactor. . . . Today I should be run in, fined £10, and sent to gaol for a month for being in unauthorised possession of a narcotic drug. I never heard of anybody, in those days, larking about with white drugs or using them for any other purpose than that of easing the pains and agonies of daily life. Of course it may have been that the abuse of white drugs was coming. . . . It may be we were in for a wave of white drug debauchery if the law hadn't said "No." But it also may be that we weren't in for it at all; that we should never have taken to it anyhow. It may be that no people anywhere would have taken to it, as a body-and-soul-destroying habit, had it not been for the passing of the laws against it.'

The League of Nations' Permanent Central Opium Board admitted that 'the present system of fighting the drug traffic has broken down entirely,' and the late Professor Hilton foresaw, correctly, that their way of dealing with this failure would be 'more laws, more police, more Customs officers, more Secret Service money, more arrests, heavier punishment.' The real solution, he urged, was to end the illicit traffic by the simple process of making it entirely unprofitable—that is to say, by removing all the restrictions without which the world existed so long and yet did not drug itself into 'an idiotic trance.'

Such a step, I may add, besides being a sure and instantaneous checkmate to the traffickers, would do much to remove the primary *psychological* cause of addiction—namely, the consciousness of degradation with its attendant sense of hopelessness insidiously working to make the habit inveterate. Advances in the chemistry of hypnotic compounds are faithfully accompanied by an increase of bogy-bogyism concerning their use. Doctors are frequently so ominous in their warnings when prescribing such medicines, fears are so played upon from childhood, that any slight abuse is likely to produce a state of mind favourable for despairing surrender.

Brought up with all the usual inhibitions against treating drugs lightly, I well

---

[1] Reprinted in *The Listener*, May 6th, 1936.

remember my surprise when a robust old gentleman of seventy-seven told me how he and his brother in their youth had experimented with hashish and had smoked opium. 'Weren't you afraid,' I asked, 'of getting addicted to them?' He replied simply, 'Oh no, we didn't *hear* so much about addiction in those days. You could buy opium across the counter. Very few people injured themselves with it.'

Byron openly took laudanum at various times and did without it at other times. Had he lived in the twentieth century, his mild partiality for this sedative would have been regarded as a deadly peril, and out of mingled self-disgust and defiance he would probably have developed a real craving. This once established, he would have met on every hand a firm conviction that he was totally degenerate, unfit for further work, and useless to society. Under such an overwhelming weight of suggestion mental decay would have been almost inevitable. Besides Byron, Coleridge, de Quincey, and a dozen other great artists and writers who were fortunate in being born before the use of drugs was controlled by law, would have drifted very early, perhaps, into sterile ruin.

APPENDIX 27

The Pass Laws only operate in the Orange Free State and the Transvaal. The native in Natal and Cape Province is comparatively a free man. In the Transvaal, he must hold an Employment Pass which must be stamped by the Pass Office every month, and produced for inspection by any police constable at any time. This Pass entitles the holder to stay out till nine in the evening. The Transvaal Pass Laws demand that a native male is not allowed at large after nine without a 'special Pass' from his employer stating the purpose for which he is out and the time at which he must return to his place of residence. (A very few natives hold highly-prized certificates of exemption.) Policemen have a right to stop any native after nine p.m. and demand his 'special Pass.' If the hour stipulated for his return is expired, he may be arrested. A scene which recurred several times in my childhood, when I believe the curfew hour was eight, was the arrival home under police escort of one or other of our house-boys who had ventured out without a Pass or overstayed the specified time. During the half-year ended December 31st, 1940, the number of natives arrested in the Transvaal alone for breaches of the Pass Laws was 45,292. In the subsequent three years there were 318,000 convictions.

A South African authority who has been good enough to supply me with data writes: 'Many white people of by no means un-liberal tendencies regard the Pass Laws as the law-abiding male native's outstanding charter, as well as the European employer's safeguard against indescribable conditions due to broken service and large-scale dishonesty; and many employers would welcome an extension of the system to native women employees.'

The constant appalling increase in native criminality, however, appears to some observers to be due to poverty, hunger, poor social services, and a sense of grievance occasioned by harsh and inequitable laws. Speaking publicly again in 1944, Mr. Justice Krause stated that the Pass System manufactured criminals, and had 'degenerated into a convenient taxing-machine to swell the Revenue . . . an unbearable burden on the under-paid, under-fed, un-sophisticated and illiterate native.'

One of the reasons formerly advanced for maintaining close restrictions was the 'Black Peril,' the South African myth that all natives were desirous of committing rape upon white women, who would be utterly unable to emerge from their houses after dark if the comings and goings of black men were freely permitted. Actually, such crimes have always been rare considering the size of the native population. In 1938 there were 15 cases in the Union of South Africa, 7 of rape and 8 of attempted rape of 'European' women, among 6,000,000 natives. When any such unfortunate incident does take place, there is a blaze of raging publicity, and an outbreak of hysteria among the white population very similar to that described by E. M. Forster in *A Passage to India*.

The penalty for rape of a white woman by a native is death. The penalty for rape of a native woman by a white man is less drastic.

APPENDIX 28

It is customary for farmers to provide the food of their native labourers, which consists chiefly of an allowance of 'mealie-meal' (maize flour which is made into porridge) and cash wages of sometimes not more than a few pence a day. Meat and its equivalents are by no means regular constituents of the diet.

In a recent survey of farm labour in the Free State conducted by the Institute of Race Relations it is stated that 'for married men the usual ration is half a bag of mealie-meal per month, as much separated milk as is available, and salt. . . . Very occasionally a meat ration is given. It takes the form either of a sheep once a fortnight for all the labourers together, or else it simply means any animals that die.'

Under-nourishment is the most important factor in native ill-health, according to Public Service reports. The second great factor is venereal disease, which was once a white man's monopoly.

Every investigation of the physical condition of the native races affords evidence of a terrible deterioration. For example:

'A preliminary survey . . . among the Xosa of the Eastern Province carried out by the Government in 1938 reveals that the general physique of the Xosas has declined during 10 years as a result of unsatisfactory, and often too little, food.'[1]

The Municipal Public Health Department of Benoni published early in 1940 the results of its study of native ill-health and high infantile mortality. Among native men, it was found that the incidence of latent syphilis alone was 34·2 per cent. The incidence among non-European women was 42·8 per cent. In 1937, General Smuts had publicly stated that 'the natives were rotten with venereal disease,' and that as this was becoming a menace to civilization, the Government would at last have to take some steps to counteract it. Apparently at this time practically nothing was being done under government sponsorship for native venereal cases, and the only means of awakening the white population as a whole to any sense of responsibility in the matter was either to disclose the prospect of their contracting venereal diseases themselves from native nursemaids and

---

[1] South African *Sunday Times*, January 14th, 1940.

servants, or to convince them that economic loss would follow the disablement of a high proportion (sometimes not less than 25 per cent.) of the native labour supply.

Mr Gordon Hemming, one of the three members of Parliament who represent the natives in the Cape, in commenting on General Smuts's admission said it was pitiful to think that, 'while an army of veterinary experts, stock inspectors, dipping supervisors, and foremen were actively engaged in combating stock diseases, the health needs of the people were almost ignored.' Dr Ranch, Medical Officer of Health for Germiston, presented figures which showed that 42 per cent. of expectant native mothers whose blood was tested gave positive results for syphilis. In consequence there was an enormously high infantile death-rate. No organized clinics for these women were then in existence.

It will take many generations to repair the ravages which have been spread across the whole continent by the white man's almost total indifference to the well-being of the native. Some indeed doubt whether such repair is possible.

APPENDIX 29

The South African *Sunday Times*, in January 1940, announced that, according to a committee of the Medical Association in Johannesburg, minimum monthly diets for native families cost substantially more than wages under Industrial Agreements would provide for, but native workers had no facilities for making representations to Industrial Councils, 'though a rise in the cost of food affects them to the point of starvation.'

'A contributory factor to the growth of gangsterdom is that an urbanized native who is out of work for any length of time may be sent by the Native Affairs Department [working through the Pass Office] to another urban area, although he may have to leave his wife and children behind. . . . The native family as an economic unit is in many instances disrupted, resulting in the increase of native juvenile delinquency. Another consequence is that un-employed natives who do not wish to be sent away from their families become desperate and resort to any expedients in order to stay.'

On another page of this journal we may read, not very surprisingly, revelations of the success of Nazi propaganda among the negro population. An earlier issue for the same month states that more than thirty thousand native youths on the Rand alone were being driven to crime through poverty and lack of educational and recreational facilities, and the fact that unscrupulous traders in the locations were profiteering in foodstuffs though native wages had not been increased.

When Mr W. C. Foster was Mayor of Capetown in 1939, he had the courage to declare in the City Hall that the life of a native farm labourer was very little different from that of slaves a century or more ago. Needless to say, protest resolutions were sent to him asking for a denial of his statement. The farmers of Worcester (Cape Province) naïvely pointed out that, among the many benefits they had conferred or attempted to confer on the natives, there were even liquor restrictions, 'as they knew that only healthy, sober, and educated labourers were worth their wages.'

It is notable that hardly anyone in South Africa ever seems to think of the negro as a human being with a right to the pursuit of happiness, and even his champions—perhaps for diplomatic reasons—stress primarily the need of keeping up an ever-increasing supply of cheap and healthy labour.

APPENDIX 30

It is regarded as one of the functions of the press in all countries to bolster up nationalistic vanities, but English journalists in particular have the habit of prefacing their braggings with a complacent reminder that we are naturally a modest people, are not given to boasting, find it difficult to refer to our own excellences, etc. Selections of interesting and often intensely funny examples are gathered in *The English Press* by Jane Soames, *Man is My Theme* by Cyril Scott, and *The English: Are They Human?* by Dr G. J. Renier.

'It is a *sine qua non* [says Jane Soames] in the English Press that we are superior to every other country, and that our institutions are the best in the world. These beliefs are repeated and emphasized on every possible occasion—and particularly does the Press seize the opportunity of making an overt or covert comparison between some British performance or method or characteristic and that of the foreigner. Once one has noticed this tendency and is on the look-out for it, one finds it cropping up continually in every kind of likely and unlikely connection. The statement and restatement of our perfection (at all events by comparison with the rest of the world) has become half mechanical; and yet at the same time is often cleverly used to put us in a good conceit of ourselves when things do not seem to be going well.'

Kingsley Martin, in *The Magic of Monarchy*, describes the editorial effusions in praise of the 'astonishing sobriety, judgment, self-restraint' with which we behaved over the abdication of Edward VIII. 'Foreigners, it was implied, would have kicked over the traces in all sorts of unthinkable ways. . . . This self-congratulation on our own modesty, reticence, and other sterling gifts always masks a British recovery from a shock. The crisis is resolved and the process of self-assurance begins.'

Dr Renier pokes fun at the insistence of our leader-writers, under the guise of diffidence, that almost everything we make or have is 'The Best in The World,' and more still 'at the cool conviction with which the English believe that foreigners share these assumptions. Every opinion uttered in an unguarded moment, every compliment deliberately paid with the well-known insincerity of the Continental conversationalist, is lapped up and printed for the edification of the English reader.'

In wartime self-applause through the press rises to feverish crescendo, but the effect is less amusing than when we merely make such claims as the following:

'For at least two centuries we have set the world's standard not only in sport but in things that matter, from personal cleanliness downwards. We, the least military nation in Europe, have had our field uniform copied by all countries, and the cut of our riding-breeches and boots is the abiding marvel of the age.'

And:

> 'Out of our sad crisis [the Abdication] came some real good. The Continent was much impressed, and realized once more that we are not as other people.'

Or:

> 'Why is our country respected by the whole distracted world even in the agony of its spiritual torments and terrors? Because as a race we try to put Christian principles into practice.
> As a people we have a Christian conscience and it feels a stain like a wound.
> The shivering, trembling, fear-stricken peoples look up to us as the guardians and defenders of the Christian concept.' [1]

APPENDIX 31

My favourite illustration of non-sportsmanship belongs to the history of women's long struggle to attain the right to practise medicine. When an early batch of female medical students had at last, after infinite toil and trouble, procured themselves a school and staff of teachers, they were obliged to face the fact that they could not take any degree, there being no hospitals in which they were allowed to practise and no examining body which would accept them as candidates. In 1875, however, these determined women found a loophole. It appeared that the Midwifery Licence had the same legal status as the Licence of the Royal College of Surgeons, and obviously it could not be refused to women. A number of them decided, therefore, to take a degree in midwifery, having no other channels of approach to legally recognized Medicine. In 1876 three women applied for examination, and were necessarily accepted. Having accepted them, but being resolute that they should somehow be prevented from becoming qualified, the whole board of examiners then resigned. Without examiners, there could, of course, be no examination and consequently no degree. Yet to achieve this spectacular frustration of the female students involved the complete and final dissolution of the Midwifery Board!

APPENDIX 32

A study of breach of promise, seduction, and enticement cases will show how completely the male is still regarded as being the responsible party in all relationships with women.

In 1936 a widow of forty-five brought an action for breach of promise against a man ten years her junior, whose mistress she had been for a considerable time. As the case was of great 'human interest,' she was interviewed, after losing it, by many reporters. I quote from the *Daily Mail's* version of her statement,

---

[1] The first and second extracts are from the *Sunday Pictorial*, and the third, by the late James Douglas, is from the *Daily Express*. All appeared in the *New Statesman's* 'This England' column.

which gives in miniature the sentimental reactionary's whole point of view on the character, the position, and the rights of women:

'I am not ashamed. I loved—and I did what seemed natural in a love like mine [i.e. she brought a breach of promise action]. It is, to my mind, the only redress a woman has for so many wasted years. A woman in love does not think in ordinary terms, you know. To her the man she loves is someone she could worship and trust with her all.

It is true that a woman's love is all her life. She does not think in terms of what it costs her or of binding contracts. She believes in the one man who is everything to her. That is why a breach of promise action is her one protection.

A man may love—but not with that entire disregard of self with which a true woman can and does in so many cases. He does not forget everything or sacrifice everything.

Woman does it properly and gladly—with whole heart, mind, and soul—fixed only on that one man's love to her. I believe that obtains even in these modern days. If a woman is of the truly feminine type she can love very deeply.

. . . I am not overcome by the decision of the court in this case. I shall take it smiling. But for many a woman of 45 life might be very bleak and hard in these circumstances. She might have sacrificed her best years to a man. She may be losing her looks. . . . If, as is most likely, she is one whose life is bound up in the truest of a woman's occupations—the care of her home and her man—she is left stranded with only a hopeless future to face.

In her devotion to one man she has probably sacrificed all her friends. I have done. She has nowhere to turn. The future must be a bitter one.

Then there is the ordeal of having to stand before the court and tell of things which happened when you were very young. It needs courage to bring an action like this. It puts a woman in a pillory—for something which I think it is only right she should have. . . .

In spite of so-called equality woman will still want to sacrifice herself for the man she loves, and must have the protection of the law to prevent that being imposed upon.'

N.B.—The sacrifices which the lady had made for the company director were never specified, so we have no means of estimating their gravity.

APPENDIX 33

The belief that women are actually incapable of displaying the highest type of genius is so tenaciously held that its tottering basis is still evidently disregarded. The opinion of a biologist is therefore appended to that which is quoted in the chapter:

'Everything we have learned in genetics . . . proves conclusively that any combination of "superior" genes that could occur in a man could also occur in a woman; in fact, that as women carry more genes, the combination would be even likelier to occur. We must therefore conclude that (a) our social environment, in which women have always been kept subordinate to men, is responsible for suppressing their potentialities, or (*b*) that something constitutional—possibly hormonal, or such factors as motherhood—acts as an inhibitory influence. As to the latter, we have seen that in hardly more than a generation since women have been given comparative freedom in careers, but not yet equality, they have produced many notable persons. Until they are given *full* equality and full opportunity we cannot conclude that there is something inherent in women which prevents their being geniuses.'

(From *You and Heredity* by Amram Scheinfeld, edited by J. B. S. Haldane.)

APPENDIX 34

It has been constantly said that when women lose their natural tenderness they are more bloodthirsty than men. This is one of those statements we hear so often that we are inclined to assume they are axioms and need no investigation. Nevertheless, I am sure it is false and has gained currency only because physical cruelty in a woman is always so surprising as to seem monstrous, even when the actual degree it attains is less than that which we know to be common among males. (In the same way, we are told that a drunken woman is more disgusting than a drunken man—an entirely subjective impression based on astonishment that a woman can be publicly drunk at all.)

Unfortunately, however, the masculine standards being aimed at by some women—not necessarily feminists—are resulting in a cult of ruthlessness rather different from the vicarious militancy which is to be expected of non-combatants, that willingness to sacrifice other people's lives in battle which has at times turned mothers and wives into such formidable recruiting officers. There is a movement towards feminine participation in the destructive aspects of warfare, as opposed to the traditional tasks of healing, ministering, cheering, and inspiring. How much this movement is genuine and how much it is a newspaper fiction I cannot pretend to guess, as I personally have never heard any woman profess the smallest desire to join in the fighting, but editors at least suppose there is a public for articles on the following lines:

'If The Parachutists Come
I WANT TO FIGHT
says SHELAGH HOWARTH.[1]

'With rifle—or a rolling pin—I'd fight like fury any over-laden sky devil who touched a blade of grass on my lawn . . . I read with understanding the report that Belgian women had lynched a parachutist. I felt for them and would do as they did if given the chance. . . .

A women's corps of "Parashooters" would prove invaluable to civil defence, and I feel that the privilege of dealing with possible sky murderers should not be entirely reserved for men. . . .

There will be no stopping the women of Britain if Hitler chooses to send his suicide troops over here with their sub-machine-guns and bicycles. . . .

---

[1] *Yorkshire Evening News*, May 22nd, 1940.

Surely our men do not want to think of us slinking through woods like animals from a hunter. Rather give us a gun and a chance.'

The one small thing that can be said in favour of the softer sex emulating the sterner in violence is that it can then no longer be thought to require protection, so that one of the great rallying-cries of the warriors will lose what slight conviction it still possesses.

APPENDIX 35

In this place I may offer a larger instalment of the history of the Dionne Quintuplets, a subject which will not, I trust, prove unattractive to my reader merely because it is popular (for that would imply an inverted sentimentality). The five children are now fully restored to their parents, but their formative years were passed under the guardianship of the Canadian Government which had confided them to the doctor who, undeniably I believe, was responsible for their being alive and healthy. Mr and Mrs Dionne, however, kept up a persistent agitation to get them back into their own care. Two facts are to be borne in mind—that, when these five children so astonishingly arrived, Mr and Mrs Dionne already had a substantial family and were dependent on Government relief, and that, even with a much better start than they could have afforded to give them, the chances that all five would survive were remote. As always with multiple births, the children were extremely delicate, and the Government was having them cared for expertly under special and exemplary conditions.

According to the newspaper reports by which I am guided, it was when the father signed a contract for the public exhibition of the quintuplets at the age of seven days that the Government stepped in and passed a Bill making them wards of the King, since it was considered that the fulfilment of the engagement would mean almost certain death. The parents still managed to earn £200 a week by appearing without them in vaudeville shows, and the children were furnished by means of grants and gifts with a comfortable fortune. Mrs Dionne, however, was for some time dissatisfied and made an insistent demand for the return of the five.

Now here was a clear case upon which to exercise judgment. Could these children be better cared for by their mother than by the doctor who had managed their affairs with such marked ability from the moment of their birth? Controversy ran high, a questionnaire was published in Canada, and 90 per cent. of the people who answered it agreed emphatically that the babies should be given back. When I read this result, I was inclined to blame the Canadians for a blatant sentimentality which would not have been shared by the English, but I was wrong. Among the many comments on this verdict which appeared in the press was one by my friend, Margaret Lane, in which, assessing parental claims, she wrote:

'Our right . . . to our own children should depend on whether or not we are capable of doing the best that is possible for them. . . . To believe that children should never be parted from their parents implies a belief in a sort of divinity of parenthood—as if there were a magic influence flowing from all parents to all children which cannot be replaced. To me such a belief seems not only ignorant but sentimental.'

No sooner had these very moderate words appeared than the wish-fulfilment experts began to spring to the defence of their illusions. It is true that sympathizers also wrote in, but dissentients were in the majority. I quote in full one of the protesting letters, a typical working out of the Sentimentality Formula :

'Sir,—Margaret Lane's article suggests more of an outpouring of the brain than of the heart, but the upbringing of children is more a question of the latter.

No, the magic influence of parentage is there all right, but it needs experience to comprehend this. There is no better atmosphere for the rearing of a child than that generated by its own parents, happy in the bond of mutual understanding ; such happiness is the rule, not the exception.

Margaret Lane should not belittle sentiment in these matters, for it is the basis of the Christian faith. It is the thing to which we turn when cold reason fails us—it is the difference between the machine and the man.

J. H. M——.'

I regard this as an excellent specimen of the simplifying and idealizing process. There is a tacit dismissal of all material that might undermine the writer's occult creed ; as, for example, the fact that one society alone deals, even in peacetime, with about 120,000 suffering children a year, of whom a large proportion owe their miseries to the cruelty or neglect of one or both of their parents. (And there must be an enormously greater number of cases which are never reported.) There is also a complete inability, very general among wishful thinkers, to see that reason as well as sentiment may differentiate men from machines.

APPENDIX 36

A single anecdote will perhaps not be superfluous. A girl of about eight was brought to the hospital for the removal of tonsils and displayed a speechless horror and bewilderment. After the operation, she lay strangely silent and still for many hours, and although she complained of no pain, tears were constantly seen upon her cheeks. She appeared afraid of being moved and showed no desire to sit up in bed even when invited to do so. At length, encouraged, it seemed, by the nurse's cheerful overtures, she took herself in hand with what was evidently a great effort and tremulously asked : 'Did I look awful with my head off ?' The nurse was then able to elicit the cause of her misery. Her father had told her that to perform the operation on her throat the surgeon would have to cut her head off and stitch it on again. This gruesome joke, taken quite seriously by the child, had reduced her to a state of mental anguish which, if she had remained inarticulate, might have had permanent ill effects.

APPENDIX 37

Two or three examples will convey, though faintly, an impression of the public backwardness.

In May 1939, at Brentford Police Court, a boy cyclist was summoned for holding on to a lorry. The policeman who gave evidence said, 'When I saw the father he immediately dealt with his son in the approved manner.' There was a question from the Bench as to what this meant, to which the policeman replied (and we detect a note of relish in his phrasing): 'The father soundly belted his son. He gave him a jolly good leathering.' One of the magistrates then remarked, it is to be hoped not facetiously, 'I think you should have said "in the disapproved manner."' As the boy was fined five shillings over and above the punishment he had already received, it may be presumed that the Bench had little confidence in its deterrent value.

On April 10th, 1941, the *Yorkshire Evening News* reported the case of a fourteen-year-old boy who was charged with stealing a bicycle from school premises. His mother said she had thrashed him so severely that if others had not got him away from her she might have been brought before the Court herself on a manslaughter charge. No one suggested that this violent woman was not a fit person to direct the conduct of her family.

In August 1937, at Stockport Juvenile Court, a father appeared with a boy of thirteen who was accused of loitering on enclosed premises with intent to commit a felony. 'I thrashed him till he could not stand,' he told the magistrate. 'He will remember it for many a long day.' The Chairman, instead of having the case investigated by the N.S.P.C.C., commended him warmly. 'We are very pleased,' he stated, 'that you saw fit to thrash your son for committing this offence.' The boy's subsequent career would be an interesting study for a psychologist.

It is not surprising, when magistrates show themselves so completely out of sympathy with the findings of modern research, that the police frequently display a set of ideas adapted rather to the eighteenth than the twentieth century, chief constables being known to appeal for more and severer beatings in the home to keep down juvenile crime, and policemen not seldom showing in evidence concerning difficult children that they regard plenty of 'jolly good leatherings' as synonymous with sound training and wise care.

Incidentally, it is a gross injustice, calling urgently for legislation, that children are permitted to suffer twice for the same offence, the sentence of the Court and whatever chastisement may be inflicted by a parent who is often less angered by the offence itself than by the disgrace of Court proceedings. Public prosecution should automatically cancel out the parent's right to take the law into his own hands. Still less should the schoolmaster be permitted to impose additional punishment; yet this, too, sometimes happens.

APPENDIX 38

So greatly has woman as mother been glorified that there even appears to be some vague belief among the extremists that women are the sole procreators. Captain Henderson-Livesey, for example, protesting against the intrusion of childless women into public life, writes:

'We should not dream of allowing people who have not paid the entrance fee to serve on the committee of our clubs, and it is surely equally ridiculous to allow a number of women, most if not all of whom have avoided the maternal function, to claim to speak in the name of the whole female sex.'

This is not accompanied by any vestige of a suggestion that a man should be debarred from speaking in the name of the male sex unless he can prove his masculinity by showing children of his own begetting: so we must presume the author has forgotten that there is a paternal as well as a maternal function to be fulfilled if breeding is to continue. Or else he considers men entitled to exist for their own sakes but women dependent for all rights and privileges upon genital productiveness. It is a difference of status hard to justify, particularly as women must be solicited by men before they can thus acquire eligibility. But the world of Henderson-Livesey, like the world of Hitler and Mussolini, was created for the pleasure and aggrandizement of the male, and if woman is to grasp any of its prizes, she must creep in after them by the back door. Consider the implications of the following paragraph, which is culled, not from some Hitlerite's address to a Youth Movement, but from one of the English captain's 'Social Service' publications:

'The great majority of women who take an active part in political life are those whose activities are inspired by the desire to help husbands, fathers, brothers or friends; their party affiliation depending on that of their male relatives. In these cases political interest is due to a really womanly motive and we find such women to be normal and agreeable people.'

To women who have not been content to exercise petticoat influence in protected seclusion the captain gives short shrift. Of Joan of Arc he says, 'If we look upon her as a general and judge her performances purely from a military standpoint, she would hardly pass as fit to command a cadet battalion on the occasion of some elementary field exercises.' Gertrude Bell he called an eastern intriguer, and he once asked Taleb Pasha why, in accordance with 'the healthy realism' of Oriental politics, she was not murdered. Taleb replied that the etiquette of Iraq did not sanction the murder of women, so the captain wistfully remarks, 'she had an unfair advantage as women in men's positions always do.'

APPENDIX 39

The humourless pomposity with which certain eminent psycho-analysts have advanced hypotheses of the most risible character has naturally militated against the acceptance of their more sagacious judgments. Many of the assumptions of Freud himself are loose and inconsistent, though there is always in his work a residue which claims our respect. He had the greatness to retract some of his earlier exaggerations, such as the quasi-universality of the Oedipus complex, but unhappily the terms of his recantations are never likely to be so well known as his original dogmas; and theories concerning infantile eroticism, phallic symbolism, the castration complex, etc., are still extant which appear to have been worked out under the influence of a taboo upon all moderate conclusions and coherent reasoning.

Professor Flugel of the University of London, more than any other psycho-analyst, has afforded me the perverse pleasure of laughter unintentionally evoked. His *Psychology of Clothes* (which displays a very much more limited knowledge of fashion than we are entitled to expect in one who is laying down the law about it, and illustrates dress appeal with photographs of as plain a lady as I ever saw) is enlivened with the most agreeably startling interpretations of ordinary customs and habits.

We learn, for instance, that a woman who removes her hat at the earliest opportunity is suffering from 'the female form of the castration complex (i.e. the fear that the penis *has* been lost, instead of fear that it may be lost, as in the male).' 'In men castration itself is symbolized by the removal of garments, while the possession or display of the corresponding garments serves in virtue of their phallic symbolism, as a reassurance against the fear of castration.' A man takes off his hat as a sign of respect, the hat being phallic and the wearing of it regarded as a proud piece of display.

The Professor is troubled, however, by the fact that soldiers retain their head-dress even in a Christian church. He admits that this is a little difficult to explain, but proceeds to explain it thus:

'The military uniform, with its sword and helmet, contains in an unusual degree the element of phallic symbolism which, as we have seen, belongs to so many articles of clothing. The removal of the helmet would, like the removal of the sword, constitute a painfully clear symbol of castration: too painful indeed to be tolerated, so that the soldier proudly displays his military glory even in the house of the Almighty, trusting perhaps that the righteous ends for which he is prepared to fight (in the last resort—glorification of the Father [ruler] and protection of the Mother [country] . . .) will induce the Divine Father to take paternal pride in an exhibition in which he might otherwise have been offended.'

Equally remarkable is his diagnosis of the feminine practice of making up the face in public as narcissistic and implying 'a preoccupation with self and a relative indifference to other things and persons . . . in fact, a withdrawal from the outer world that is hostile to the higher forms alike of work and love and sociality.' It is curious for a psychologist not to observe that, on the contrary, make-up implies a preoccupation with appearances (i.e. outwardness) and women who frequently have recourse to powder and lipstick are clearly concerned with the impression they are making upon others. Withdrawal from the outer world indeed! As to the reason why public attention to make-up is annoying to men, the Professor has one of his inimitable footnotes:

'. . . Another factor in this irritation may come from the auto-erotic elements involved in the practice, in virtue of which "powdering the nose," like any other manipulation of the person's own body, is apt to be unconsciously identified with (genital or anal) masturbation (sometimes, of course correctly, for the identification may unconsciously exist for the manipulator also).'

Another footnote tells us that dickies and false cuffs are seldom worn in English 'respectable' society because, being detachable, they have a castration significance. This distaste being admittedly stronger in England than elsewhere, we are to presume that Continental men are more tolerant towards the idea of castration. The mystery of the detachable collar, worn everywhere, is not solved.

Yet another footnote accounts for the retention of the post-war fashion of high heels on the grounds, *inter alia*, that they make it impossible to protrude the abdomen—which is simply untrue; and 'an unconscious phallic symbolism attaching to the heel' in harmony with the adoption of masculine short hair and general boyishness of line—which begs the question of why heels grew considerably higher when boyish fashions went out and feminine ones returned. According to Professor Flugel himself, high heels were originally brought in to give erotic prominence to the bosom (how, I cannot tell, though I have worn them all my adult life), and if this is their function, it is difficult to see how they could have been appropriate with the flat chests of the post-war era.

It is undeniable that high heels are a phallic symbol *to some people*, and are sexually exciting to them. So are riding boots, rubber mackintoshes, and cotton underwear, but surely no one (except perhaps a psycho-analyst) would suggest that these garments were introduced *because* of their titillating associations.

The exponent of the psychology of clothes should know that mere delight in change for its own sake is the motive of many fashions and that modistes will continue to lay emphasis upon a variation which has been successful—such as the raising or lowering of heels, the diminution of waists, the enlargement of skirts—until no further extension of the style is possible. To deduce the normal from the abnormal is a regrettable propensity of psycho-analysts, due perhaps to the special nature of their clinical practice. Nevertheless I wholeheartedly endorse the verdict thus expressed by Leonard Woolf:

> 'Many absurd and exaggerated things have been said and many wild theories propounded in the name of psycho-analysis, but that kind of thing invariably happens whenever any field of human knowledge is being rapidly widened, and it is certain that, though one may hesitate to accept particular psycho-analytical theories and doctrines, psycho-analysis has thrown extraordinarily important light upon the way in which the human mind works.'

APPENDIX 40

Severity against offences directly actuated by sexual desire is only slightly relaxed when that desire follows a normal course. At an Assize Court in the north of England I saw a man sentenced to nine months' imprisonment with hard labour for having seduced a girl of nineteen under a promise of marriage, he being already a married man. His defence, which carried some conviction to me but not to the jury, was that the young woman knew perfectly well he was married, and that if she had told her parents—at whose instance the prosecution had been brought—that he was a single man, then she had, for obvious reasons, been lying to them. The trial took place in an atmosphere charged through and through with virtuous indignation.

In the same Court on the same morning a similar sentence was meted out to another young man, a soldier, who had thrown vitriol over a girl's face with the intention of blinding her. He had only succeeded in disfiguring her for life. He was treated with a considerable degree of sympathy by the Court as one who had acted under the compulsion of a not altogether reprehensible jealousy; although, as he had carried the vitriol about in his pocket for several days, and had quietly asked the girl to take off her glasses 'as she wouldn't need them again when he had done with her,' there did not seem to me to be much of uncontrollable impulse about his conduct.

I should mention that, in the first of these two cases, the girl had not become pregnant nor contracted any harm beyond the loss of her virginity—a loss which her parents had chosen to advertise in the law courts. Until I witnessed this trial, I was not aware that seduction of a female over the age of consent could be a criminal offence.

APPENDIX 41

The psychological fallacy of preserving peace by intensive arming has been repeatedly exploded, but seldom better than by Lord Grey of Fallodon (Sir Edward Grey, Foreign Secretary at the outbreak of the First Great War). I quote briefly from his reminiscences of *Twenty-five Years*:

'. . . Great armaments lead inevitably to war. . . . Each measure taken by one nation is noted and leads to counter-measures by others. The increase in armaments, that is intended in each nation to produce consciousness of strength, and a sense of security, does not produce these effects. On the contrary it produces consciousness of the strength of other nations and a sense of fear. Fear begets suspicion and distrust and evil imaginings of all sorts, till each Government feels it would be criminal and a betrayal of its own country not to take every precaution, while every Government regards every precaution of every other Government as evidence of hostile intent. The enormous growth of armaments in Europe, the sense of insecurity and fear caused by them—it was these that made war inevitable. This, it seems to me, is . . . the warning to be handed on to those who come after us.'

Whatever may be thought of the necessity for the armaments programme so costly to the country, so profitable to share-holders, and, we have since been informed, so inefficiently carried out from the time of the National Government's election in 1935 to the outbreak of war in 1939, there must be some who wish it had not been coupled with the Fools' Paradise assurance, 'Britain's rearmament is the guarantee of peace.' But peculiar uses of the word 'guarantee' might have a chapter to themselves.

APPENDIX 42

Though I have little hope of convincing any reader who enjoys believing that Germany had spent forty years arming for the First Great War while we were completely off our guard, I append here a mere hint of the available evidence to the contrary, which is enormous. Mr Winston Churchill in his essay on Sir John French [1] remarks:

'Ever since the Algeciras conference of 1905, technical relations—declared non-committal in policy—had existed between the French and British General Staffs. Both Sir John French and I were fully informed upon these secret matters. We therefore discussed the future and its potent menace in the

---

[1] *Great Contemporaries.*

freedom of exclusive confidences. [At the beginning of the essay Mr Churchill had stated, rather ominously, that Sir John French's "single purpose, which was achieved to an extent far beyond his utmost dreams . . . was to command a great British Army in a European war"—a task "for which he had hoped and laboured throughout a long adventurous career."] After the Agadir crisis of 1911, I was sent to the Admiralty for the express purpose of raising our naval precautions to the highest pitch of readiness and—only less important —to establish effectual co-operation between the Admiralty and the War Office for the transport of the whole Army to France in certain contingencies. . . . We discussed every aspect, then conceivable, of a possible war between France and Germany and of British intervention by sea and land.'

In the meantime, Mr Churchill explains, the growing tenseness of the situation was 'concealed from the public eye by the bland skies of peace and platitude.'

Harold Nicolson's biography of his father, *The First Lord Carnock*, a diplomat whose correspondence and diaries are of first-rate interest, contains the following passage:

'Our preparations were in fact far more advanced than was realized by British public opinion. . . . The extent of this preparedness can be gauged by the letter which he [Sir Arthur Nicolson] wrote to Lord Hardinge on September 14th [1911]:

"I spent a week at Balmoral last week, but nothing very important occurred during my visit. I was glad to find that the King is perfectly sound as regards foreign affairs. I have had some talks since my return with Haldane, Lloyd George, and Winston Churchill; I am glad to find that all three are perfectly ready—I might almost say eager—to face all possible eventualities, and most careful preparations have been made to meet any contingencies that may arise. . . . I may tell you in confidence that preparations for landing four or six divisions on the Continent have been worked out to the minutest detail. On the other hand, reports which we have received from our various military informants all point to the fact that the French army has never been in a better state of equipment, organization and armament, or been inspired by so strong a feeling of perfect confidence and unity, and in short they would enter into a campaign feeling that they were able to meet their adversary on very nearly equal terms. . . ."'

As we were continuously engaged in the amassing of armaments from that date, when an exceedingly well-informed observer already regarded our preparations as excellent, till the conflagration broke out three years later, the pretence of guileless unreadiness could only have been a cloak for incompetence or a means of fixing guilt more securely upon the enemy.

APPENDIX 43

We are quite persuaded, in every war, that the enemy is led by the worst men who ever lived, and the only difference between one set of villains and the next is that the language of accusation grows, on the whole, less lurid. I have already remarked on the detestation of the Kaiser, the Crown Prince, and their entourage in the First Great War; portrayals of these symbolical figures in newspaper cartoons were actually far more repulsive than most which have so far appeared of Hitler, Goering, and Goebbels. Yet no one now seriously supposes that the Hohenzollerns were the sole cause, or even an essential cause, of Pan-European slaughter. As for Napoleon, the bogy of a hundred years earlier, he rapidly became one of our favourite 'great men,' and by the time our invasion of the Crimea had elevated the Czar of Russia to the status of Chief Monster, it was hard to recall that our ogre had once been Corsican. How much he was hated in his day we may judge from a piece of 1814 propaganda—a pamphlet published in Berlin and London, purporting to be *Memoirs of Buonaparte, His Imperial Family, Great Officers of State and Great Military Officers*. Here are some specimen extracts:

'NAPOLEON BUONAPARTE. . . . The greatest vagabond, and the worst public and private character, in ancient or modern history. . . . He commenced his career of murder at the age of sixteen by poisoning a young woman at Brienne, who was with child by him. . . .

LETITIA RANIOLINI, *Mother of the Imperial Family*, a most notorious prostitute. At fifteen years of age she had a child by a friar. After her marriage with Carlo Buonaparte, she was kept by Count Marbœuf, by whom she had Napoleon and Lucien. She afterwards kept a public brothel at Marseilles.

PAULINA BUONAPARTE, Princess Borghese, eldest sister of the Emperor, with whom she had incestuous intercourse. . . . In 1796 was a common prostitute in Paris. [Eliza, the Emperor's second sister, was, according to the biographer, 'a milliner and prostitute at Marseilles.']

JOACHIM MURAT, King of Naples, a most infamous, sanguinary villain; son of an Innkeeper at Cahors in Provence; himself originally a postillion, then scullion in the Prince of Condé's kitchen.

SAVARY, Duc de Rovigo, Minister of Police, a most infamous villain, a common bravo, who, by Buonaparte's orders, stabbed General Dessaix in the back at the battle of Marengo, and afterwards kidnapped the whole royal family of Spain; the person whom Buonaparte employs in all his secret murders.

MARSHAL NEY, Prince of Moskwa, Duc of Elchingen, originally an ostler at a livery stables in Paris, from whence he stole two horses and ran away. He is still a robber in every particular, but has the reputation of an excellent officer.

THE DUCHESS OF ELCHINGEN was debauched by Lucien Buonaparte and is still a lady of pleasure.

MARSHAL LEFEVRE, Duc of Danzig, formerly a private soldier in the old French service, afterwards a most notorious robber. He is a man of the lowest and most brutal manners. . . .

GENERAL SABASTINI, Count of the Empire . . . of a bloodthirsty cruel disposition; frequently employed in secret and murdering expeditions.

GENERAL HULIN, Count of the Empire and Governor of Paris, whose wife took in washing: the leader of most of the massacres in Paris since the Revolution, and one who has been a *swindler, coiner, robber*, and *murderer*.'

Compared with these diatribes, the attacks on the present German and recent Italian rulers are mild and, like other kinds of war propaganda, show a distinct ethical advance. Perhaps we shall ultimately arrive at a stage when we are able to perceive that war is not made by a handful of unscrupulous individuals but by a series of incorrigible situations which bring these individuals into prominence.

'If we look back over the course of history [writes G. Lowes Dickinson] we find war to be a normal part of its process; and historians are so hypnotized by that fact that they commonly consider, not the fundamental conditions which make war inevitable, but the superficial occasions out of which this or that war happened to arise. These occasions, of course, vary indefinitely in detail; but underneath them all lies a general situation which makes it certain that war will come, though it is always doubtful by what particular circumstances or at what precise date it may be precipitated.'

APPENDIX 44

I have arranged a batch of newspapers in chronological order and I give here a very brief résumé of their interpretation of important current events:

On the verge of the war, Germany's loan to Russia: This was described as a purely normal commercial transaction which readers must not imagine to have any political significance whatever. The Hitler-Stalin pact, coming immediately afterwards, was admitted to be a great surprise, but 'experts' were quick to explain that it was a meaningless gesture which would strengthen rather than weaken the position of the Poles. A Liberal journal said it was 'grotesque' to suspect that Russia had any designs upon Poland.

The resistance of Poland: Glowing reports at first assured us that the German offensive was making very little headway and that we should be able to provide the Poles with everything necessary in the way of support. Declarations from the Polish Government that they would go on fighting to the customary last man were received here as if words alone would hold the enemy at bay.

An abortive outburst in Czecho-Slovakia was reported as a great riot and rebellion, and hints were thrown out that the end of the Nazi régime was imminent. More, indeed, than hints! The general tone of the press was voiced in such headlines as 'NAZI REGIME CRACKING UP'—'HITLER LIKE A CAGED ANIMAL.' (Later there were similar premature estimates of the strength of anti-Nazism in Rumania, Holland, Norway, and elsewhere, and throughout the war, cheering press rumours of Hitler's death, disappearance, total insanity, and incurable illnesses.)

Absence of severe aerial fighting in the first months of the war was constantly interpreted as a proof of the impotence of the German air force. Hitler was taunted with having threatened a blitzkrieg which he 'hadn't the nerve' to carry out. Our defences against air attack were supposed to be magnificent and London practically invulnerable. (A new optimism was instantly found to replace the one which became quite untenable. During the autumn and winter of 1940-1941 an 'answer' to the night bomber was always just within sight.)

Some changes in the Italian Cabinet in late 1939 were represented as an attempt to root out the pro-Germans and put in pro-English Ministers, since Italy was almost certainly about to break away from the Axis rather than enter the war.

A meeting of the Dutch and Belgian monarchs in November was held to be for the purpose of forming a strong alliance against Germany: it would actually appear to have been for the purpose of framing another peace appeal.

At this period, to give an impression of confusion and division among the enemy, almost every German high official, one after another, was described as being out of favour with Hitler and about to be dismissed.

Britain's success in Norway was exaggerated to the degree of sheer irresponsibility, and when after repeated 'victorious' actions we suddenly withdrew, the bewilderment of the public was pitiful.

'BRITAIN TO THE RESCUE' was the headline successively applied to our 1940 operations in Norway, Belgium, and Holland. Our claims to be saving the situation were, in each case, soon destined to look as embarrassing as our term 'guarantee' in its application to Poland.

I cite these examples, not with the slightest intention of sneering at the failures of the well-meaning commanders and forces who strove to achieve the impossible, but to expose the deceptions and self-deceptions of those who manipulate the current of public opinion.

Until a few days before the French debacle, no theme was more insistently harped upon in the press than the fraternization of the armies of France and Britain. The phrase 'side by side' was used in this connection with endless repetition. The defection of France was unthinkable; the friendship of the two countries was eternal. Placed 'side by side' with subsequent bitter revilings, and still later reports of our heavy bombing attacks upon French territory, newspaper articles of the mutual admiration period make tragi-comic reading. The recovery of France has, of course, produced another *volte face*.

Here are a few further reminders of the fallibility of journalist prophets: For several months all moves by the enemy in the Balkans were supposed to be rousing Russia to attack Germany and perhaps to bring Turkey into the conflict on our side. Italian bombers coming over England with German squadrons were thought by some editorial writers to be proving the exhaustion of the German air force, which in reality was being husbanded for a vast attack on Russia. When a newly formed and not fully accredited Italian Government capitulated in 1943—a capitulation which had been due at any moment during the preceding three years—no further difficulties in that country were anticipated by the popular press, which simply reckoned Italy as being 'out of the war' and foretold the rapid advent of a similar catastrophe to the German rulers. The political entanglements in countries recaptured in 1944 were glossed over or misrepresented. Very heavy bombing of Germany during 1943 and 1944 was said to be leading swiftly to chaos and industrial dislocation, of which, however, at the time of writing, 1945, the signs are not yet apparent. It was freely suggested that the Germans would collapse as soon as any attack was made on their own soil which was defended chiefly by old men and young boys.

Threats of new bombing inventions which turned out to be very well grounded were received with jocular incredulity—so much so that it was never possible to regain for Londoners in 1944 the sympathy from which they had drawn support in the earlier 'blitz.' Secret weapons could be taken lightly by people who did not have to contend with them, thanks to the training their minds had received from the press.

That optimism, even of the most extravagant character, is necessary to keep a nation in the mood for war undiscouraged by reverses and errors, may be seriously contended. On the other hand, it is at least as feasible that reverses and errors are frequently due to this persistent cultivation of a rosy outlook, and when we are given the full history of the loss of Singapore, to name but one disaster, it may reveal very clearly the vulgar folly of the let-'em-all-come attitude which nations in arms always assume. I will go further and suggest that a lavish equipment of rose-coloured spectacles is so essential to any nation entering a war that, without these commodities, warfare might die out altogether.

APPENDIX 45

The pathos and absurdity of obsolete wartime newspapers is not confined to the editorial comments and the methods of interpreting news. The correspondence columns also excel themselves in silliness, though it is only fair to say that there is probably a very general practice of suppressing a large proportion of the correspondence which does not endorse the policy of the paper it is addressed to. Some journals, I think, do attempt to present both sides of the question with fairness, but others certainly only make a specious pretence of doing so.

In the belief that they will have at least a certain oddity value a few years hence, I offer a random selection of extracts from representative contemporary letters. It would be easy for anyone who took all the popular daily and weekly papers to gather some hundreds of equally curious specimens in the course of a few days.

'I have recently received a letter from a friend in New York, telling me of a rather unique scheme his circle of friends have thought of to combat Hitlerism. When answering a telephone ring instead of using the usual exclamation "Hello" they say "Stop Hitler." . . . After the recent campaign against imprudent gossipers, I was wondering whether it would be a good idea to carry out a similar plan here, by exclaiming, when answering the telephone, "No careless talk" instead of the customary "Hello."   H. L. K——.'

'In puritan England, cradle of our present liberties, the spirit of the age was expressed in giving children Biblical texts as Christian names. . . . Why not adopt the stirring slogans coined by our Premier and others to a similar purpose in this heroic hour? Christian names for 1940's children could range from the crisp "Go-to-it" Jones to "We-will-fight-on-the-hills-We-will-fight-on-the-beaches" Robinson. They would be a matter of pride to their possessors in the hour of victory.   J. T. B——.'

'Now that enemy pilots have begun their attacks upon barrage balloons the time has come to extend the spirit of the fair. Portraits of the Nazi leaders ought to be painted on the balloons; they should not be caricatures, as a German pilot might well consider himself justified in removing an insult to Nazism. . . .

How heartening it would be to the people below to know that "Hitler" had been brought down, that "Himmler" was being beaten up by German pilots, that "Goebbels" gas had given out, that "Hess" is deflated.
                                        C. T. C—— (Rev.).'

(All from *Picture Post*, September 21st, 1940.)

'I have a small (comparatively small) crater from a bomb in my garden. I have proudly stuck a Union Jack in it.

It seems to me that it would be a pleasantly symbolic way of showing how we take Goering's onslaughts if everybody were to do the same. If your house is demolished, stick a Union Jack in the ruins. Even if your windows are broken, a small Union Jack would flutter gaily in the draught so created.

S. H——.'

(*Daily Express*, September 20th, 1940.)

'Whenever I hear people engaging in careless, disloyal, or pessimistic talk I give them one of my glances. A steady, unfriendly glare works wonders. It shrivels careless or critical talk at the root. It harms no one. . . .

K. G——.'

(*Picture Post*, October 5th, 1940.)

'Some time ago I tried to find out the view of some of our working people, especially the womenfolk of mining districts, about Hitler's invasion. There was only one desire: "If we could only get hold of Hitler."

From this impression it occurred to me what a tower of strength these Amazons could be made into if an invasion took place. Dante's Inferno would be a peaceful haven compared with the action they would take. I would suggest arming each home with several hand grenades, and every approach of the enemy would be met with devastating attack. Our working women only want the arms and they will do the rest. Make each home a hornets' nest.

J. A. G——.'

(*Yorkshire Evening News*, February 6th, 1941.)

'When the war is won we should distribute all German children between three and fourteen throughout the British Commonwealth, compelling every childless couple to bring up at least one child. . . . All the expenses would be borne by the German nation.

We would thus do more to ensure everlasting peace in Europe than has ever been done before. By the time these children were 25 they would have acquired British qualities, and could then be allowed to return to Germany taking that influence with them.

LEO S——.'

(*Sunday Express*, January 30th, 1944.)

APPENDIX 46

Self-sufficiency creeds have not had the same flourishing success in England as in many other countries—at least not in the twentieth century—but they have their adherents. There is, for instance, the National Constitution Defence Movement, founded in 1910 with the motto *Intelligentia et vis Imperii*. In November 1939 its Newsletter to members consisted of a request for the suppression of the rights of organizations opposed to the government policy. 'Any Society or individual engaged in combating dangerous and subversive influences for some years past,' it ran, 'knows full well that there exists in this country a considerable body of opinion which is *definitely international in outlook and is at no pains to conceal the fact.*' (The italics are mine.) A sentence accusing the pacifists contains the curious aspersion that many of them were 'never at any time pronouncedly national or imperial in outlook.' The circular ends with an appeal to be spared the activities of '*malcontents and internationalists,*' and a suggestion that, though members may lament the sacrifice of cherished liberty, they should remain unperturbed as long as the blow fell on those who would impede the war machine.

'Freedom to think as we think' is the only sort of freedom which really excites general enthusiasm.

APPENDIX 47

H. G. Wells, in his courageous autobiography, speaks ruefully of his 1914 attitude—his 'shrill jets of journalism' indicting the enemy, his extreme belligerence and unwillingness 'to face the frightful truth' that no explosion of indignant common sense would sweep over the world and remodel it as the result of the carnage. 'The fount of sanguine exhortation in me,' he explains with candour, 'swamped my warier disposition towards critical analysis and swept me along.' He wrote a highly persuasive pamphlet called *The War that will end War*. Anatole France did the same (*Débout pour la Dernière Guerre*), and Mr Wells translated it into English.

Professor Gilbert Murray also wrote a pamphlet explaining that he 'desperately desired' to hear of German dreadnoughts sunk in the North Sea, that he should have liked to help in laying mines, and that he was disappointed, reading one day that twenty thousand Germans had been killed, to find next day it was only two thousand. 'We are fighting for that which we love, whatever we call it. It is the right.'

The late Sir Arthur Quiller-Couch gave an address at Cambridge on *The Huns and Literature*. 'The Germans,' he said, 'are congenitally unfit to read our poetry; the very structure of their organs forbids it. . . . The German who can write even passable English is yet to be found. . . . For them the great body of our literature was only the dead possession of a decadent race. . . . There can only be one way of exorcising this menace of dusty historicism—the sword in the hand of the young, who will see to it that this tumour is cleanly lanced.'

Henri Bergson meanwhile was writing: 'Should the day come when Germany, conscious of her moral humiliation, shall say, to excuse herself, that she had trusted herself too much to certain theories, that an error of judgment is not a crime, it will then be necessary to remind her that her philosophy was simply a translation into intellectual terms of her brutality, her appetites, and her vices.'

Such examples, selected strictly from the utterances of the eminent and intelligent, might be multiplied into a collection of vast dimensions. It is at least possible that similar statements being made today will eventually come to look as curious as these did after 1918.

INDEX

Curie, Mme, 143
conservatism, and, 95 n. 1
Curie, Pierre, on freedom, 143
Customs, ancient, 119-20
Czecho-Slovakia, 279

Daily Express, 129, 267 n. 1, 282
Daily Mail, 124 n. 1, 133, 145 n. 1, 213,
214 nn. 1, 2, 222 n. 1, 267-8
Dalzel, Archibald, *History of Dahomey*,
139 n. 1
Darling, Sir William Young, 155
Dataller, Roger, 160 n. 1
Davidson, J., 257
Death, 132 ff., 154
words and, 73-4
Death penalty, the, 205-6
Renier, G. J., on, 205
Debunking, 40-1
de Hubert, W. H., 209
Delusions, 35 ff., 51, 225
See also Illusions and illusionism
Democracy, 51 ff., 59, 246
Churchill, Winston, on, 52-3
Croker, J. W., on, 51 n. 2
Henderson, Sir Nevile, on, 53
Streit, Clarence, on, 52
Demos, 43 ff.
Dicey, Edward, 151
Dickens, Charles, *The Chimes*, 136
n. 1
novels of, 26-7
Dickinson, G. Lowes, 41
on annihilation, 83
on honour, 82-3
International Anarchy, The, 82-3
Magic Flute, The, 212, 227-8
on war, 279
Dionne, Mr, 178
Dionne Quintuplets, and, 178, 270-1
Diseases, euphemistic treatment of, 74
Dislike, 35
Divorce, 99 ff.
civil marriage and, 102
collusion, 99-100
compensatio criminis, 100
condonation in, 101-2
Divorce Bill, 103, 164-5
first three years of marriage and, 103

Divorce Laws, 99
Waugh, Evelyn, on, 103
'Dole,' the, 74-5
Domestic servants, 73
Donegall, Lord, 221-2
Douglas, James, 249, 267 n. 1
Drugs, 126, 128, 262-3
Drummond, 'Lt. Commissioner' Flora,
121 n. 1
Drunkenness, 126
Duncan, Isadora, 125
Duty, discussion of, 79

East, W. Norwood, 209
Economic system, the, 50-1
Education, 61, 97, 148, 231 ff.
female, 163, 165
history, teaching of, 234 ff.
independence, and, 226 ff.
patriotism, and, 151-2
pictures suitable for a boy's room,
232 n. 1
public school, 35
religious, 109
renunciation, weighing of value of, 130
Eighteenth century, the, 14, 24, 39,
46, 113, 127
Electoral system, the, and the elec-
torate, 55 ff., 60-1
See also Government
Ellis, Havelock, 187
Man and Woman, 171 n. 1
Emotion, 7, 12, 19, 34-5, 178, 213-14
Engelbrecht, H. C., and Hanighen,
F. C., *Merchants of Death*, 212 n. 2
English Justice. See 'Solicitor'
Englishwoman's Domestic Magazine, The,
169 n. 2, 194
Entertainments, 124-5
'love interest' and, 167-8
men and women and, 172, 175
Epstein, 'Genesis,' 36, 37
Equality, 52
France and, 253
Espionage, 215
Eugenics, 186-7
Euphemisms, 72
Evasion, 72-3
Ex-Servicemen, 133-4

Women: marriage, and conception of dependence of, 29-30
married women and laws concerning, 112 n. 1
medical students' struggle, 267
Nightingale, Florence, on, 166-7
nineteenth-century writers on position of, 164 ff.
Rathbone, Eleanor F., on, 167
Renier, G. J., on monogamy of, 168-9
rights of, 164
voting, and, 75
war, and, 167, 173 ff., 212, 269-70
Women's Movement, 182, 195
See also Strachey, Ray, The Cause
Women's Suffrage, 165
Debate on (1870), 163
Woolf, Leonard, 46, 94
on intellectuals, 241

on psycho-analysis, 275
on self-glorification, 148
Words, 65 ff.
changing or misapplying of, 70 ff.
Chase, Stuart, on, 65, 67, 73-4, 89, 174
death and terminology for, 73-4
Fowler, H. W., and, 251
Ogden and Richards on, 89
word-magic, 36, 67, 72, 73 ff., 78 ff., 217, 251

Xosa (Xhosa), 264

York, Archbishop of, 84
Yorkshire Evening News, 97 and n. 1, 158, 180 n. 1, 219 n. 2, 220 n. 3, 269 n. 1, 272, 282
Young Lady's Book, The (1829), 167 n. 1
Youth, vilifying of, 38